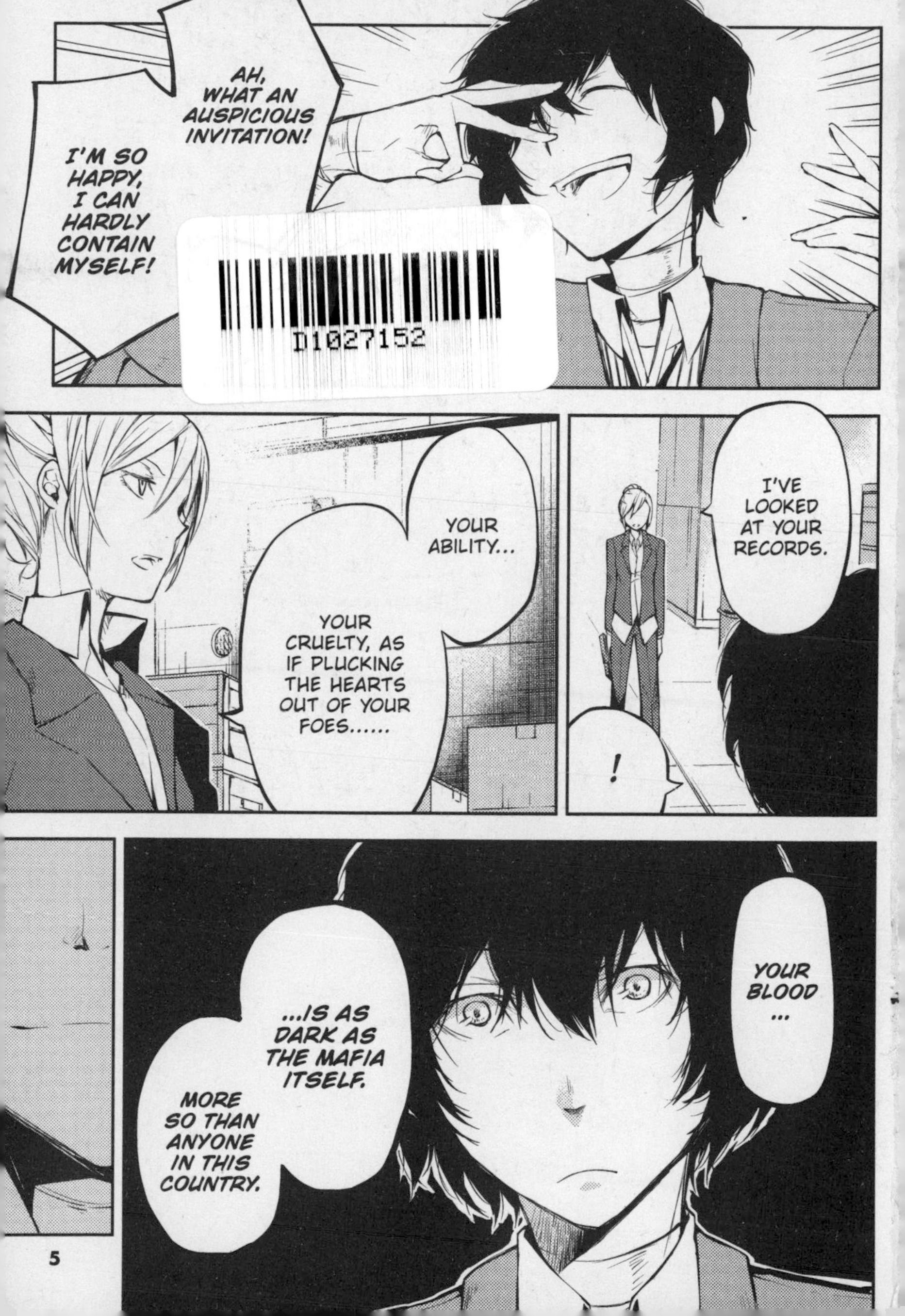
AH, WHAT AN AUSPICIOUS INVITATION!
I'M SO HAPPY, I CAN HARDLY CONTAIN MYSELF!
I'VE LOOKED AT YOUR RECORDS.
!
YOUR ABILITY...
YOUR CRUELTY, AS IF PLUCKING THE HEARTS OUT OF YOUR FOES......
YOUR BLOOD ...
...IS AS DARK AS THE MAFIA ITSELF.
MORE SO THAN ANYONE IN THIS COUNTRY.

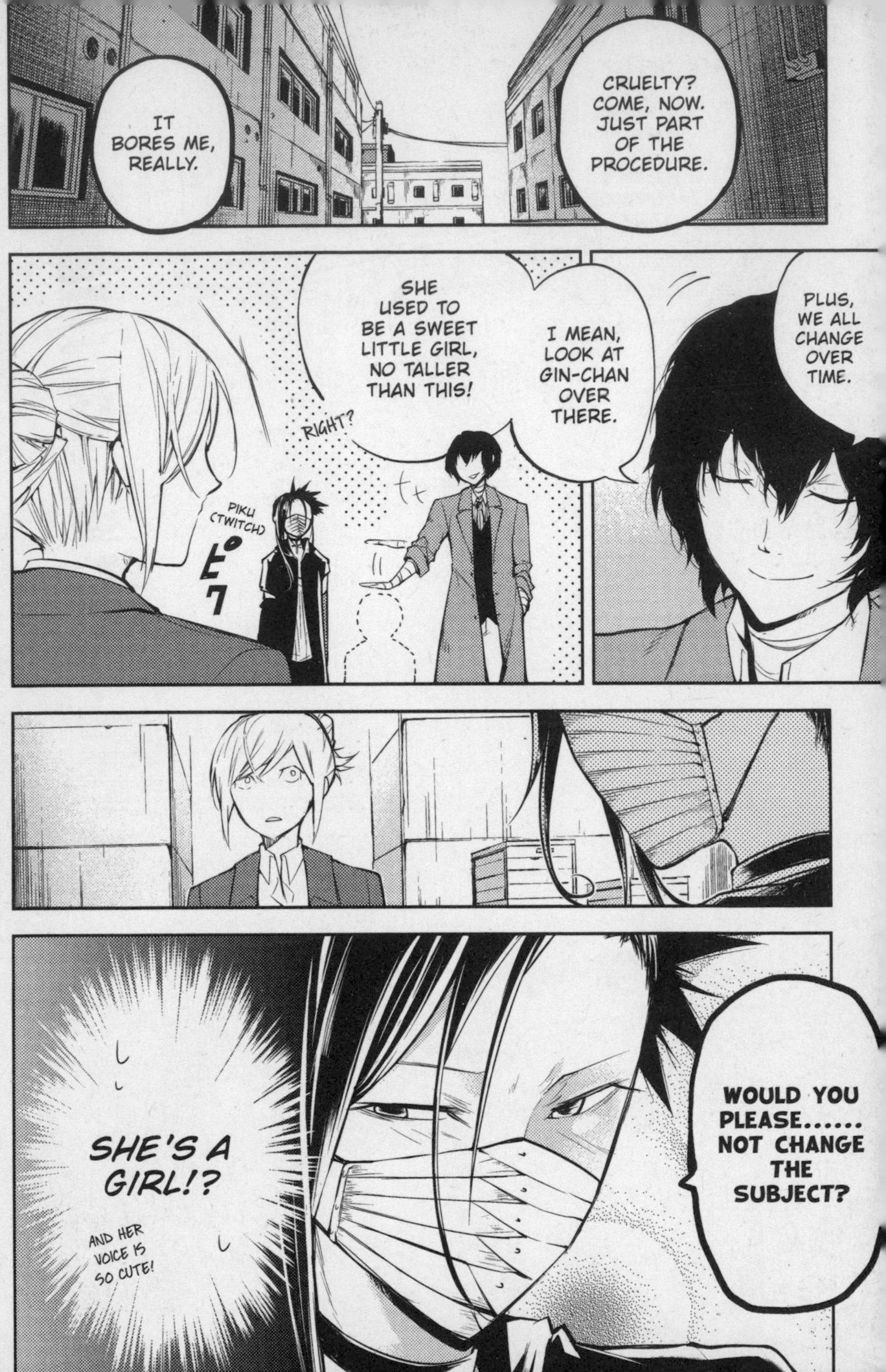
CRUELTY? COME, NOW. JUST PART OF THE PROCEDURE.
IT BORES ME, REALLY.
PLUS, WE ALL CHANGE OVER TIME.
I MEAN, LOOK AT GIN-CHAN OVER THERE.
SHE USED TO BE A SWEET LITTLE GIRL, NO TALLER THAN THIS!
RIGHT?
PIKU (TWITCH)
WOULD YOU PLEASE...... NOT CHANGE THE SUBJECT?
SHE'S A GIRL!?
AND HER VOICE IS SO CUTE!

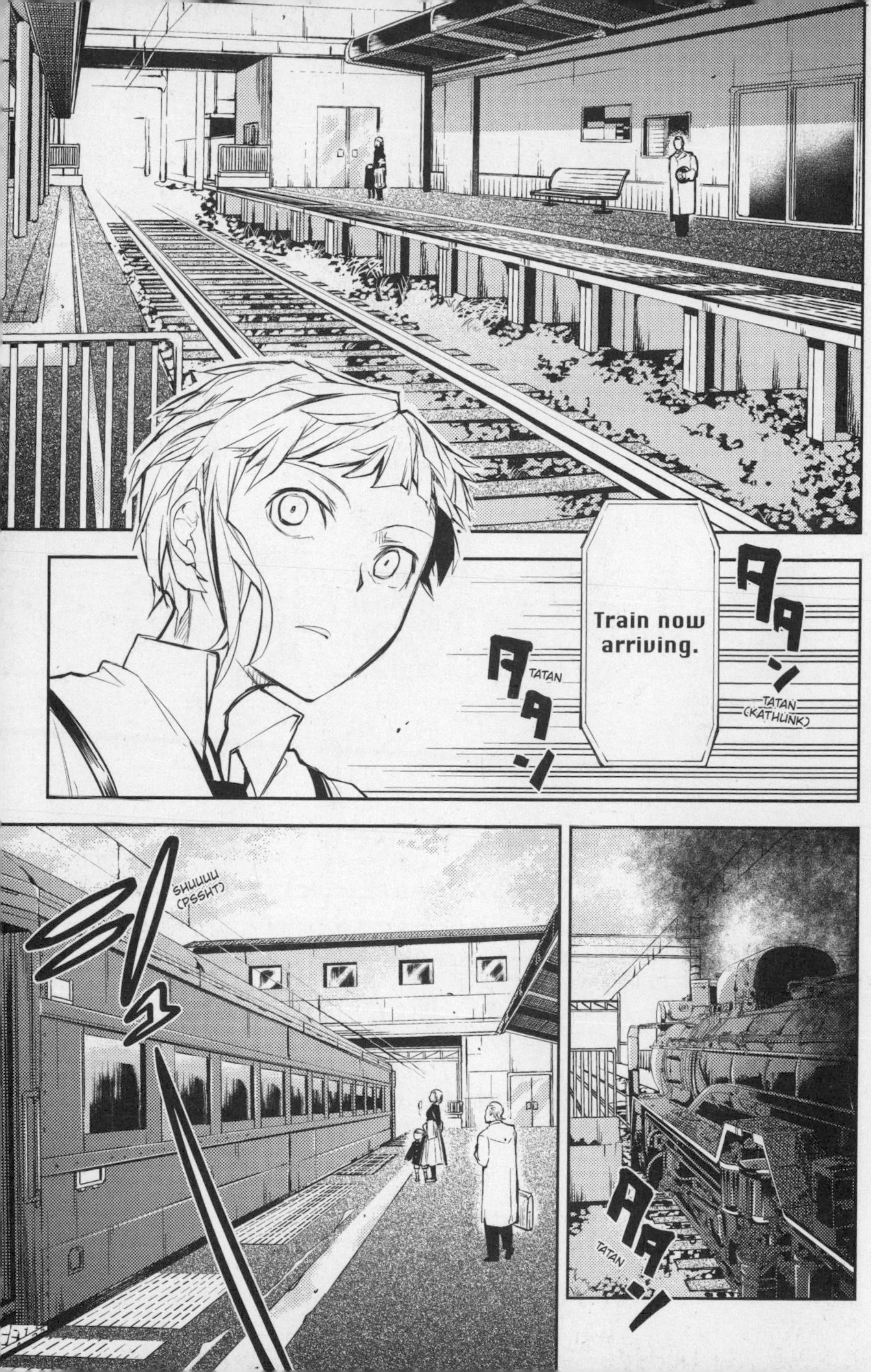
Train now arriving.
TATAN (KATHUNK)
TATAN
TATAN
SHUUUU (PSSHT)

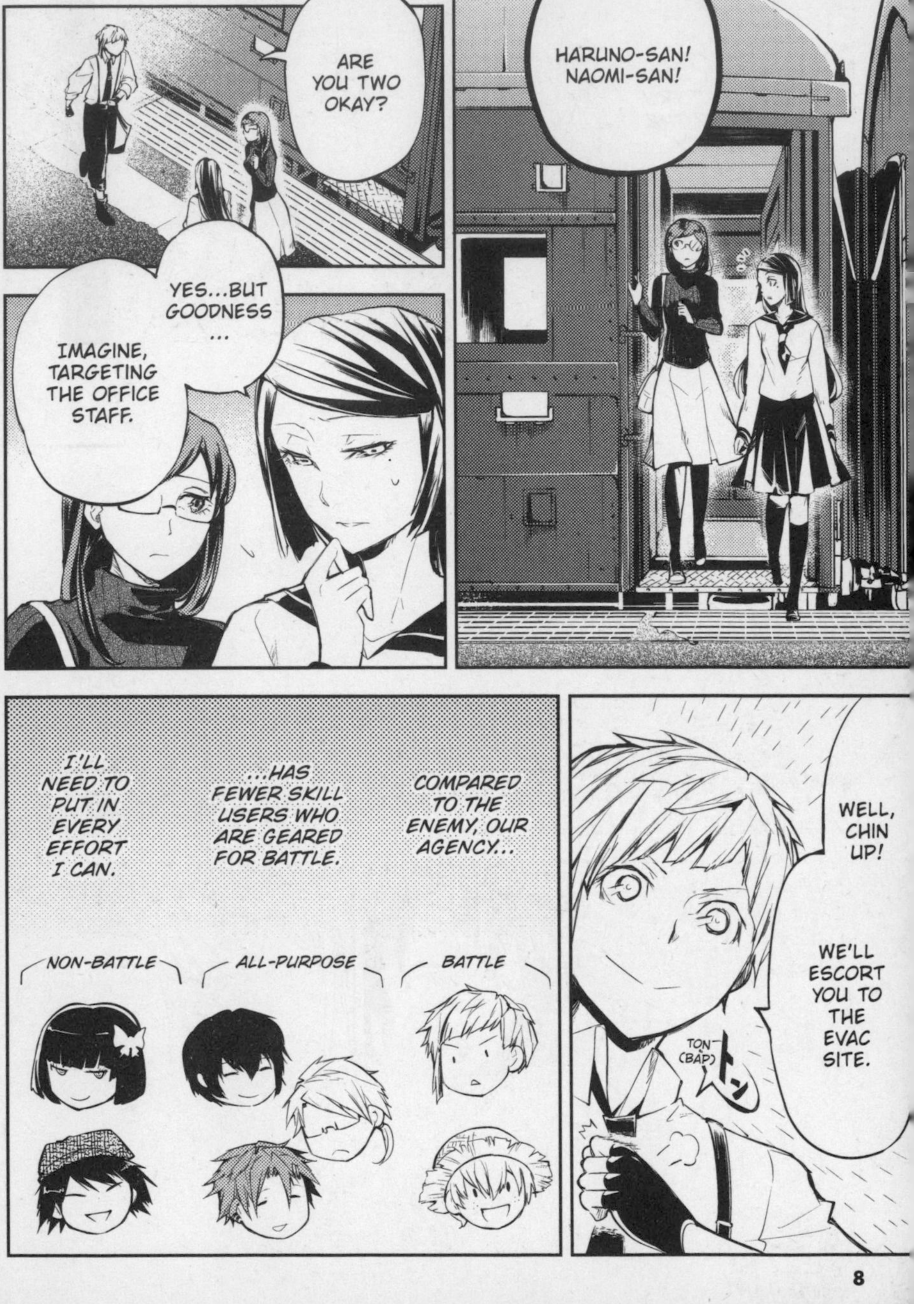
HARUNO-SAN! NAOMI-SAN!
ARE YOU TWO OKAY?
YES...BUT GOODNESS...
IMAGINE, TARGETING THE OFFICE STAFF.
WELL, CHIN UP!
WE'LL ESCORT YOU TO THE EVAC SITE.
TON (BAP)
COMPARED TO THE ENEMY, OUR AGENCY...
...HAS FEWER SKILL USERS WHO ARE GEARED FOR BATTLE.
I'LL NEED TO PUT IN EVERY EFFORT I CAN.
BATTLE
ALL-PURPOSE
NON-BATTLE

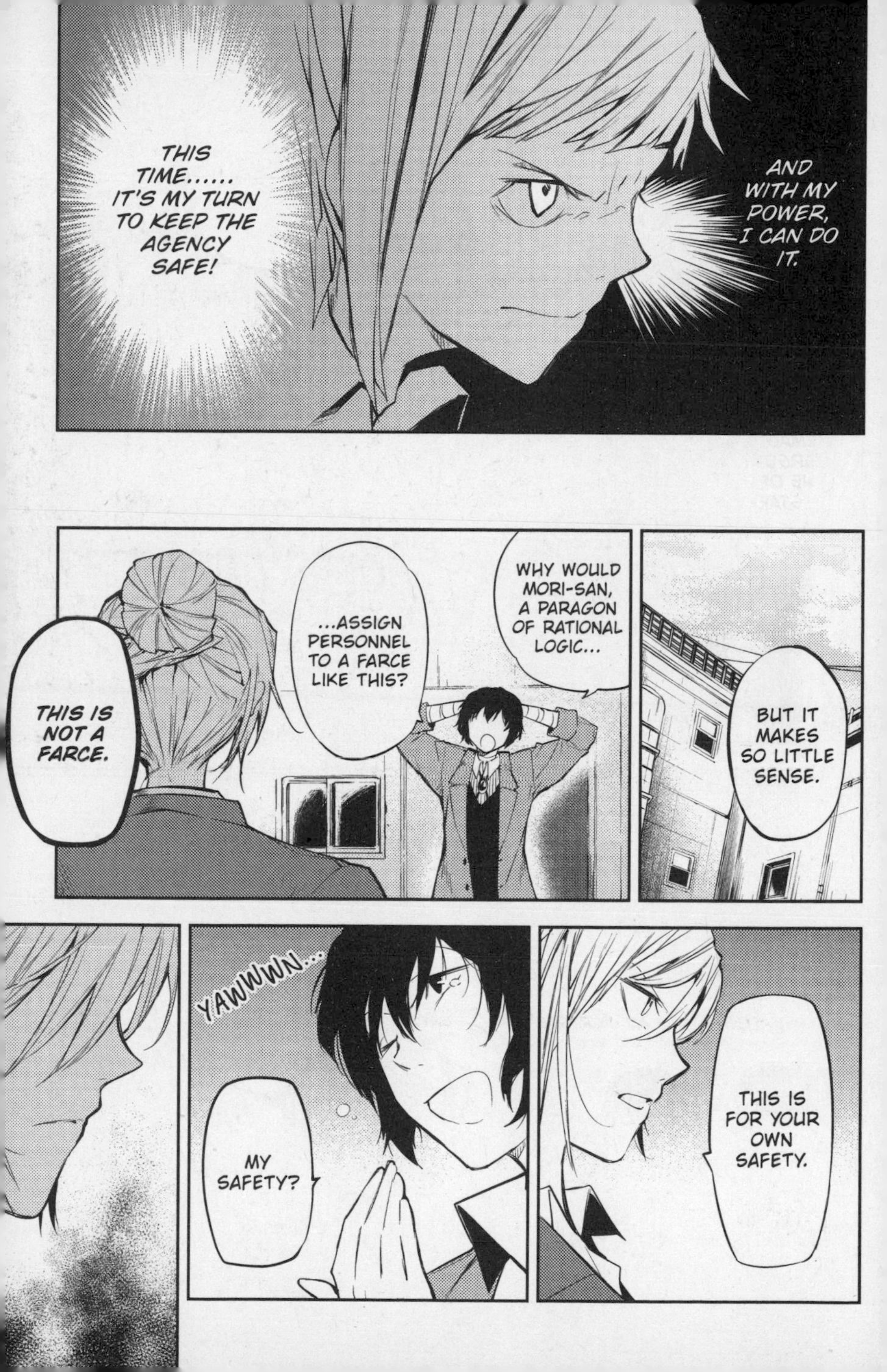
AND WITH MY POWER, I CAN DO IT.
THIS TIME...... IT'S MY TURN TO KEEP THE AGENCY SAFE!
BUT IT MAKES SO LITTLE SENSE.
WHY WOULD MORI-SAN, A PARAGON OF RATIONAL LOGIC...
...ASSIGN PERSONNEL TO A FARCE LIKE THIS?
THIS IS NOT A FARCE.
THIS IS FOR YOUR OWN SAFETY.
YAWWWN...
MY SAFETY?

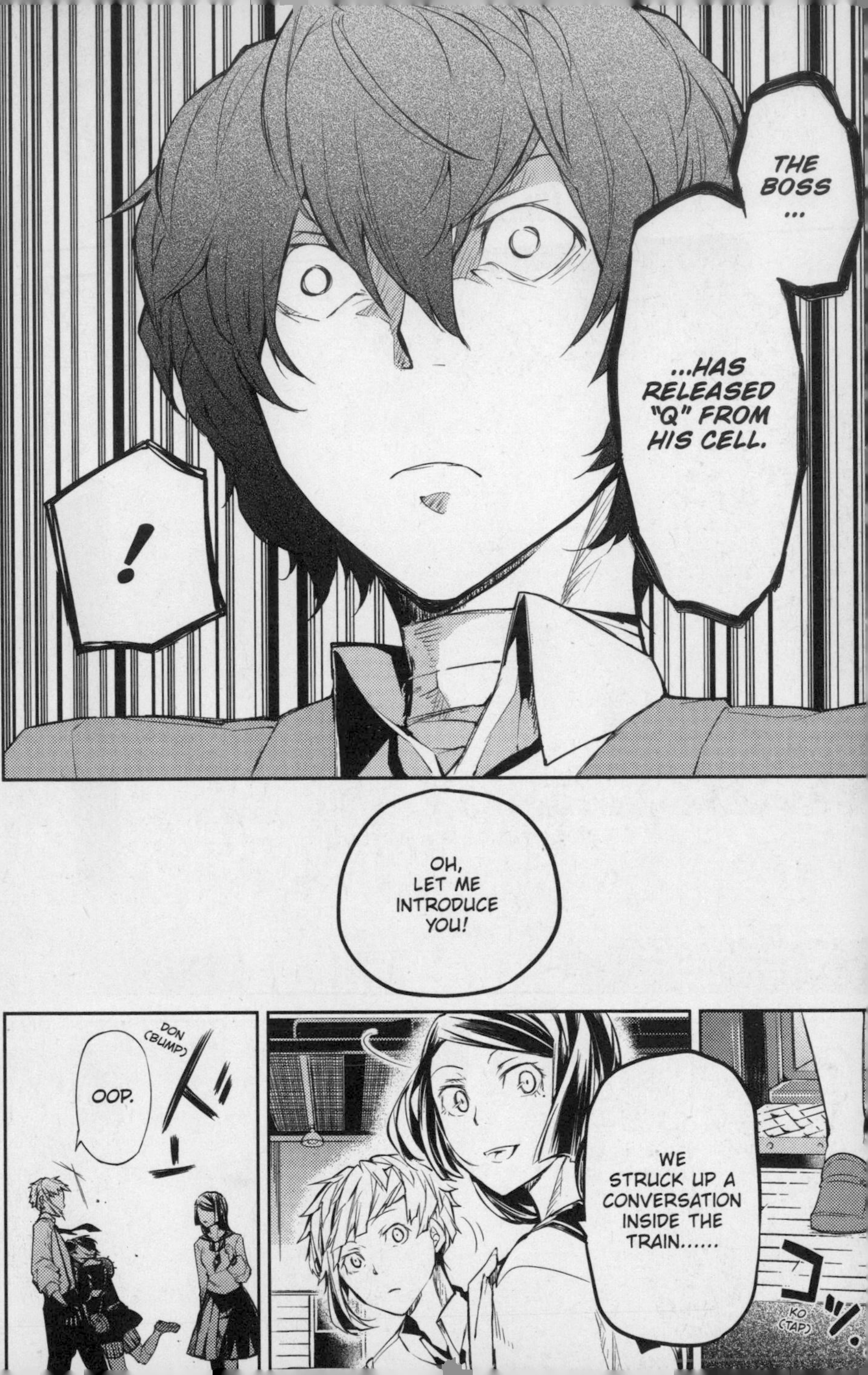
THE BOSS...
...HAS RELEASED "Q" FROM HIS CELL.
!
OH, LET ME INTRODUCE YOU!
KO (TAP)
WE STRUCK UP A CONVERSATION INSIDE THE TRAIN......
DON (BUMP)
OOP.

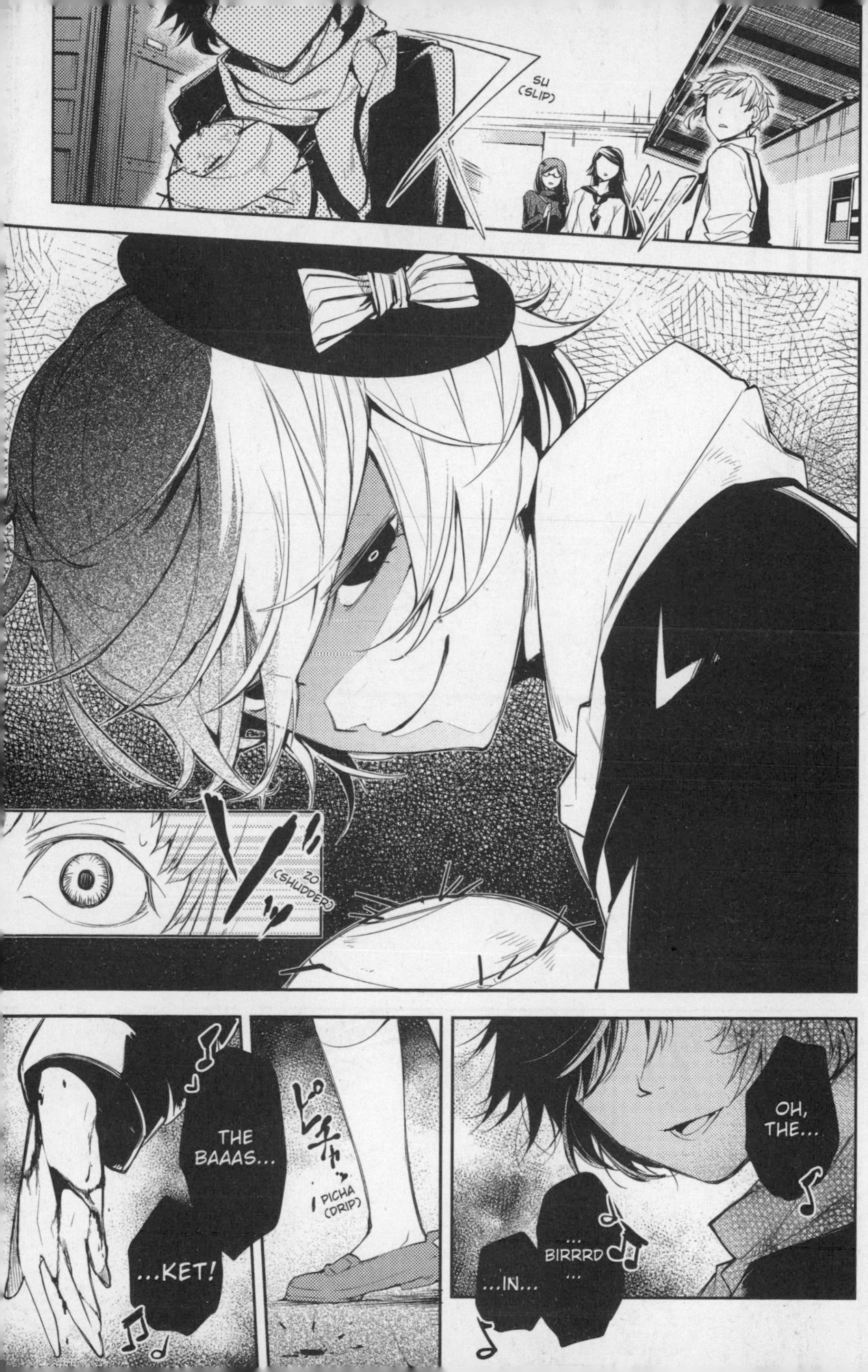
SU (SLIP)
ZO (SHUDDER)
OH, THE...
... BIRRRD ...
...IN...
ピチャ
PICHA (DRIP)
THE BAAAS...
...KET!

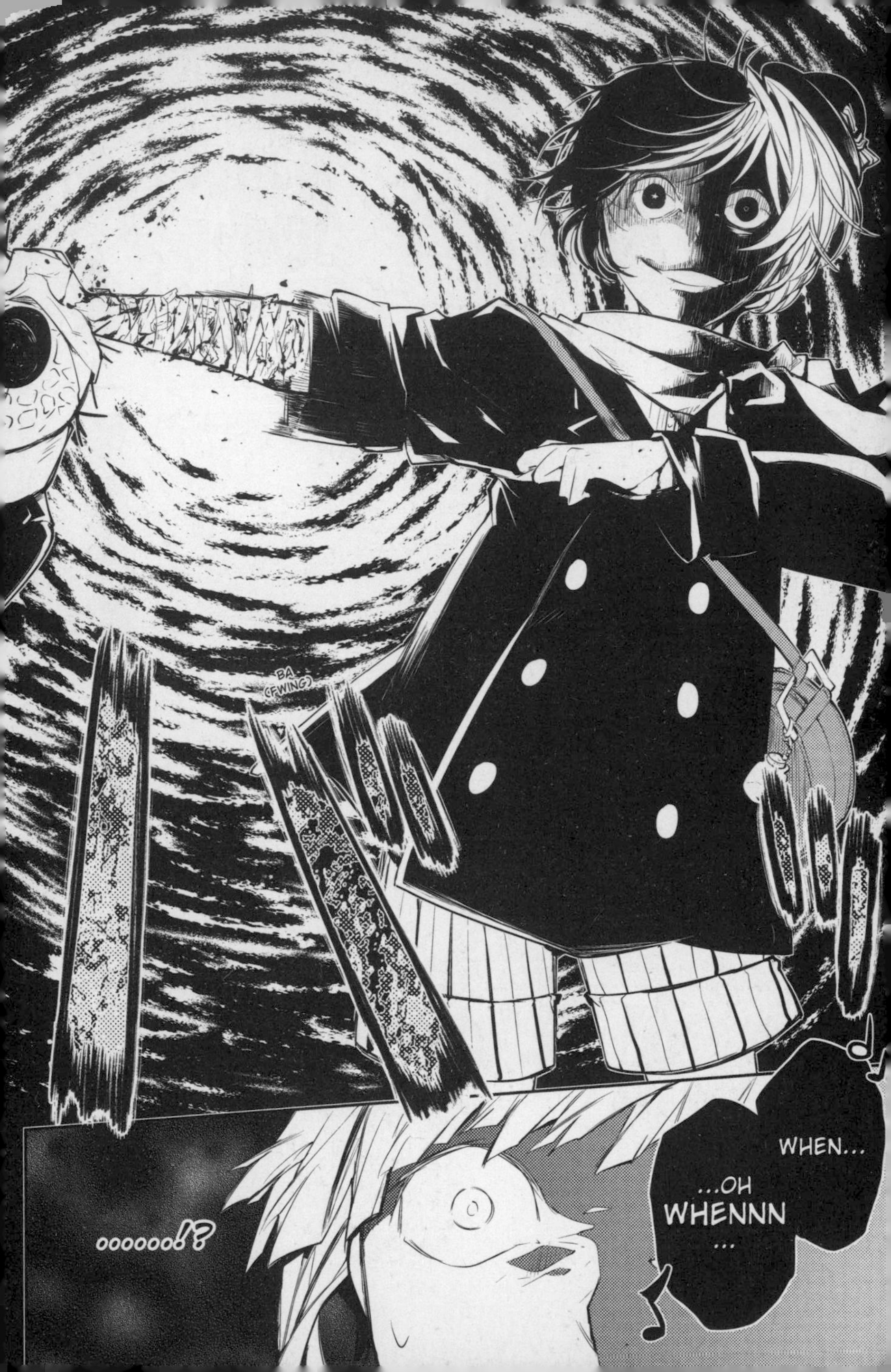
BA (FWING)
WHEN...
...OH WHENNN ...
OOOOOO!?

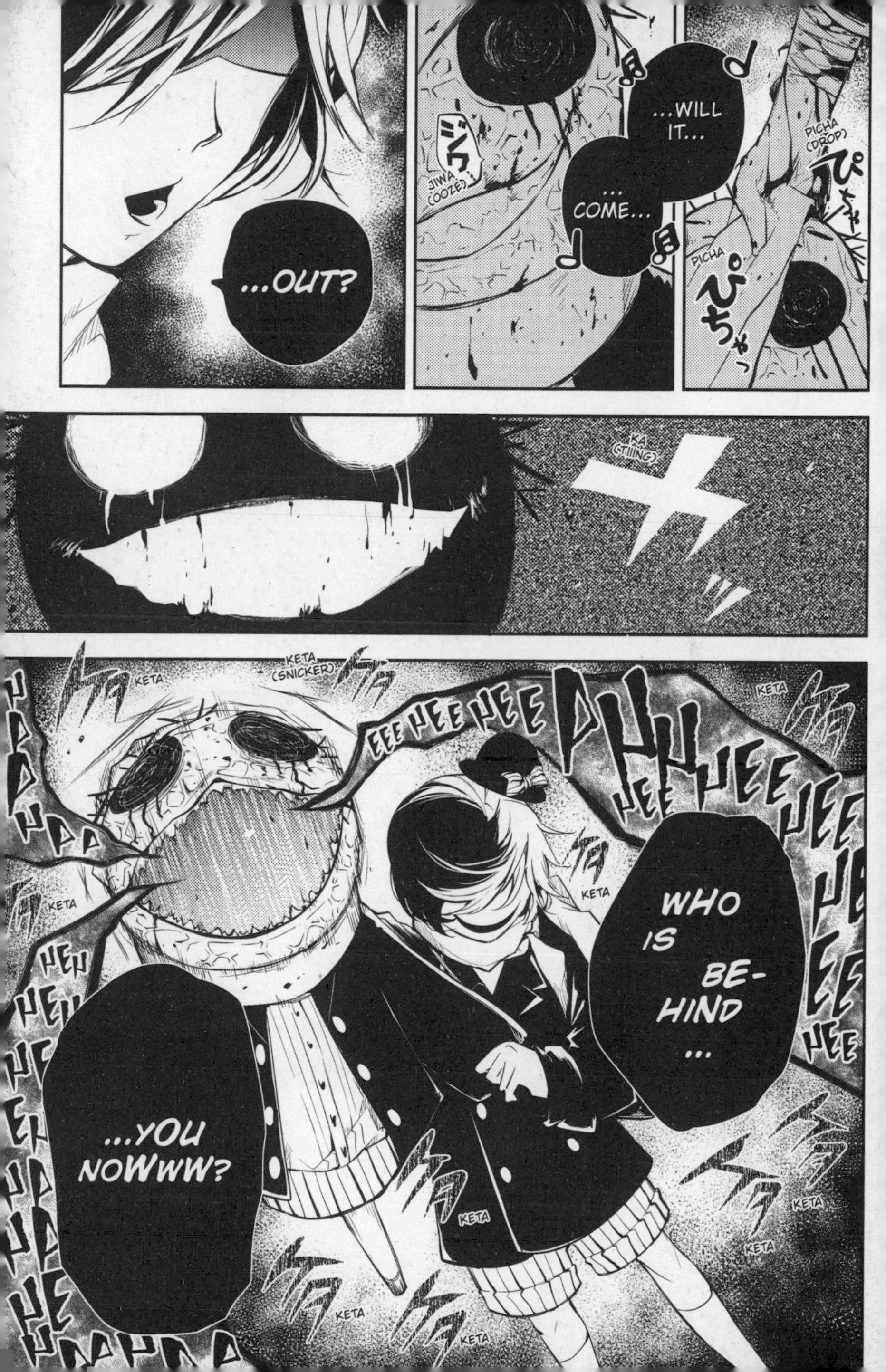
PICHA (DROP)
ぴちゃ
PICHA
ぴちゃっ
...WILL IT...
...COME...
JIWA (OOZE)
ジワ
...OUT?
KA (TIIING)
KETA (SNICKER)
KETA
WHO IS BE-HIND...
...YOU NOWWW?

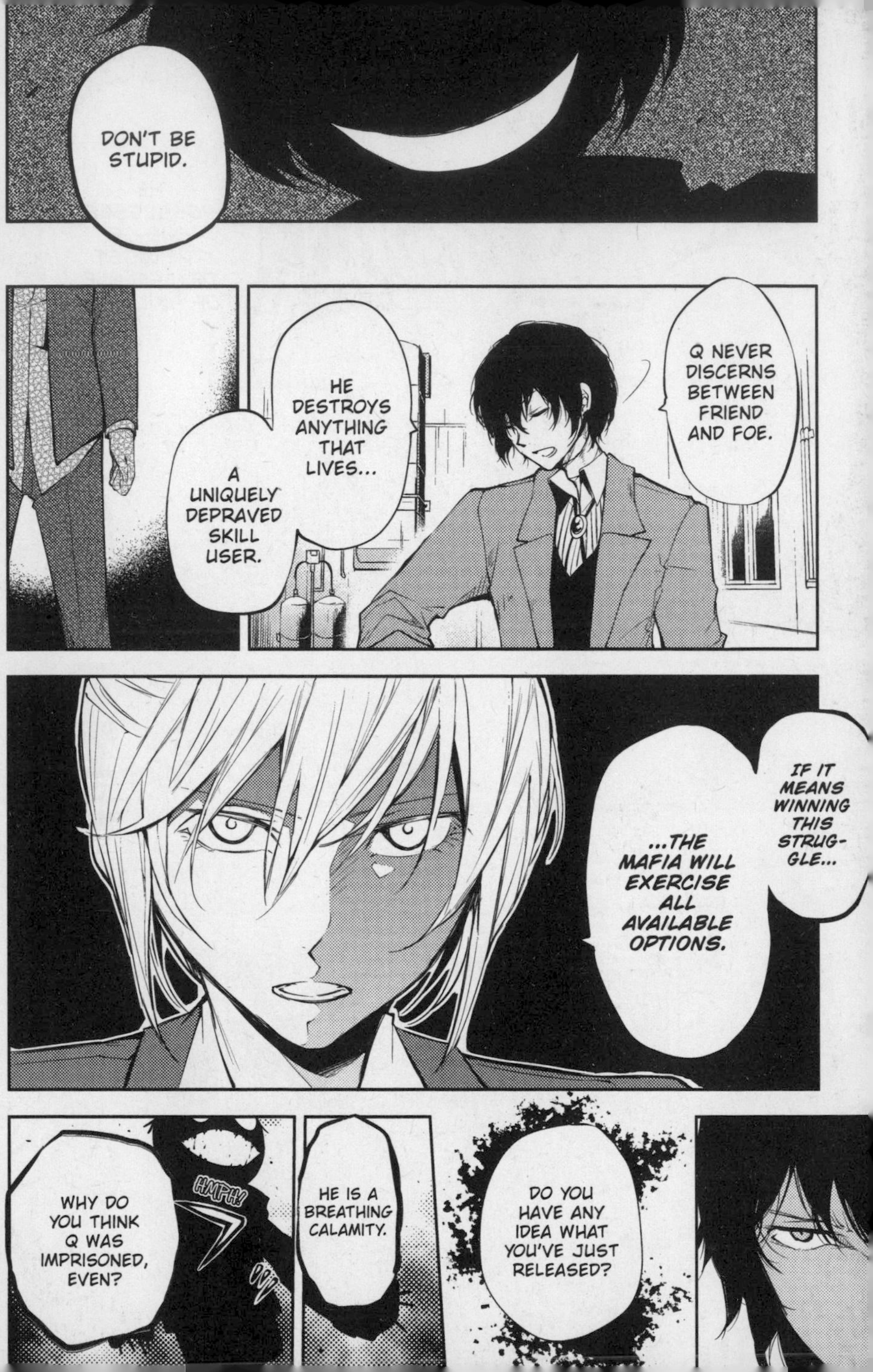
DON'T BE STUPID.
Q NEVER DISCERNS BETWEEN FRIEND AND FOE.
HE DESTROYS ANYTHING THAT LIVES...
A UNIQUELY DEPRAVED SKILL USER.
IF IT MEANS WINNING THIS STRUG-GLE...
...THE MAFIA WILL EXERCISE ALL AVAILABLE OPTIONS.
DO YOU HAVE ANY IDEA WHAT YOU'VE JUST RELEASED?
HE IS A BREATHING CALAMITY.
HMPH!
WHY DO YOU THINK Q WAS IMPRISONED, EVEN?

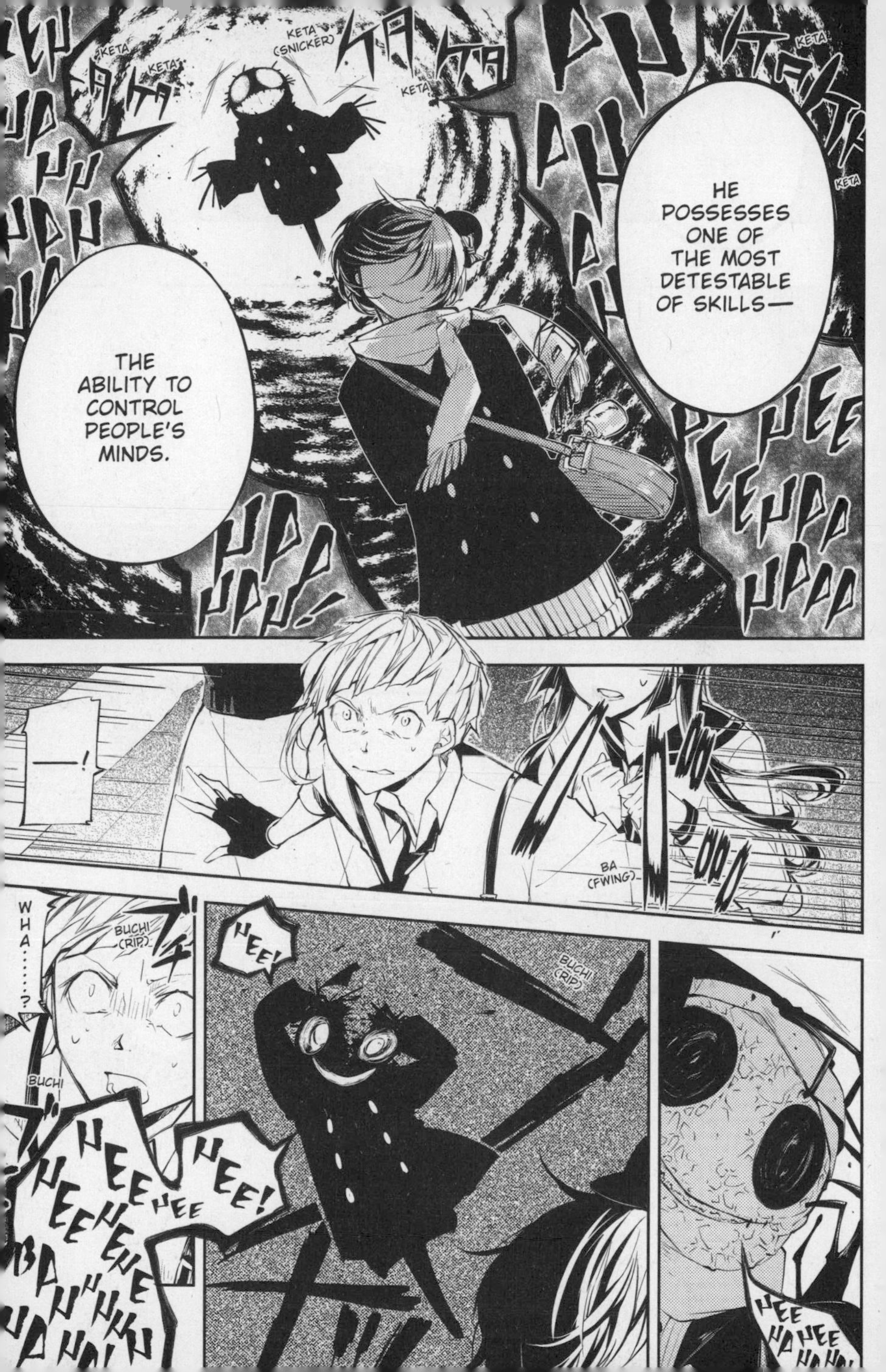
KETA
KETA
HE POSSESSES ONE OF THE MOST DETESTABLE OF SKILLS—
KETA
KETA (SNICKER)
KETA
KETA
THE ABILITY TO CONTROL PEOPLE'S MINDS.
BA (FWING)
——!
HEE!
BUCHI (RIP)
WHA......?
BUCHI (RIP)
BUCHI

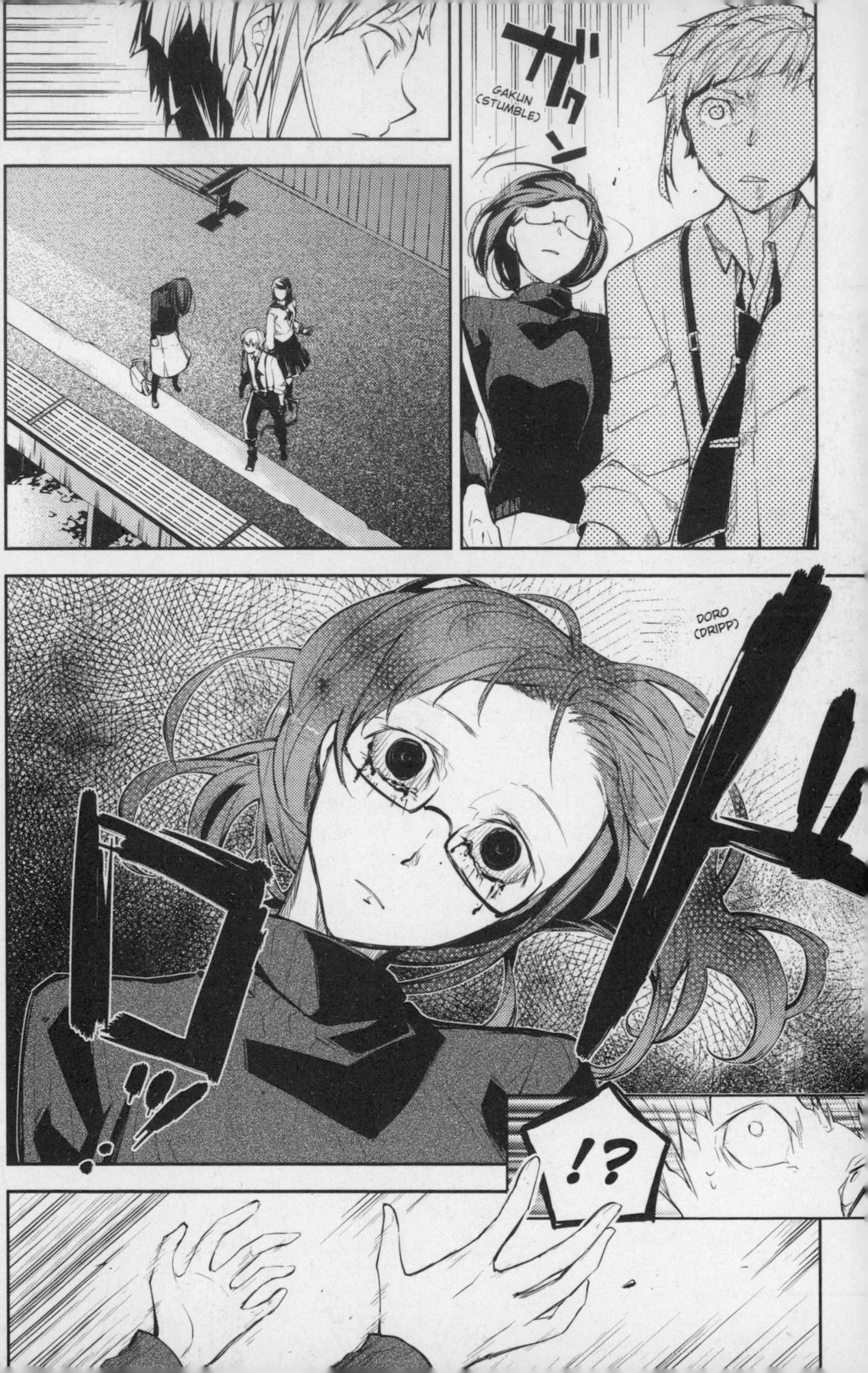
ガクン
GAKUN (STUMBLE)
DORO (DRIPP)
!?

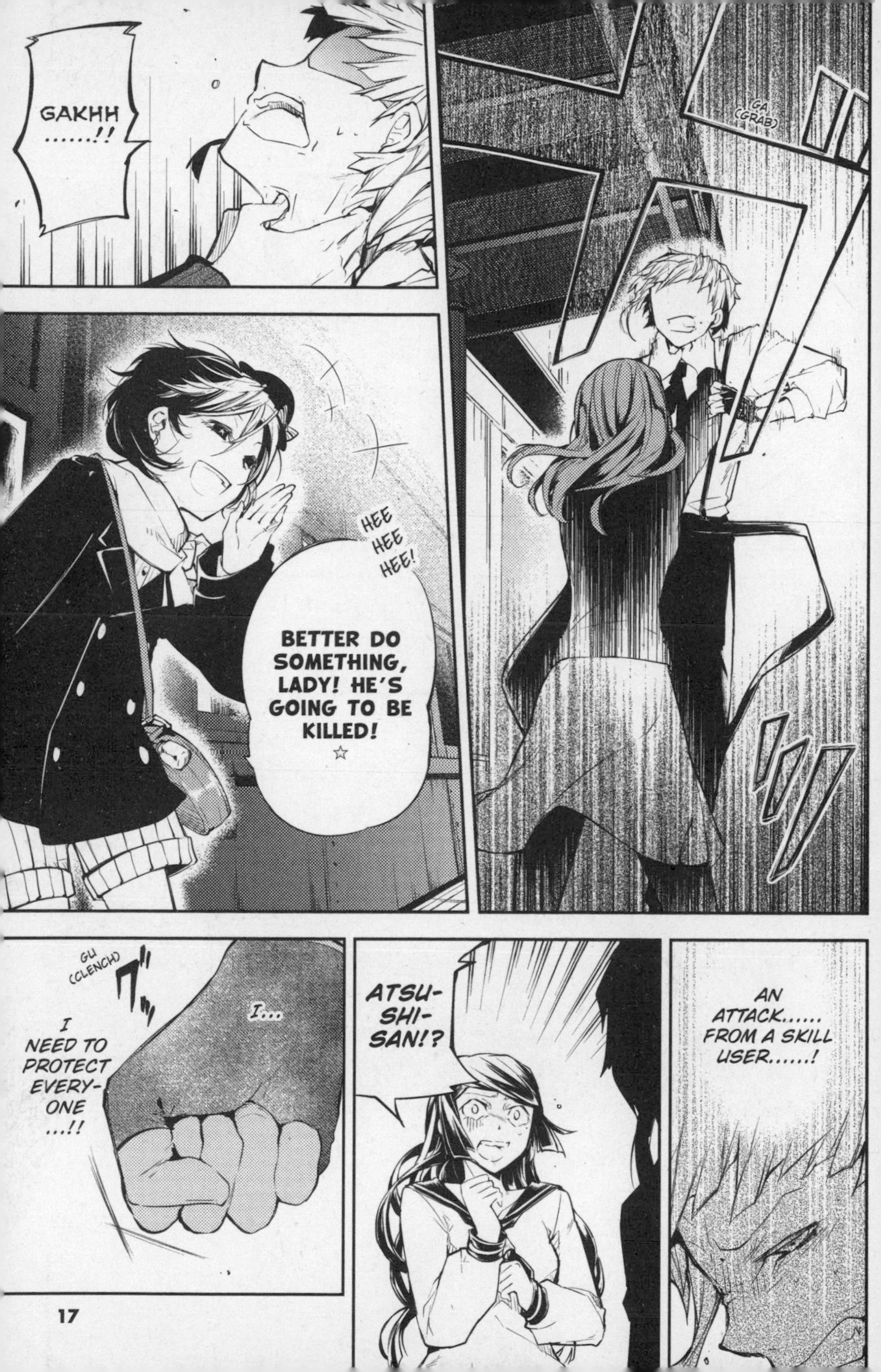
GA (GRAB)
GAKHH ......!!
HEE HEE HEE!
BETTER DO SOMETHING, LADY! HE'S GOING TO BE KILLED! ☆
AN ATTACK...... FROM A SKILL USER......!
ATSU-SHI-SAN!?
GU (CLENCH)
I...
I NEED TO PROTECT EVERY-ONE ...!!

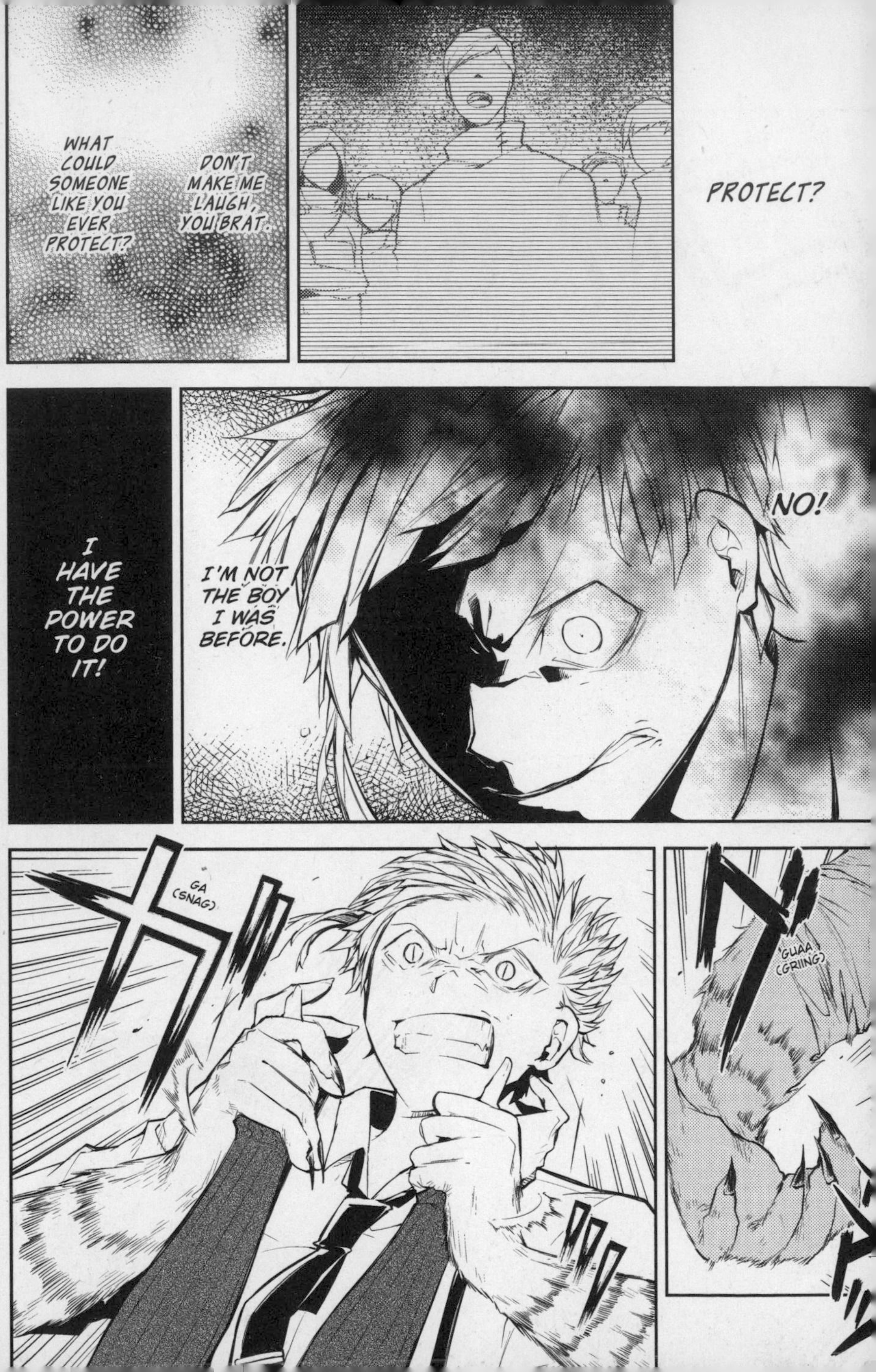
PROTECT?
DON'T MAKE ME LAUGH, YOU BRAT.
WHAT COULD SOMEONE LIKE YOU EVER PROTECT?
NO!
I'M NOT THE BOY I WAS BEFORE.
I HAVE THE POWER TO DO IT!
GUAA (GRIING)
GA (SNAG)

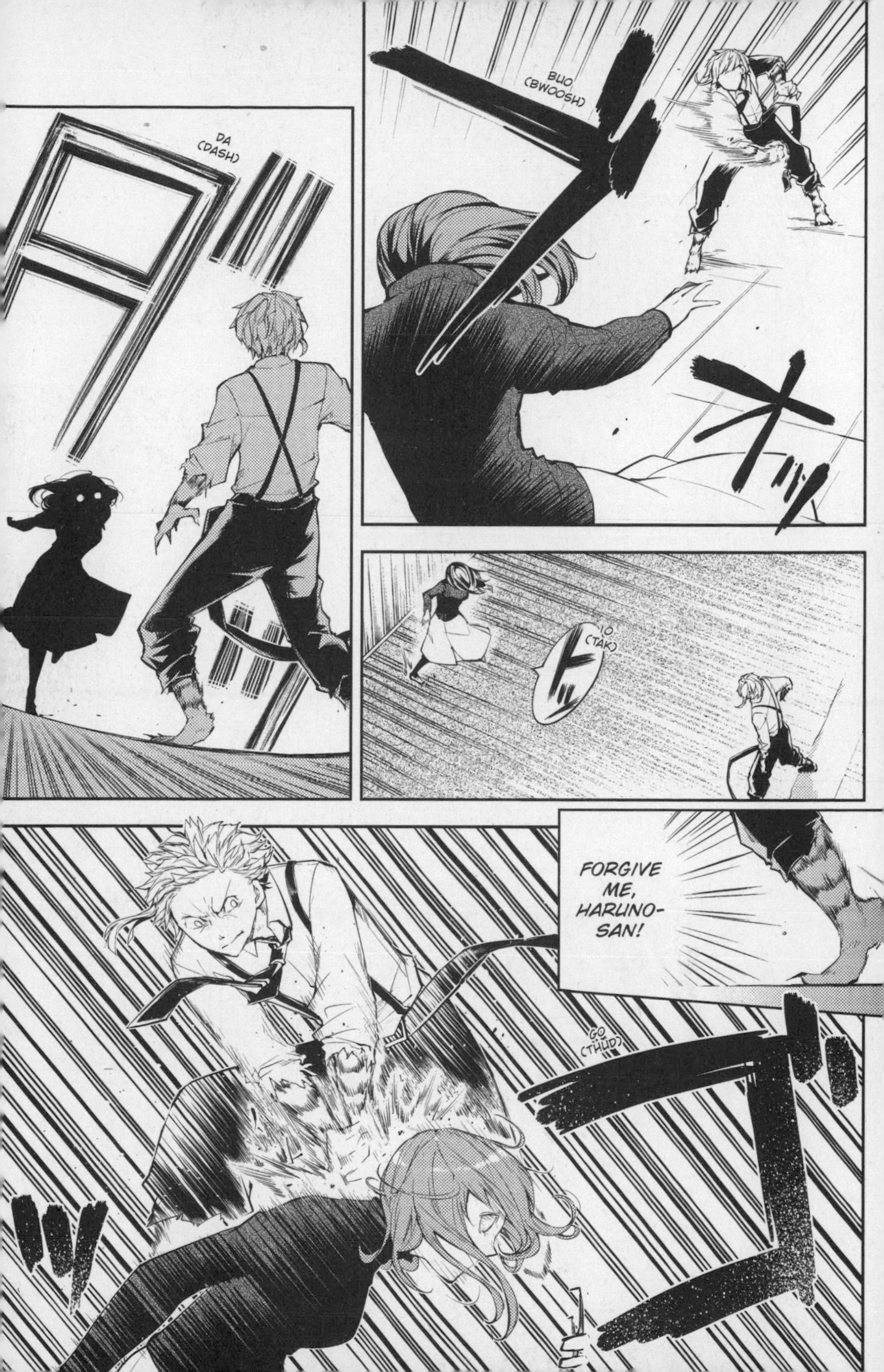
BUO (BWOOSH)
TO (TAK)
DA (DASH)
FORGIVE ME, HARUNO-SAN!
GO (THUD)

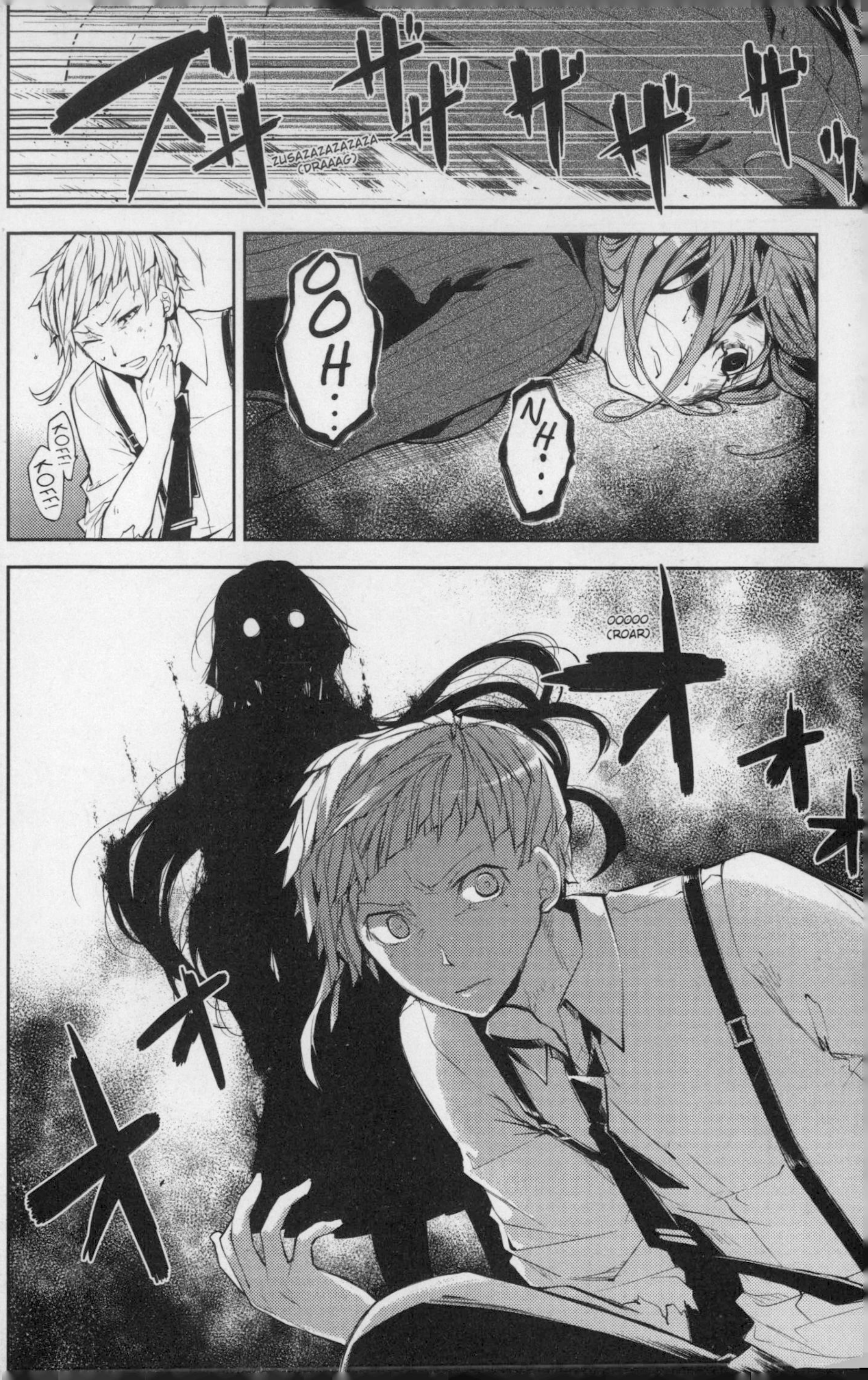
ズザザザザザッ
ZUSAZAZAZAZAZA
(DRAAAG)
OOH...
NH...
KOFF! KOFF!
オオオオ
OOOOO
(ROAR)

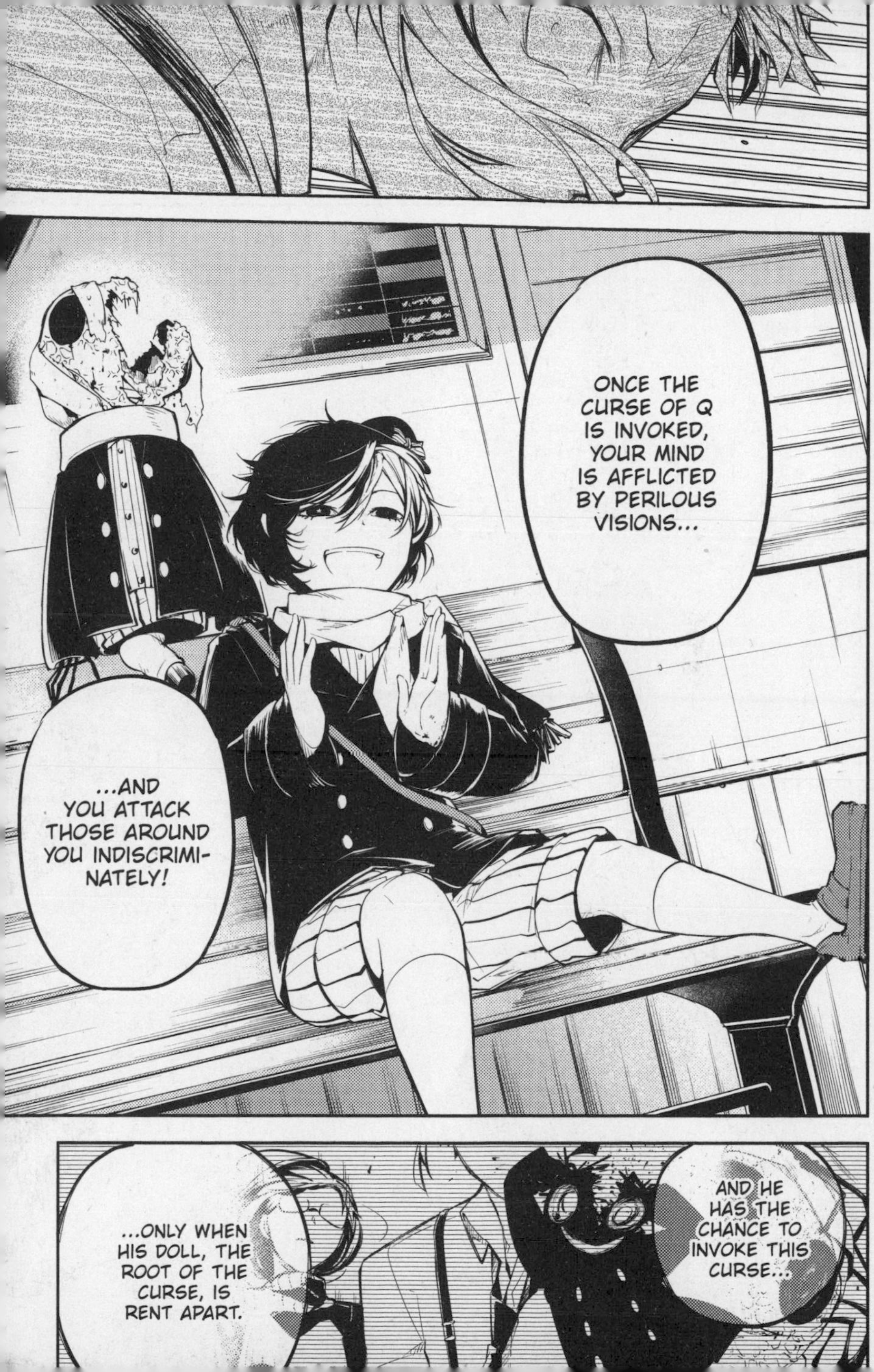
ONCE THE CURSE OF Q IS INVOKED, YOUR MIND IS AFFLICTED BY PERILOUS VISIONS...
...AND YOU ATTACK THOSE AROUND YOU INDISCRIMI-NATELY!
AND HE HAS THE CHANCE TO INVOKE THIS CURSE...
...ONLY WHEN HIS DOLL, THE ROOT OF THE CURSE, IS RENT APART.

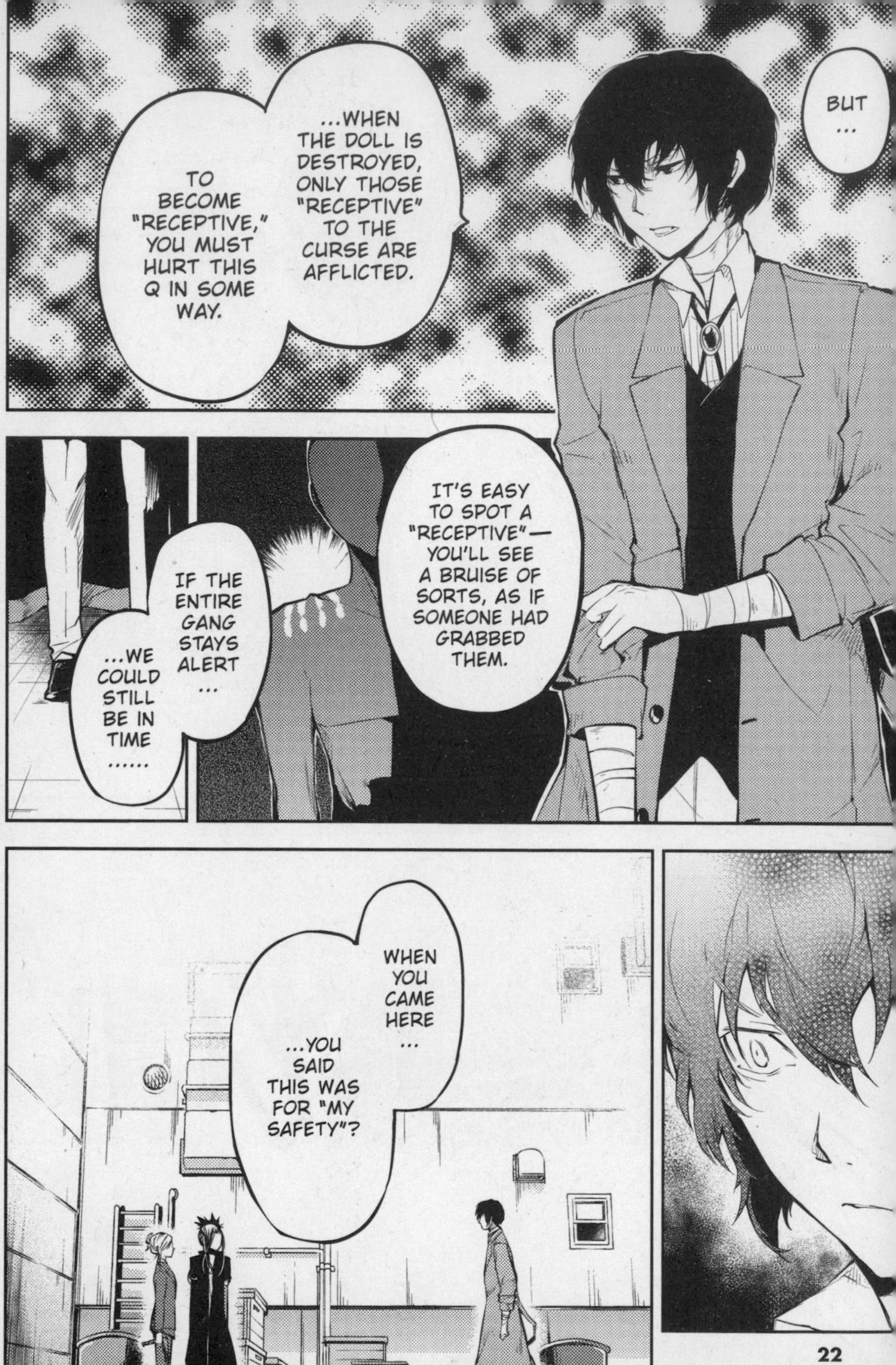
BUT ...
...WHEN THE DOLL IS DESTROYED, ONLY THOSE "RECEPTIVE" TO THE CURSE ARE AFFLICTED.
TO BECOME "RECEPTIVE," YOU MUST HURT THIS Q IN SOME WAY.
IT'S EASY TO SPOT A "RECEPTIVE"—YOU'LL SEE A BRUISE OF SORTS, AS IF SOMEONE HAD GRABBED THEM.
IF THE ENTIRE GANG STAYS ALERT ...
...WE COULD STILL BE IN TIME ......
WHEN YOU CAME HERE ...
...YOU SAID THIS WAS FOR "MY SAFETY"?

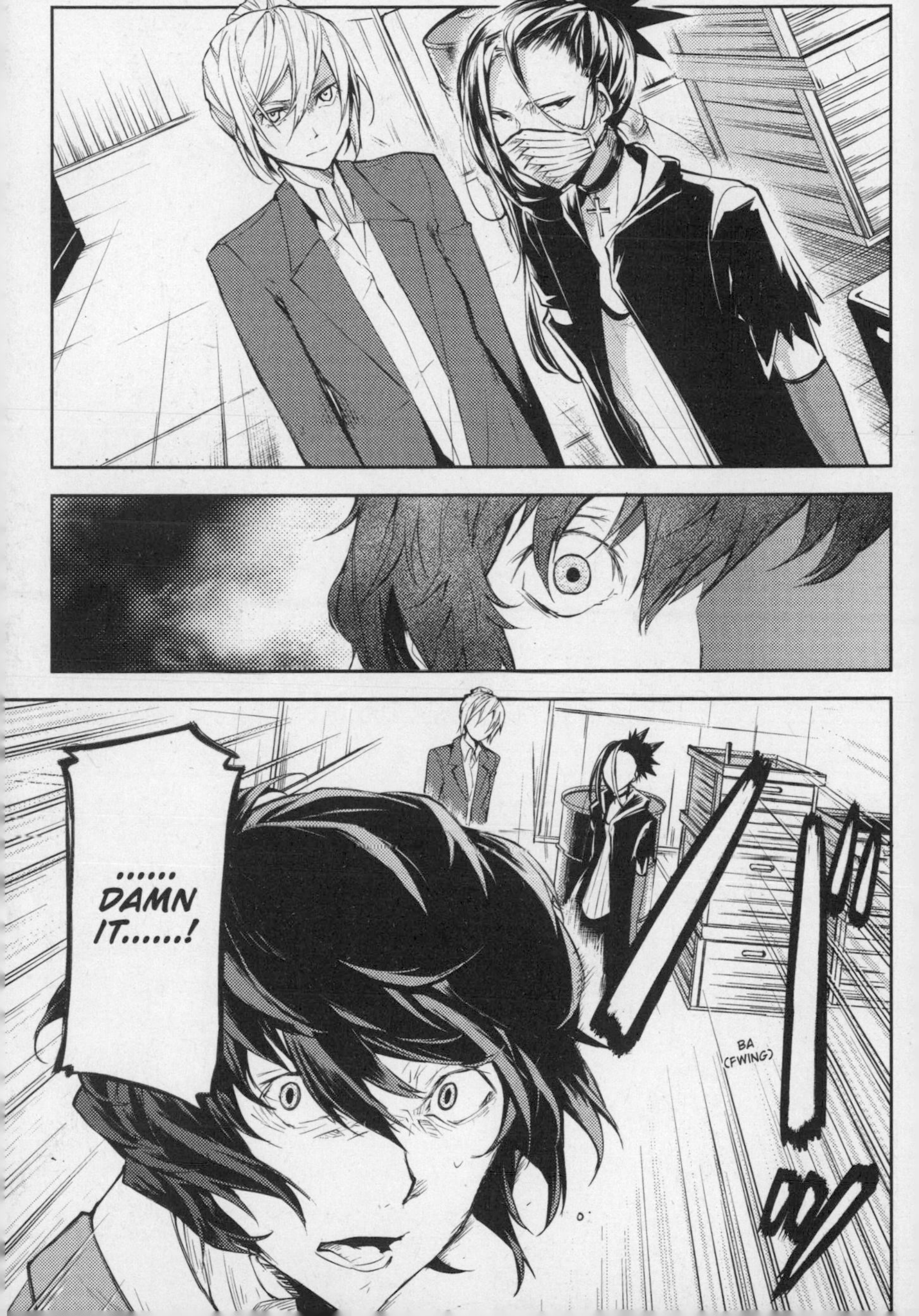
......
DAMN
IT......!
BA
(FWING)

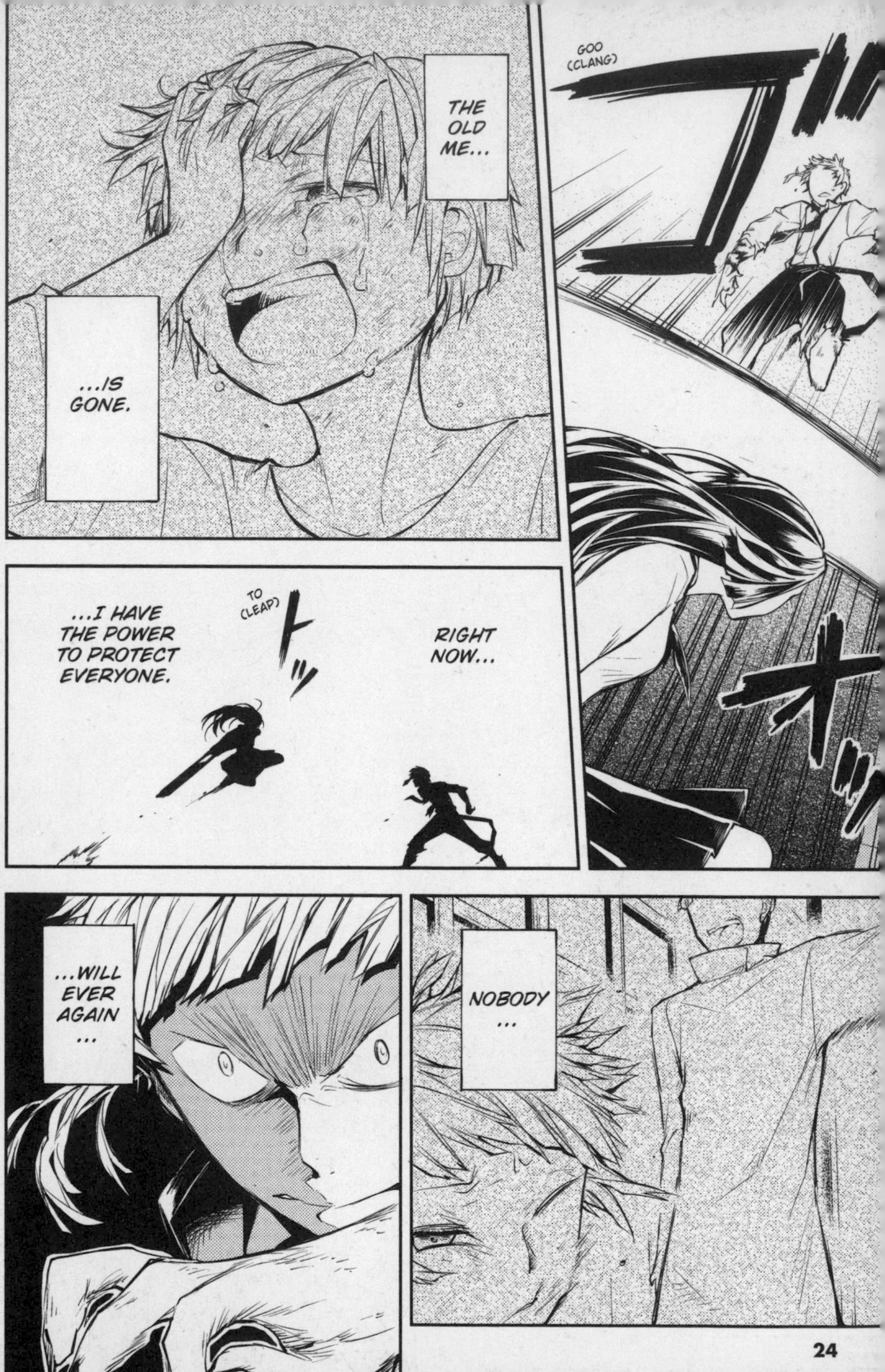
GOO (CLANG)
THE OLD ME...
...IS GONE.
RIGHT NOW...
TO (LEAP)
...I HAVE THE POWER TO PROTECT EVERYONE.
NOBODY ...
...WILL EVER AGAIN ...

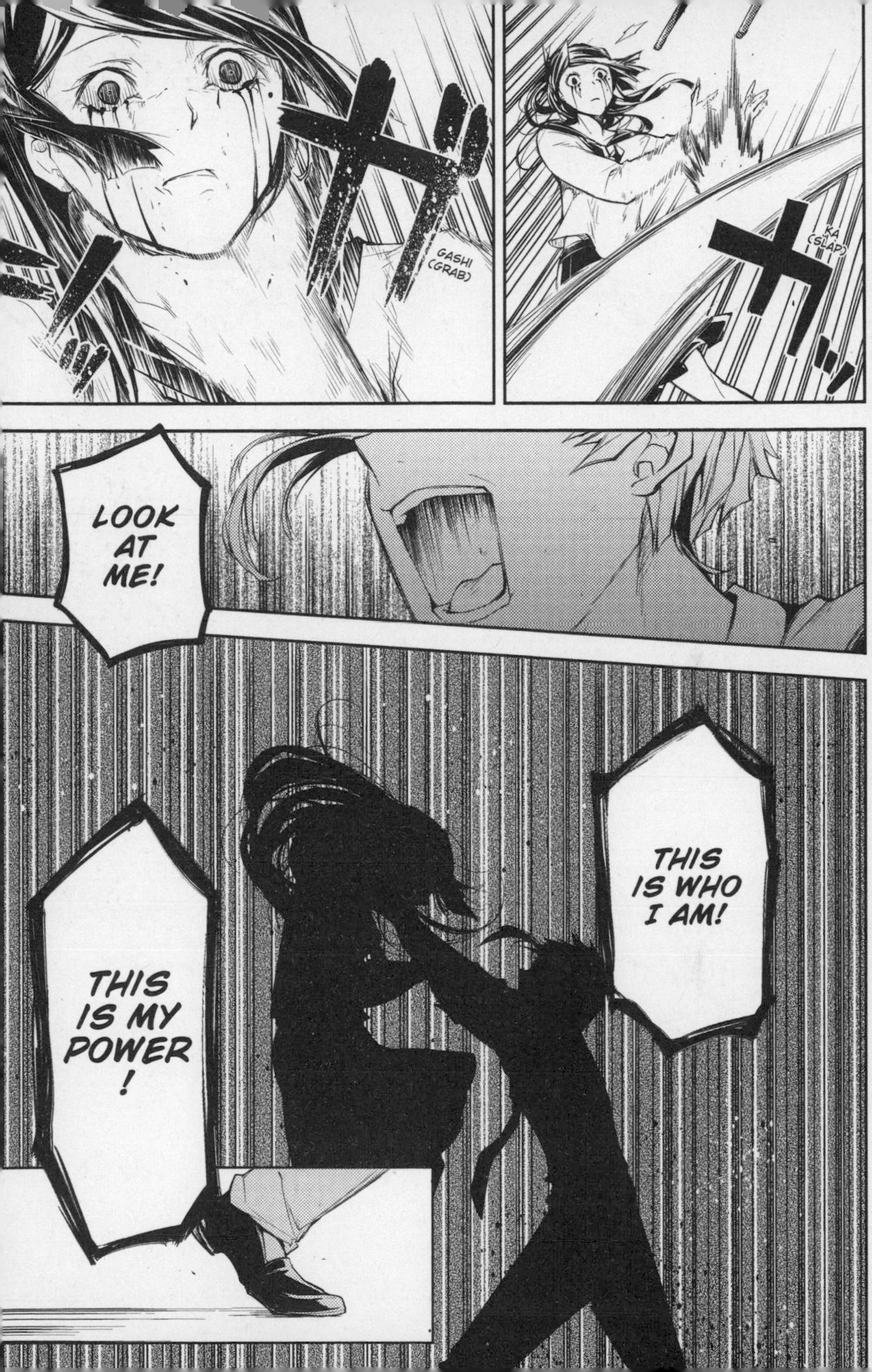
KA (SLAP)
GASHI (GRAB)
LOOK AT ME!
THIS IS WHO I AM!
THIS IS MY POWER!

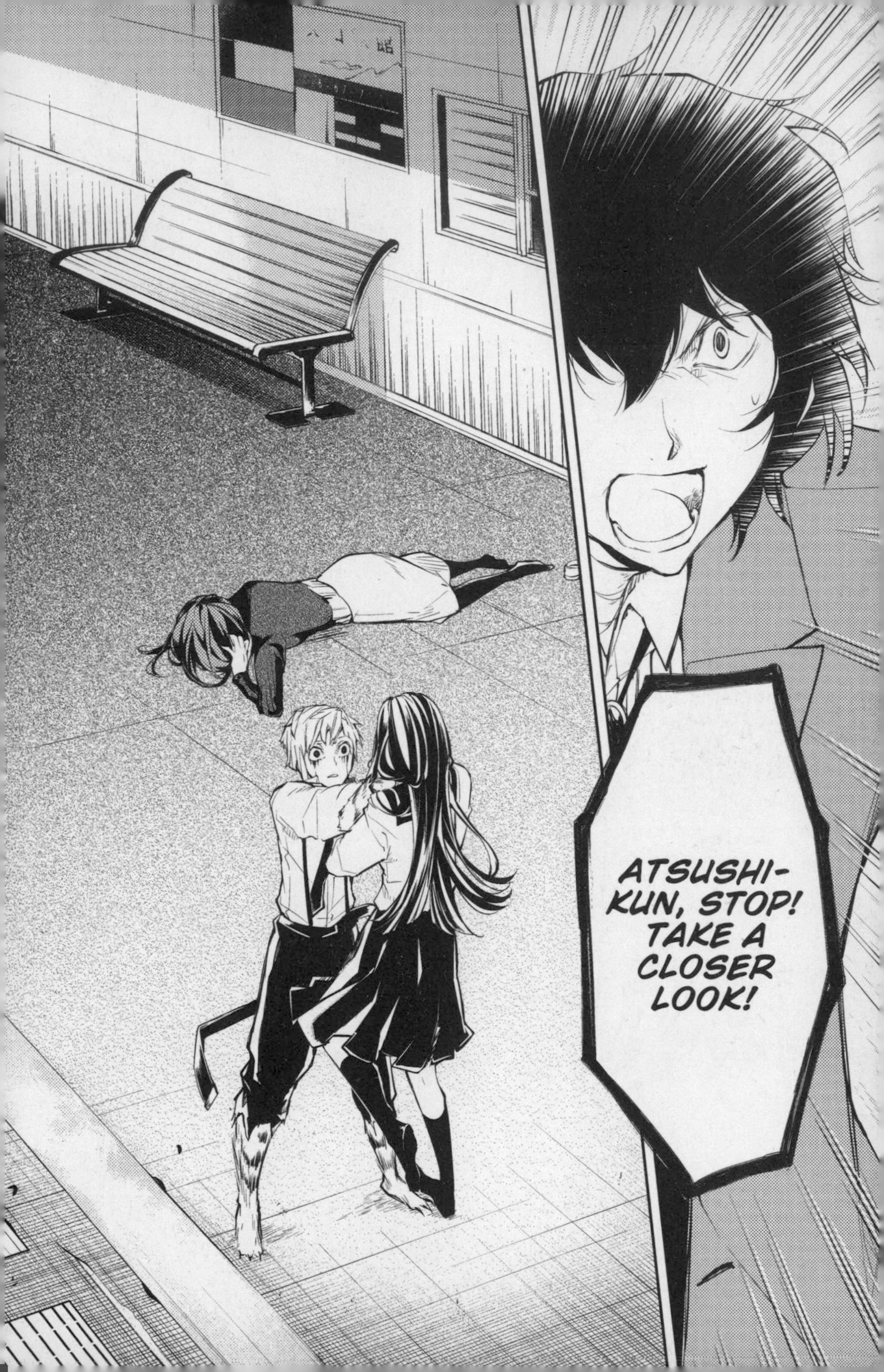
ATSUSHI-KUN, STOP! TAKE A CLOSER LOOK!

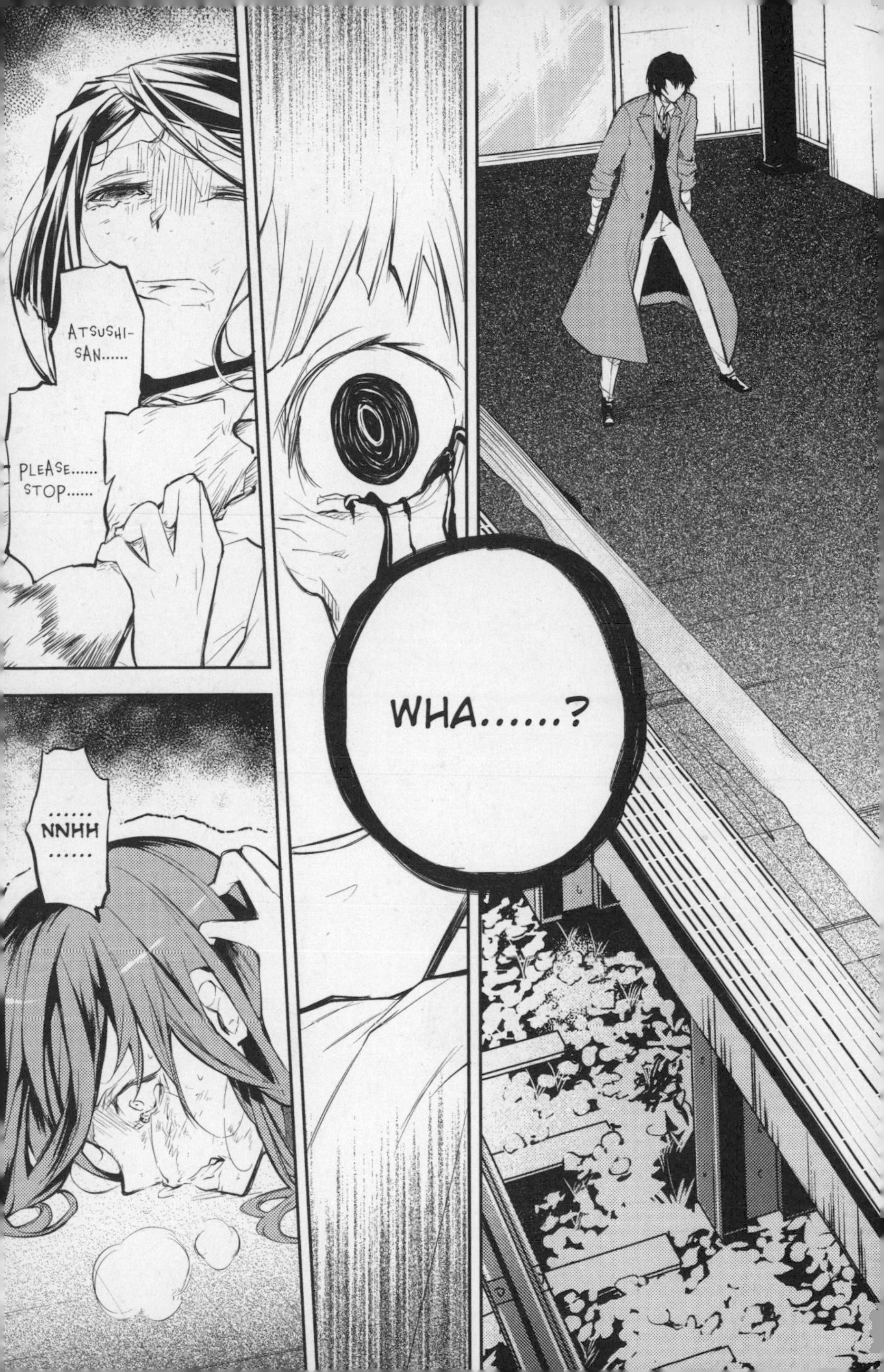
WHA......?
ATSUSHI-SAN......
PLEASE...... STOP......
......NNHH......

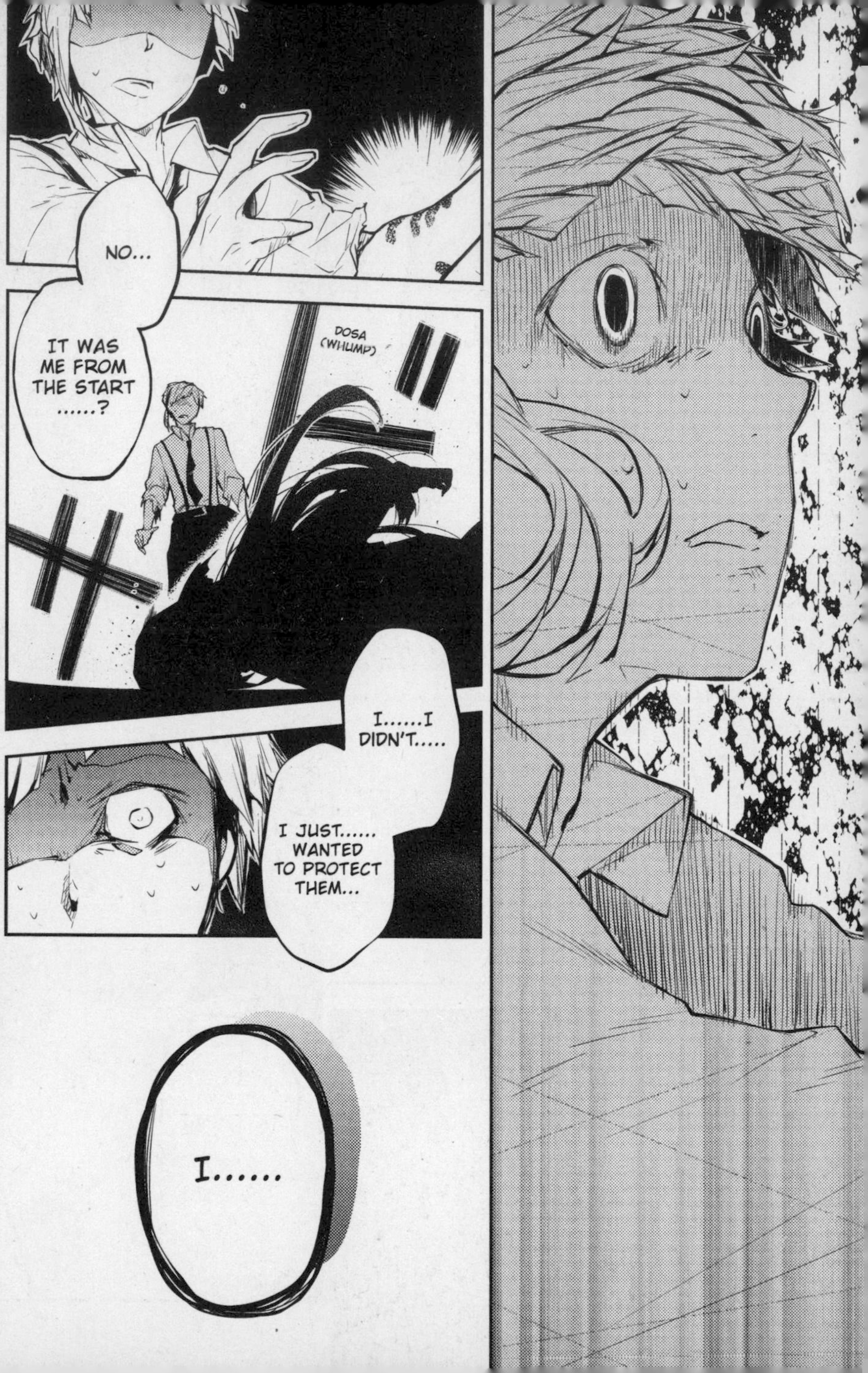
NO...
IT WAS ME FROM THE START ......?
DOSA (WHUMP)
I......I DIDN'T.....
I JUST...... WANTED TO PROTECT THEM...
I......

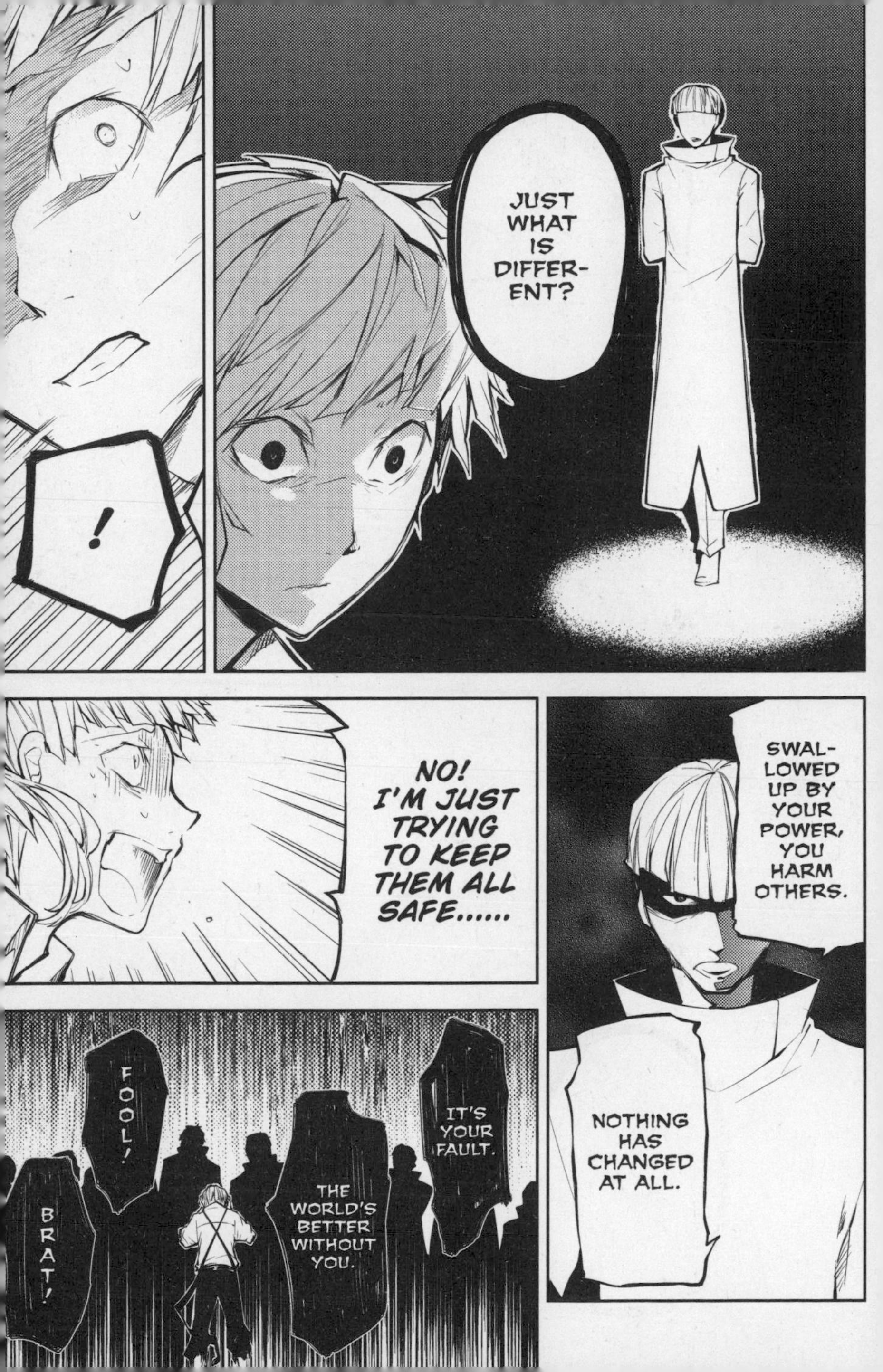
JUST WHAT IS DIFFERENT?
!
SWALLOWED UP BY YOUR POWER, YOU HARM OTHERS.
NOTHING HAS CHANGED AT ALL.
NO! I'M JUST TRYING TO KEEP THEM ALL SAFE......
IT'S YOUR FAULT.
FOOL!
THE WORLD'S BETTER WITHOUT YOU.
BRAT!

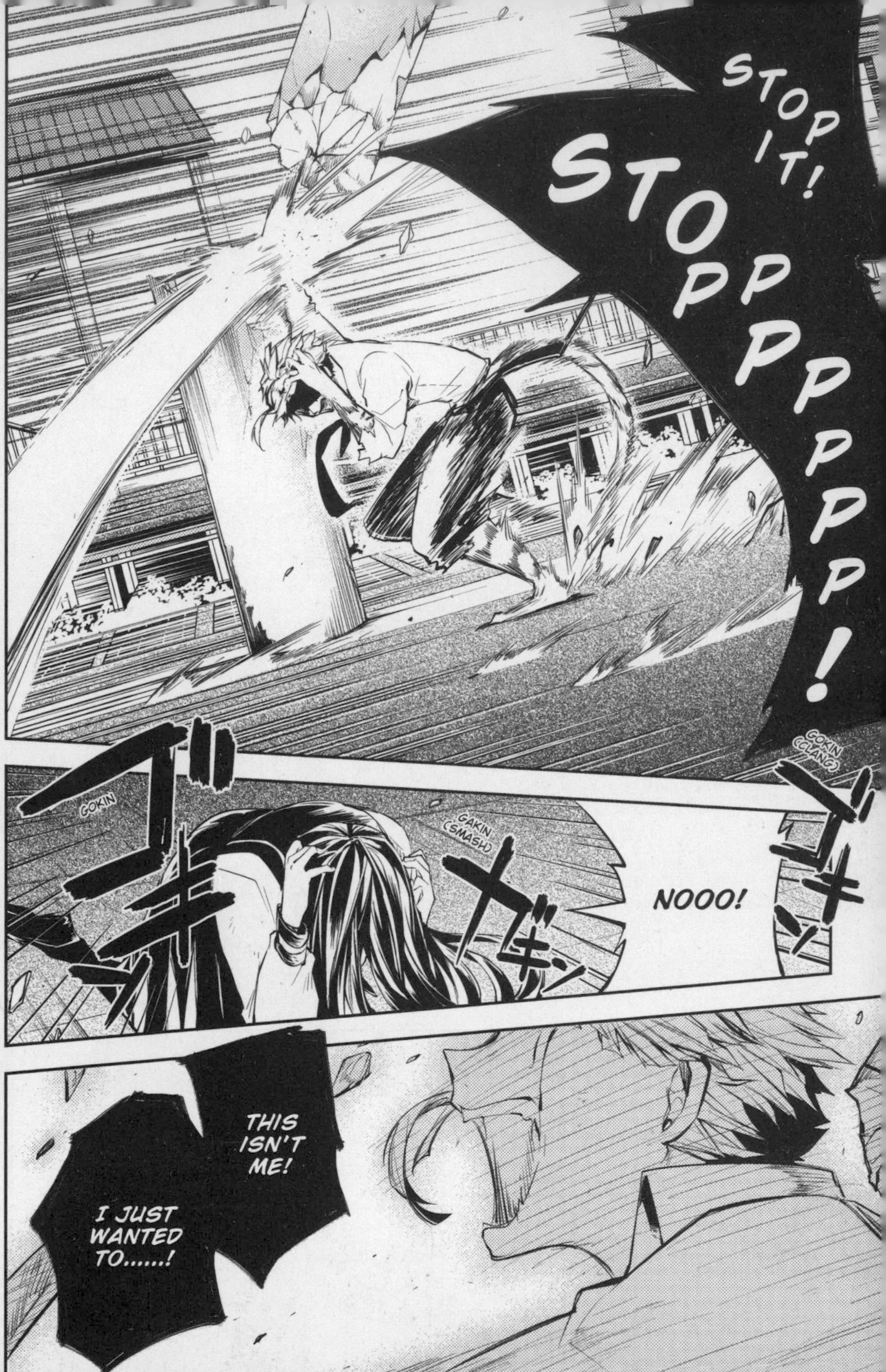
STOP IT!
STOPPPPPPPPP!
GOKIN (CLANG)
NOOO!
GAKIN (SMASH)
GOKIN
THIS ISN'T ME!
I JUST WANTED TO......!

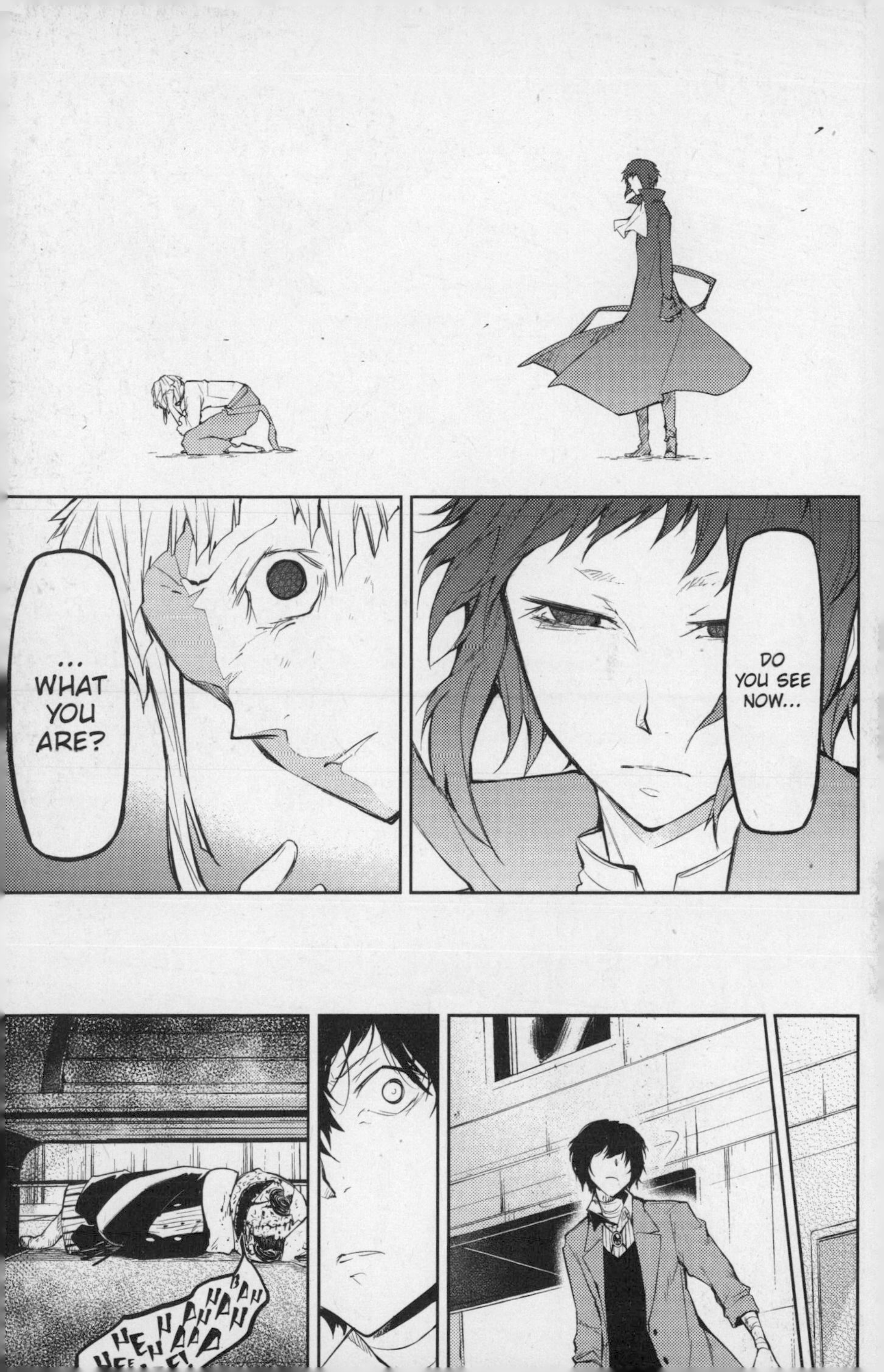
DO YOU SEE NOW...
... WHAT YOU ARE?

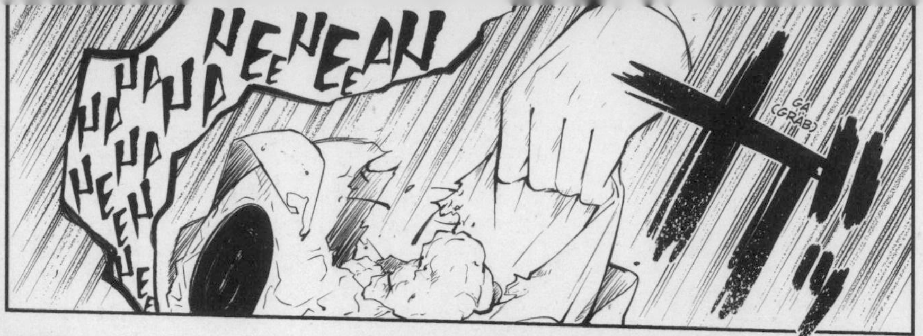
GA
(GRAB)
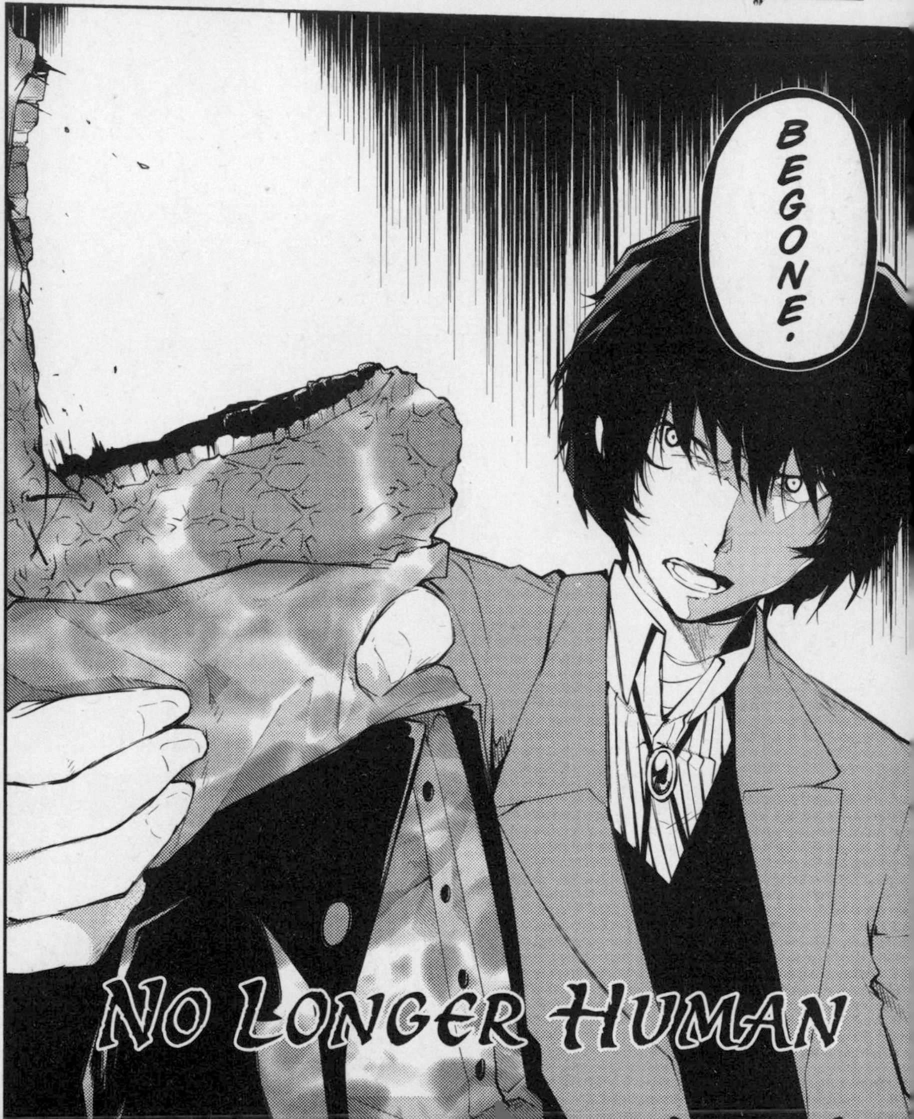
BEGONE.
NO LONGER HUMAN

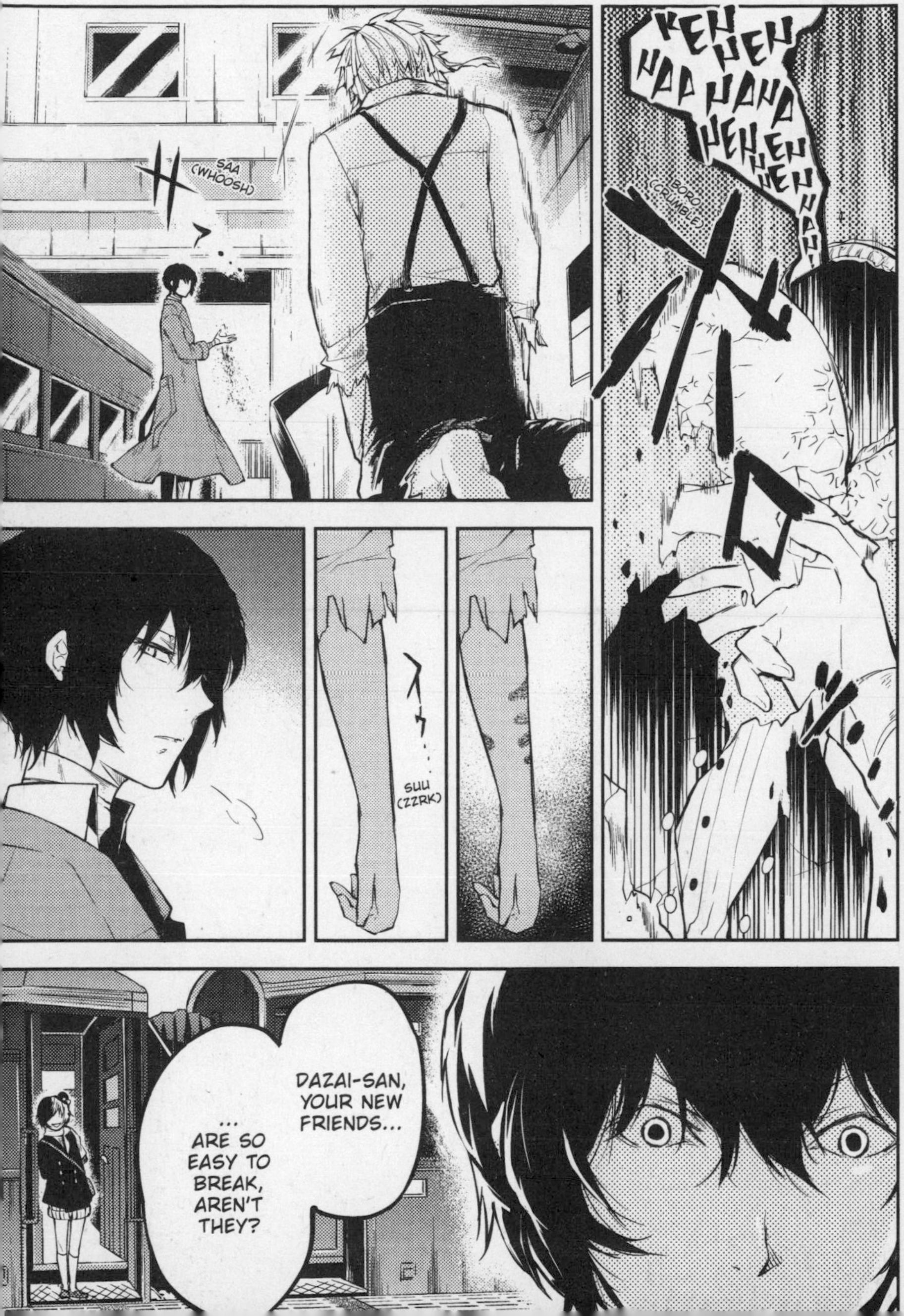
KEH HEH HEH HAH HAHA HEH HEH HEH HAH!
BORO (CRUMBLE)
SAA (WHOOSH)
SUU (ZZRK)
DAZAI-SAN, YOUR NEW FRIENDS...
... ARE SO EASY TO BREAK, AREN'T THEY?

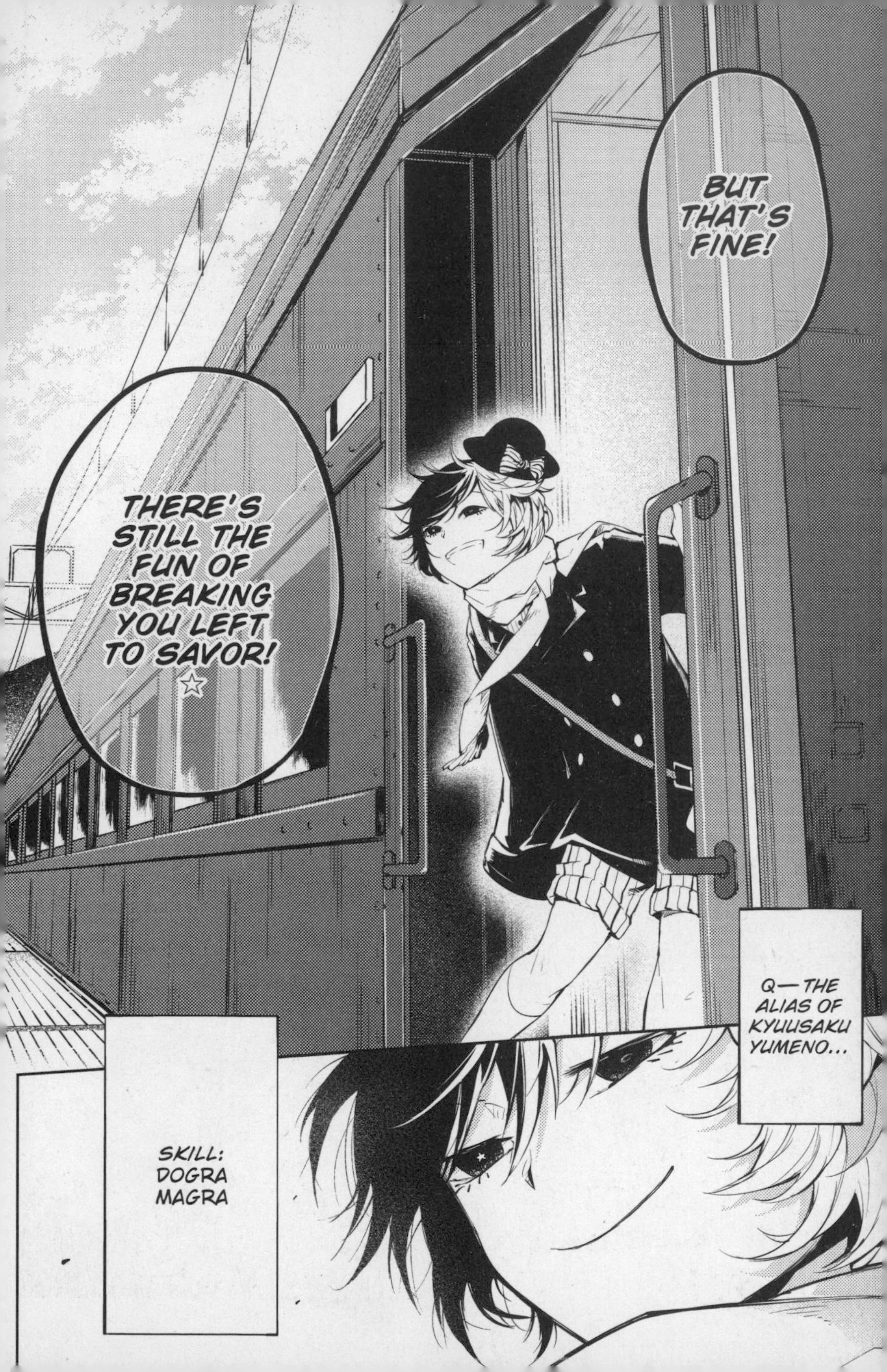
BUT THAT'S FINE!
THERE'S STILL THE FUN OF BREAKING YOU LEFT TO SAVOR! ☆
Q—THE ALIAS OF KYUUSAKU YUMENO...
SKILL: DOGRA MAGRA

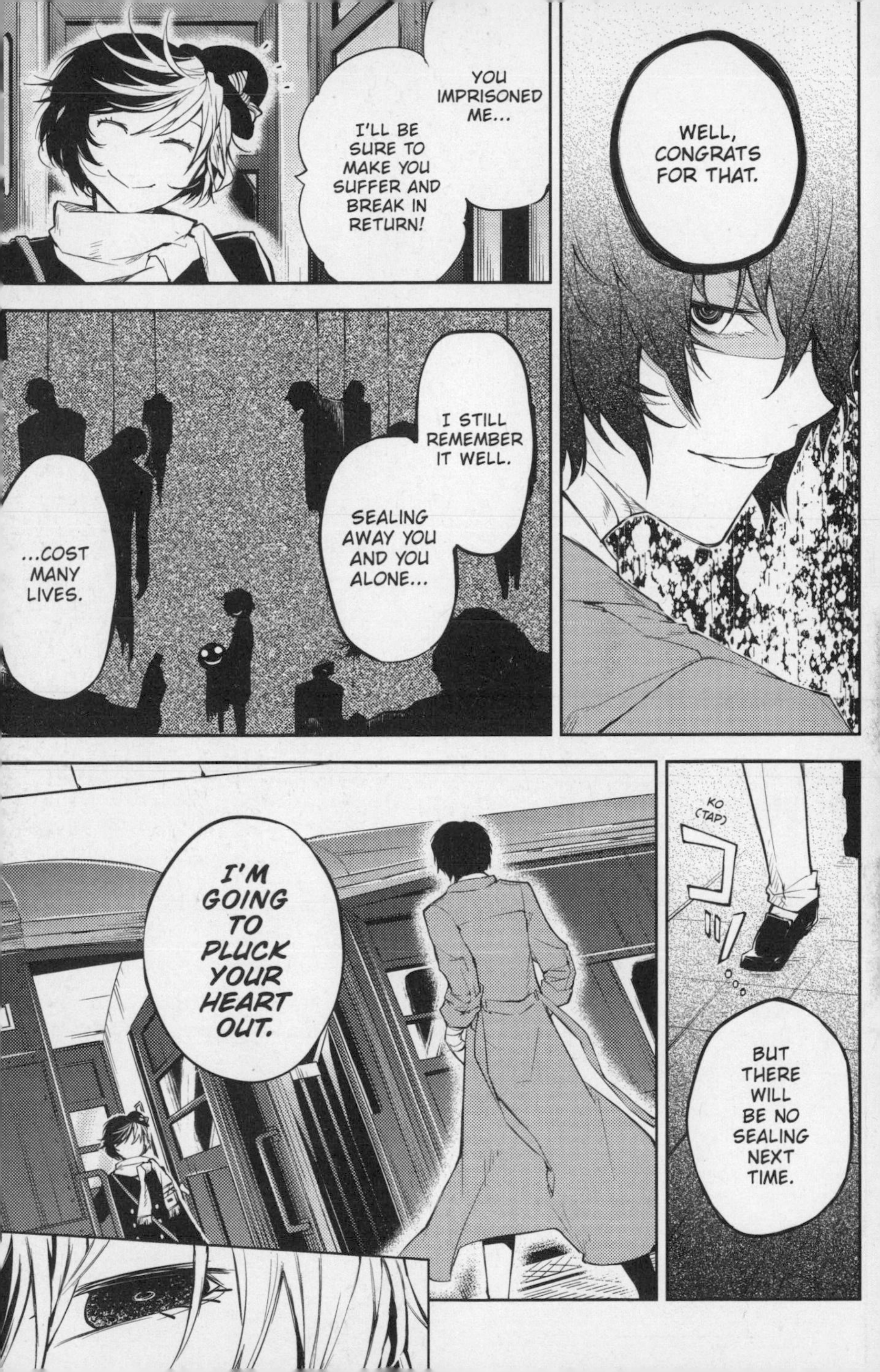
WELL, CONGRATS FOR THAT.
YOU IMPRISONED ME...
I'LL BE SURE TO MAKE YOU SUFFER AND BREAK IN RETURN!
I STILL REMEMBER IT WELL.
SEALING AWAY YOU AND YOU ALONE...
...COST MANY LIVES.
KO (TAP)
BUT THERE WILL BE NO SEALING NEXT TIME.
I'M GOING TO PLUCK YOUR HEART OUT.

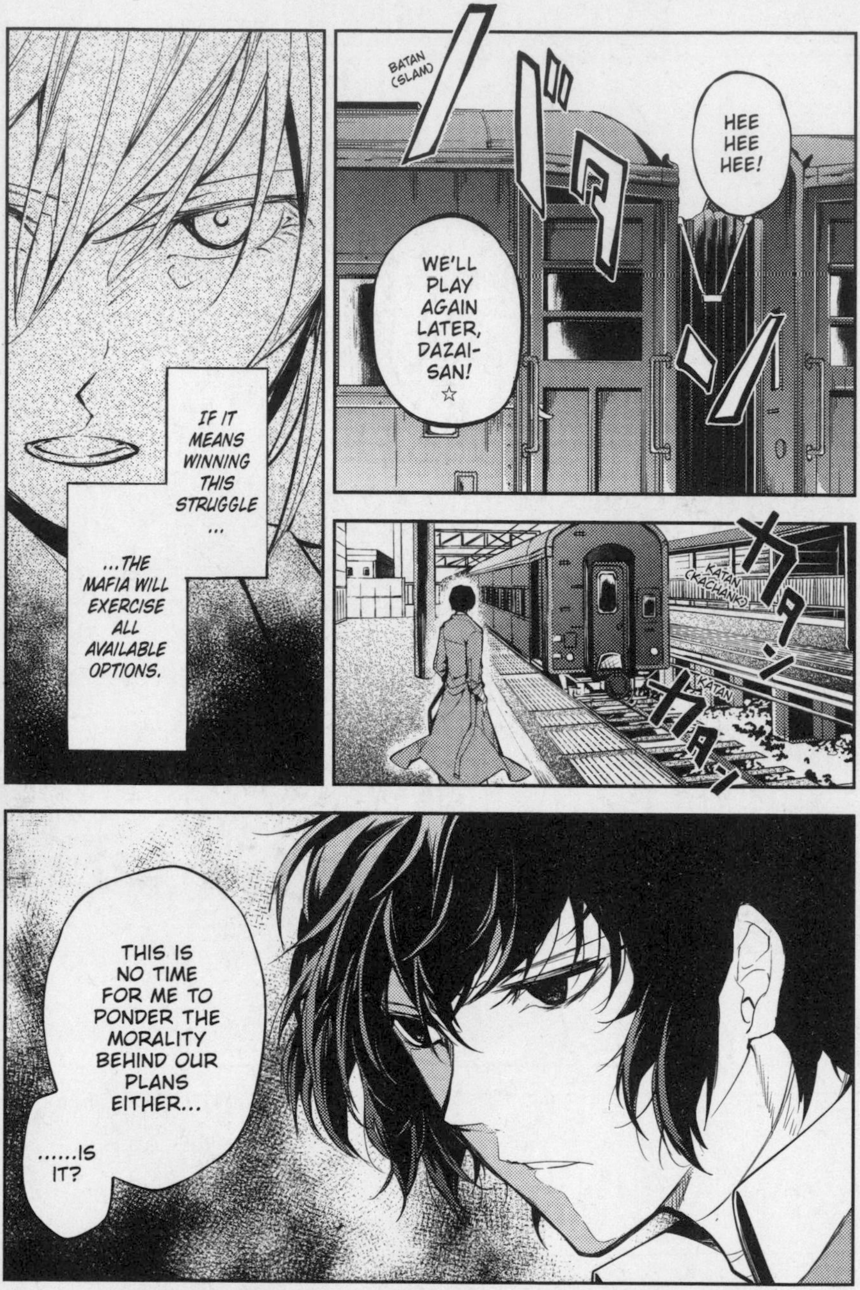
HEE HEE HEE!
BATAN (SLAM)
WE'LL PLAY AGAIN LATER, DAZAI-SAN! ☆
KATAN (KACHANK)
KATAN
IF IT MEANS WINNING THIS STRUGGLE...
...THE MAFIA WILL EXERCISE ALL AVAILABLE OPTIONS.
THIS IS NO TIME FOR ME TO PONDER THE MORALITY BEHIND OUR PLANS EITHER...
......IS IT?

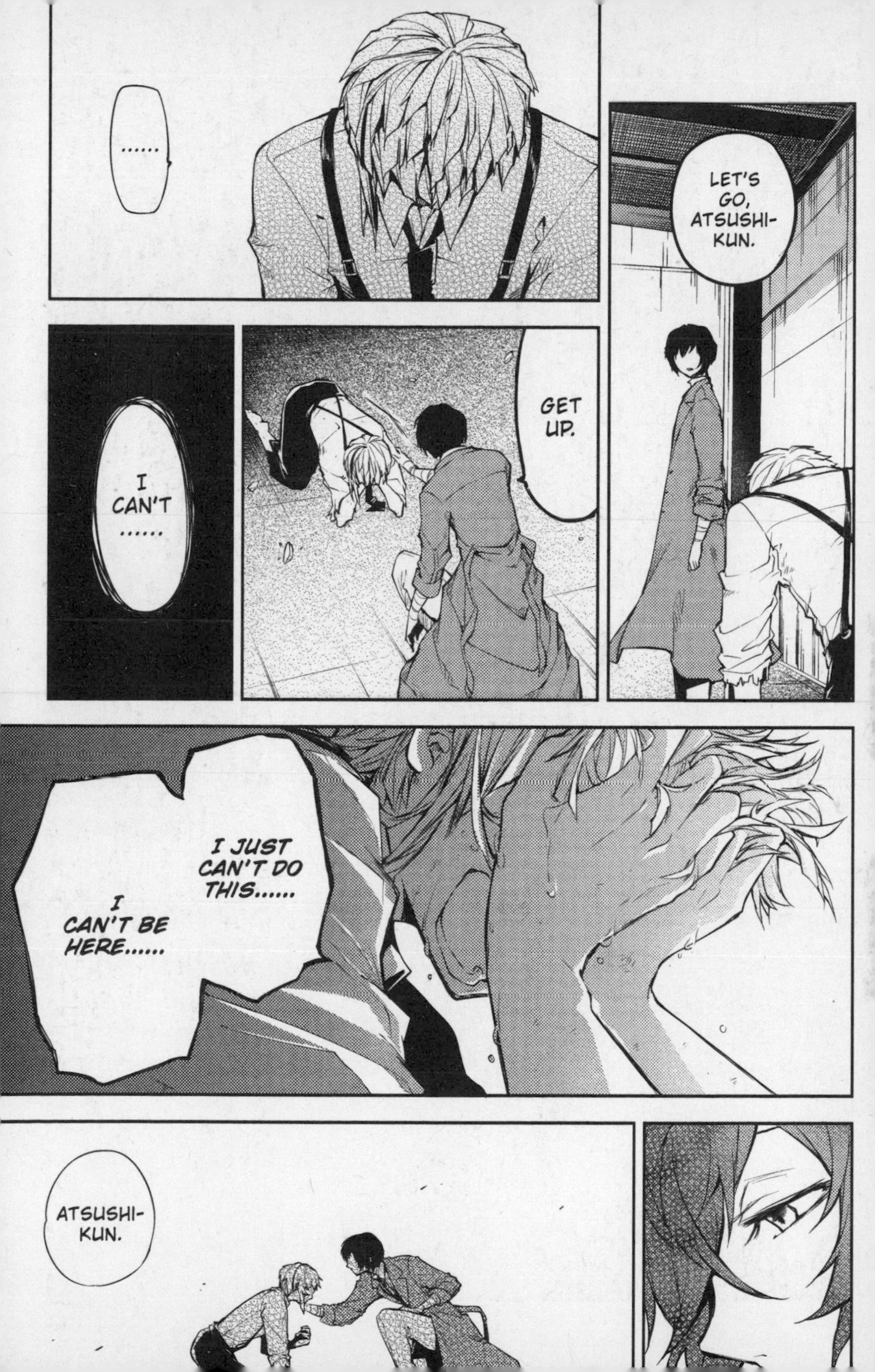
LET'S GO, ATSUSHI-KUN.
......
GET UP.
I CAN'T ......
I JUST CAN'T DO THIS......
I CAN'T BE HERE......
ATSUSHI-KUN.

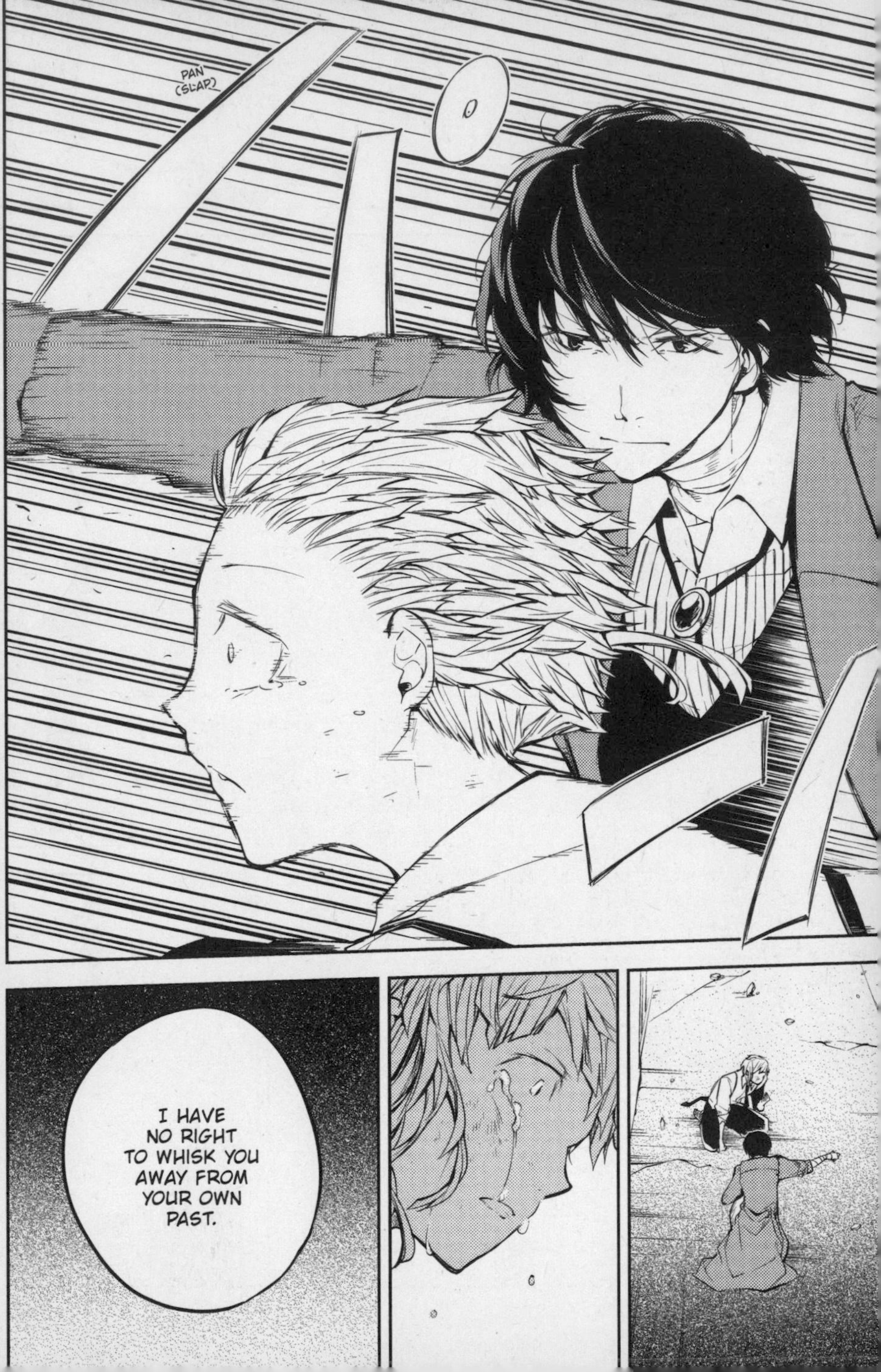
PAN
(SLAP)
I HAVE NO RIGHT TO WHISK YOU AWAY FROM YOUR OWN PAST.

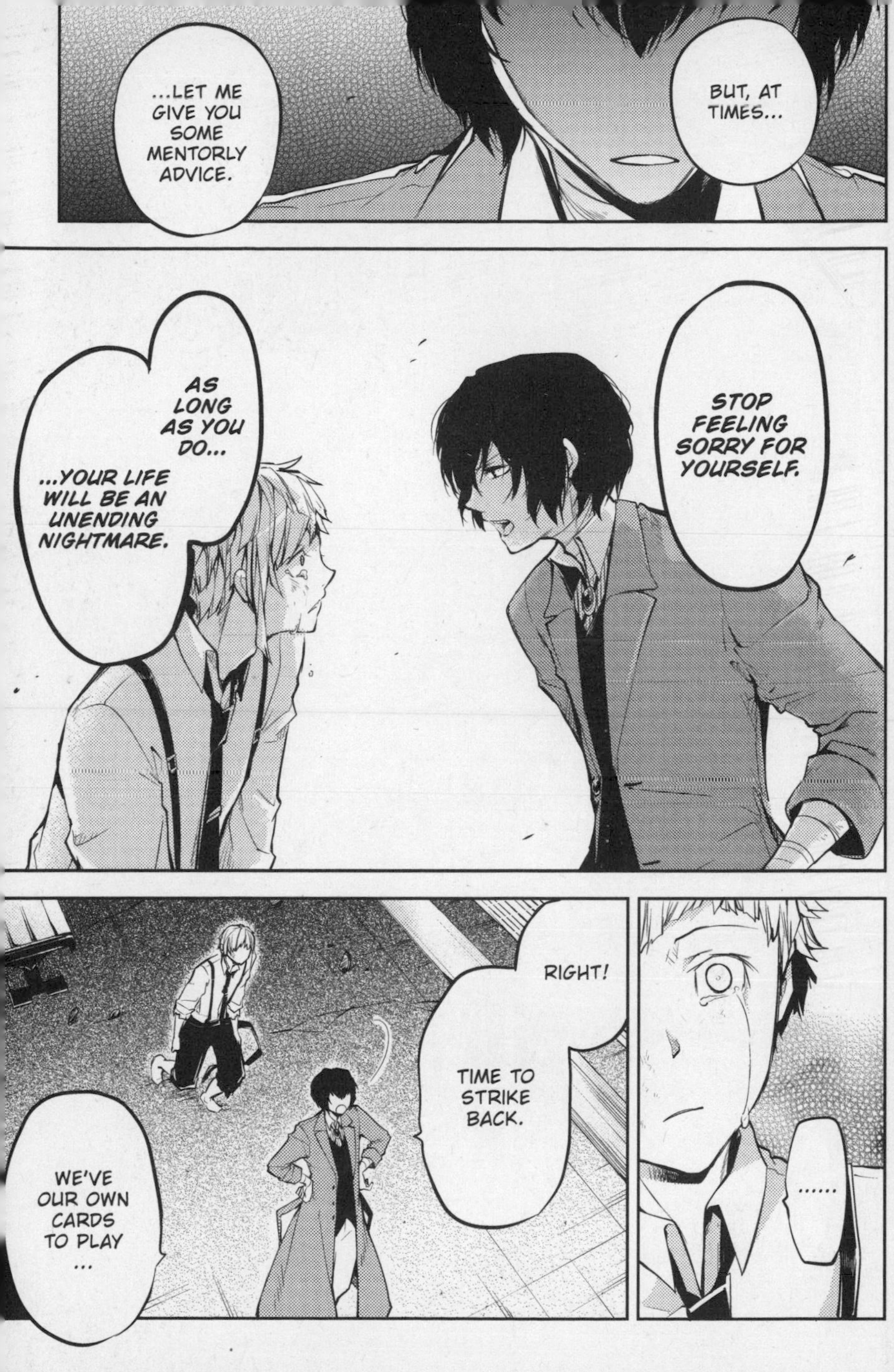
BUT, AT TIMES...
...LET ME GIVE YOU SOME MENTORLY ADVICE.
STOP FEELING SORRY FOR YOURSELF.
AS LONG AS YOU DO...
...YOUR LIFE WILL BE AN UNENDING NIGHTMARE.
......
RIGHT!
TIME TO STRIKE BACK.
WE'VE OUR OWN CARDS TO PLAY ...

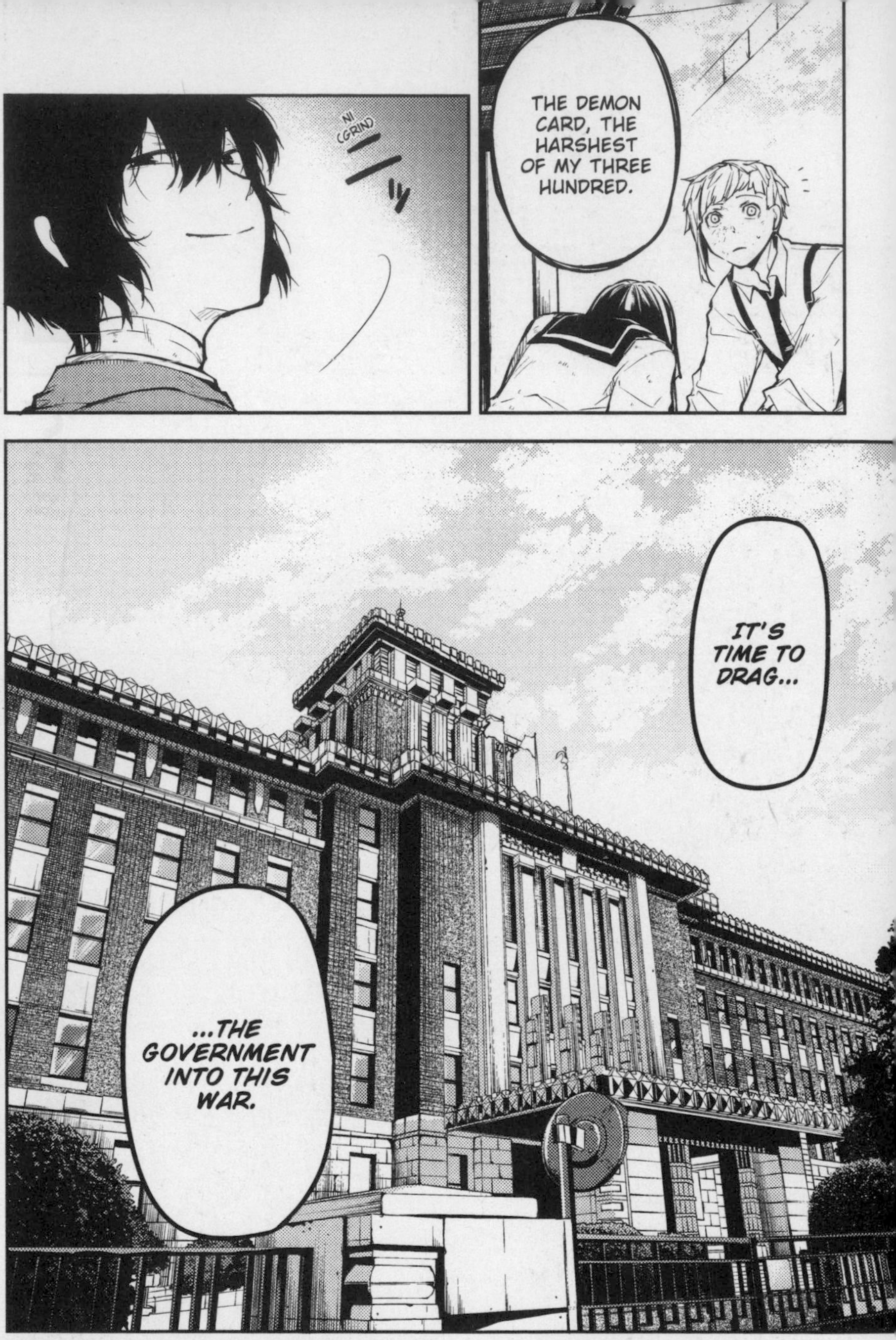
THE DEMON CARD, THE HARSHEST OF MY THREE HUNDRED.
NI (GRIN)
IT'S TIME TO DRAG...
...THE GOVERNMENT INTO THIS WAR.

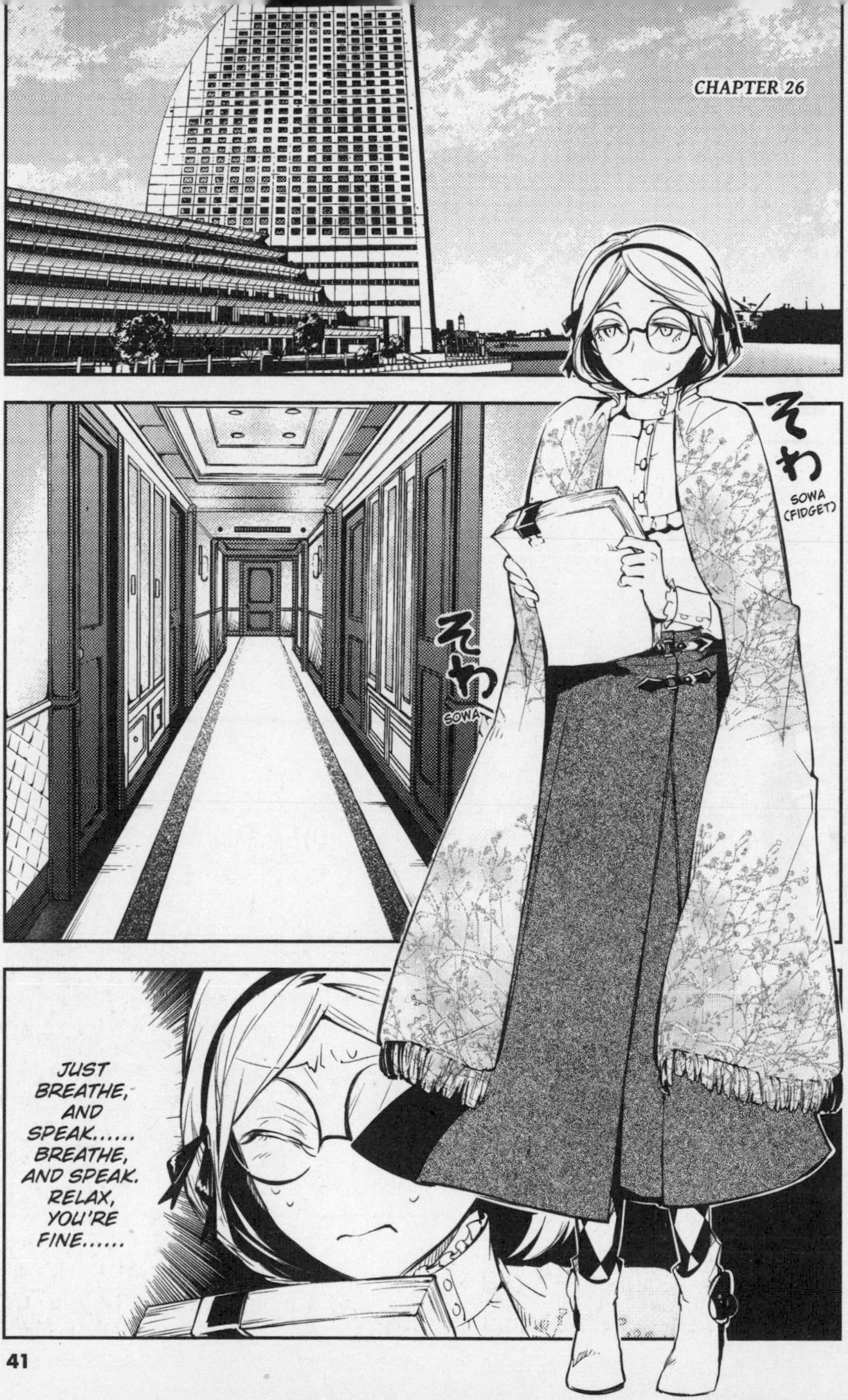
CHAPTER 26
そわ
SOWA (FIDGET)
そわ
SOWA
JUST BREATHE, AND SPEAK...... BREATHE, AND SPEAK. RELAX, YOU'RE FINE......

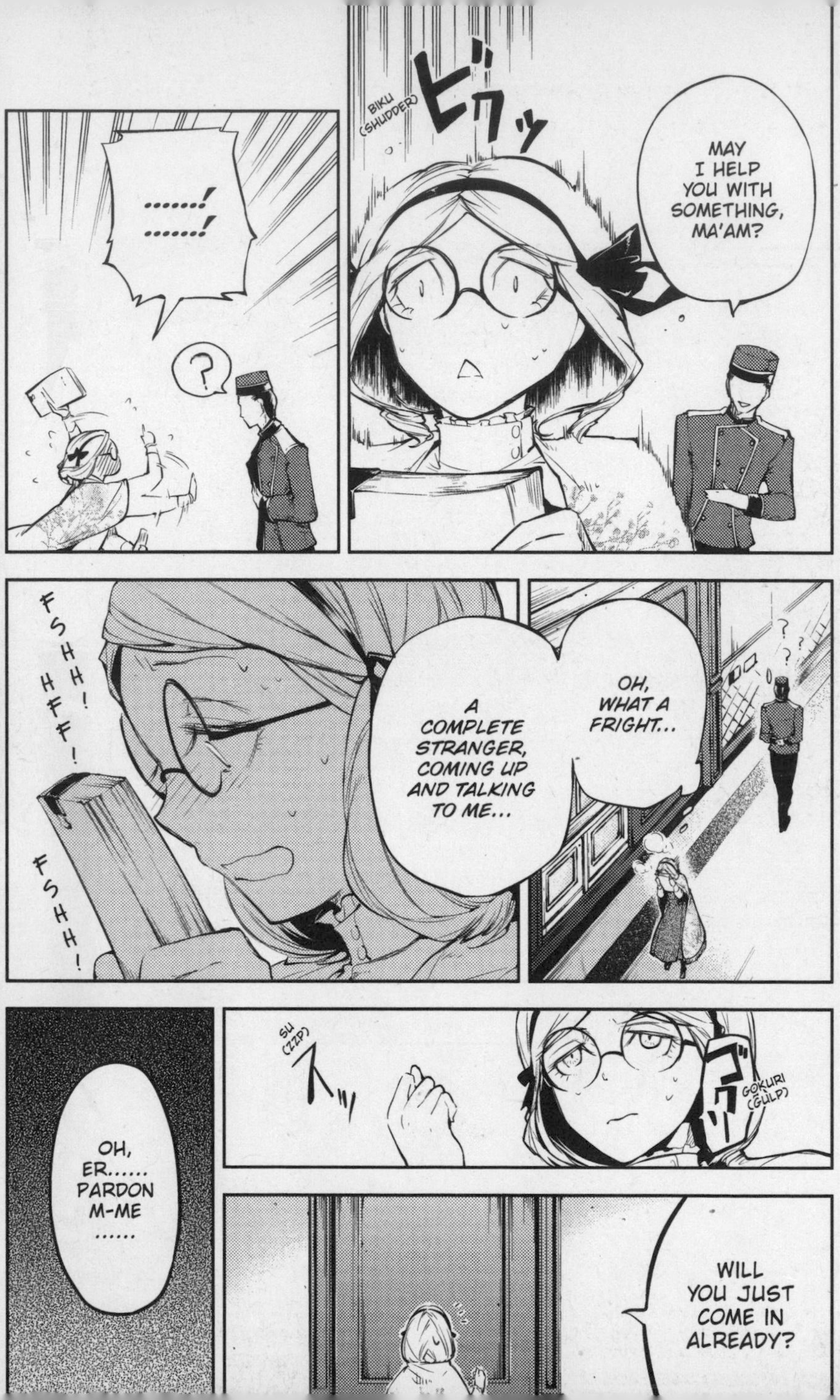
BIKU (SHUDDER)
MAY I HELP YOU WITH SOMETHING, MA'AM?
......! ......!
?
OH, WHAT A FRIGHT...
A COMPLETE STRANGER, COMING UP AND TALKING TO ME...
FSHH! HFF!
FSHH!
SU (ZZIP)
GOKURI (GULP)
WILL YOU JUST COME IN ALREADY?
OH, ER...... PARDON M-ME ......

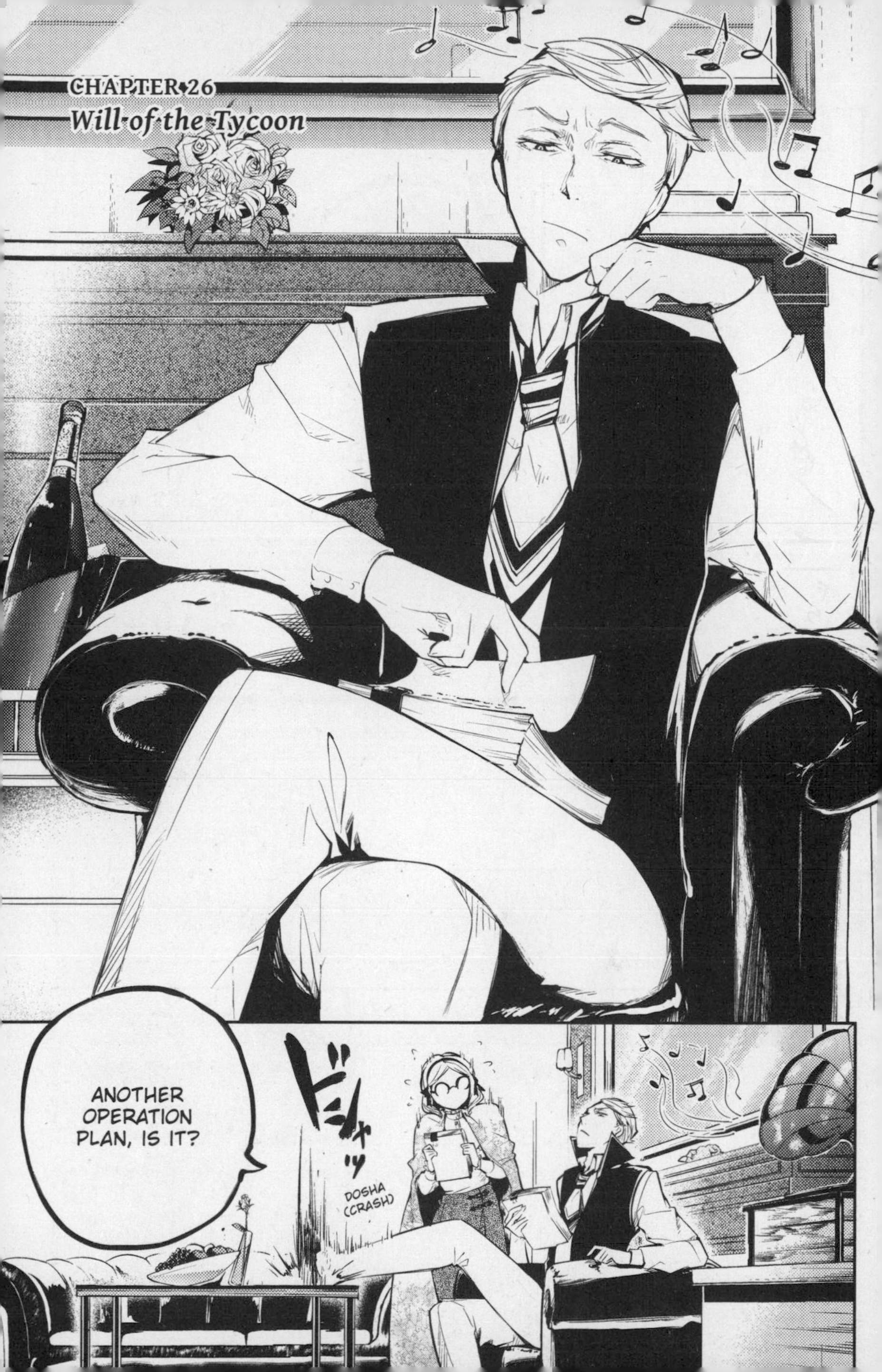
CHAPTER 26
Will of the Tycoon
ドシャッ
DOSHA (CRASH)
ANOTHER OPERATION PLAN, IS IT?

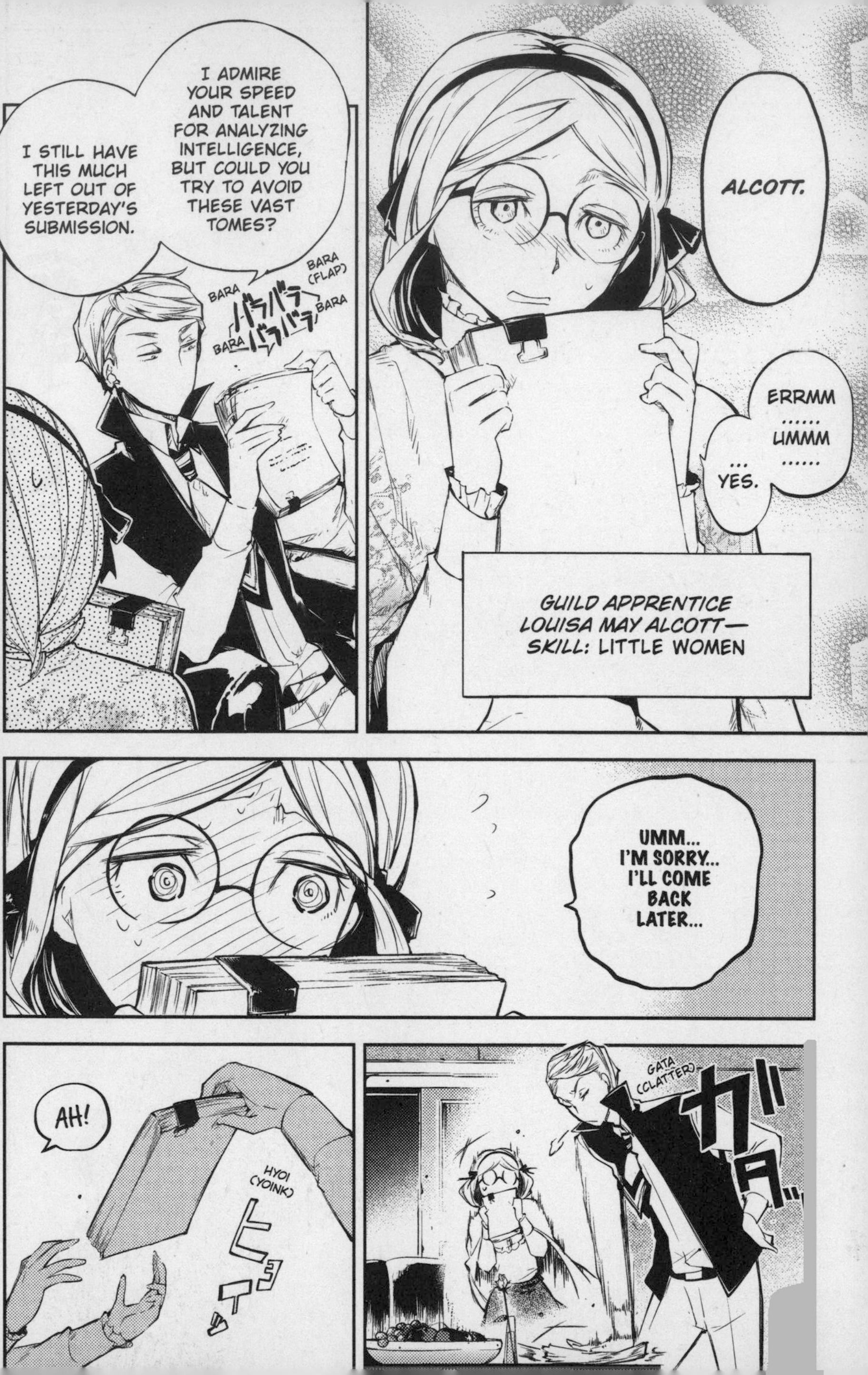
ALCOTT.
ERRMM ...... UMMM ......
... YES.
GUILD APPRENTICE LOUISA MAY ALCOTT— SKILL: LITTLE WOMEN
I ADMIRE YOUR SPEED AND TALENT FOR ANALYZING INTELLIGENCE, BUT COULD YOU TRY TO AVOID THESE VAST TOMES?
I STILL HAVE THIS MUCH LEFT OUT OF YESTERDAY'S SUBMISSION.
BARA (FLAP)
BARA
BARA
BARA
UMM... I'M SORRY... I'LL COME BACK LATER...
GATA (CLATTER)
AH!
HYOI (YOINK)

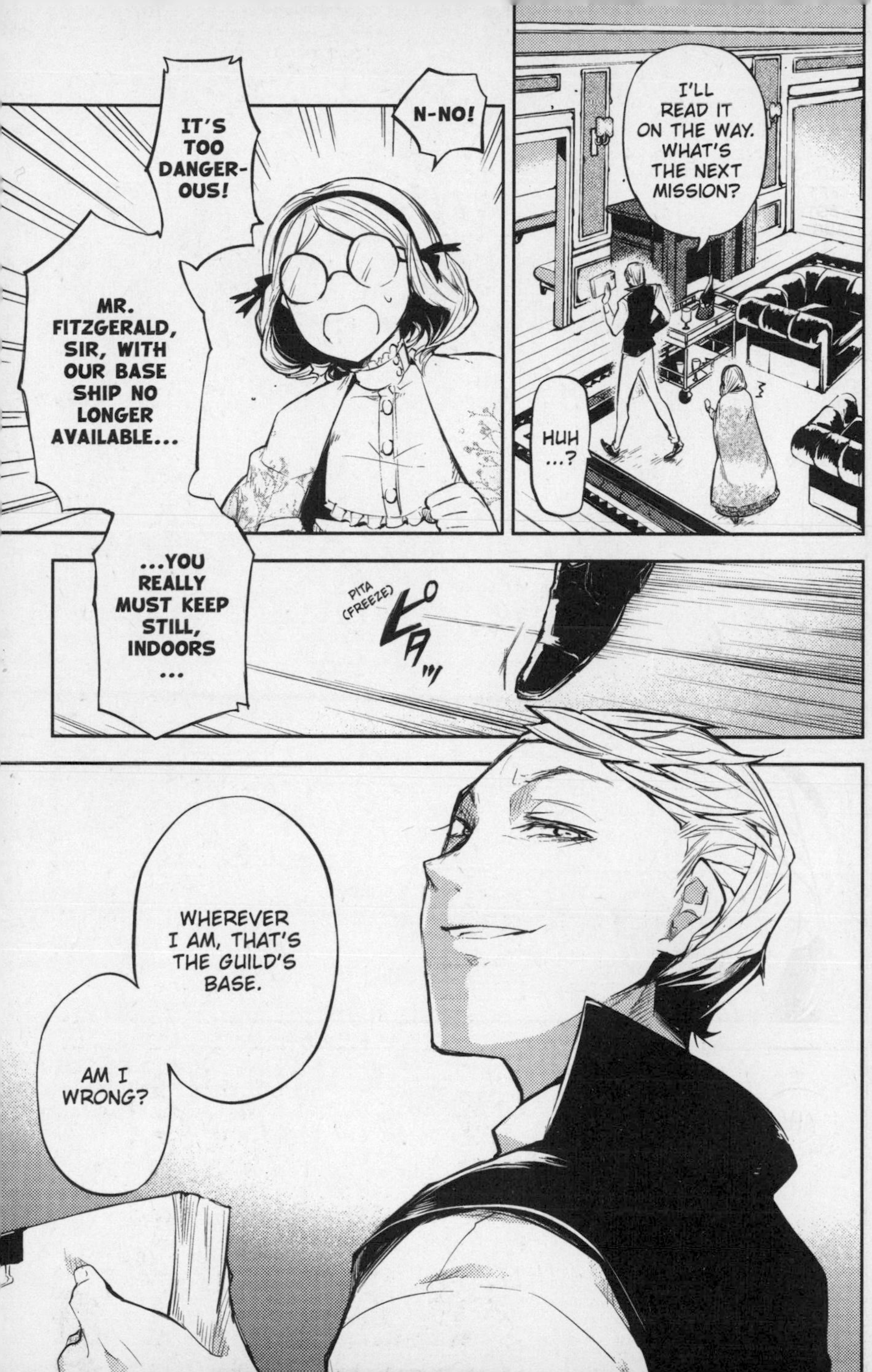
I'LL READ IT ON THE WAY. WHAT'S THE NEXT MISSION?
HUH ...?
N-NO!
IT'S TOO DANGER-OUS!
MR. FITZGERALD, SIR, WITH OUR BASE SHIP NO LONGER AVAILABLE...
...YOU REALLY MUST KEEP STILL, INDOORS ...
PITA (FREEZE)
WHEREVER I AM, THAT'S THE GUILD'S BASE.
AM I WRONG?

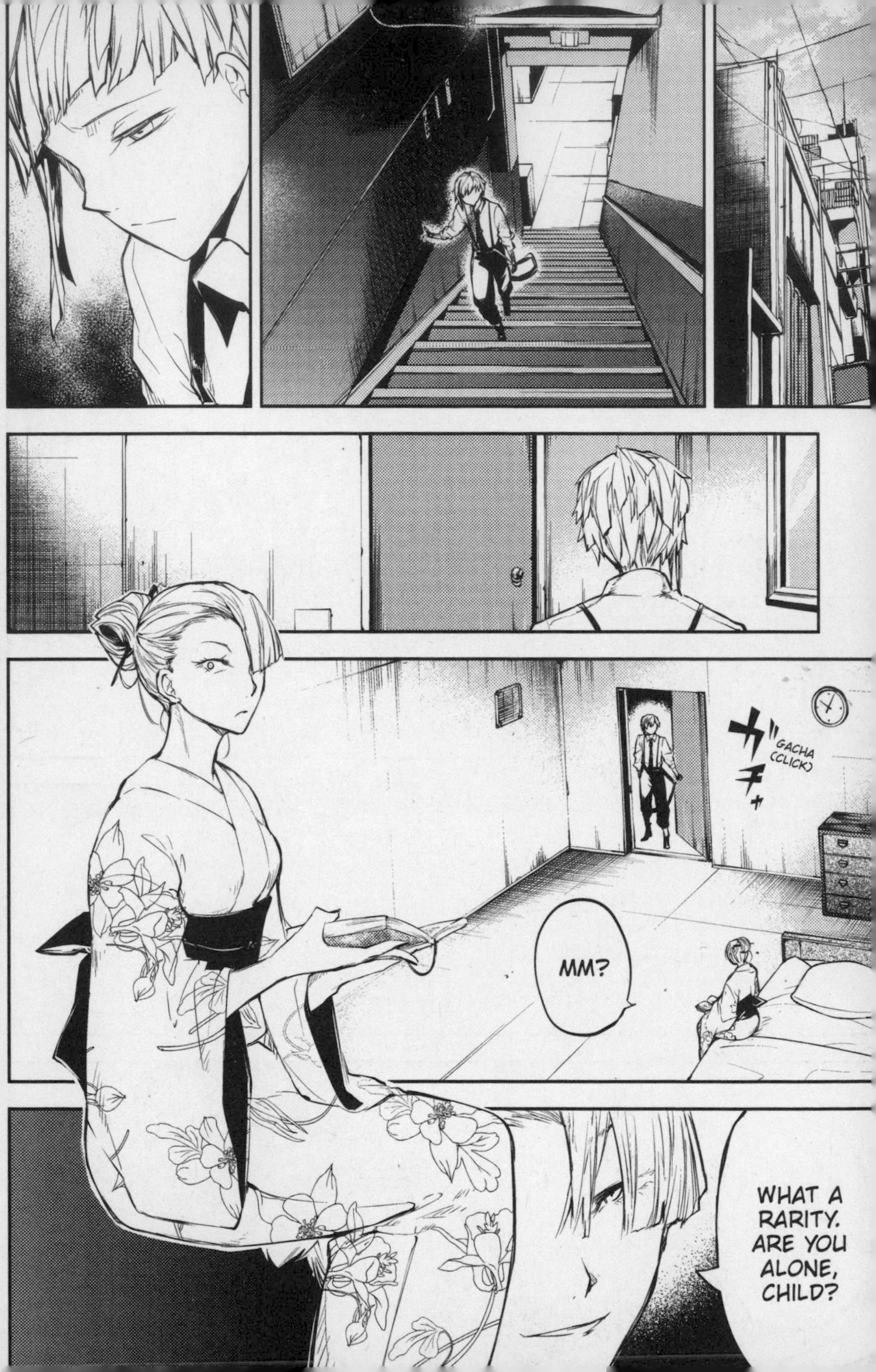
カチャ
GACHA (CLICK)
MM?
WHAT A RARITY. ARE YOU ALONE, CHILD?

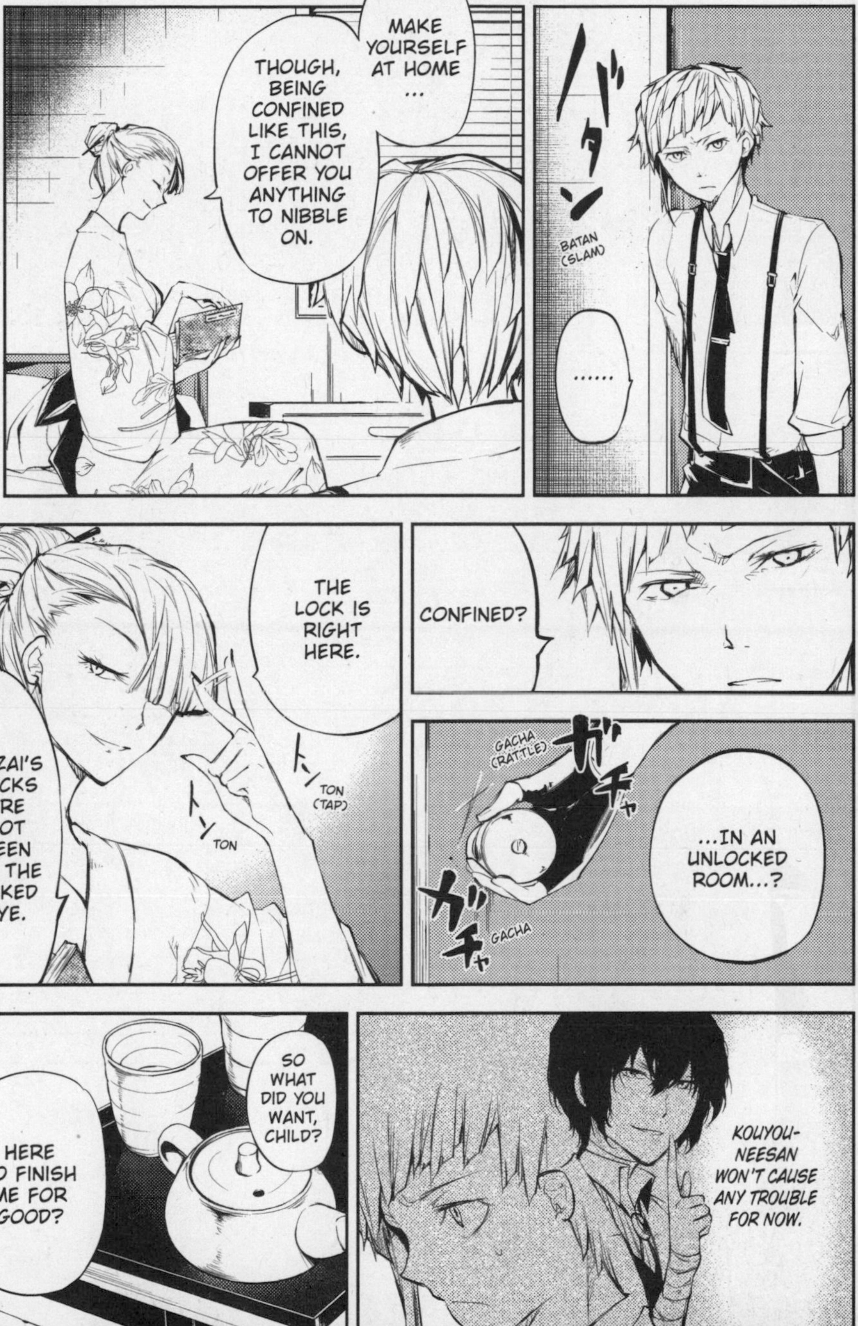
ガタン
BATAN (SLAM)
......
MAKE YOURSELF AT HOME ...
THOUGH, BEING CONFINED LIKE THIS, I CANNOT OFFER YOU ANYTHING TO NIBBLE ON.
CONFINED?
ガチャ
GACHA (RATTLE)
...IN AN UNLOCKED ROOM...?
ガチャ
GACHA
THE LOCK IS RIGHT HERE.
トン
TON (TAP)
トン
TON
DAZAI'S LOCKS ARE NOT SEEN BY THE NAKED EYE.
KOUYOU-NEESAN WON'T CAUSE ANY TROUBLE FOR NOW.
SO WHAT DID YOU WANT, CHILD?
HERE TO FINISH ME FOR GOOD?

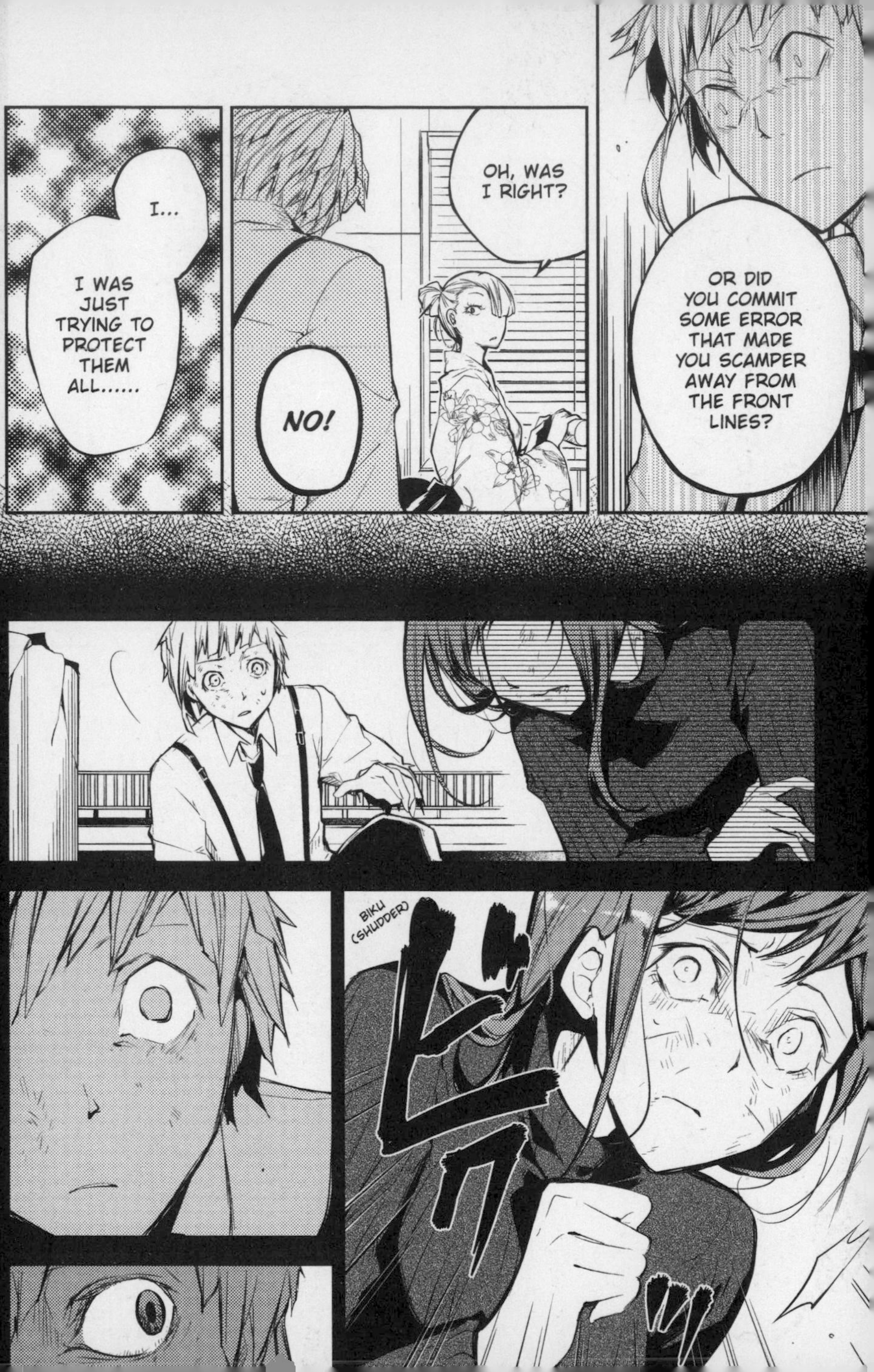
OR DID YOU COMMIT SOME ERROR THAT MADE YOU SCAMPER AWAY FROM THE FRONT LINES?
OH, WAS I RIGHT?
NO!
I...
I WAS JUST TRYING TO PROTECT THEM ALL......
BIKU (SHUDDER)

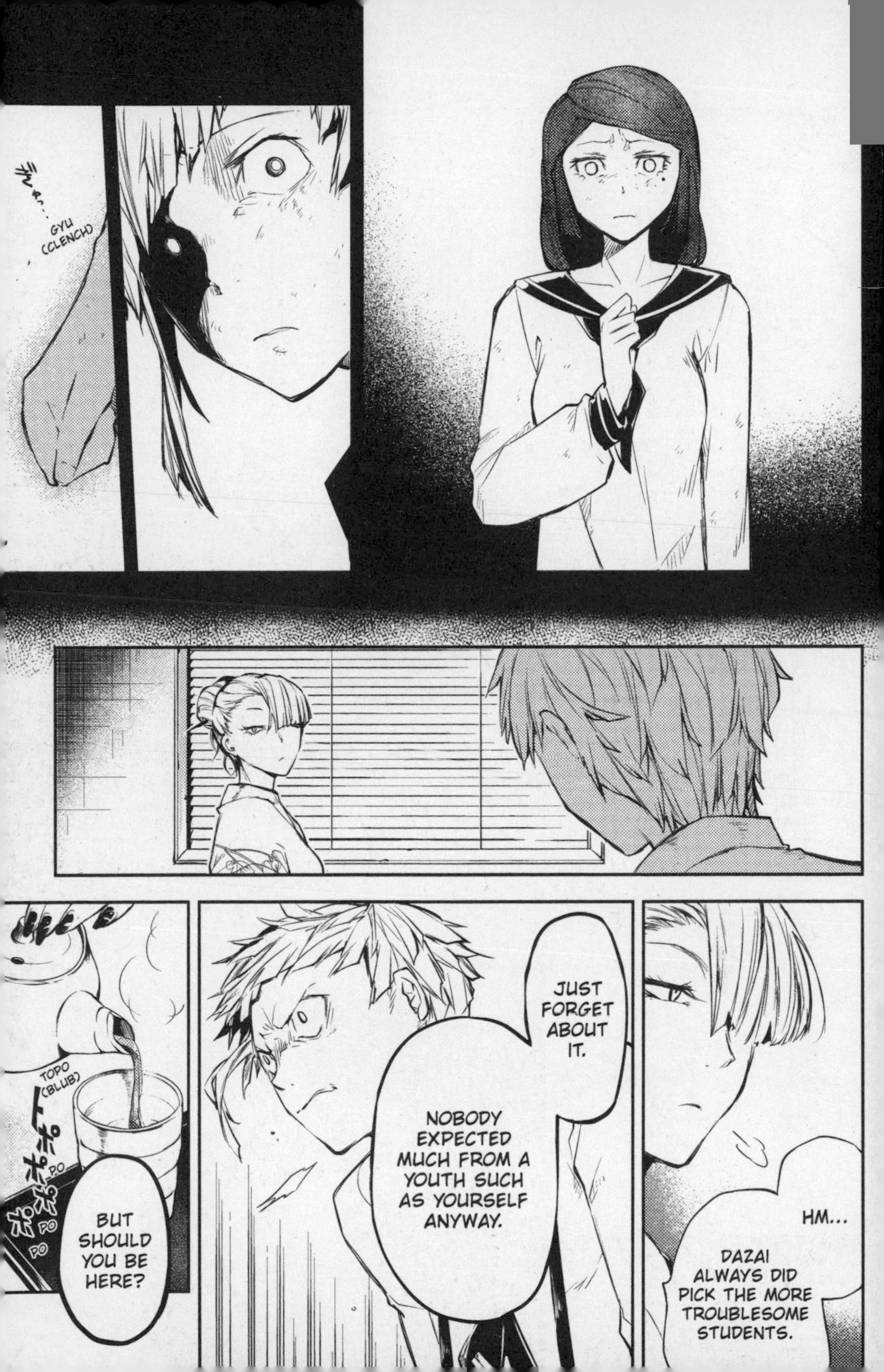
GYU
(CLENCH)
HM...
DAZAI ALWAYS DID PICK THE MORE TROUBLESOME STUDENTS.
JUST FORGET ABOUT IT.
NOBODY EXPECTED MUCH FROM A YOUTH SUCH AS YOURSELF ANYWAY.
TOPO
(BLUB)
PO
PO
PO
BUT SHOULD YOU BE HERE?

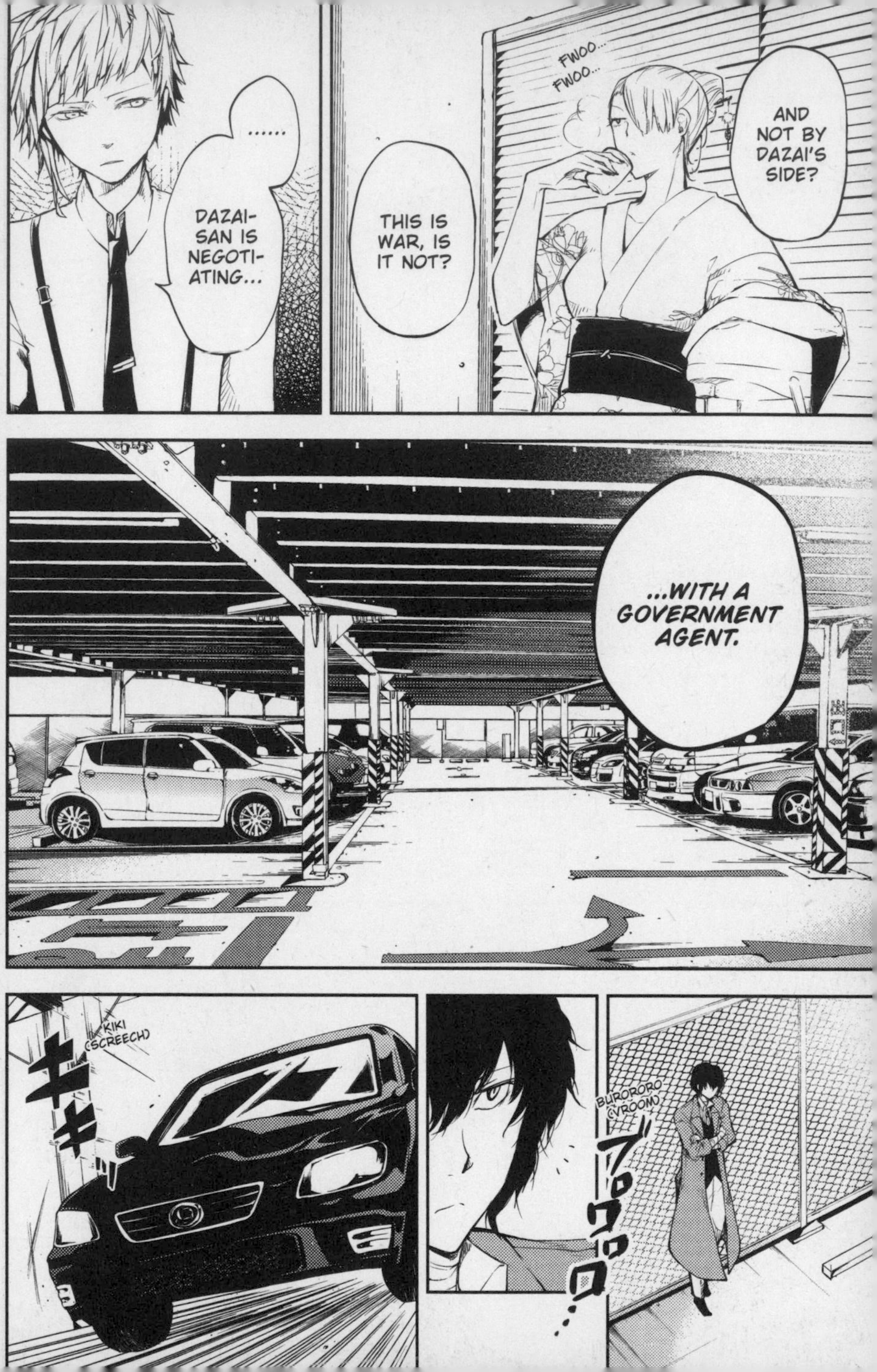
FWOO... FWOO...
AND NOT BY DAZAI'S SIDE?
THIS IS WAR, IS IT NOT?
......
DAZAI-SAN IS NEGOTIATING...
...WITH A GOVERNMENT AGENT.
BURORORO (VROOM)
ブロロロ…
KIKI (SCREECH)
キキッ

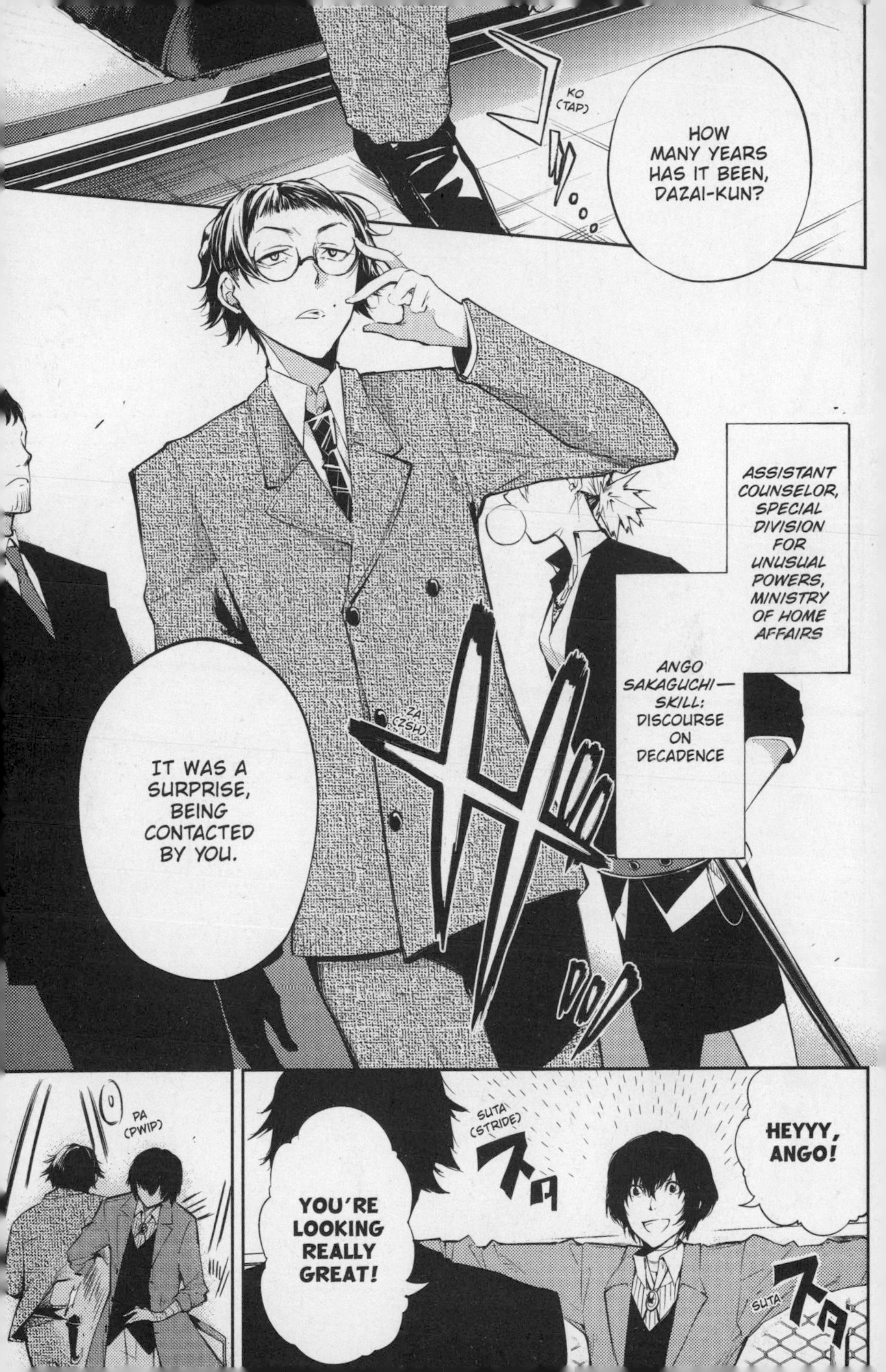
HOW MANY YEARS HAS IT BEEN, DAZAI-KUN?
KO (TAP)
ASSISTANT COUNSELOR, SPECIAL DIVISION FOR UNUSUAL POWERS, MINISTRY OF HOME AFFAIRS
ANGO SAKAGUCHI—SKILL: DISCOURSE ON DECADENCE
ZA (ZSH)
IT WAS A SURPRISE, BEING CONTACTED BY YOU.
HEYYY, ANGO!
SUTA (STRIDE)
YOU'RE LOOKING REALLY GREAT!
SUTA
PA (PWIP)

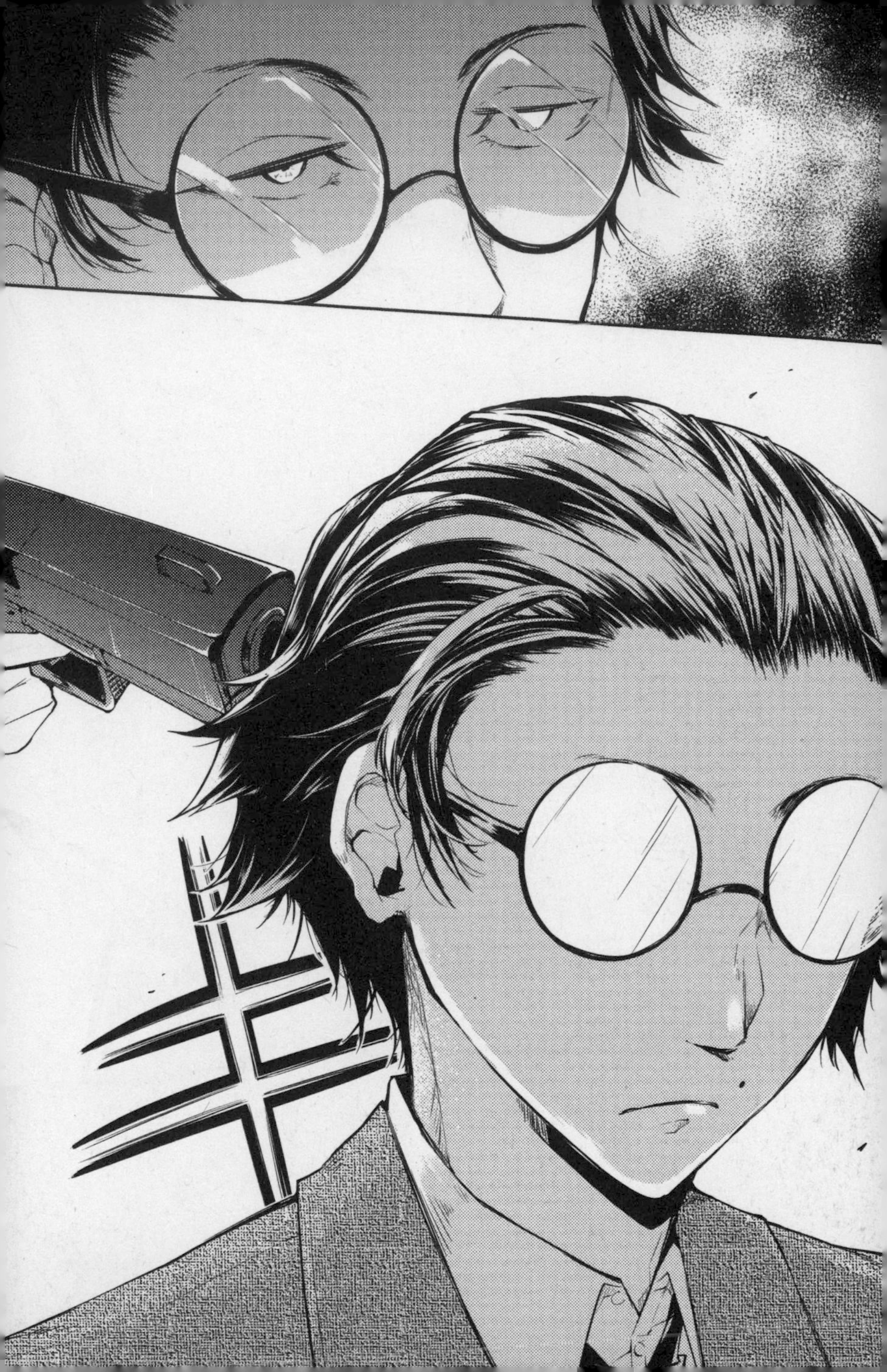

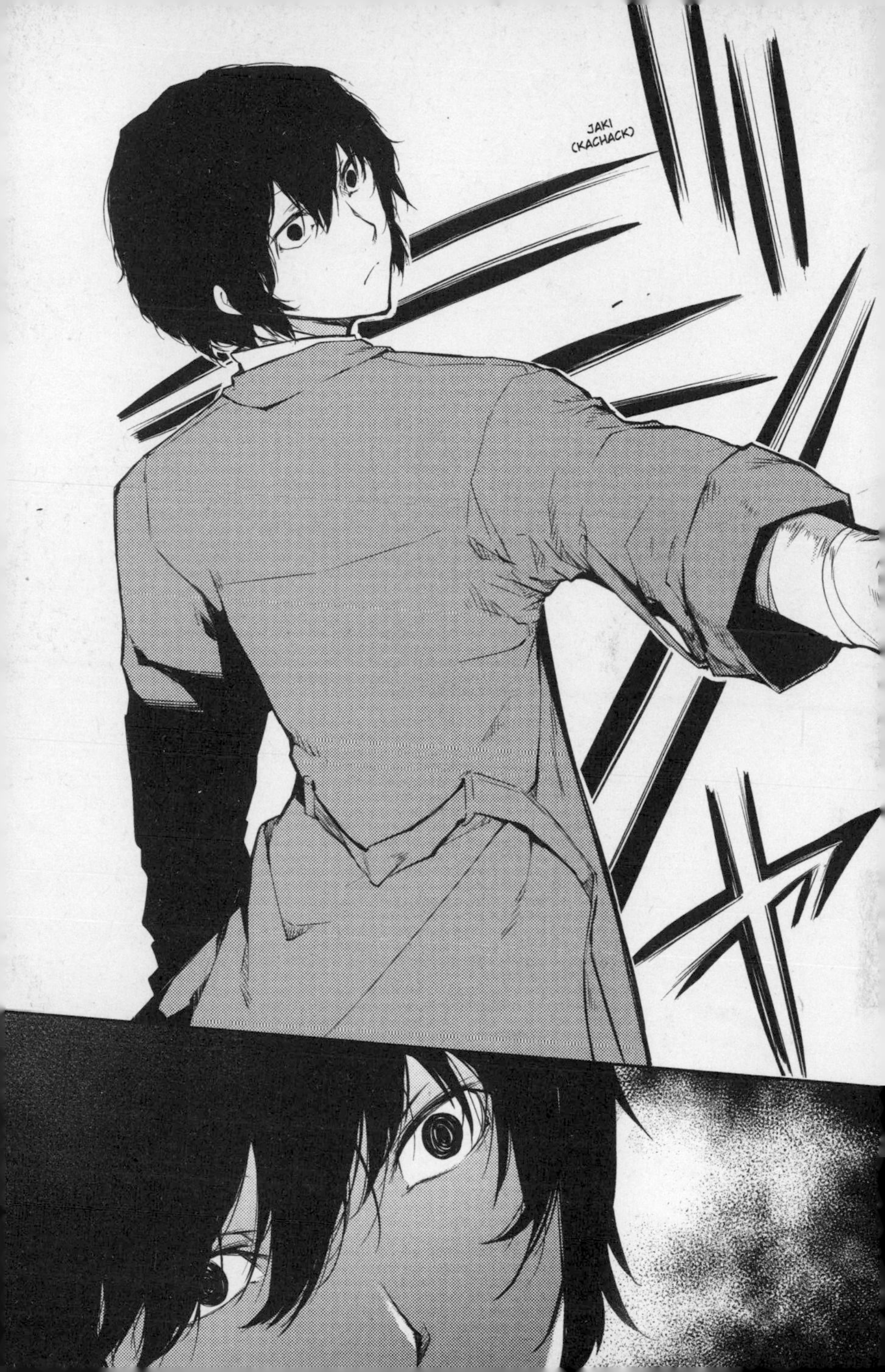
JAKI (KACHACK)

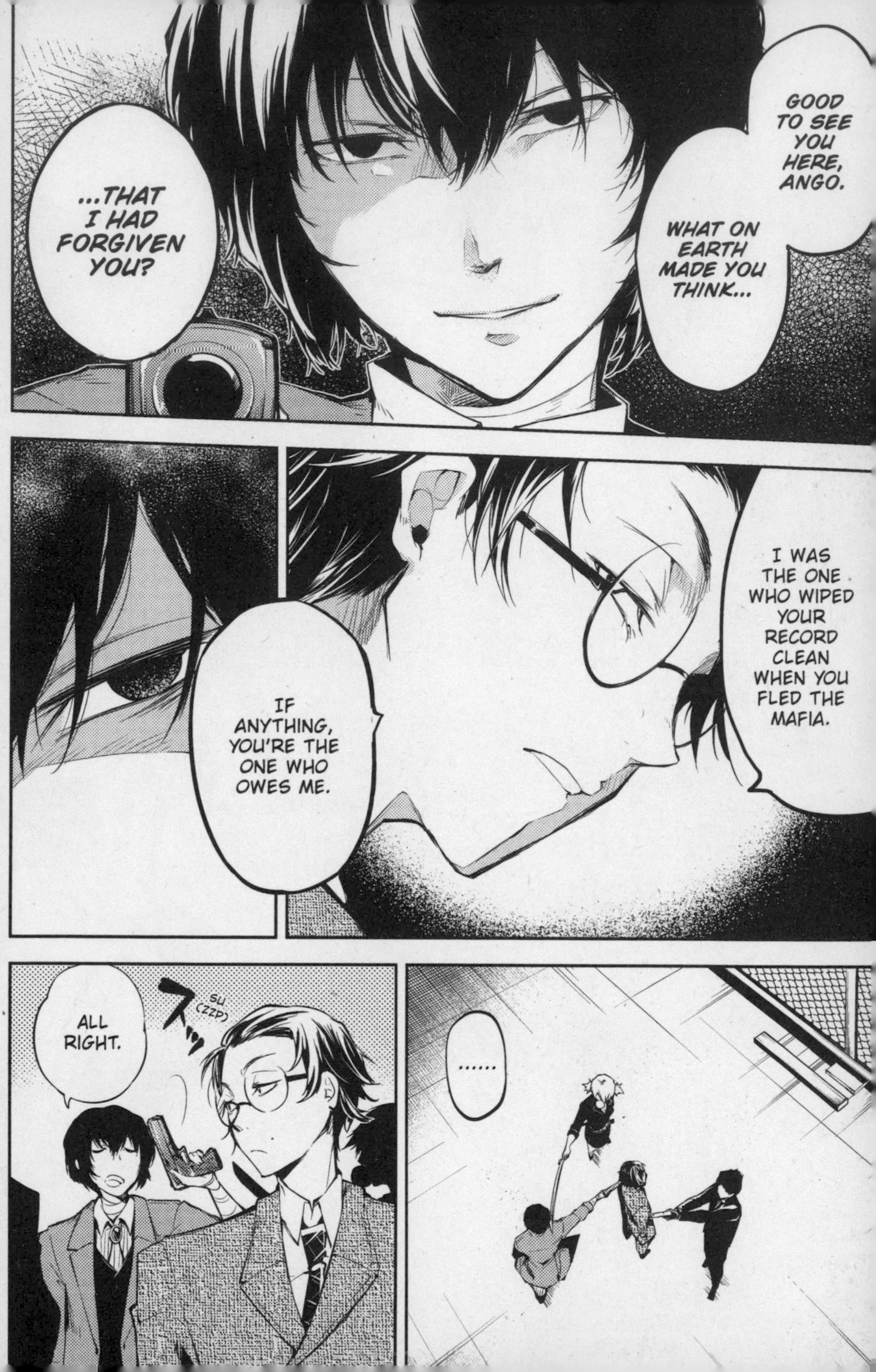
GOOD TO SEE YOU HERE, ANGO.
WHAT ON EARTH MADE YOU THINK...
...THAT I HAD FORGIVEN YOU?
I WAS THE ONE WHO WIPED YOUR RECORD CLEAN WHEN YOU FLED THE MAFIA.
IF ANYTHING, YOU'RE THE ONE WHO OWES ME.
......
SU (ZZP)
ALL RIGHT.

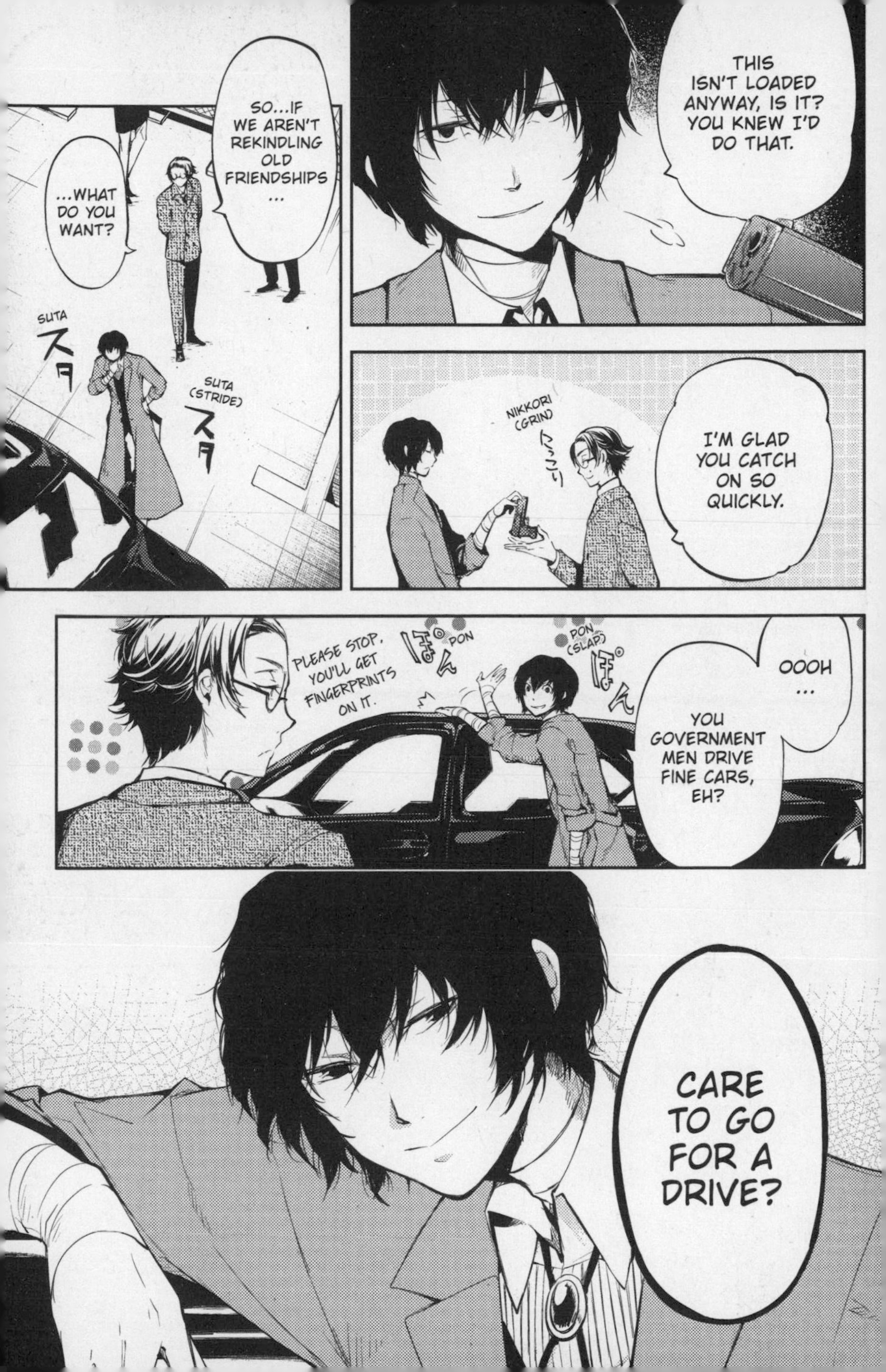
THIS ISN'T LOADED ANYWAY, IS IT? YOU KNEW I'D DO THAT.
I'M GLAD YOU CATCH ON SO QUICKLY.
NIKKORI (GRIN)
SO...IF WE AREN'T REKINDLING OLD FRIENDSHIPS ...
...WHAT DO YOU WANT?
SUTA
SUTA (STRIDE)
OOOH ...
YOU GOVERNMENT MEN DRIVE FINE CARS, EH?
PON (SLAP)
PON
PLEASE STOP. YOU'LL GET FINGERPRINTS ON IT.
CARE TO GO FOR A DRIVE?

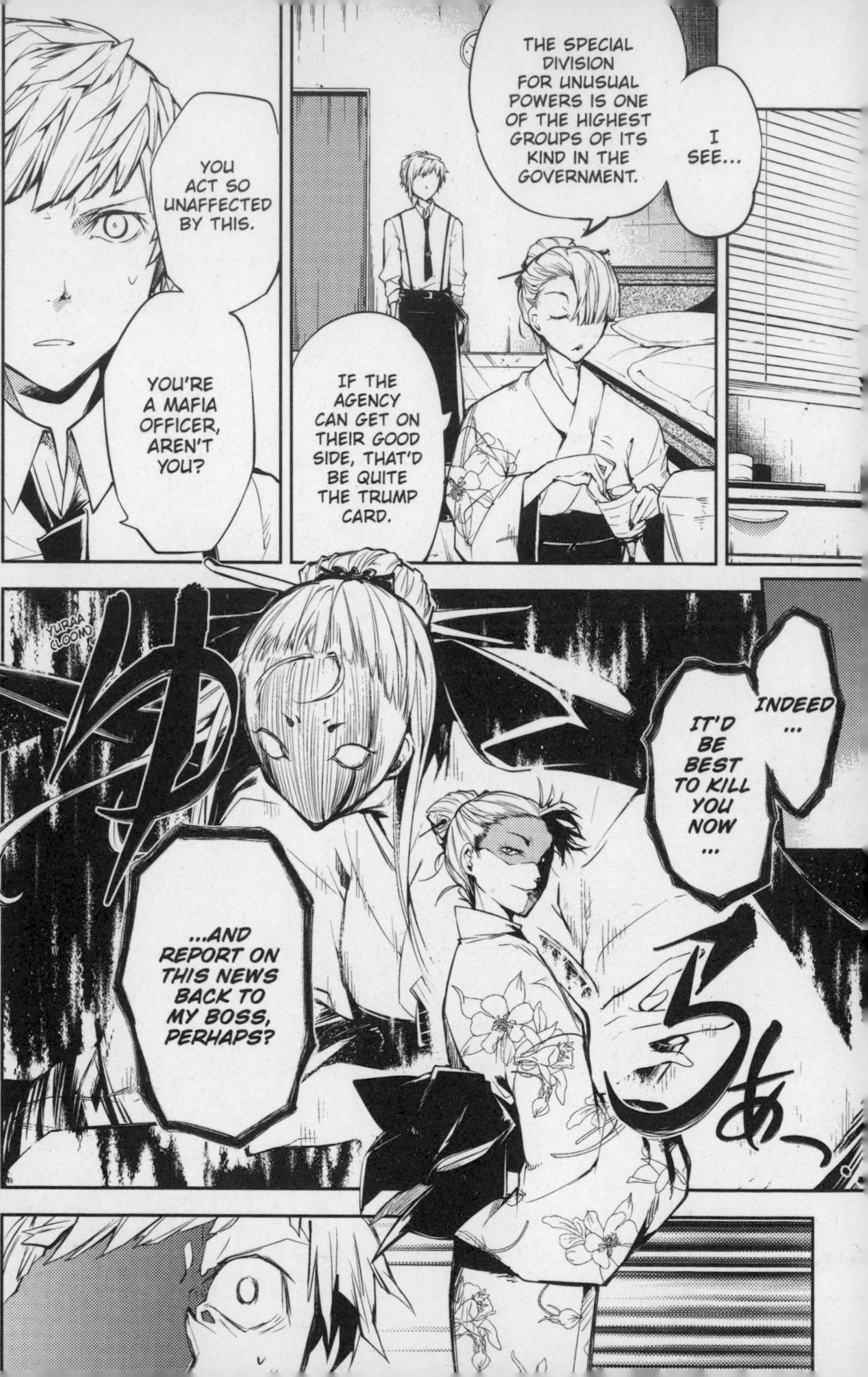
I SEE...
THE SPECIAL DIVISION FOR UNUSUAL POWERS IS ONE OF THE HIGHEST GROUPS OF ITS KIND IN THE GOVERNMENT.
IF THE AGENCY CAN GET ON THEIR GOOD SIDE, THAT'D BE QUITE THE TRUMP CARD.
YOU ACT SO UNAFFECTED BY THIS.
YOU'RE A MAFIA OFFICER, AREN'T YOU?
INDEED...
IT'D BE BEST TO KILL YOU NOW...
...AND REPORT ON THIS NEWS BACK TO MY BOSS, PERHAPS?
YURAA (LOOM)

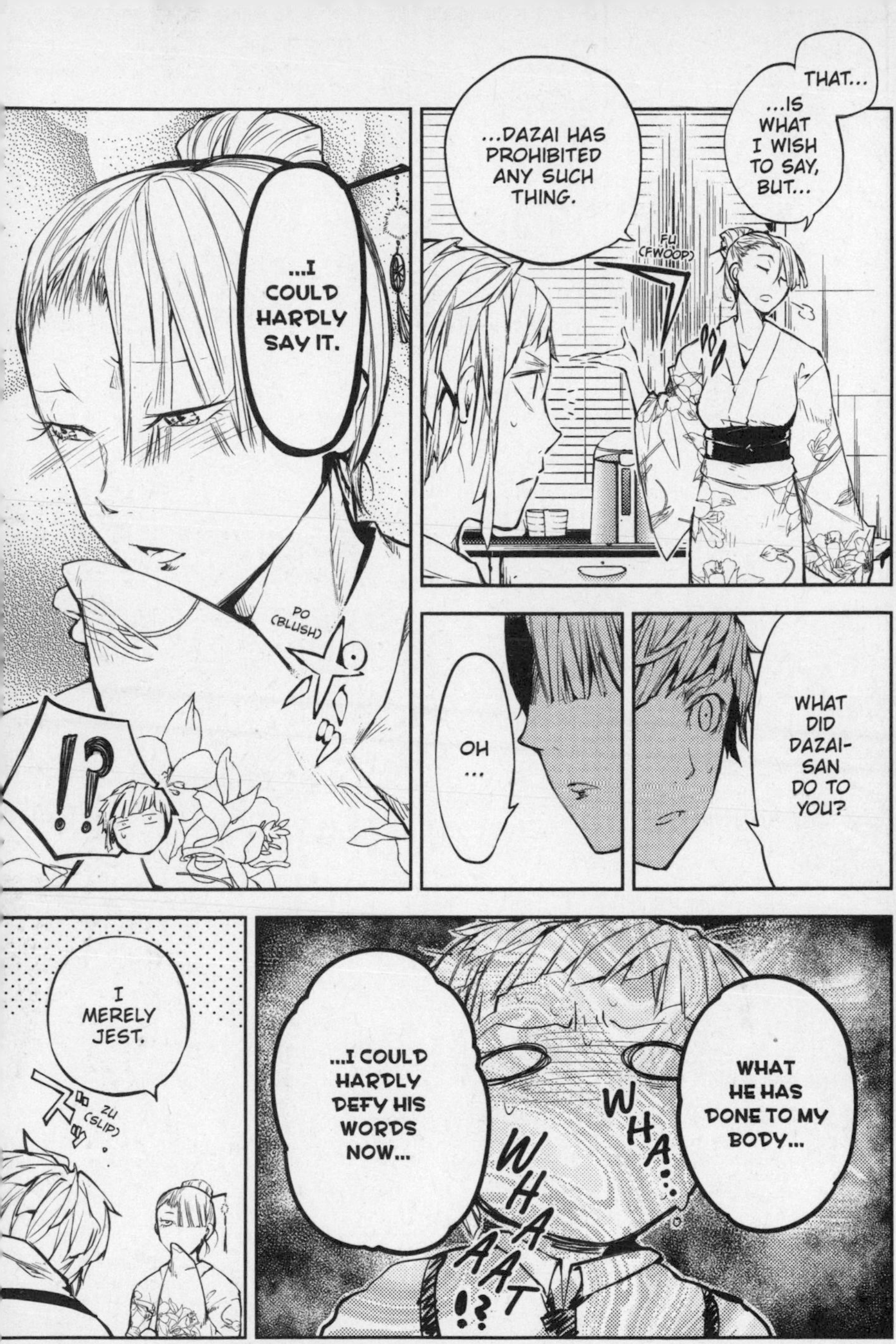
THAT...
...IS WHAT I WISH TO SAY, BUT...
...DAZAI HAS PROHIBITED ANY SUCH THING.
FU (FWOOP)
WHAT DID DAZAI-SAN DO TO YOU?
OH ...
...I COULD HARDLY SAY IT.
PO (BLUSH)
!?
WHAT HE HAS DONE TO MY BODY...
...I COULD HARDLY DEFY HIS WORDS NOW...
WHA...
WHAAAAT!?
I MERELY JEST.
ZU (SLIP)

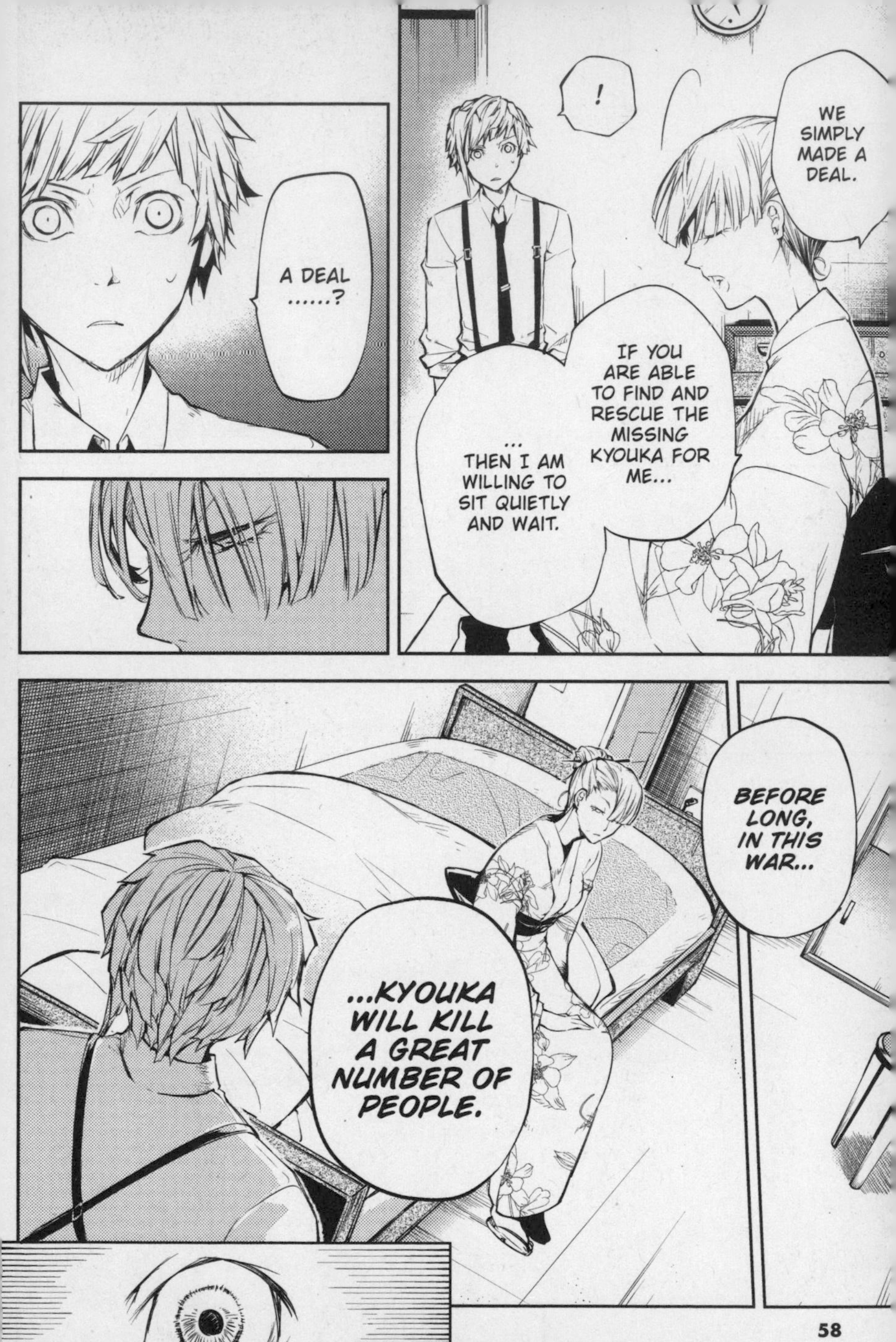
WE SIMPLY MADE A DEAL.
!
IF YOU ARE ABLE TO FIND AND RESCUE THE MISSING KYOUKA FOR ME...
...THEN I AM WILLING TO SIT QUIETLY AND WAIT.
A DEAL......?
BEFORE LONG, IN THIS WAR...
...KYOUKA WILL KILL A GREAT NUMBER OF PEOPLE.

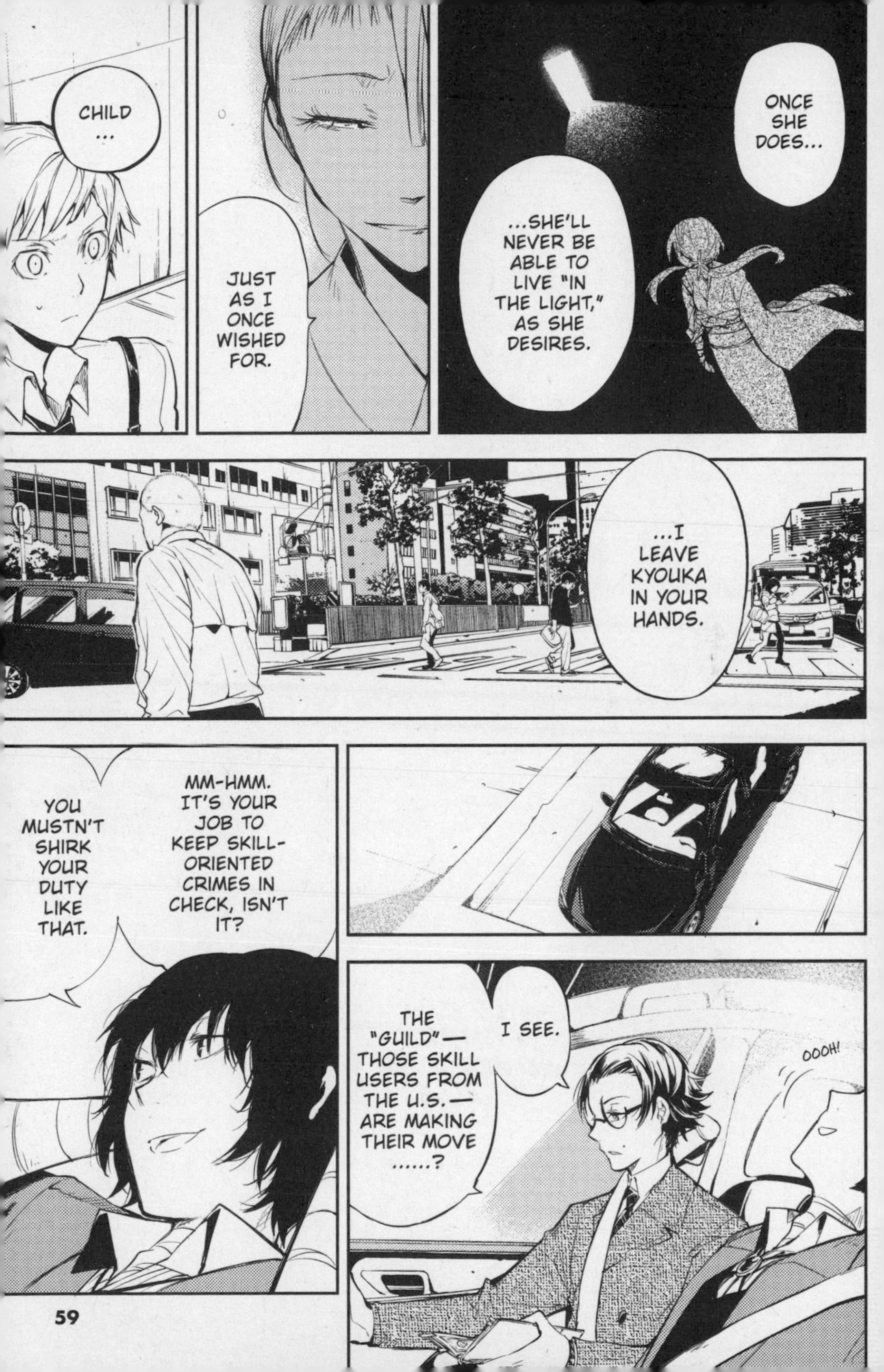
ONCE SHE DOES...
...SHE'LL NEVER BE ABLE TO LIVE "IN THE LIGHT," AS SHE DESIRES.
JUST AS I ONCE WISHED FOR.
CHILD ...
...I LEAVE KYOUKA IN YOUR HANDS.
OOOH!
I SEE.
THE "GUILD"— THOSE SKILL USERS FROM THE U.S.— ARE MAKING THEIR MOVE ......?
MM-HMM. IT'S YOUR JOB TO KEEP SKILL-ORIENTED CRIMES IN CHECK, ISN'T IT?
YOU MUSTN'T SHIRK YOUR DUTY LIKE THAT.

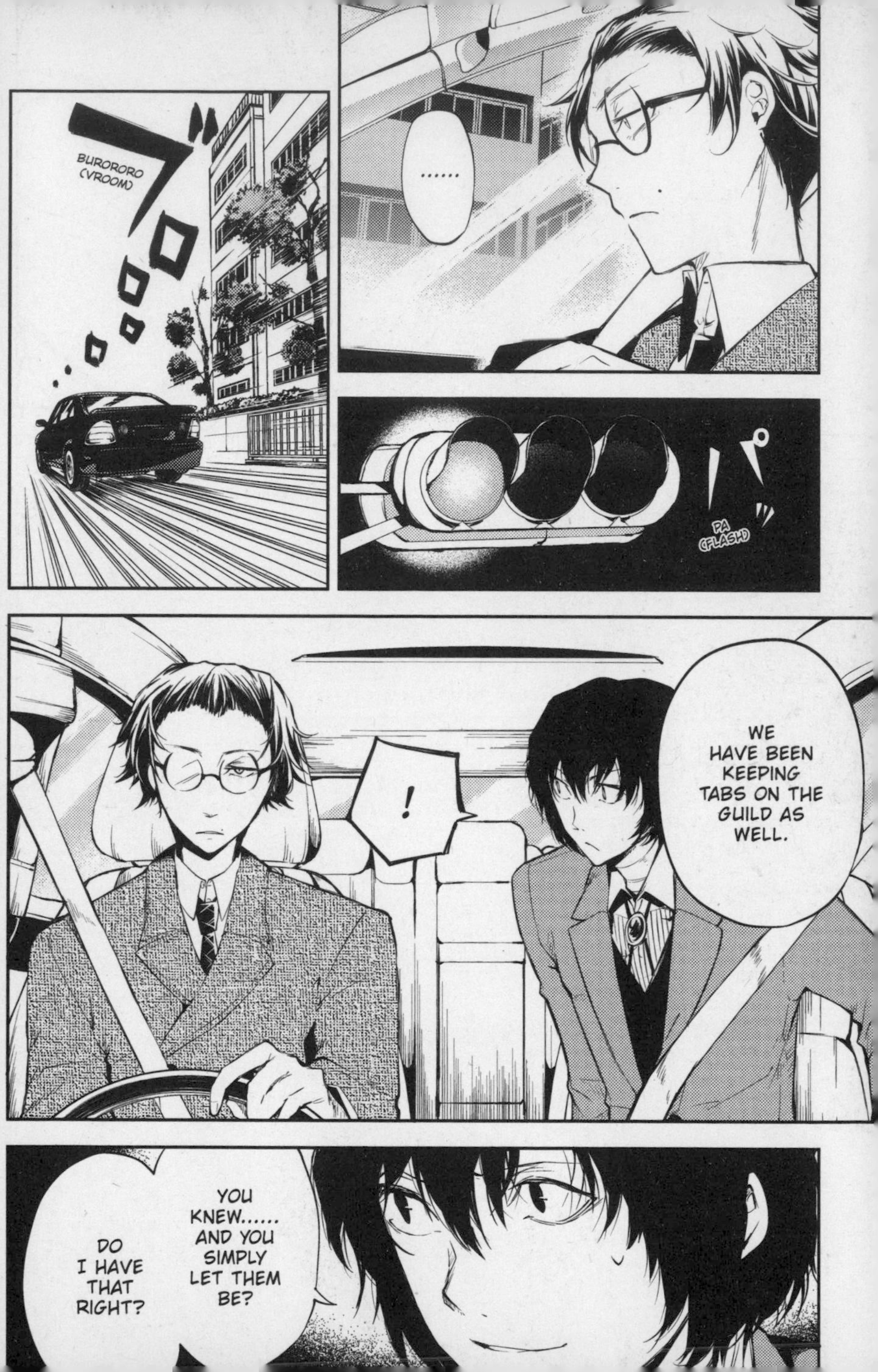
......
PA (FLASH)
BUROROROR (VROOM)
WE HAVE BEEN KEEPING TABS ON THE GUILD AS WELL.
!
YOU KNEW...... AND YOU SIMPLY LET THEM BE?
DO I HAVE THAT RIGHT?

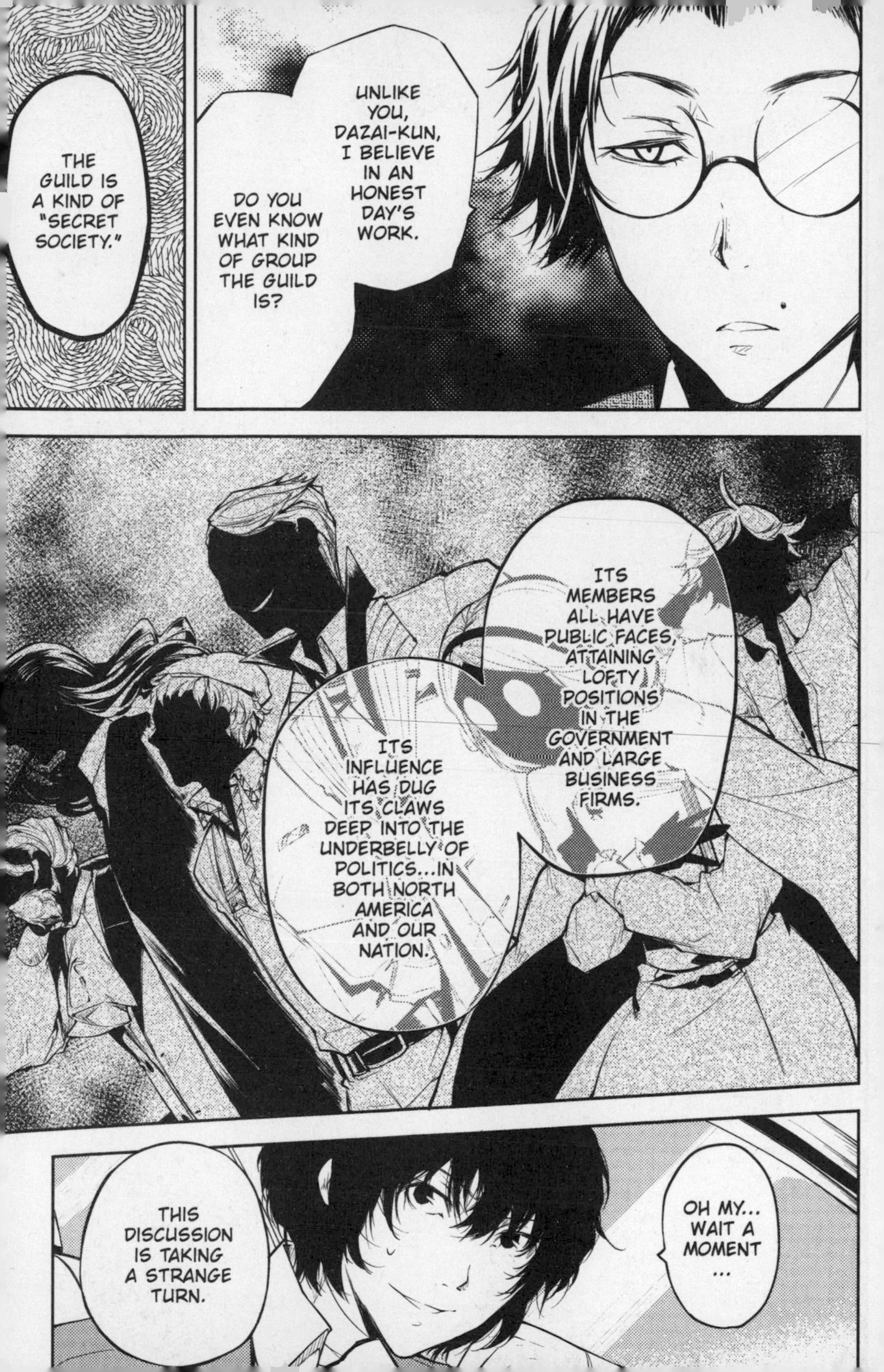
UNLIKE YOU, DAZAI-KUN, I BELIEVE IN AN HONEST DAY'S WORK.
DO YOU EVEN KNOW WHAT KIND OF GROUP THE GUILD IS?
THE GUILD IS A KIND OF "SECRET SOCIETY."
ITS MEMBERS ALL HAVE PUBLIC FACES, ATTAINING LOFTY POSITIONS IN THE GOVERNMENT AND LARGE BUSINESS FIRMS.
ITS INFLUENCE HAS DUG ITS CLAWS DEEP INTO THE UNDERBELLY OF POLITICS...IN BOTH NORTH AMERICA AND OUR NATION.
OH MY... WAIT A MOMENT ...
THIS DISCUSSION IS TAKING A STRANGE TURN.

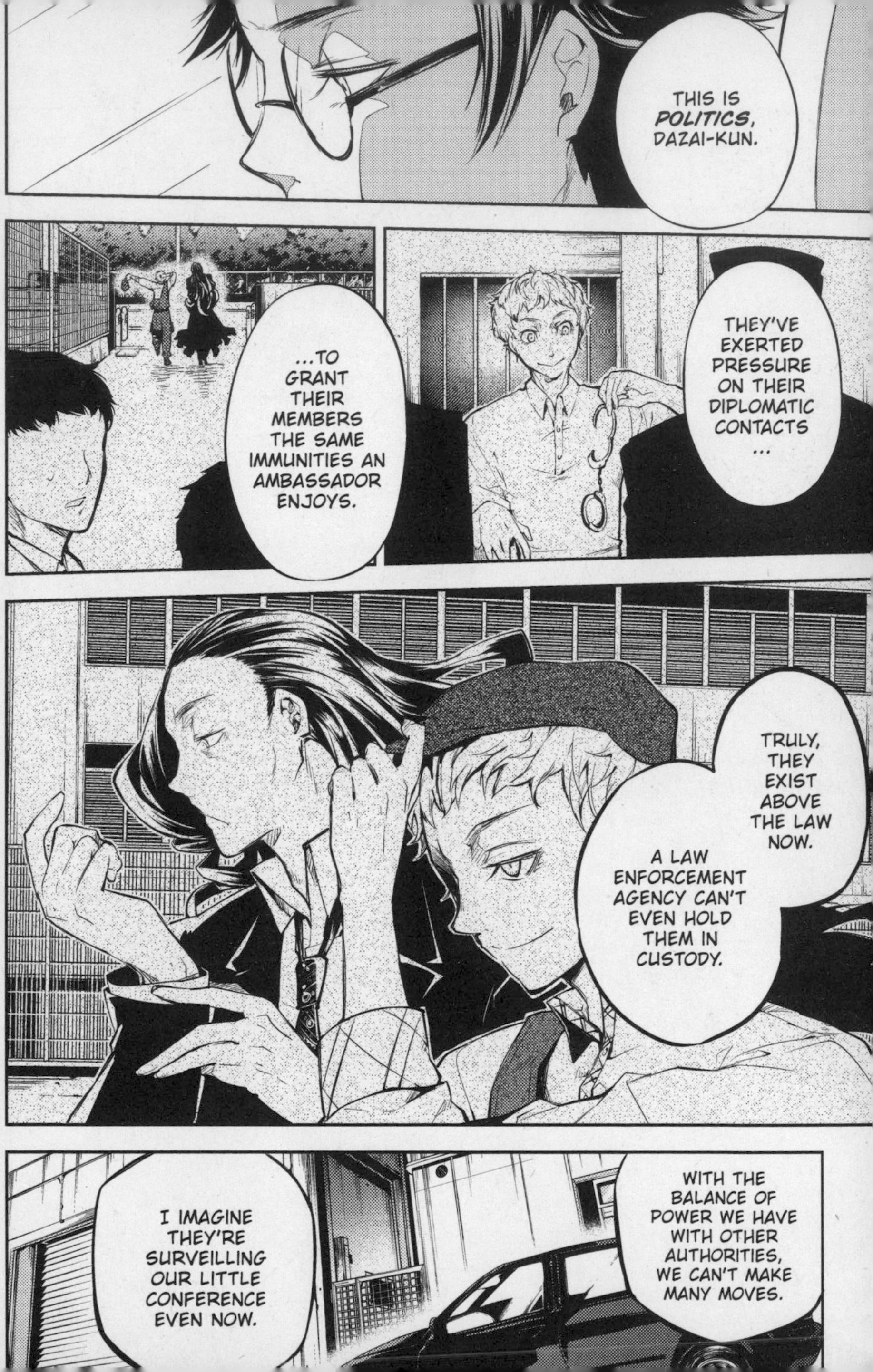
THIS IS *POLITICS*, DAZAI-KUN.
THEY'VE EXERTED PRESSURE ON THEIR DIPLOMATIC CONTACTS ...
...TO GRANT THEIR MEMBERS THE SAME IMMUNITIES AN AMBASSADOR ENJOYS.
TRULY, THEY EXIST ABOVE THE LAW NOW.
A LAW ENFORCEMENT AGENCY CAN'T EVEN HOLD THEM IN CUSTODY.
WITH THE BALANCE OF POWER WE HAVE WITH OTHER AUTHORITIES, WE CAN'T MAKE MANY MOVES.
I IMAGINE THEY'RE SURVEILLING OUR LITTLE CONFERENCE EVEN NOW.

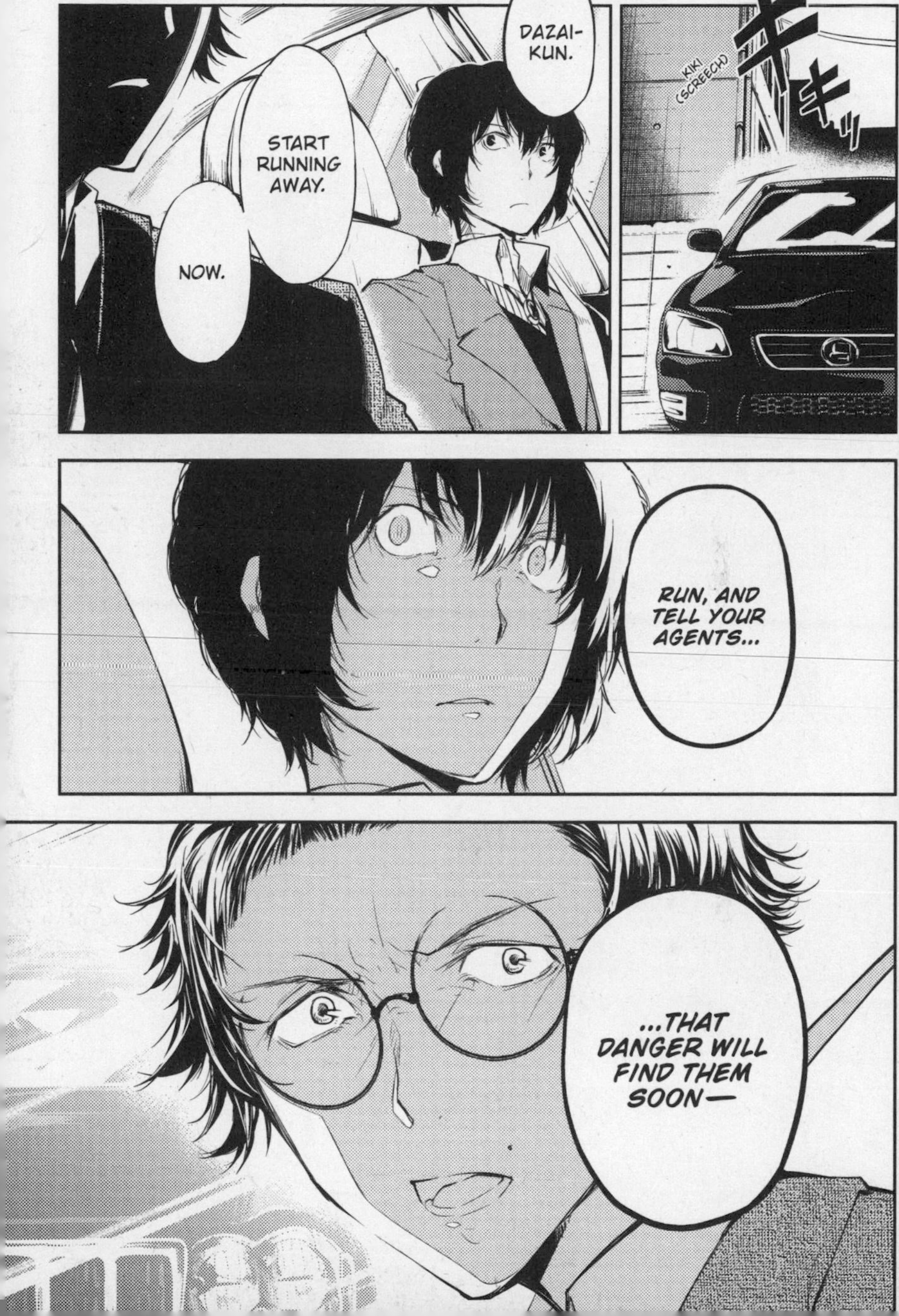
キキッ
KIKI (SCREECH)
DAZAI-KUN.
START RUNNING AWAY.
NOW.
RUN, AND TELL YOUR AGENTS...
...THAT DANGER WILL FIND THEM SOON—

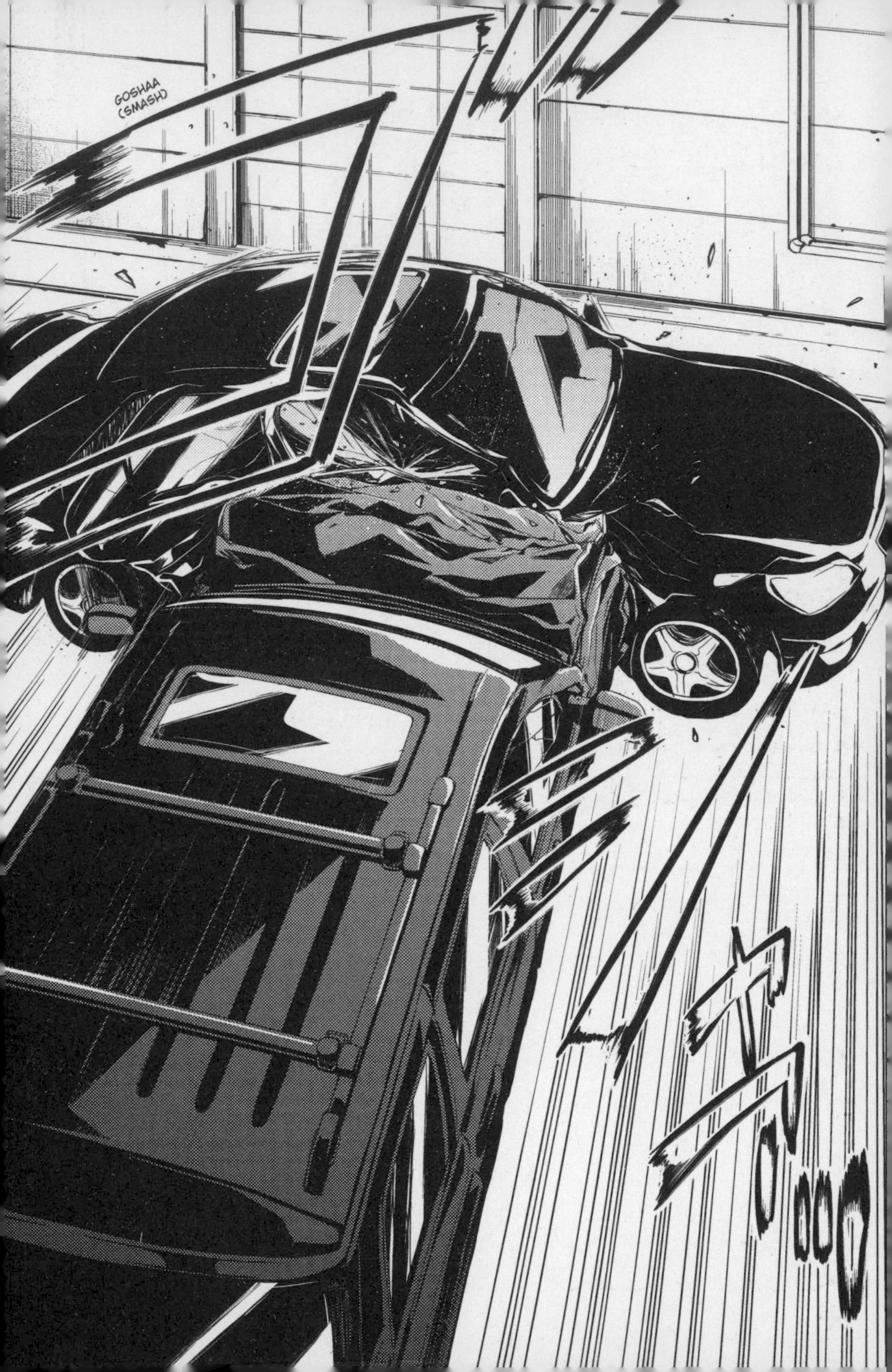
GOSHAA
(SMASH)

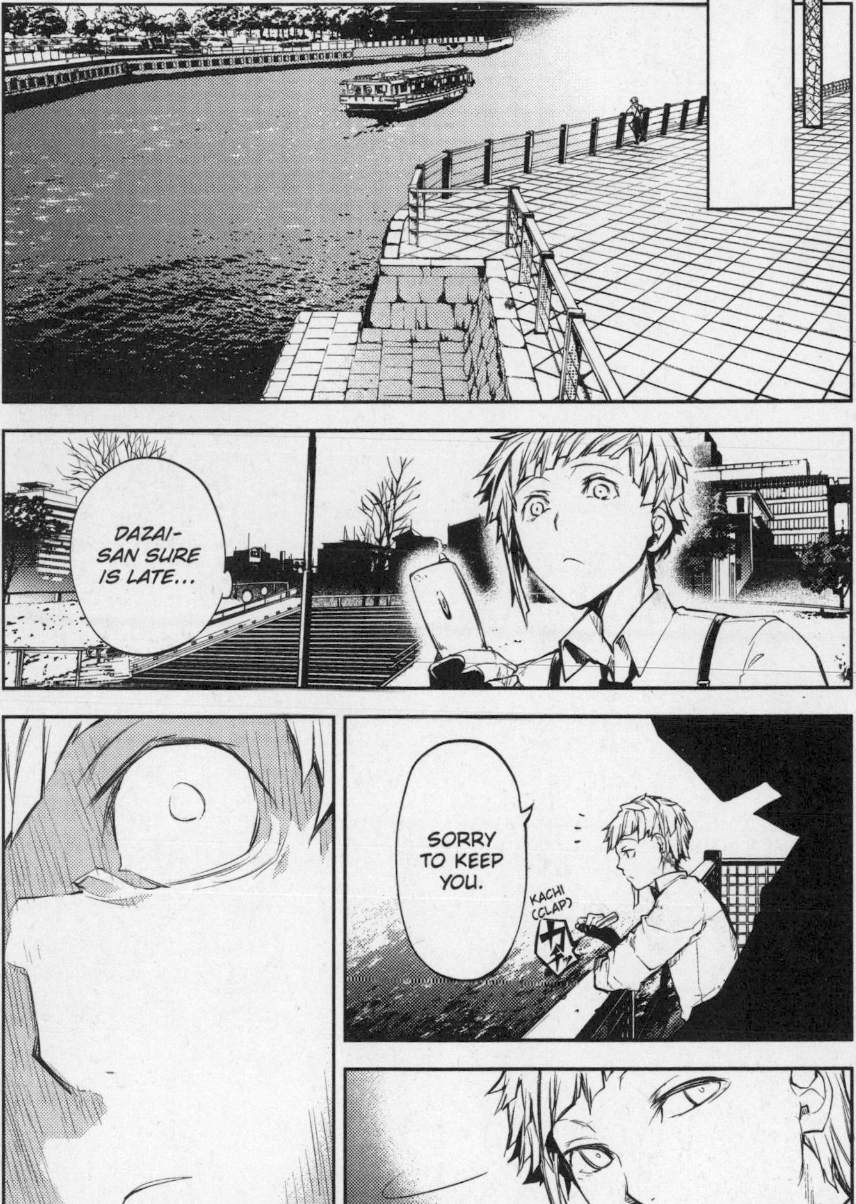
DAZAI-SAN SURE IS LATE...
SORRY TO KEEP YOU.
KACHI (CLAP)

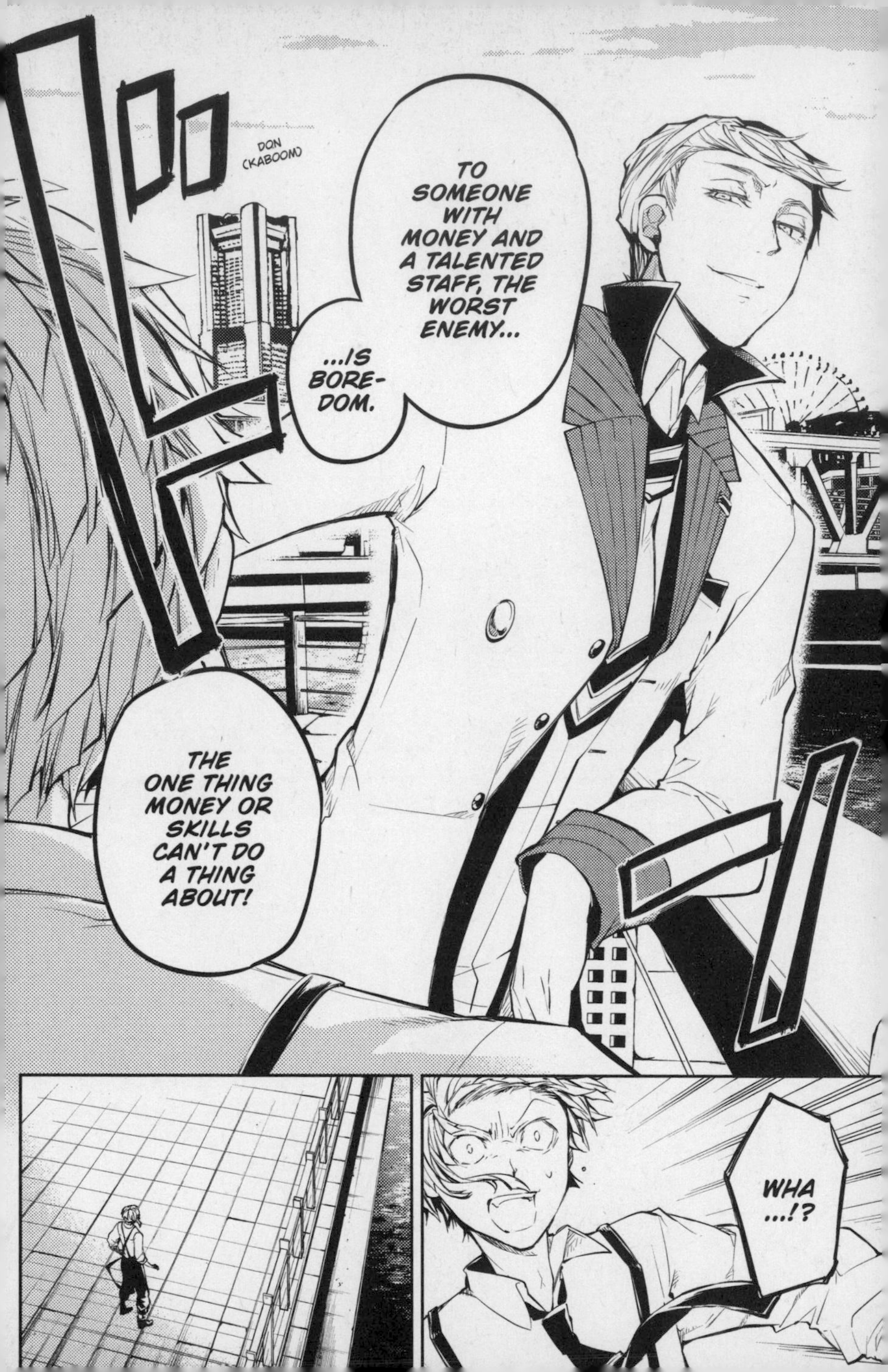
TO SOMEONE WITH MONEY AND A TALENTED STAFF, THE WORST ENEMY...
DON (KABOOM)
...IS BORE-DOM.
THE ONE THING MONEY OR SKILLS CAN'T DO A THING ABOUT!
WHA ...!?

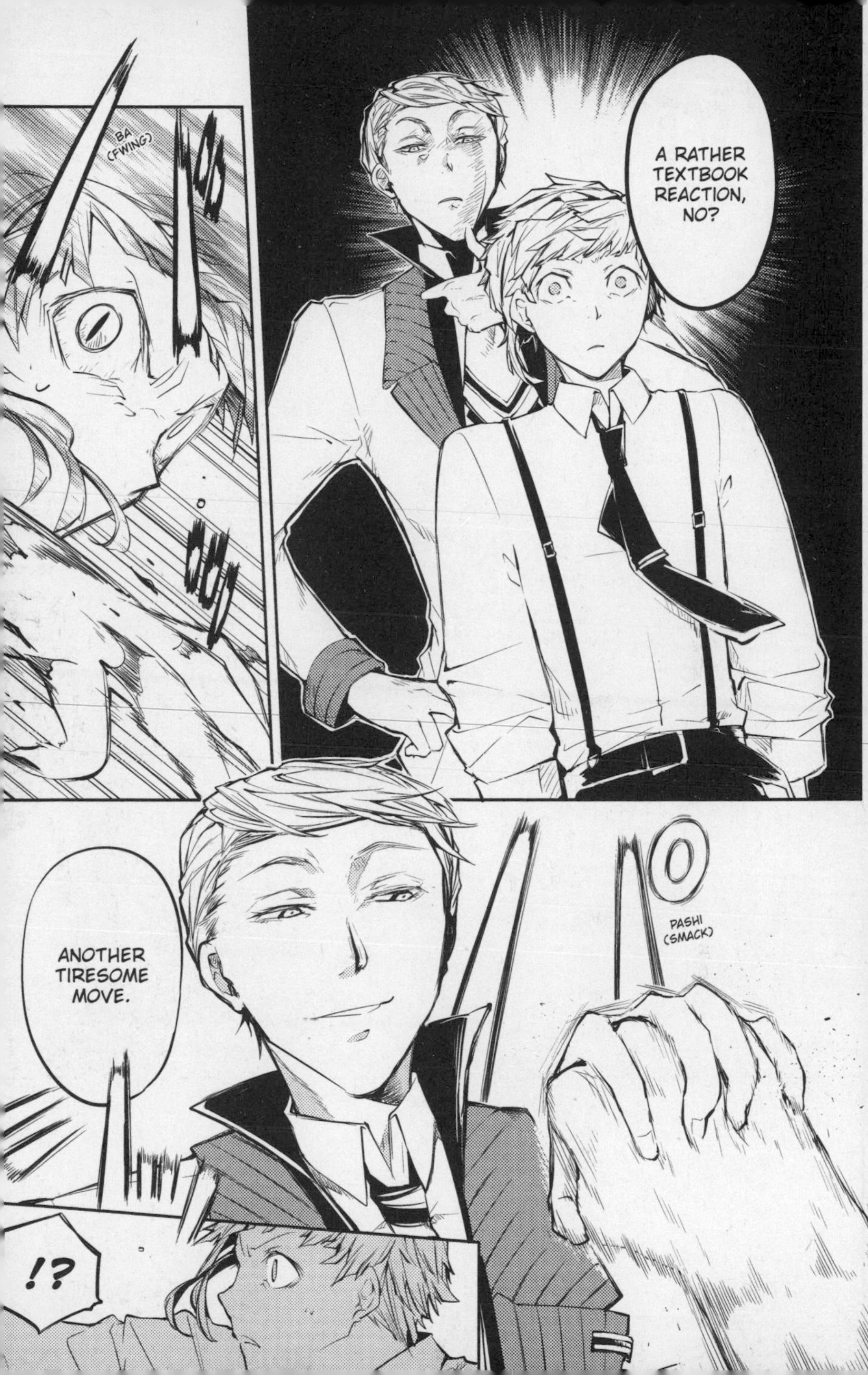
A RATHER TEXTBOOK REACTION, NO?
BA (FWING)
PASHI (SMACK)
ANOTHER TIRESOME MOVE.
!?

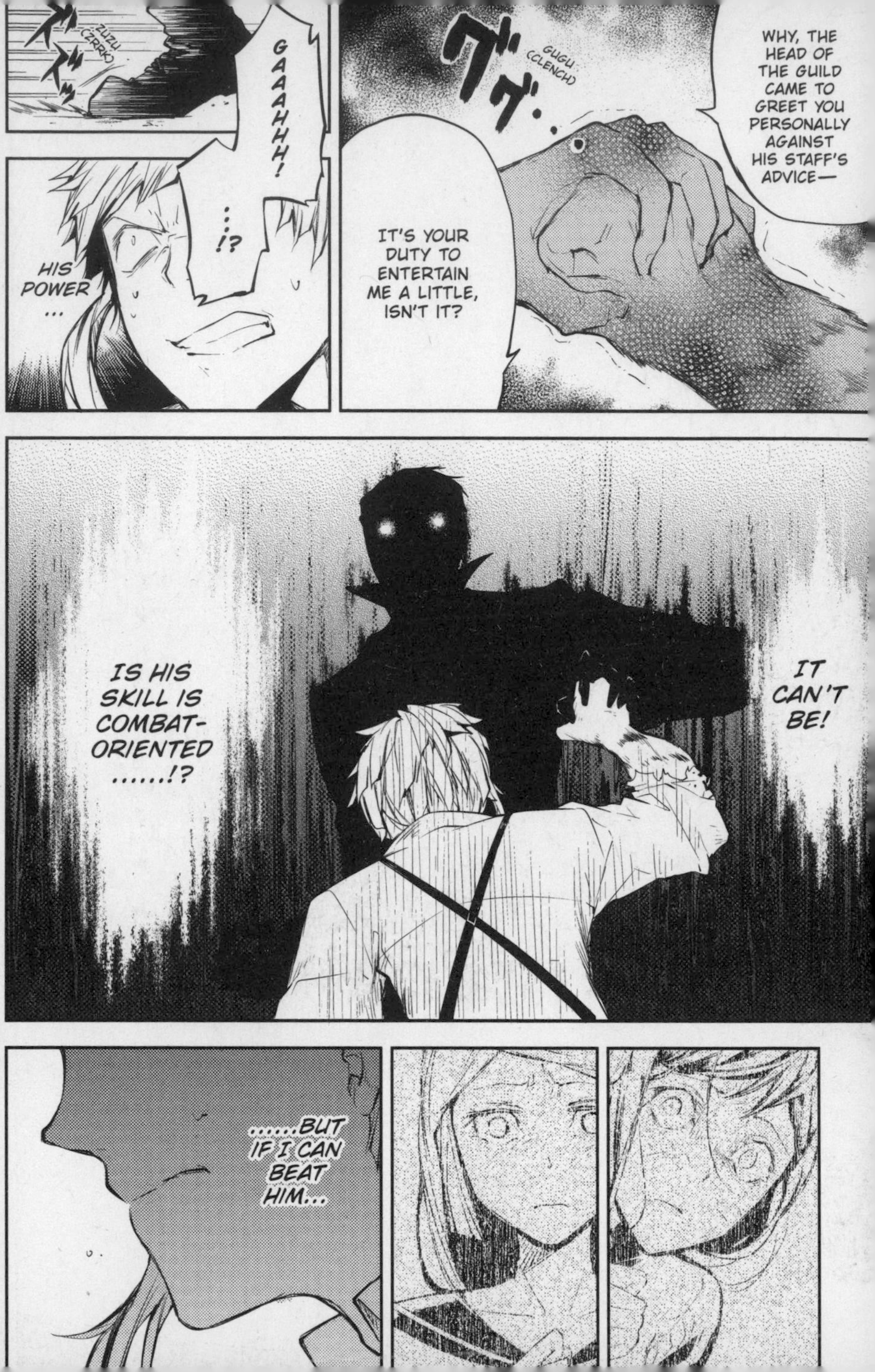
WHY, THE HEAD OF THE GUILD CAME TO GREET YOU PERSONALLY AGAINST HIS STAFF'S ADVICE—
GUGU (CLENCH)
IT'S YOUR DUTY TO ENTERTAIN ME A LITTLE, ISN'T IT?
ZUZU (CZRRK)
GAAAHHH!
...!?
HIS POWER ...
IT CAN'T BE!
IS HIS SKILL IS COMBAT-ORIENTED ......!?
......BUT IF I CAN BEAT HIM...

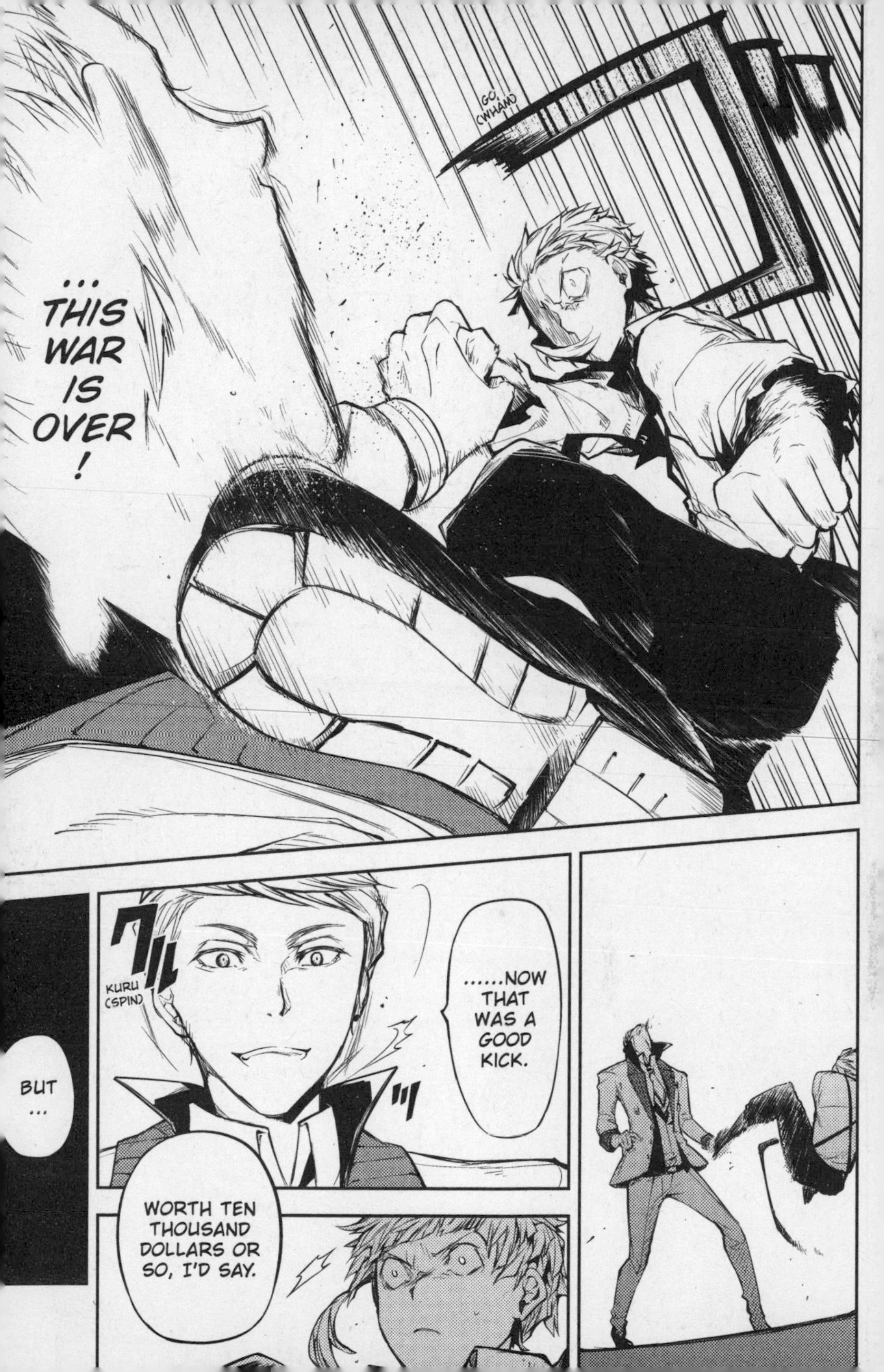
GO, (WHAM)
... THIS WAR IS OVER!
......NOW THAT WAS A GOOD KICK.
KURU (SPIN)
BUT ...
WORTH TEN THOUSAND DOLLARS OR SO, I'D SAY.

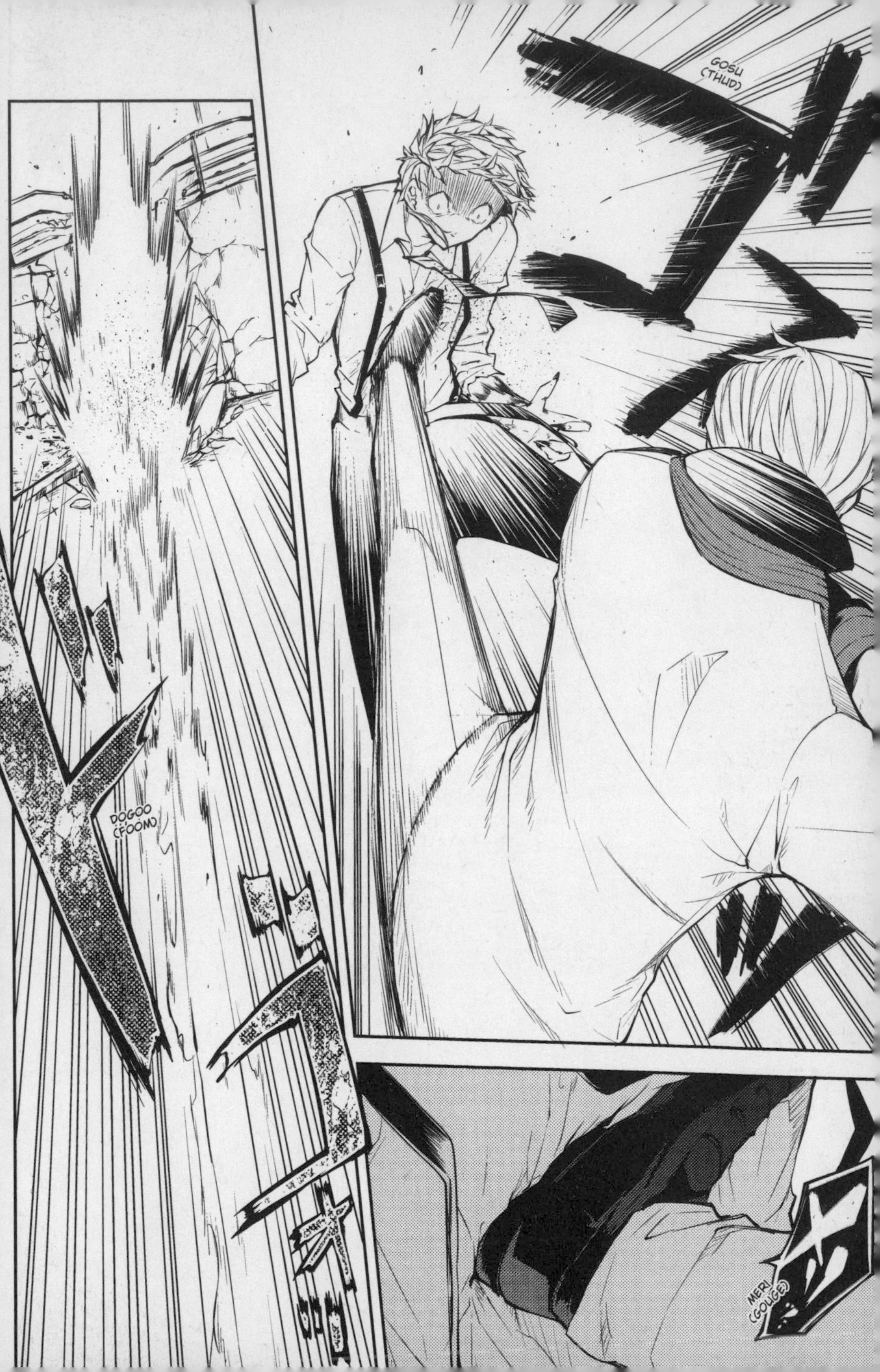
GOSU (THUD)
MERI (GOUGE)
DOGOO (FOOM)

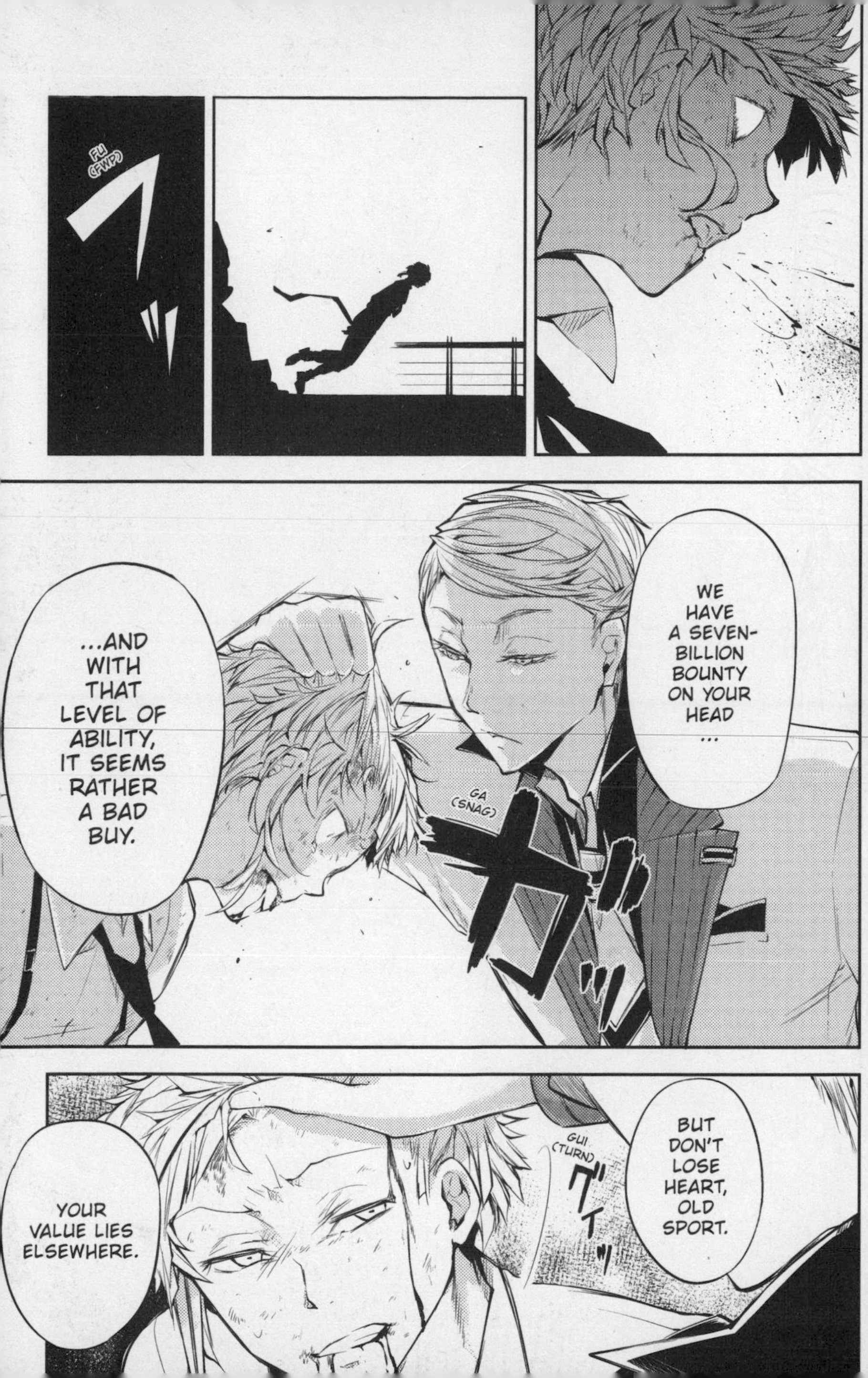
FU (FWP)
WE HAVE A SEVEN-BILLION BOUNTY ON YOUR HEAD ...
GA (SNAG)
...AND WITH THAT LEVEL OF ABILITY, IT SEEMS RATHER A BAD BUY.
BUT DON'T LOSE HEART, OLD SPORT.
GUI (TURN)
YOUR VALUE LIES ELSEWHERE.

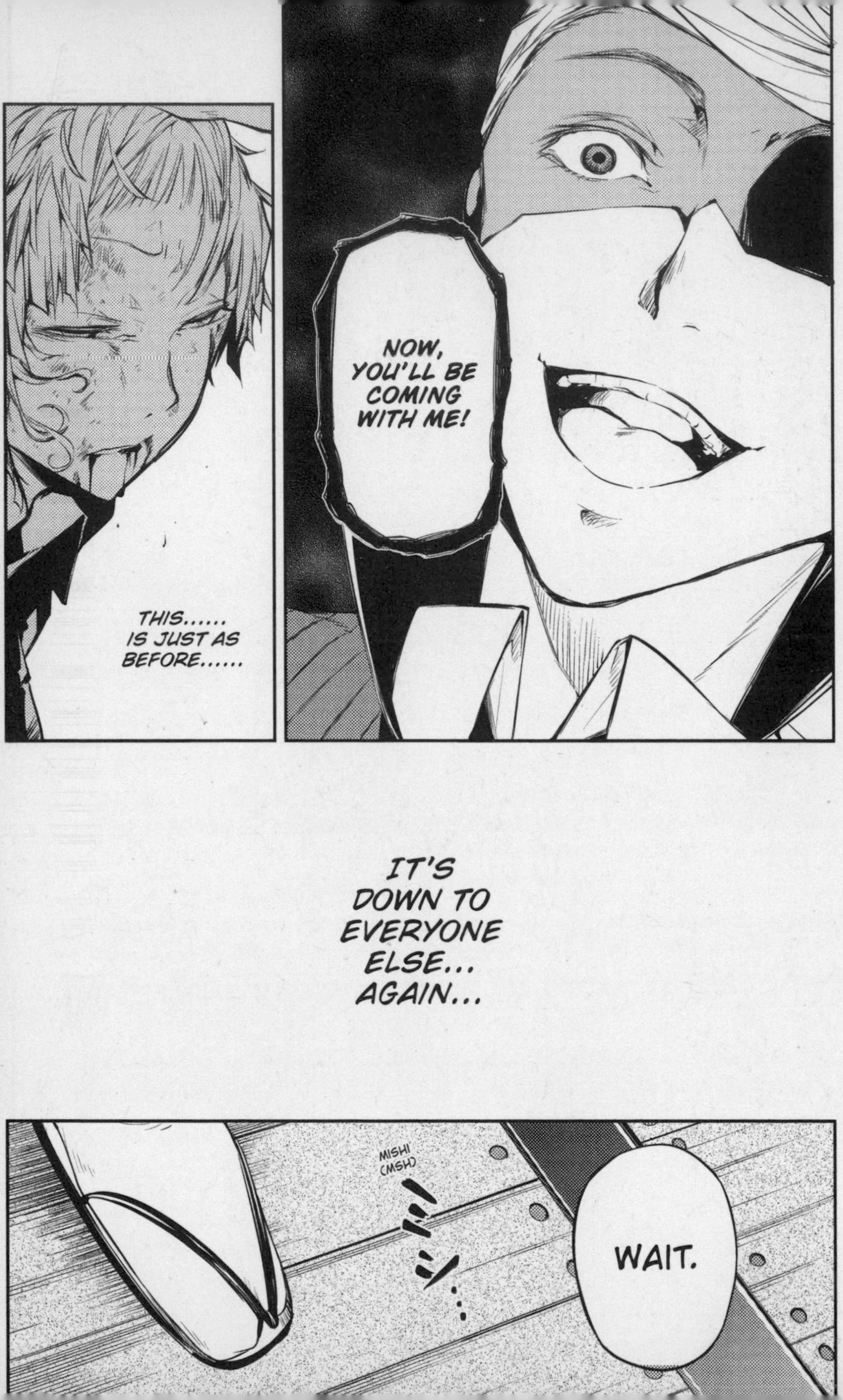
NOW, YOU'LL BE COMING WITH ME!
THIS...... IS JUST AS BEFORE......
IT'S DOWN TO EVERYONE ELSE... AGAIN...
WAIT.
MISHI (MSH)

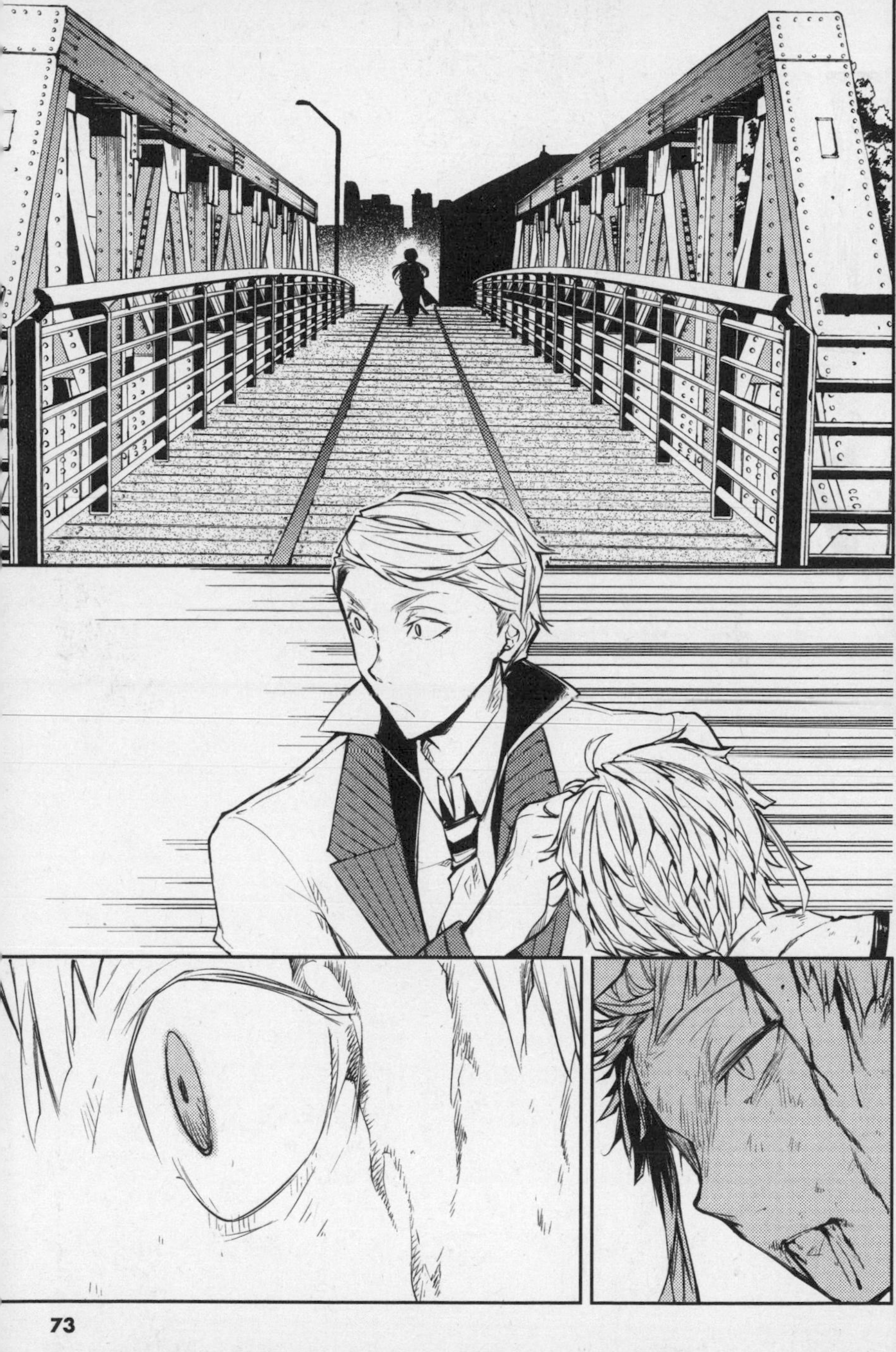

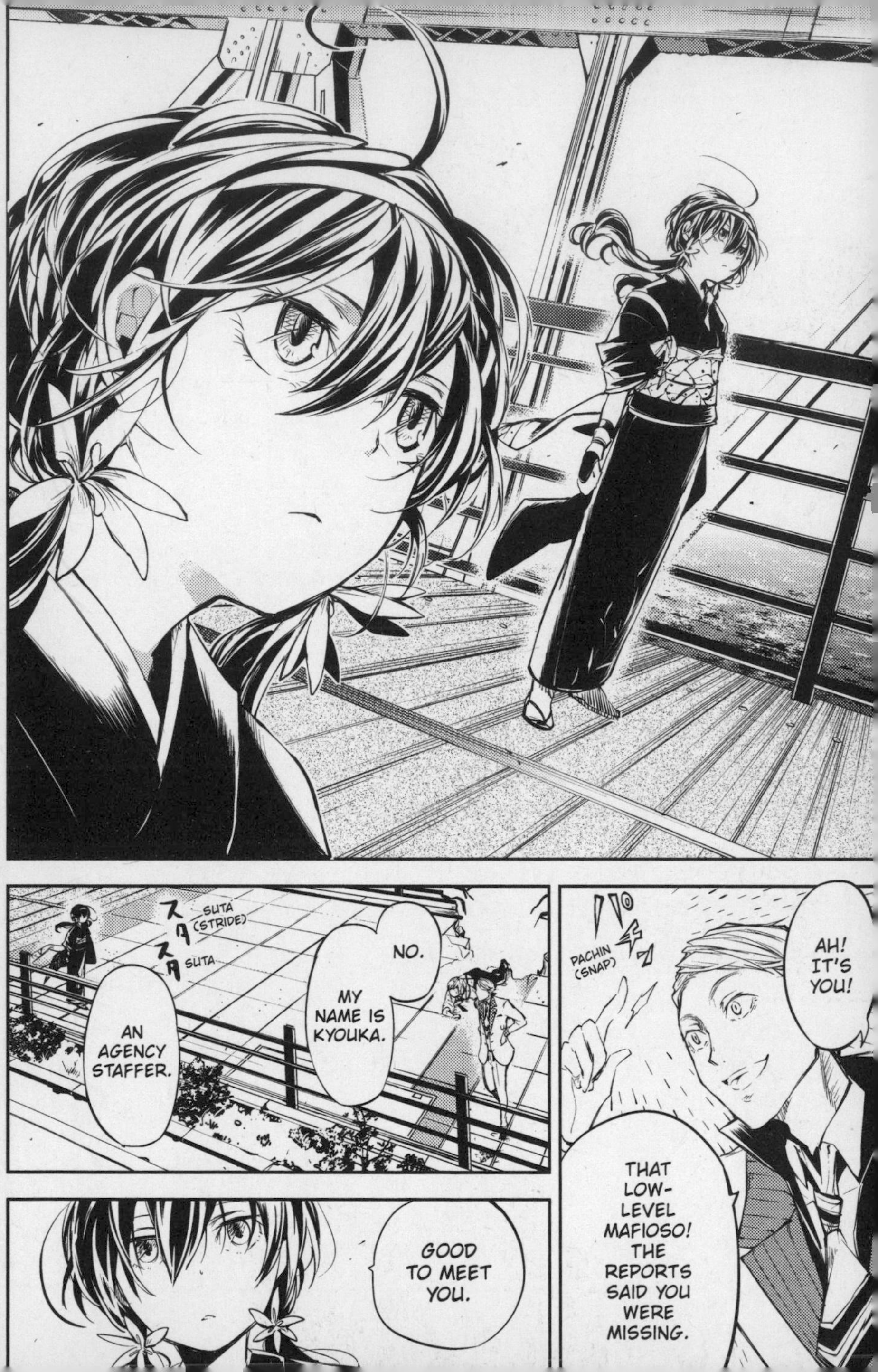
PACHIN (SNAP)
AH! IT'S YOU!
THAT LOW-LEVEL MAFIOSO! THE REPORTS SAID YOU WERE MISSING.
NO.
MY NAME IS KYOUKA.
SUTA (STRIDE) SUTA
AN AGENCY STAFFER.
GOOD TO MEET YOU.

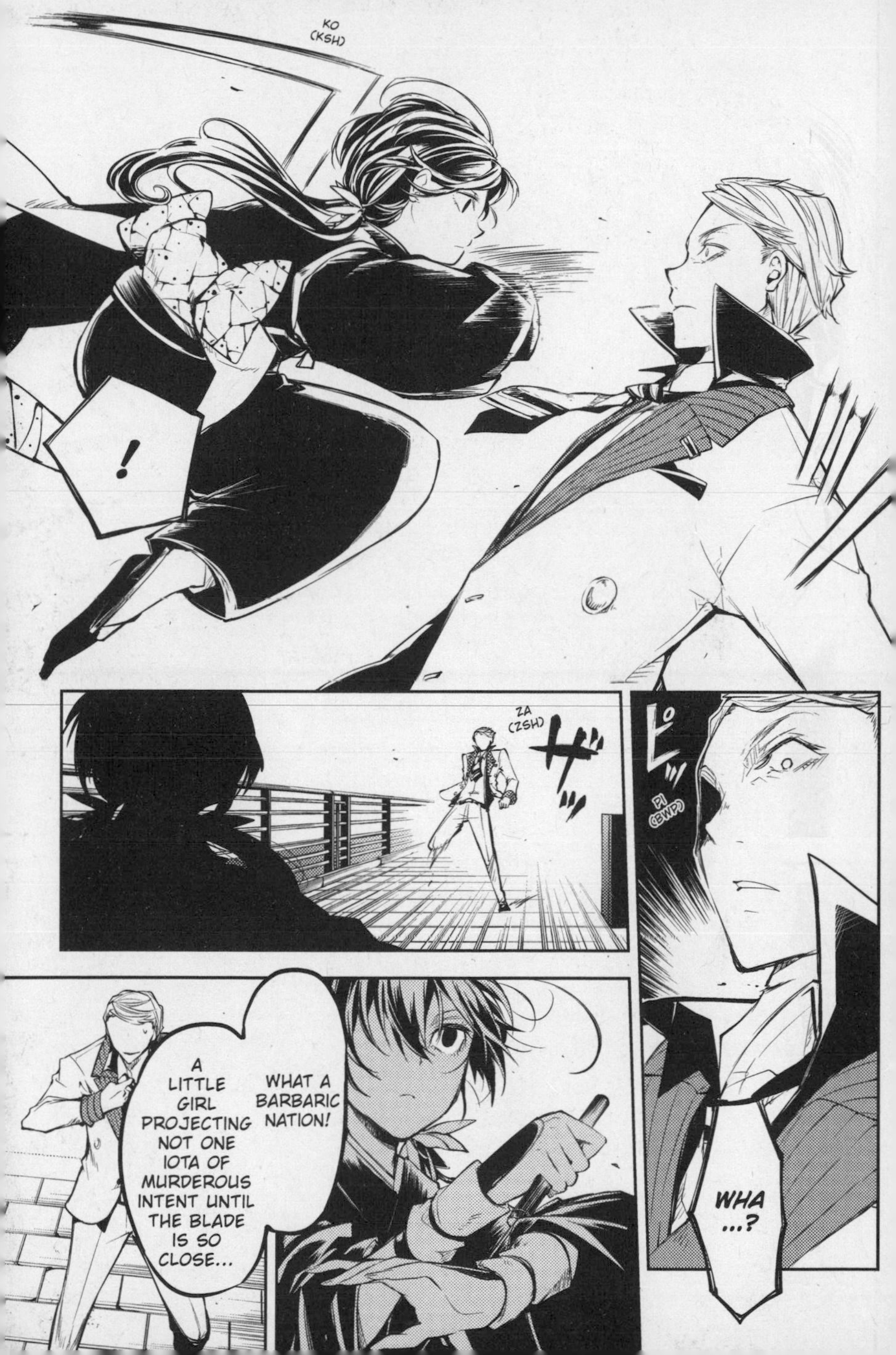
KO (KSH)
!
PI (BWP)
WHA ...?
ZA (ZSH)
WHAT A BARBARIC NATION!
A LITTLE GIRL PROJECTING NOT ONE IOTA OF MURDEROUS INTENT UNTIL THE BLADE IS SO CLOSE...

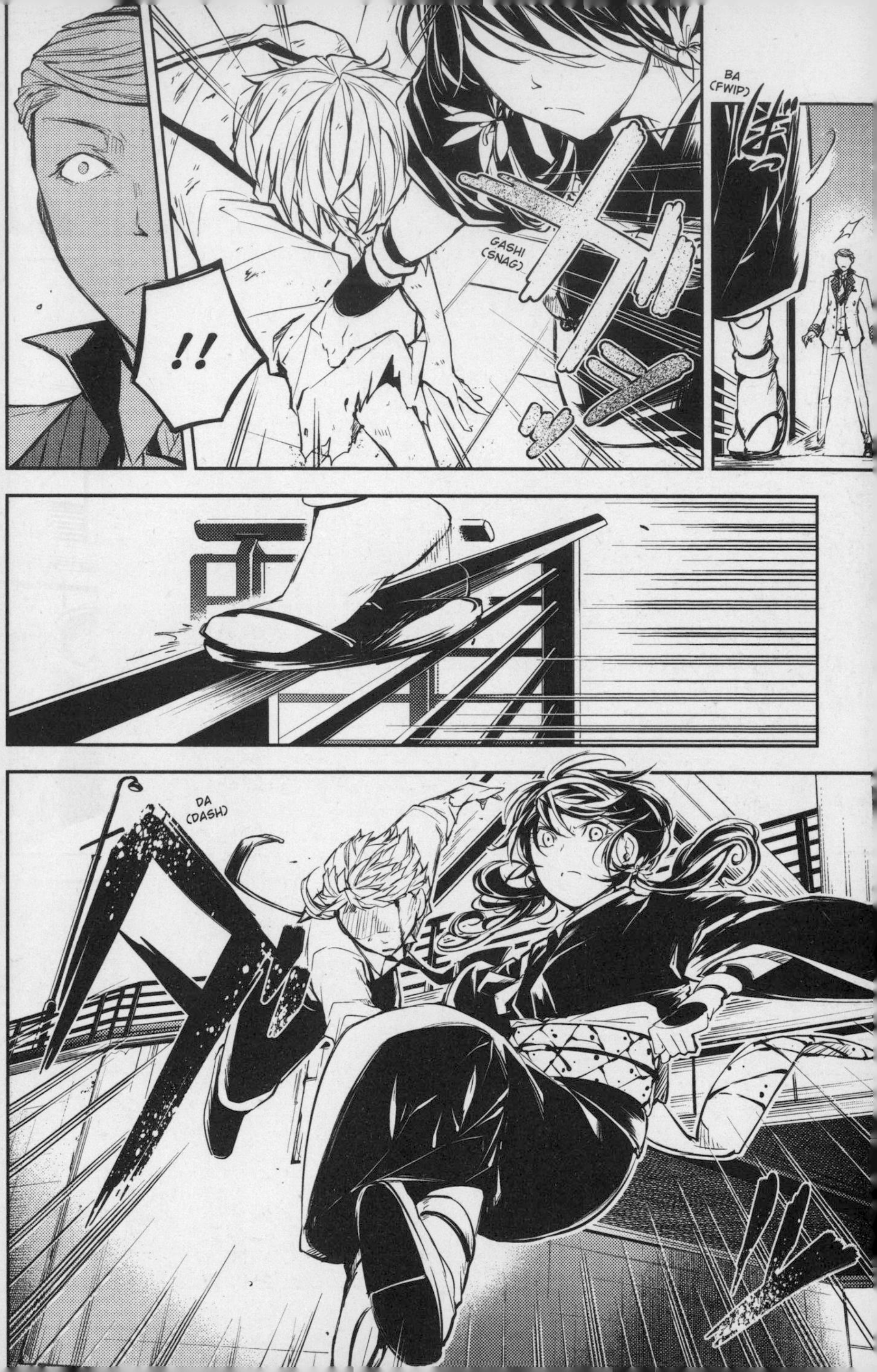
BA (FWIP)
GASHI (SNAG)
!!
DA (DASH)

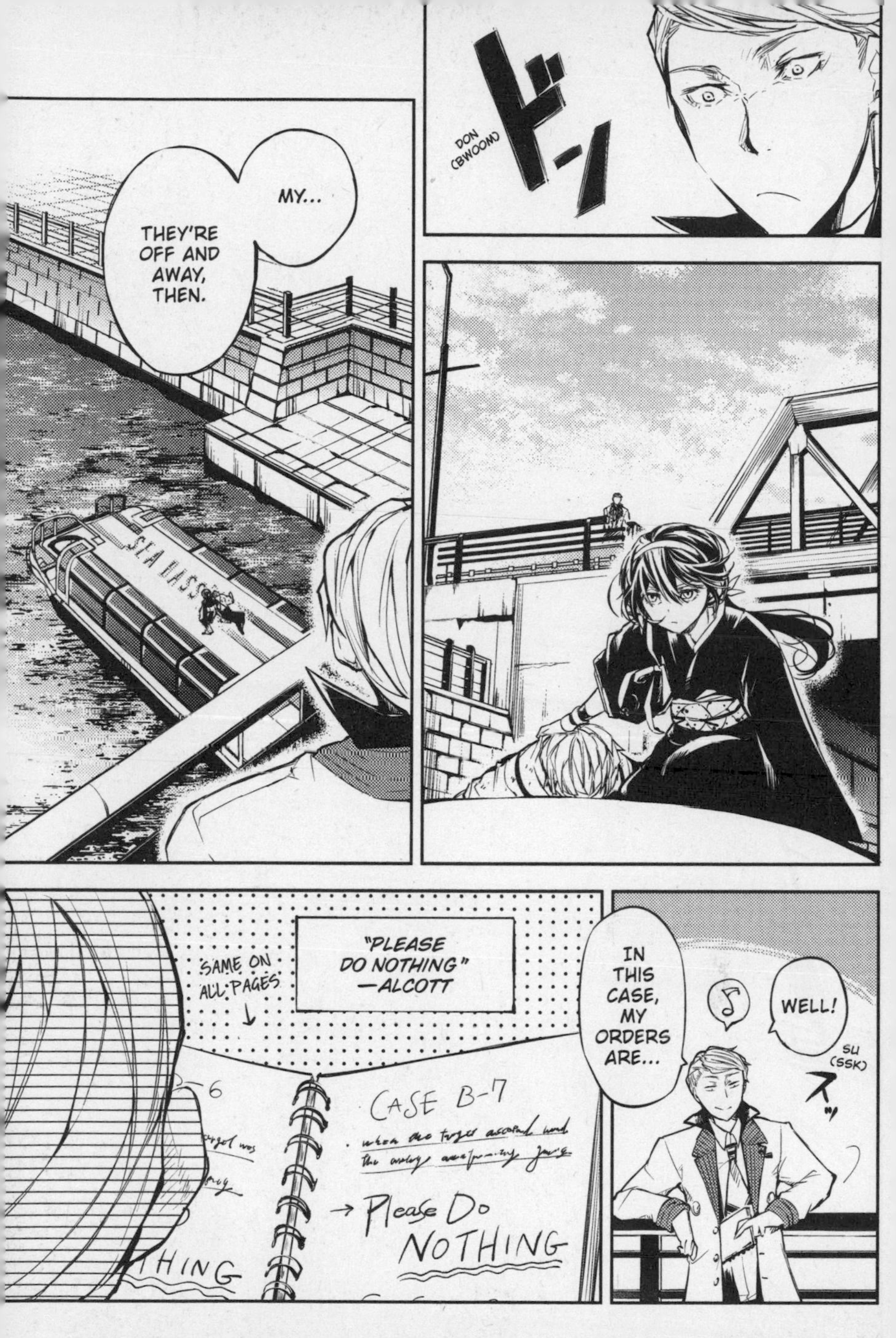
ドン
DON (BWOOM)
MY...
THEY'RE OFF AND AWAY, THEN.
WELL!
♪
IN THIS CASE, MY ORDERS ARE...
スッ
SU (SSK)
"PLEASE DO NOTHING" —ALCOTT
SAME ON ALL PAGES
CASE B-7
Please Do NOTHING
THING

# KYUUSAKU YUMENO

SKILL: **Dogra Magra**
*Able to curse anyone who physically harms him. Anyone cursed begins to sport a hand-shaped blotch on their body. Once he rips open the doll he carries with him, the cursed victim begins to wildly attack anyone around them.*

AGE: *13*

BIRTH DATE: *January 4*

HEIGHT: *146cm*

WEIGHT: *38kg*

BLOOD TYPE: *AB*

LIKES: *Himself, chaos, brown sugar*

DISLIKES: *Himself, peace, society, hospitals*

## CHAPTER 27
# *Upon the Shattering Shores*

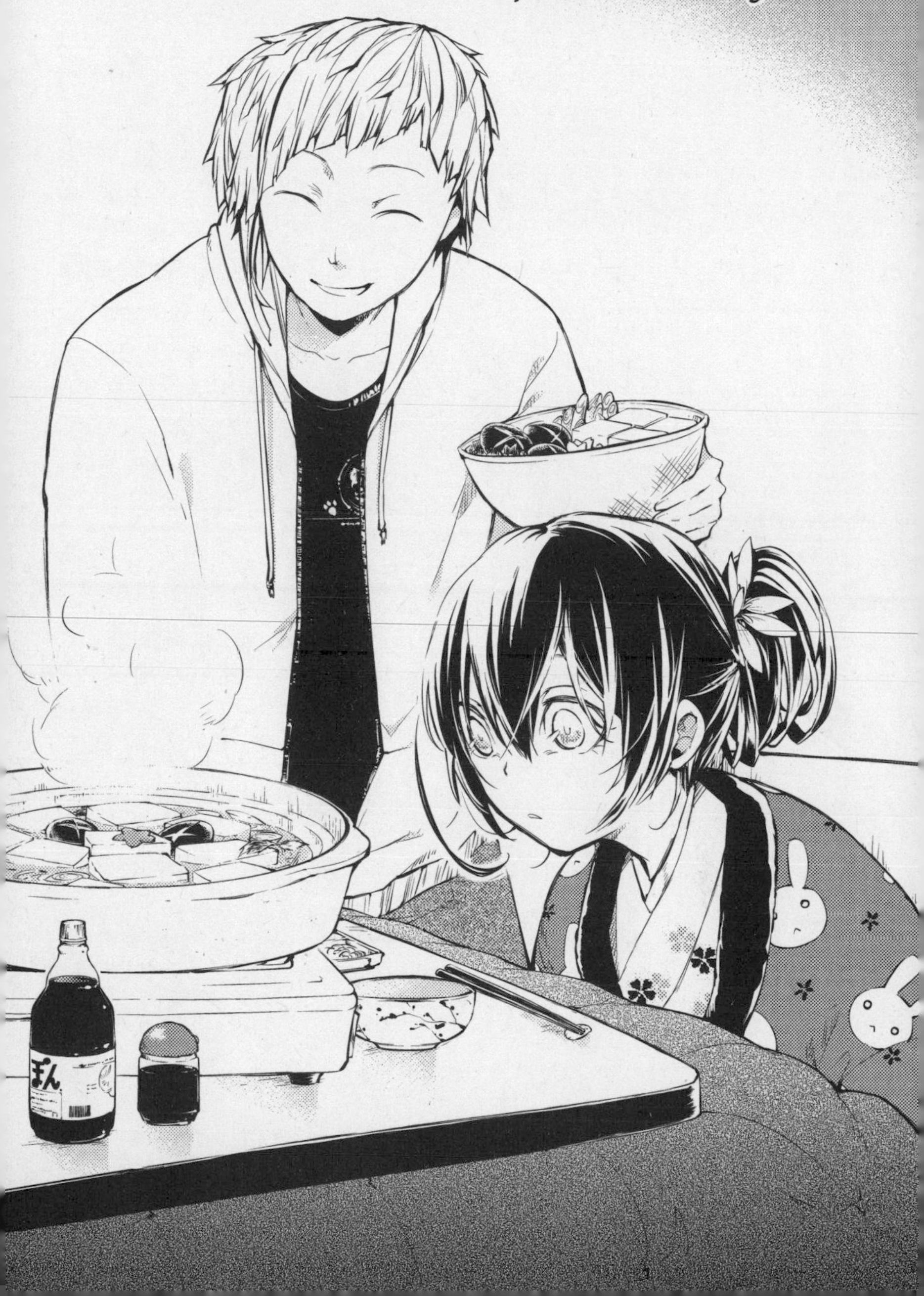

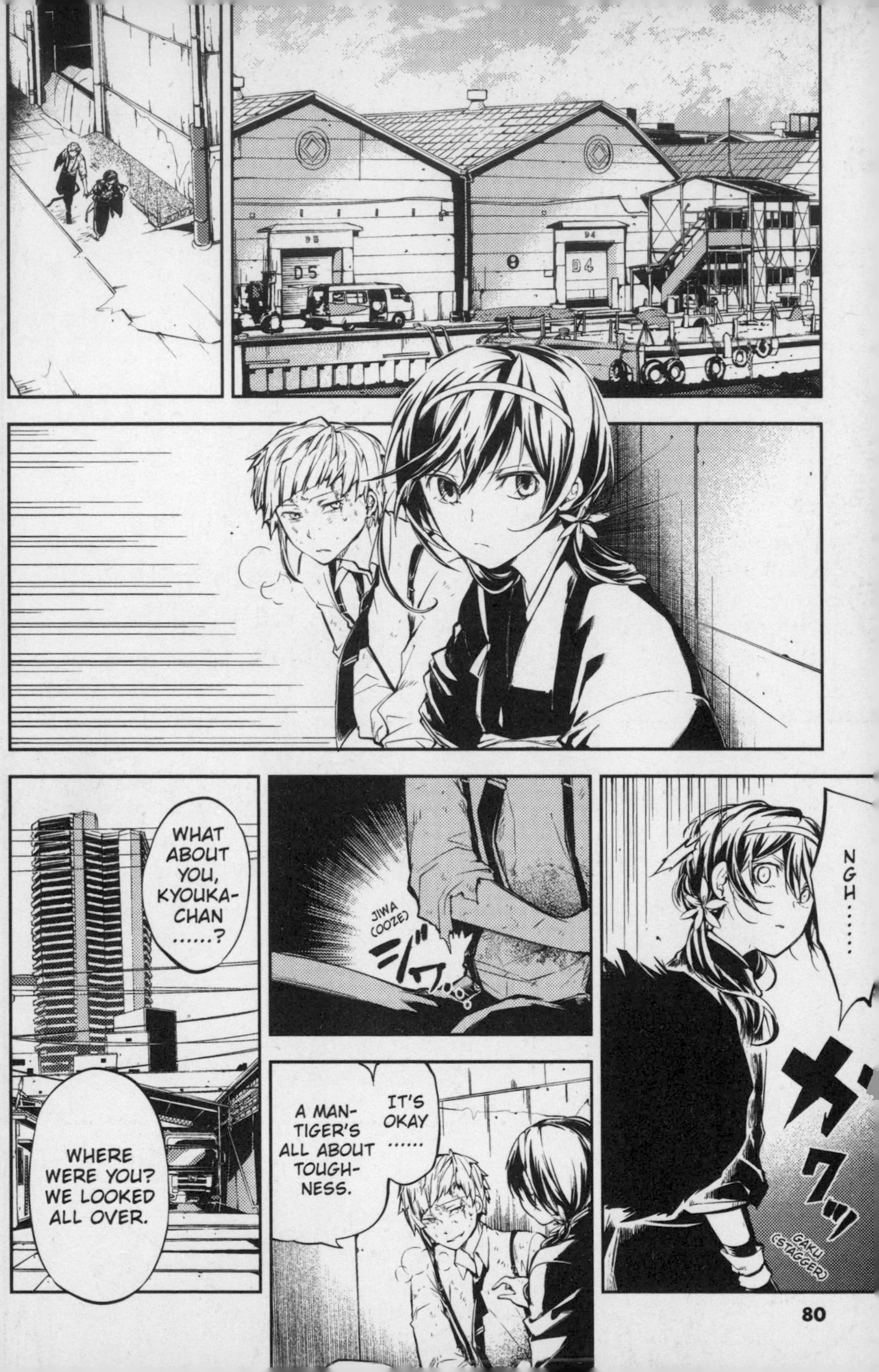
NGH......
GAKU (STAGGER)
JIWA (OOZE)
IT'S OKAY......
A MAN-TIGER'S ALL ABOUT TOUGH-NESS.
WHAT ABOUT YOU, KYOUKA-CHAN......?
WHERE WERE YOU? WE LOOKED ALL OVER.

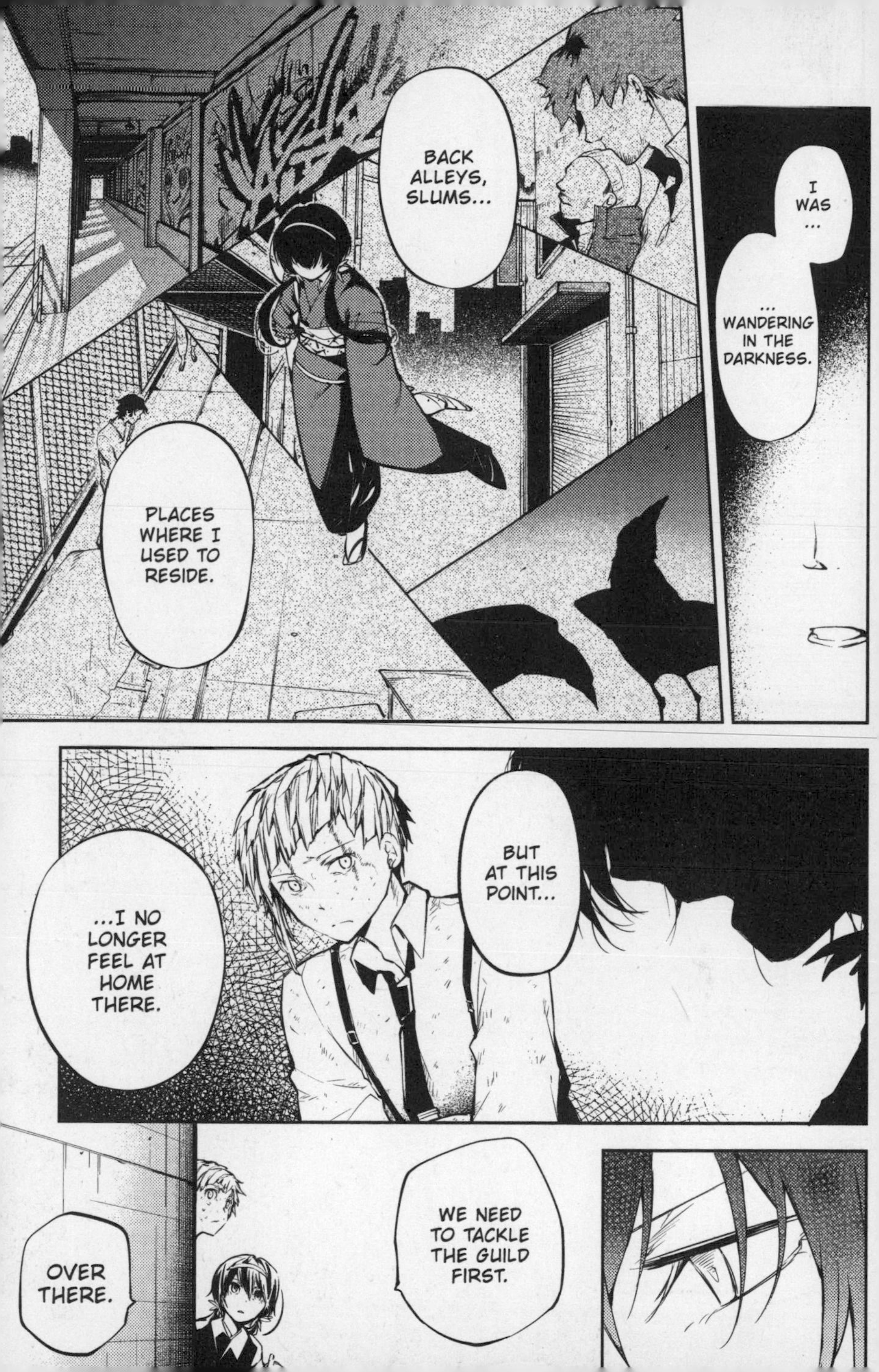
I WAS...
...WANDERING IN THE DARKNESS.
BACK ALLEYS, SLUMS...
PLACES WHERE I USED TO RESIDE.
BUT AT THIS POINT...
...I NO LONGER FEEL AT HOME THERE.
WE NEED TO TACKLE THE GUILD FIRST.
OVER THERE.

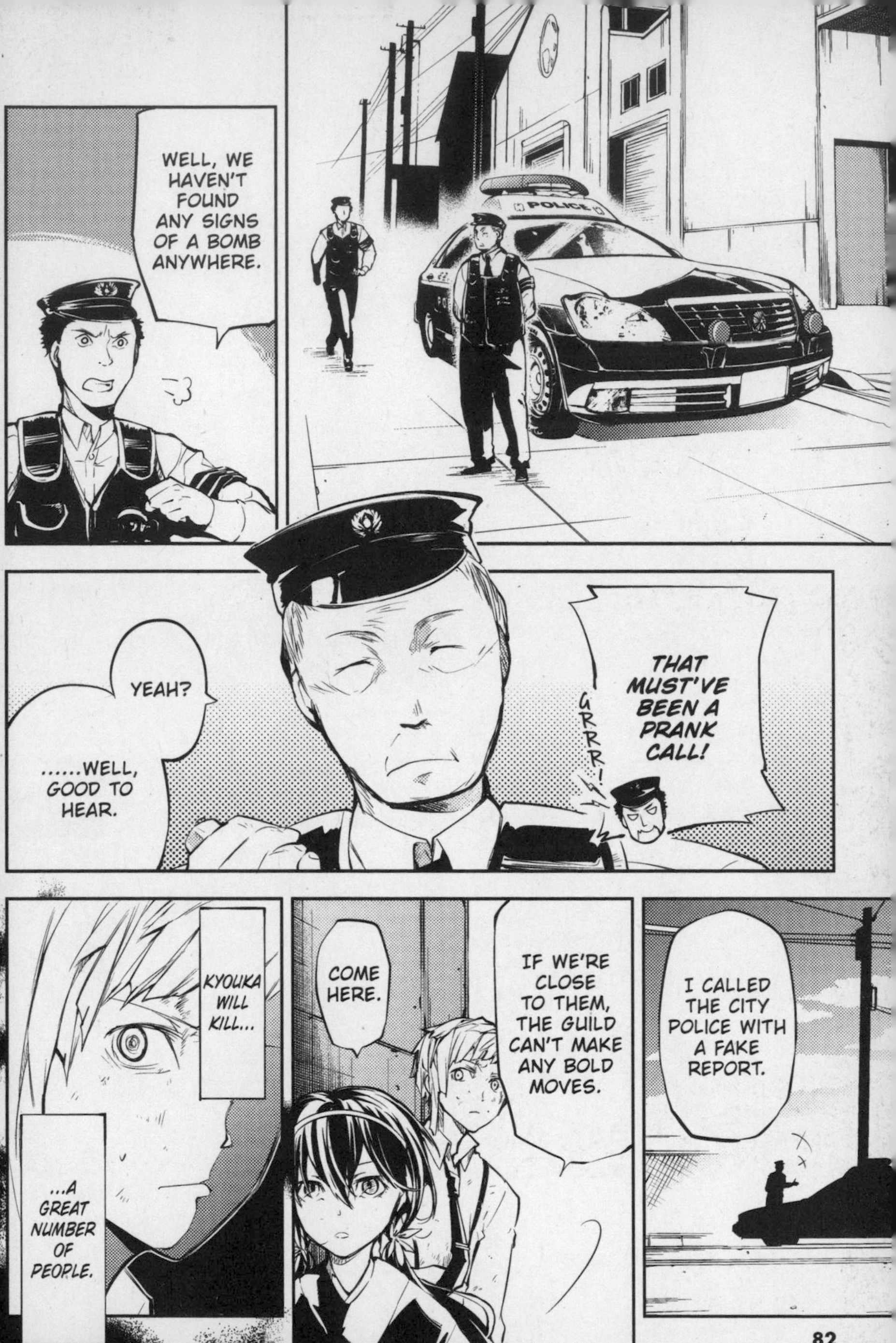
WELL, WE HAVEN'T FOUND ANY SIGNS OF A BOMB ANYWHERE.
THAT MUST'VE BEEN A PRANK CALL!
GRRR!
YEAH?
......WELL, GOOD TO HEAR.
I CALLED THE CITY POLICE WITH A FAKE REPORT.
IF WE'RE CLOSE TO THEM, THE GUILD CAN'T MAKE ANY BOLD MOVES.
COME HERE.
KYOUKA WILL KILL...
...A GREAT NUMBER OF PEOPLE.

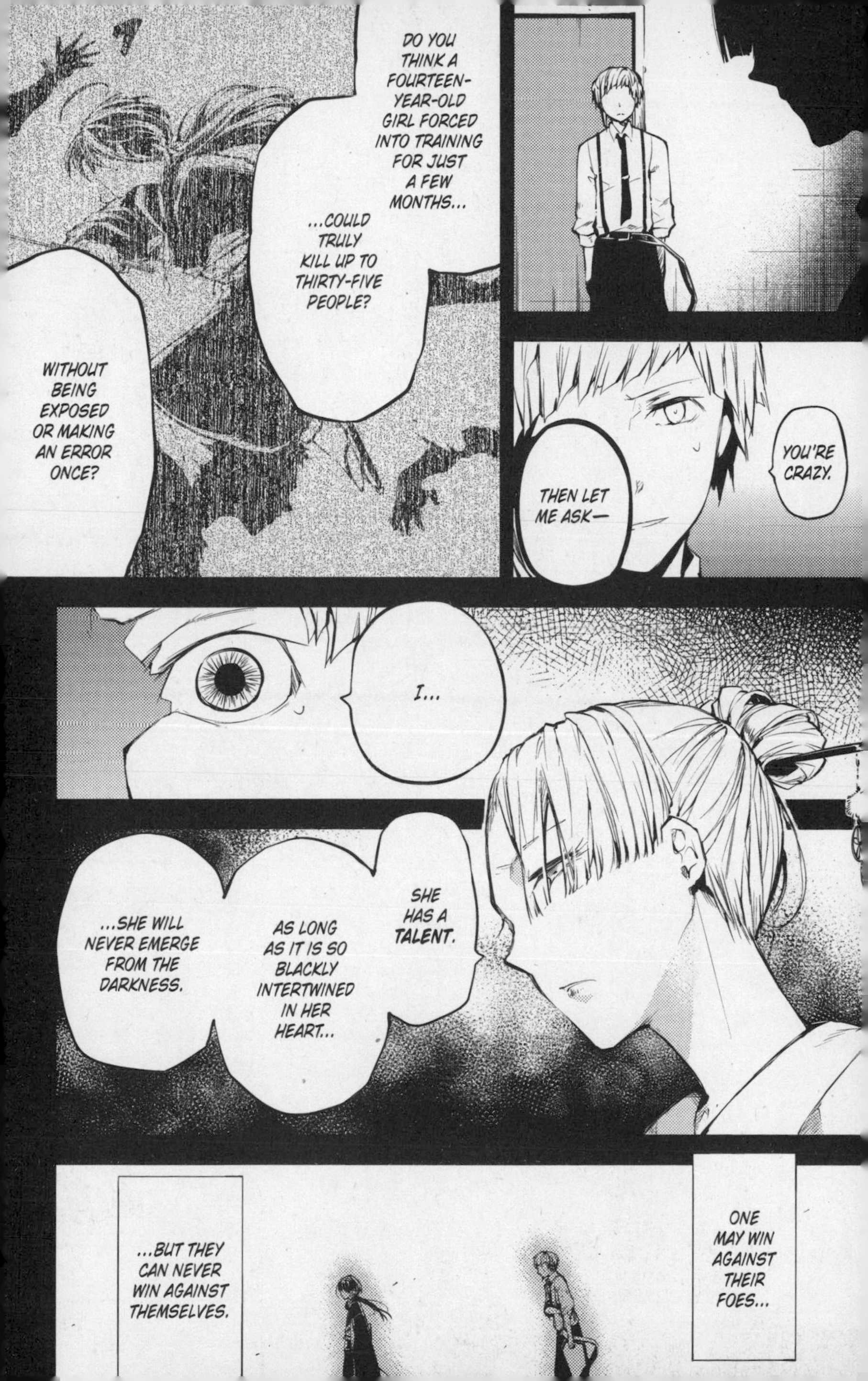
YOU'RE CRAZY.
THEN LET ME ASK—
DO YOU THINK A FOURTEEN-YEAR-OLD GIRL FORCED INTO TRAINING FOR JUST A FEW MONTHS...
...COULD TRULY KILL UP TO THIRTY-FIVE PEOPLE?
WITHOUT BEING EXPOSED OR MAKING AN ERROR ONCE?
I...
SHE HAS A TALENT.
AS LONG AS IT IS SO BLACKLY INTERTWINED IN HER HEART...
...SHE WILL NEVER EMERGE FROM THE DARKNESS.
ONE MAY WIN AGAINST THEIR FOES...
...BUT THEY CAN NEVER WIN AGAINST THEMSELVES.

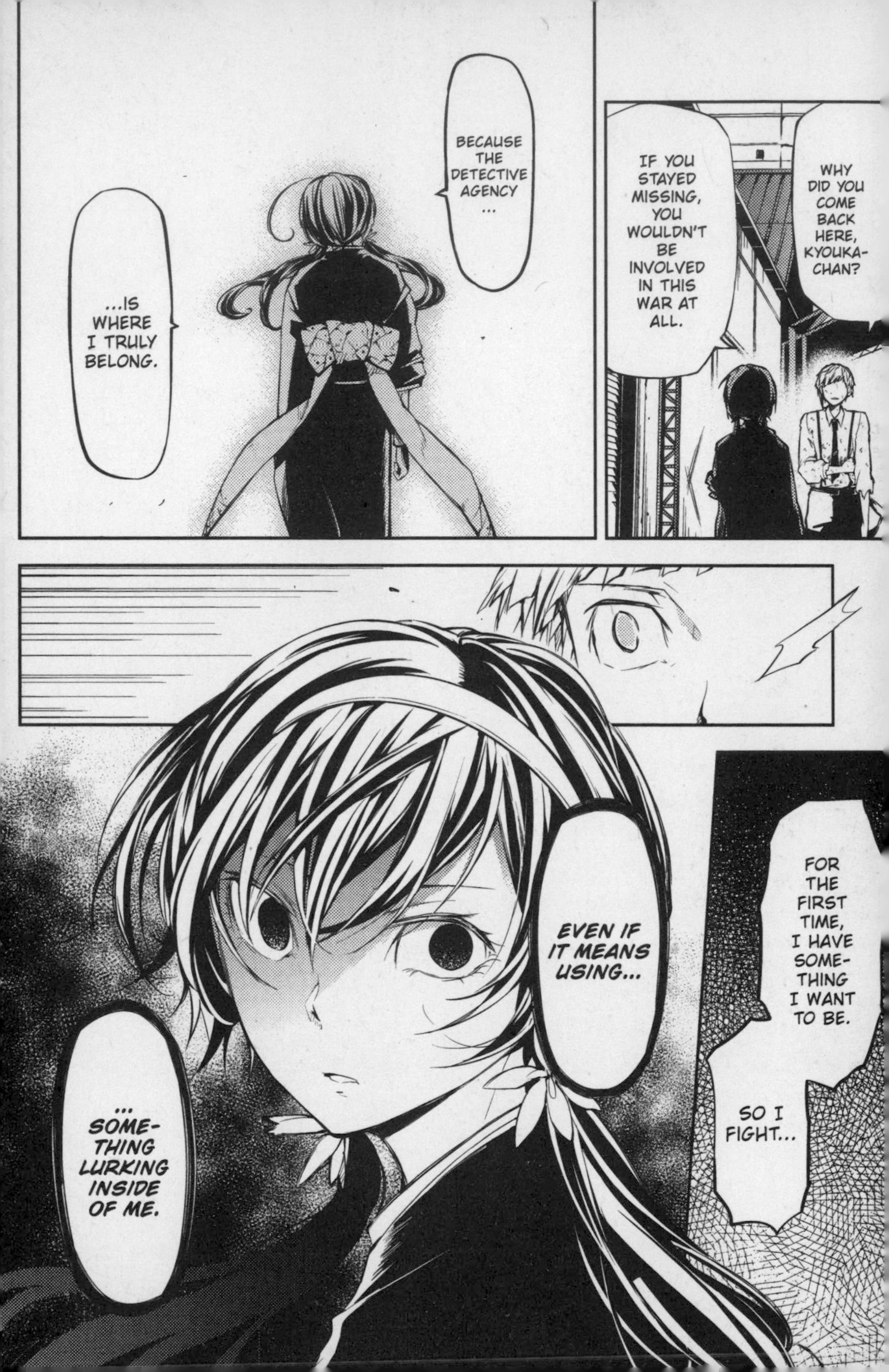
WHY DID YOU COME BACK HERE, KYOUKA-CHAN?
IF YOU STAYED MISSING, YOU WOULDN'T BE INVOLVED IN THIS WAR AT ALL.
BECAUSE THE DETECTIVE AGENCY ...
...IS WHERE I TRULY BELONG.
FOR THE FIRST TIME, I HAVE SOME-THING I WANT TO BE.
SO I FIGHT...
EVEN IF IT MEANS USING...
... SOME-THING LURKING INSIDE OF ME.

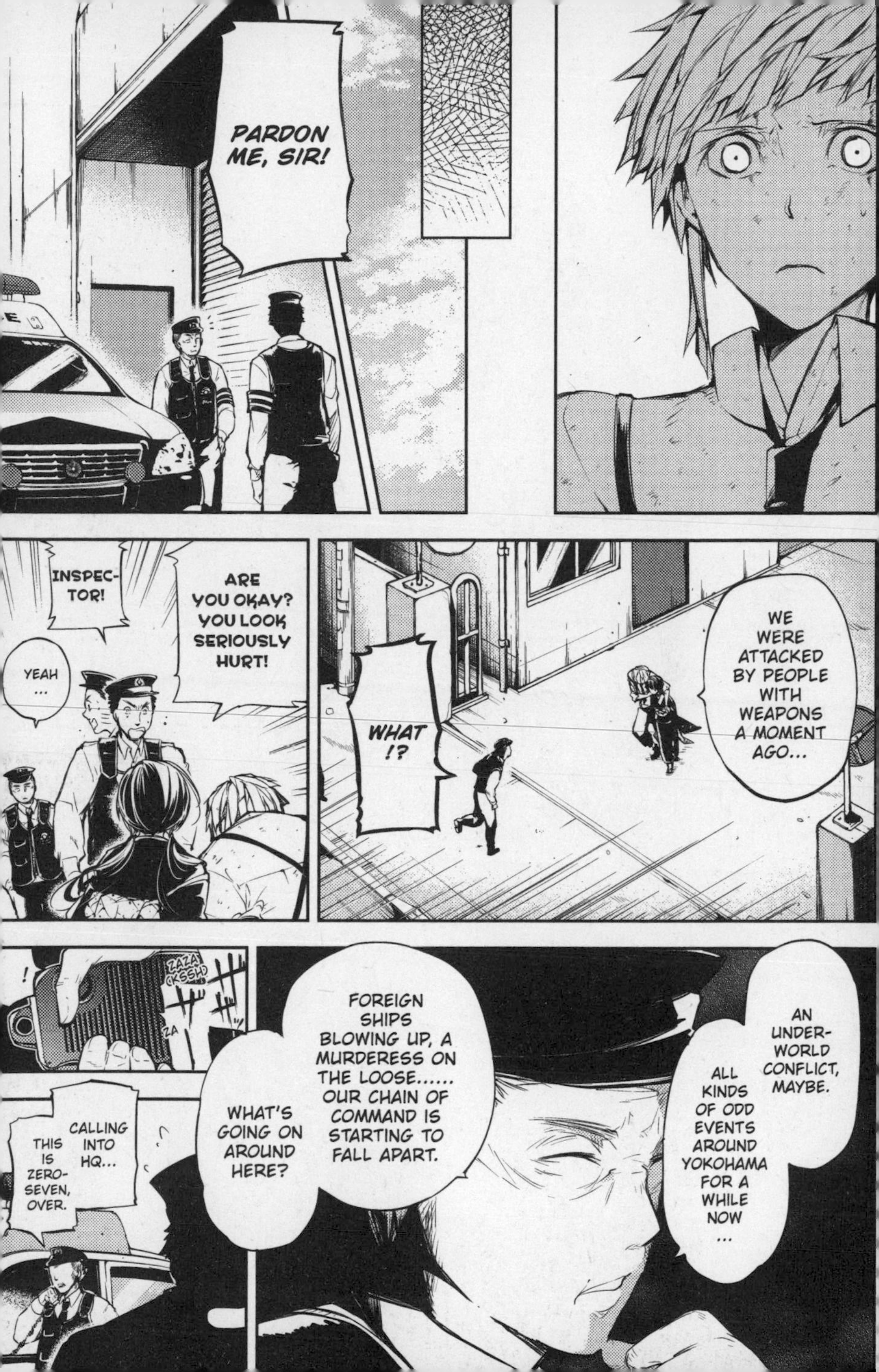
PARDON ME, SIR!
WE WERE ATTACKED BY PEOPLE WITH WEAPONS A MOMENT AGO...
WHAT!?
ARE YOU OKAY? YOU LOOK SERIOUSLY HURT!
INSPECTOR!
YEAH ...
AN UNDER-WORLD CONFLICT, MAYBE.
ALL KINDS OF ODD EVENTS AROUND YOKOHAMA FOR A WHILE NOW ...
FOREIGN SHIPS BLOWING UP, A MURDERESS ON THE LOOSE...... OUR CHAIN OF COMMAND IS STARTING TO FALL APART.
WHAT'S GOING ON AROUND HERE?
ZAZA
ZA
!
CALLING INTO HQ...
THIS IS ZERO-SEVEN, OVER.

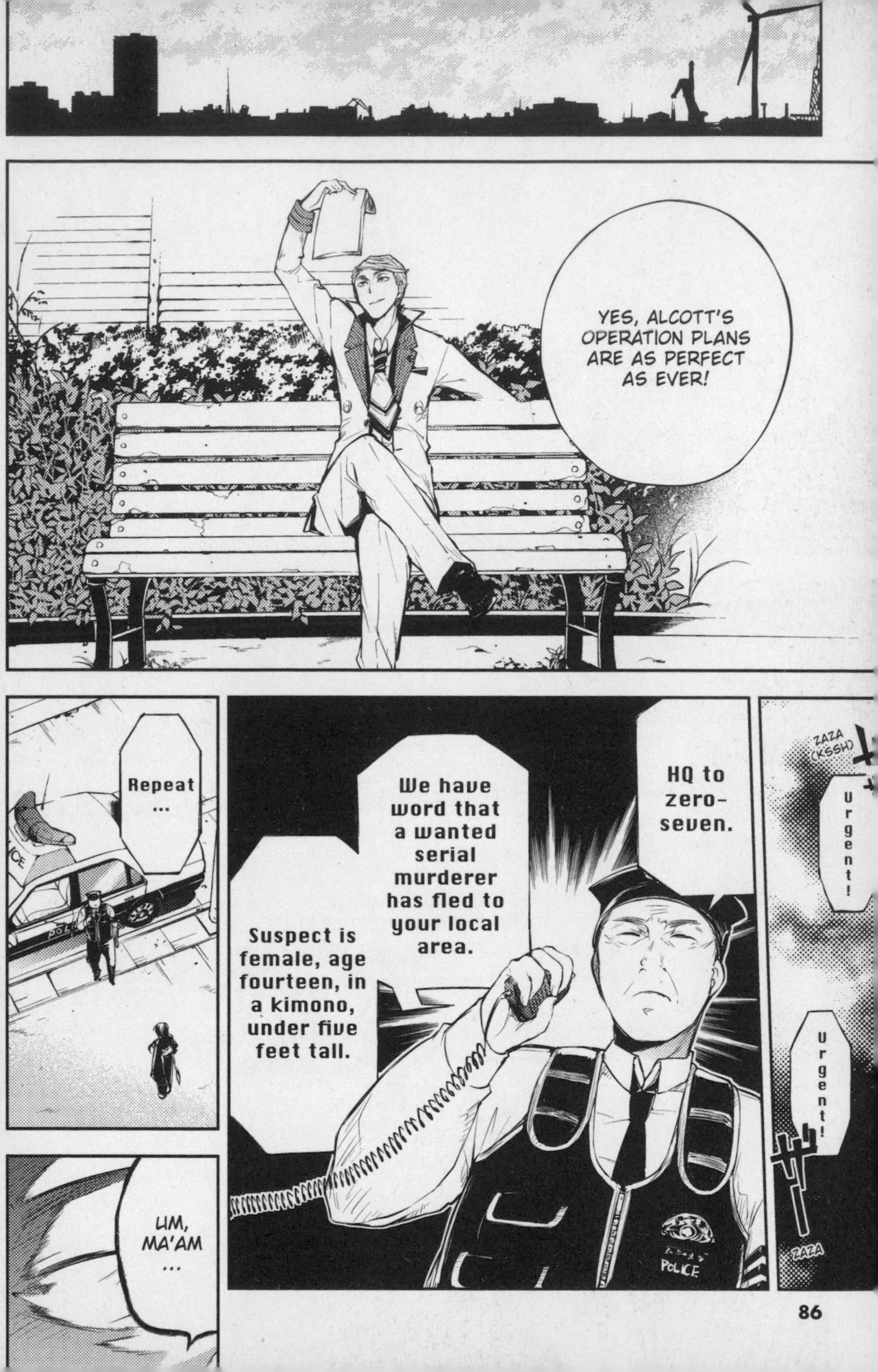
YES, ALCOTT'S OPERATION PLANS ARE AS PERFECT AS EVER!
ZAZA (KSSH)
Urgent!
Urgent!
ZAZA
HQ to zero-seven.
We have word that a wanted serial murderer has fled to your local area.
Suspect is female, age fourteen, in a kimono, under five feet tall.
Repeat ...
UM, MA'AM ...

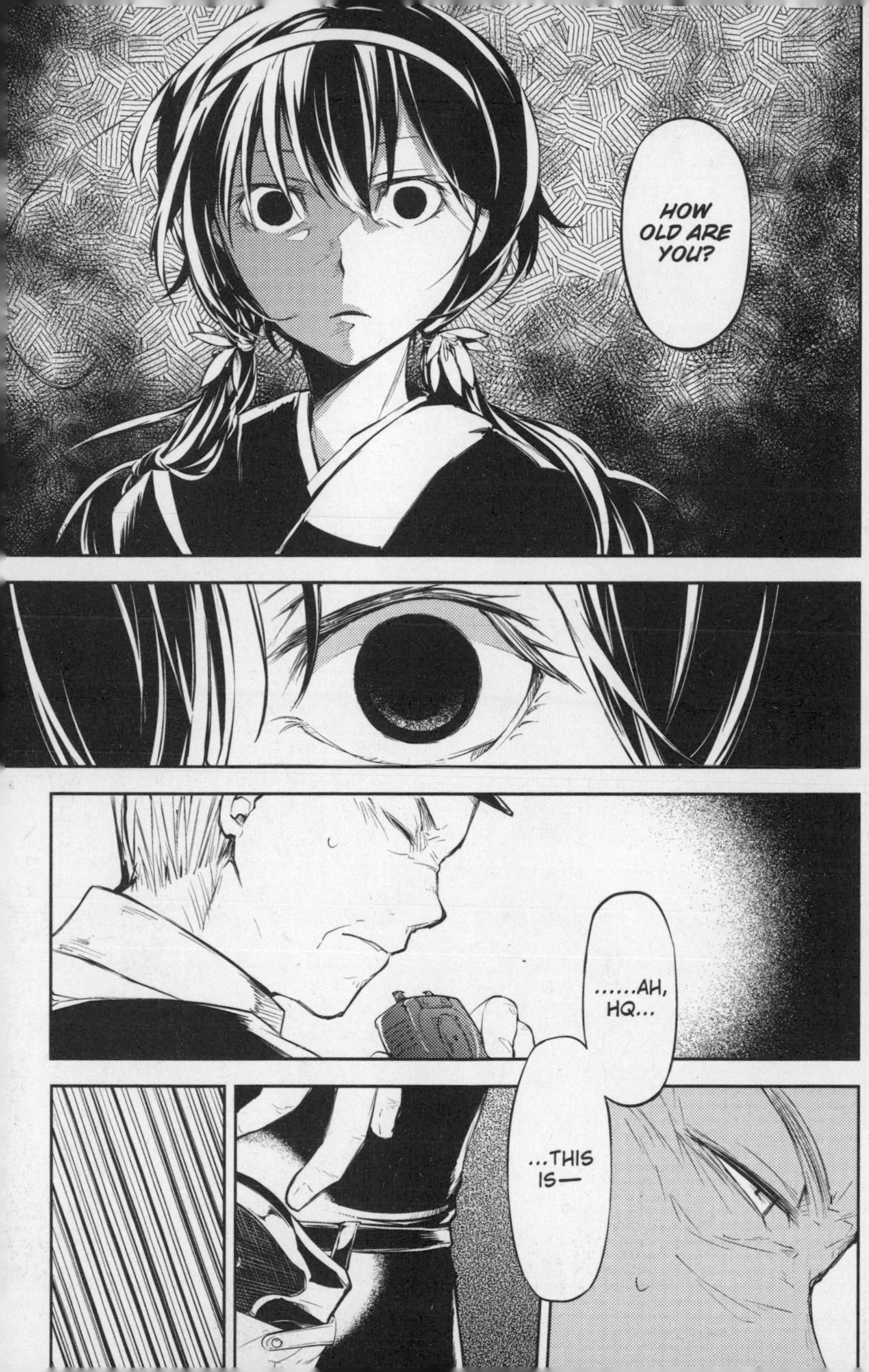
HOW OLD ARE YOU?
......AH, HQ...
...THIS IS—

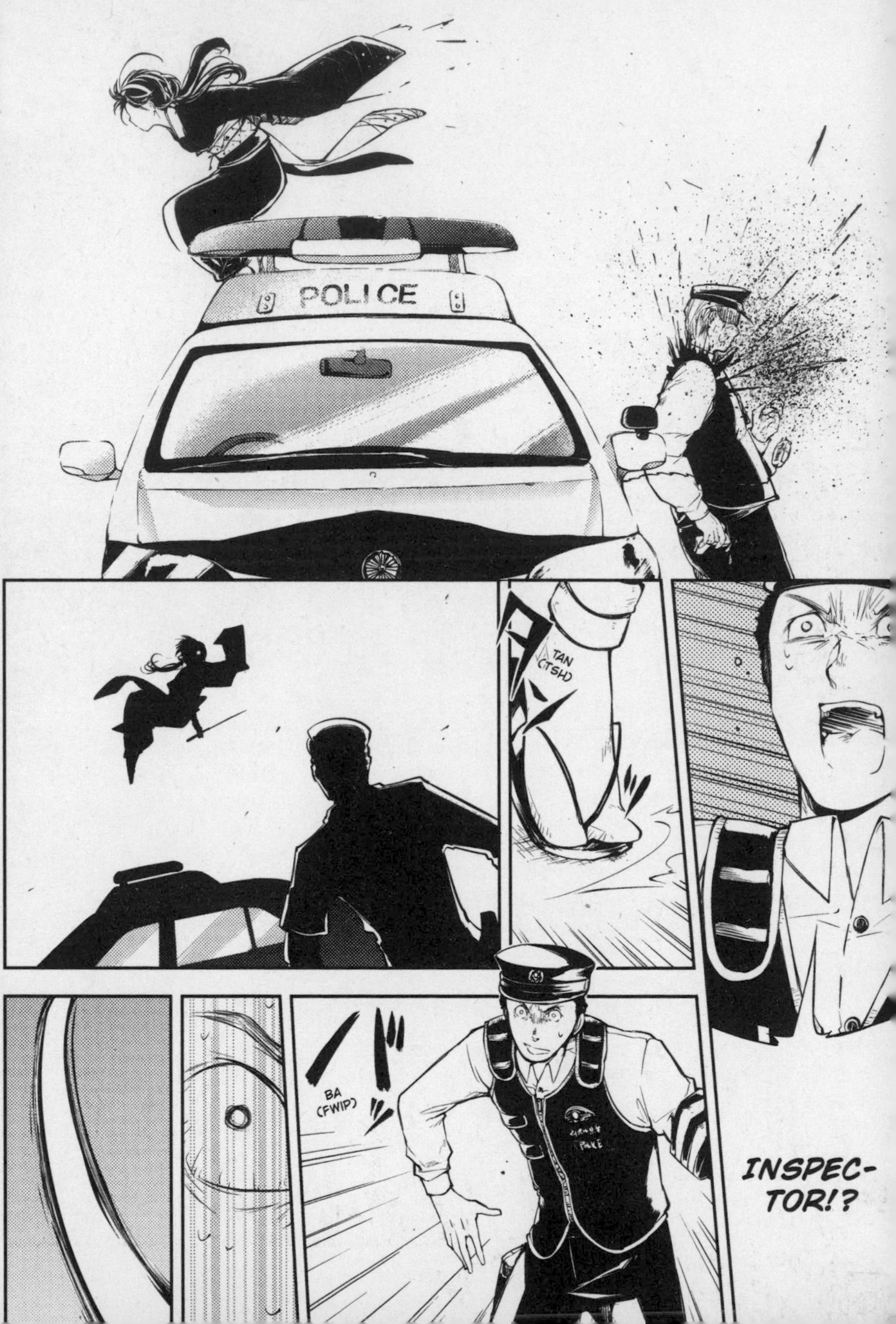
POLICE
INSPECTOR!?
TAN
(TSH)
BA
(FWIP)

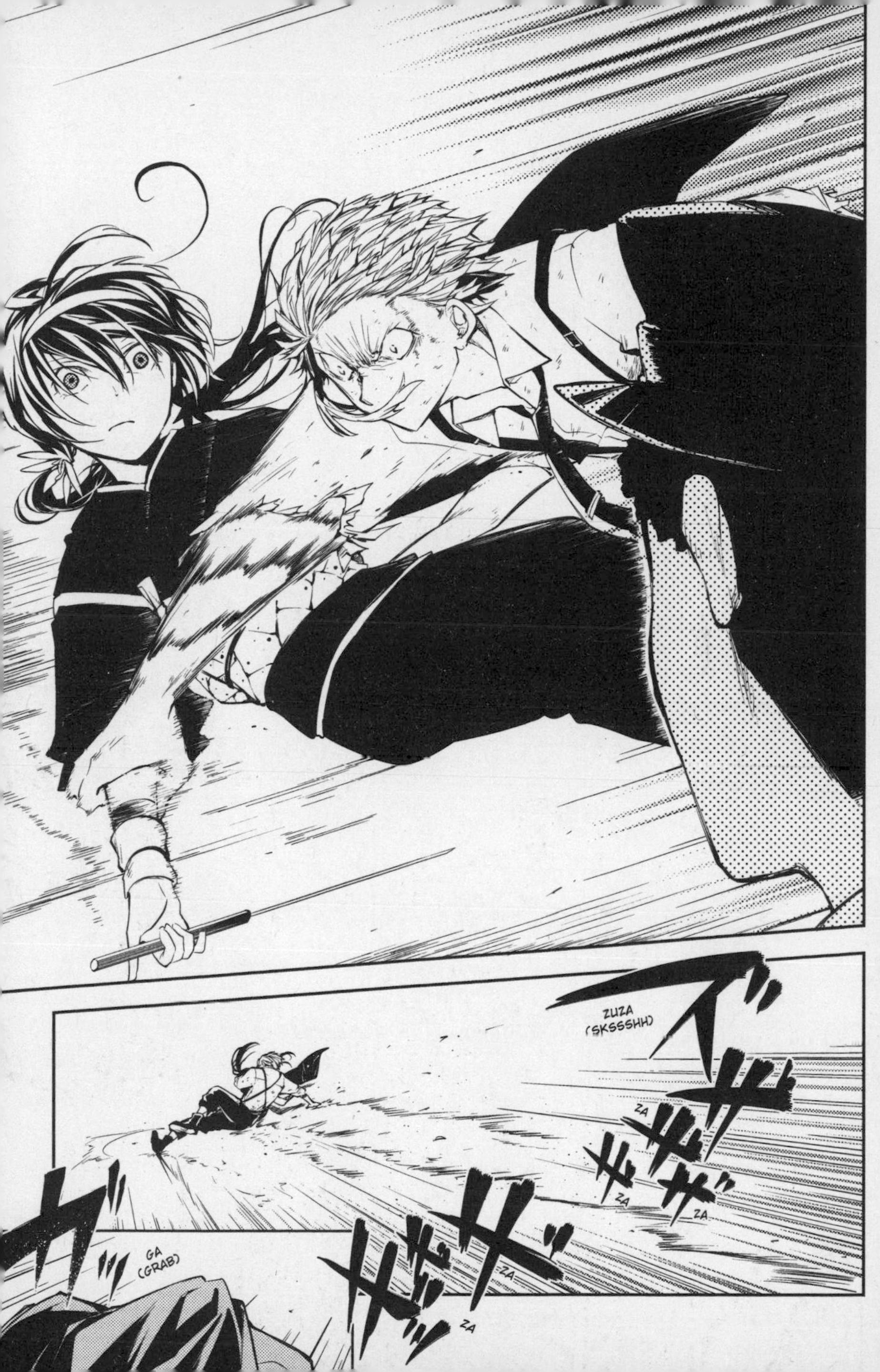

ZUZA
(SKSSSHH)
ZA
ZA
ZA
ZA
ZA
GA
(GRAB)

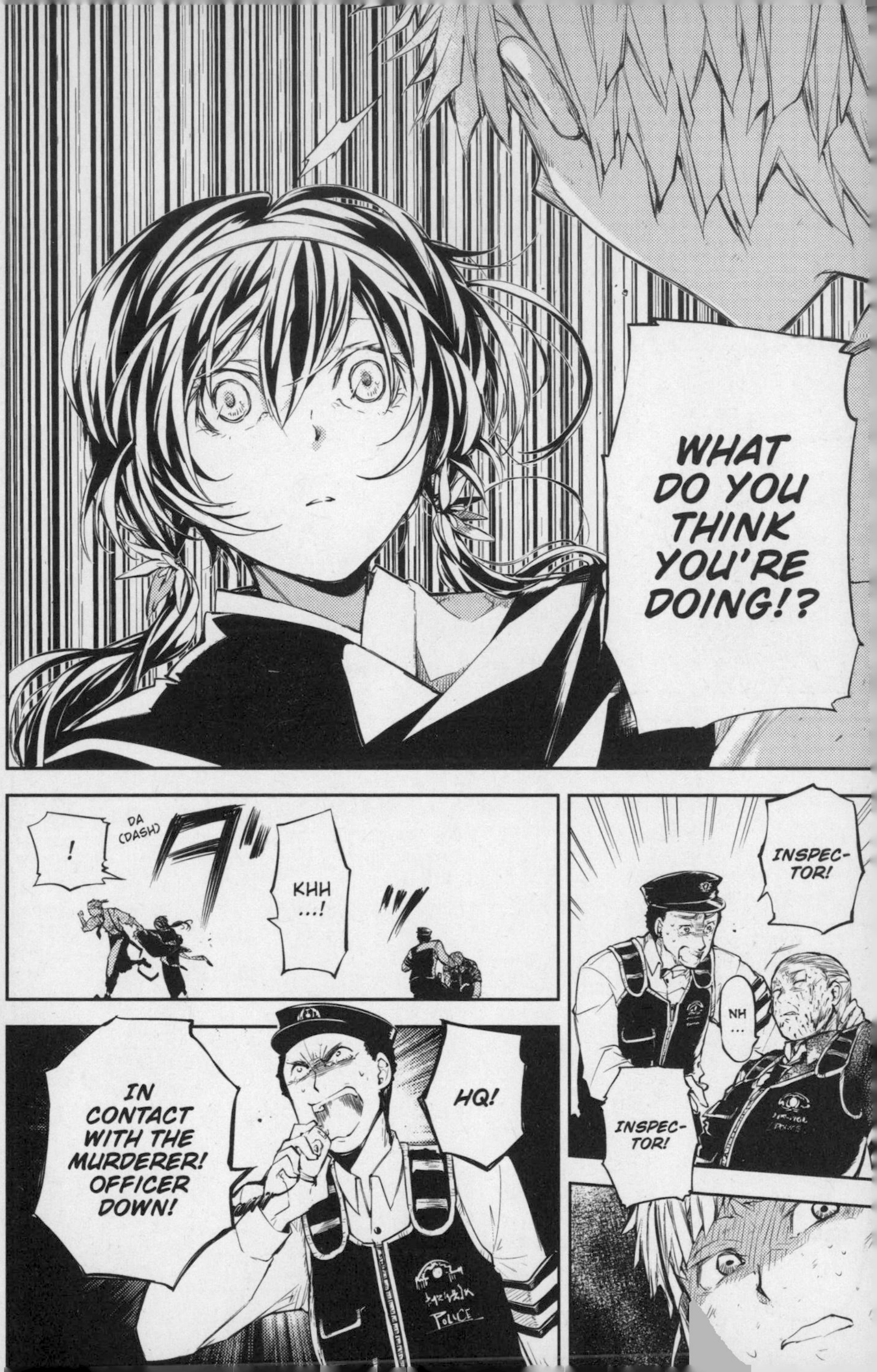
WHAT DO YOU THINK YOU'RE DOING!?
INSPECTOR!
NH ...
INSPECTOR!
KHH ...!
DA (DASH)
!
HQ!
IN CONTACT WITH THE MURDERER! OFFICER DOWN!

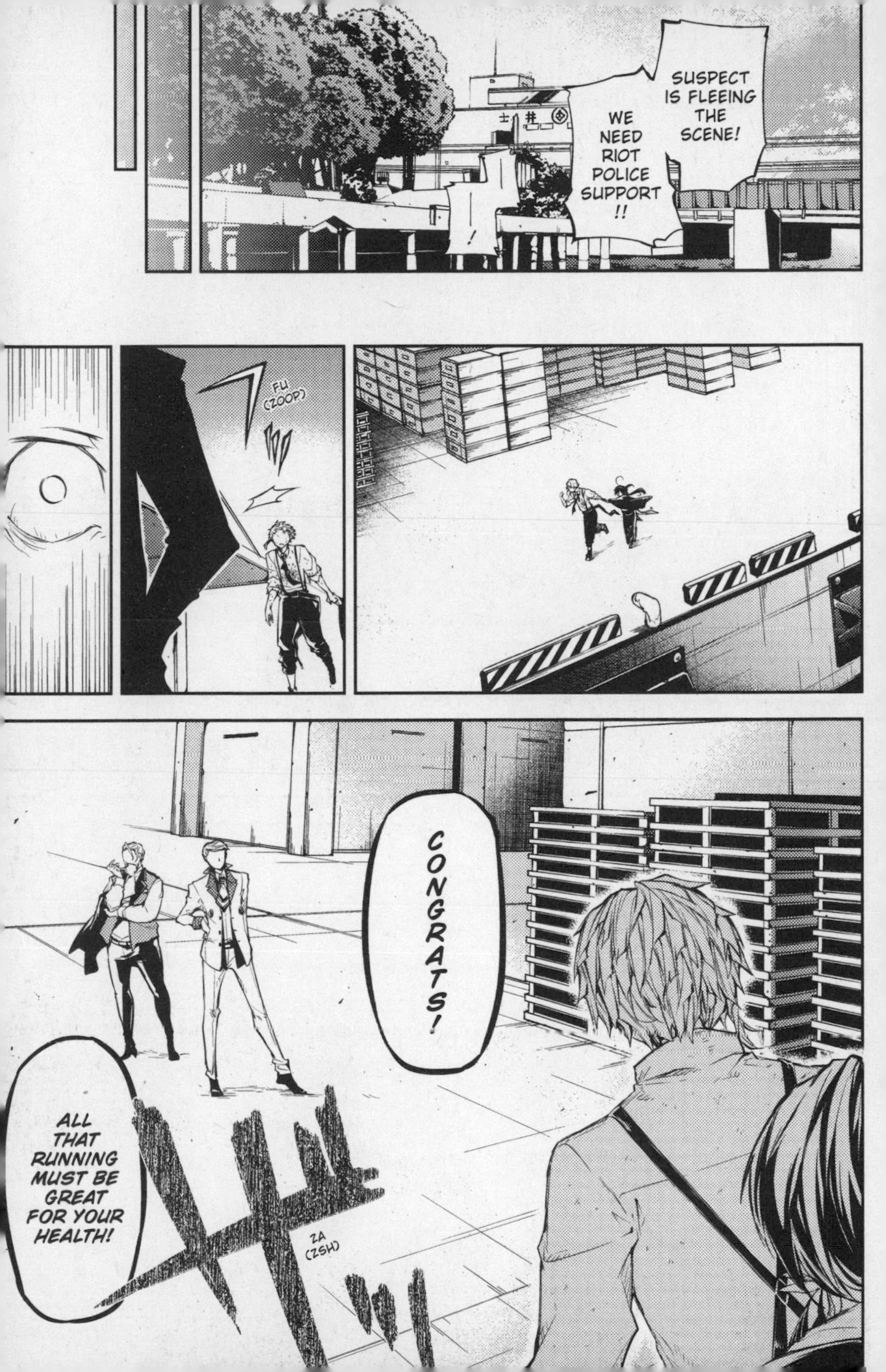
SUSPECT IS FLEEING THE SCENE!
WE NEED RIOT POLICE SUPPORT!!
FU (ZOOP)
CONGRATS!
ALL THAT RUNNING MUST BE GREAT FOR YOUR HEALTH!
ZA (ZSH)

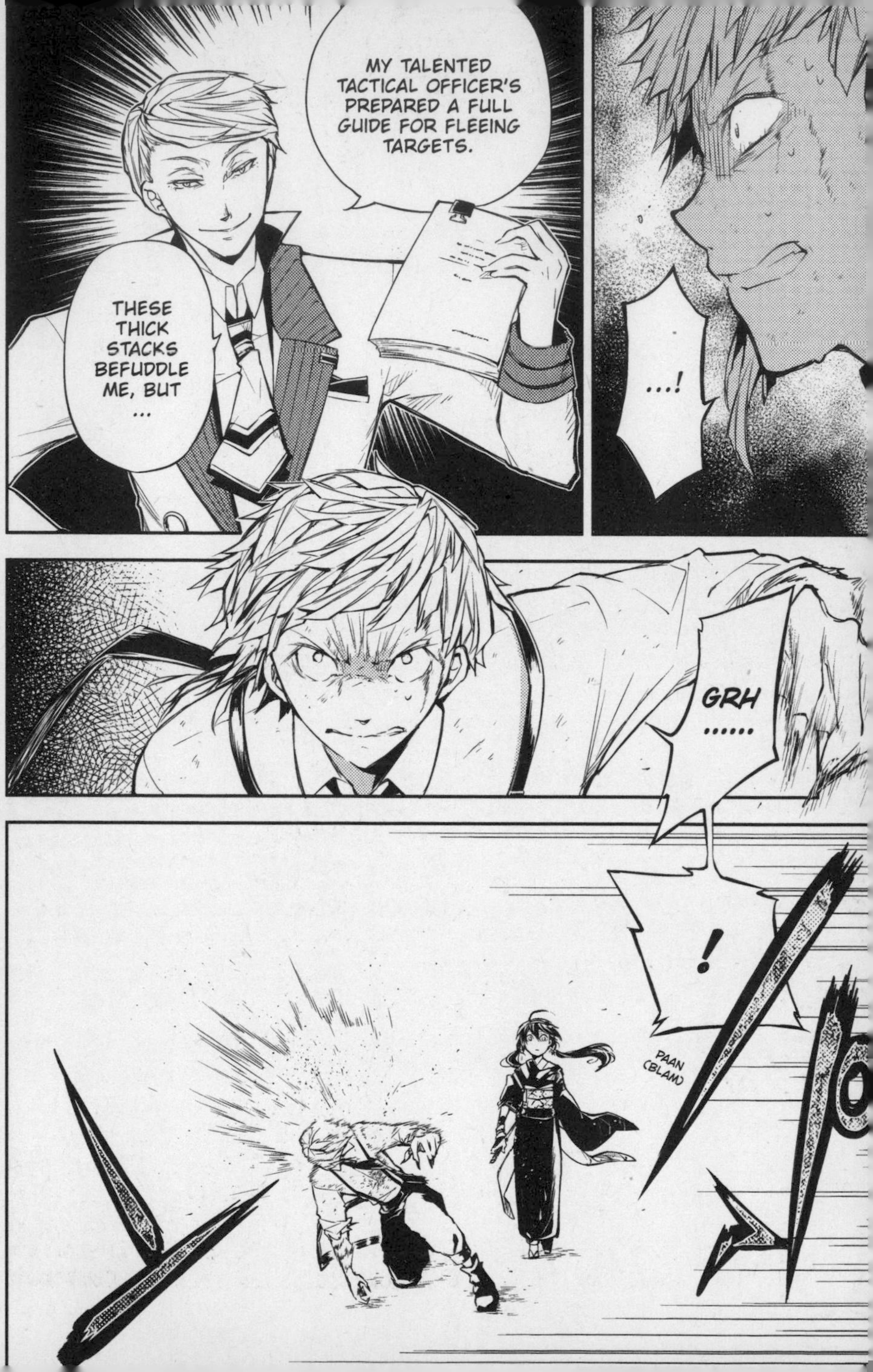
...!
MY TALENTED TACTICAL OFFICER'S PREPARED A FULL GUIDE FOR FLEEING TARGETS.
THESE THICK STACKS BEFUDDLE ME, BUT ...
GRH ......
!
PAAN (BLAM)

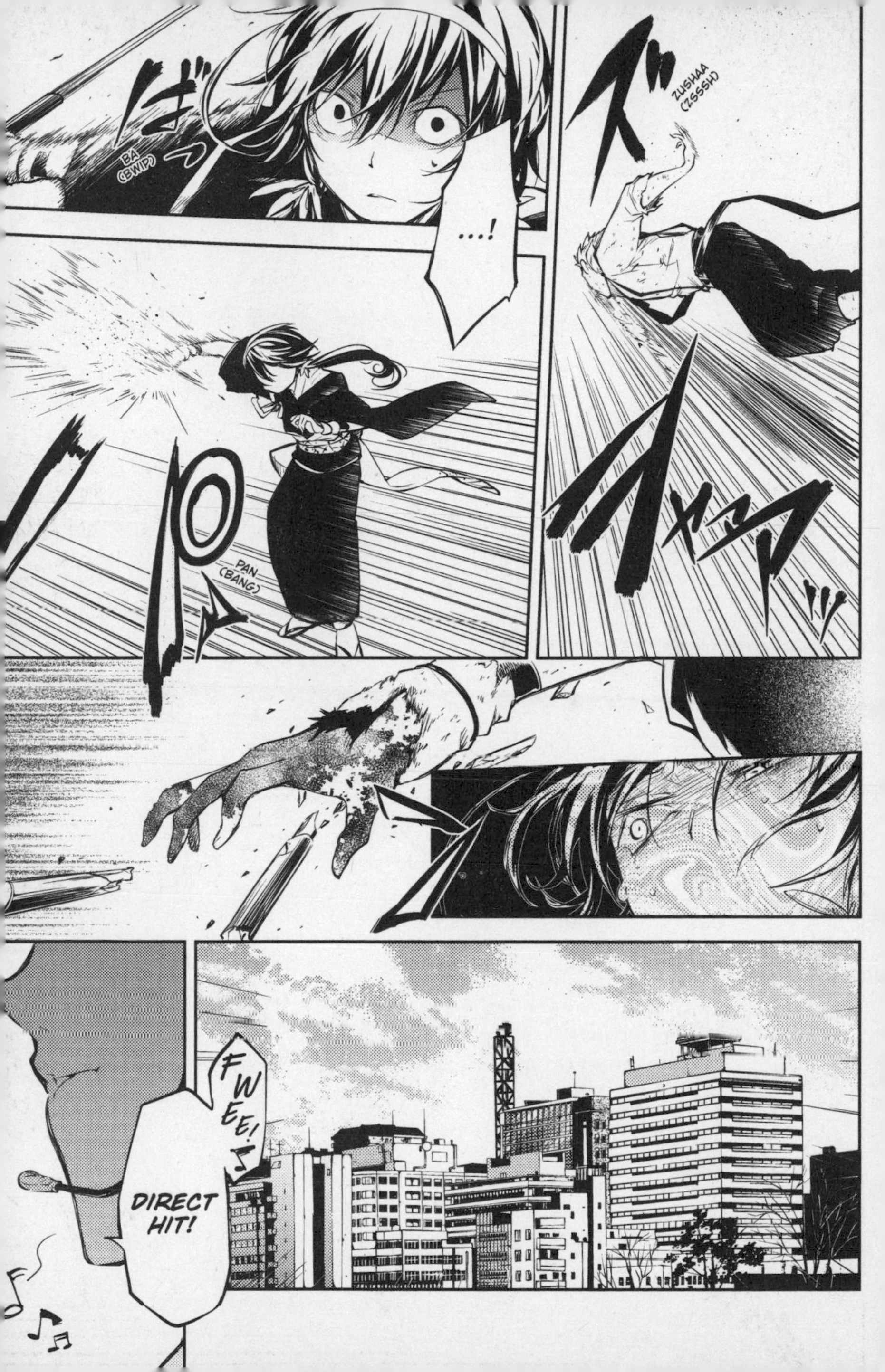
ZUSHAA (ZSSSH)
BA (BWIP)
...!
PAN (BANG)
FWEE!
DIRECT HIT!

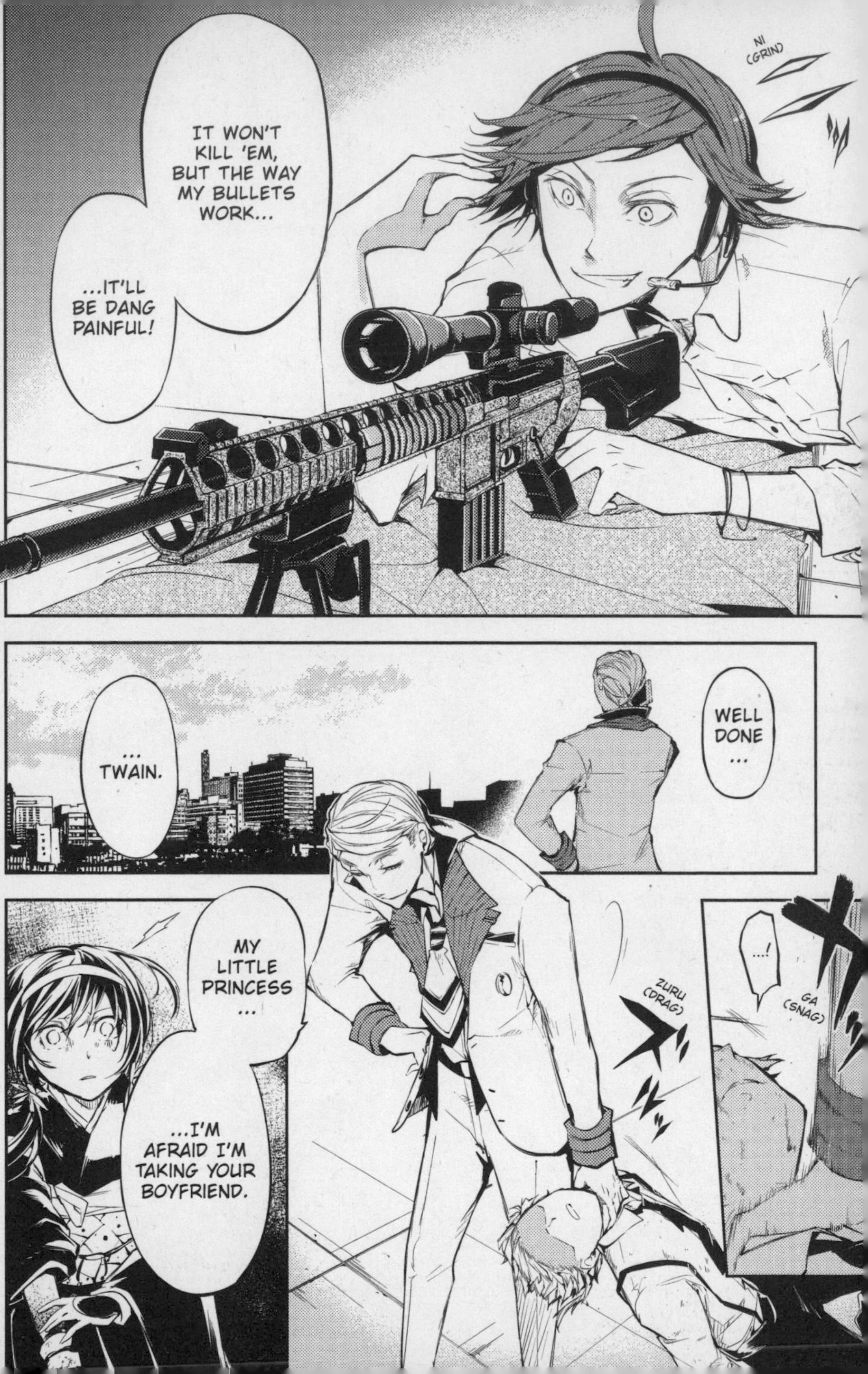
NI (GRIN)
IT WON'T KILL 'EM, BUT THE WAY MY BULLETS WORK...
...IT'LL BE DANG PAINFUL!
WELL DONE ...
... TWAIN.
...!
GA (SNAG)
ZURU (DRAG)
MY LITTLE PRINCESS ...
...I'M AFRAID I'M TAKING YOUR BOYFRIEND.

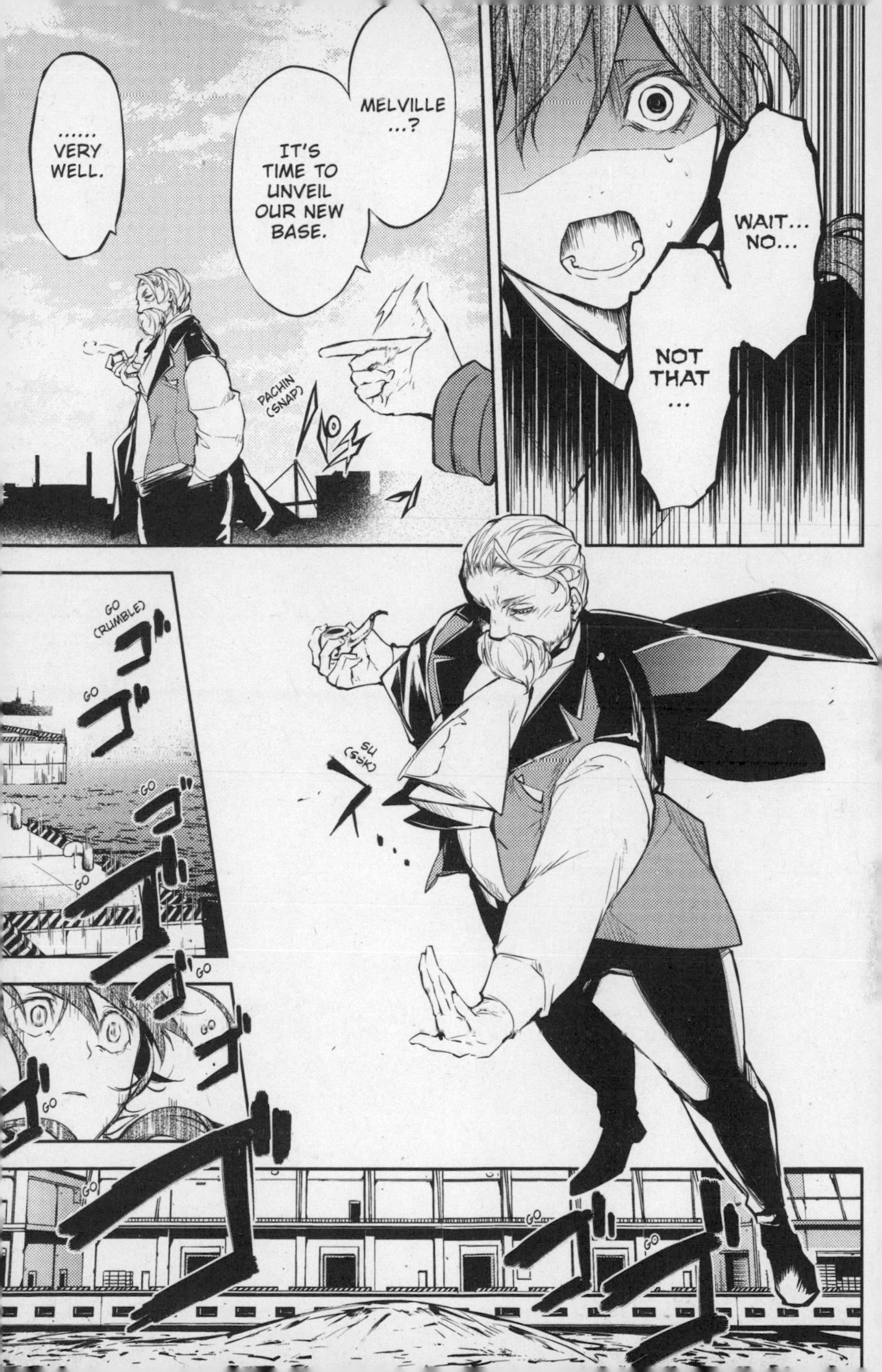
WAIT... NO...
NOT THAT ...
MELVILLE ...?
IT'S TIME TO UNVEIL OUR NEW BASE.
...... VERY WELL.
PACHIN (SNAP)
SU (SSK)
GO (RUMBLE)
GO
GO
GO
GO
GO
GO
GO
GO
GO

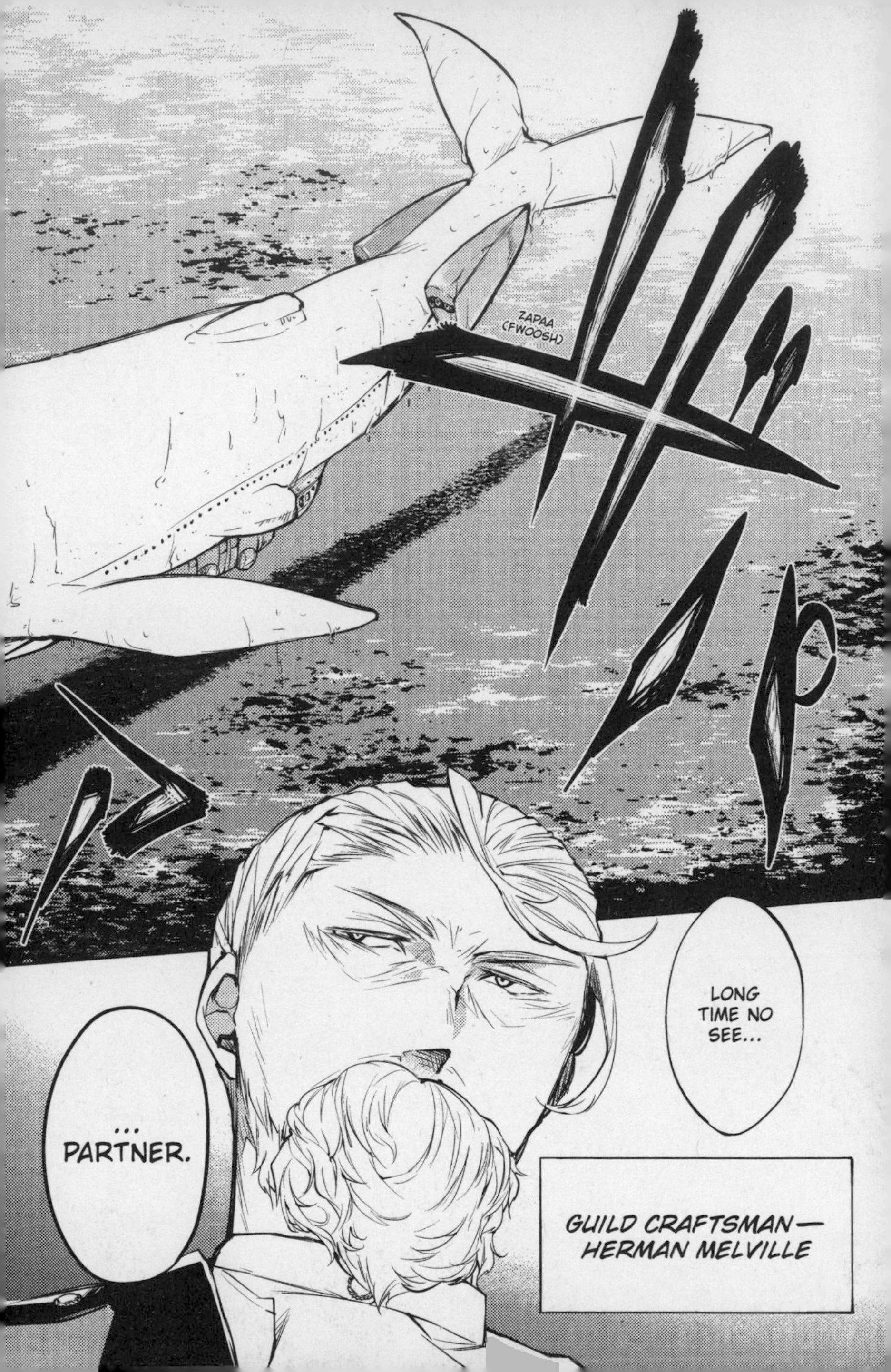
ZAPAA
(FWOOSH)
LONG TIME NO SEE...
...PARTNER.
GUILD CRAFTSMAN—
HERMAN MELVILLE

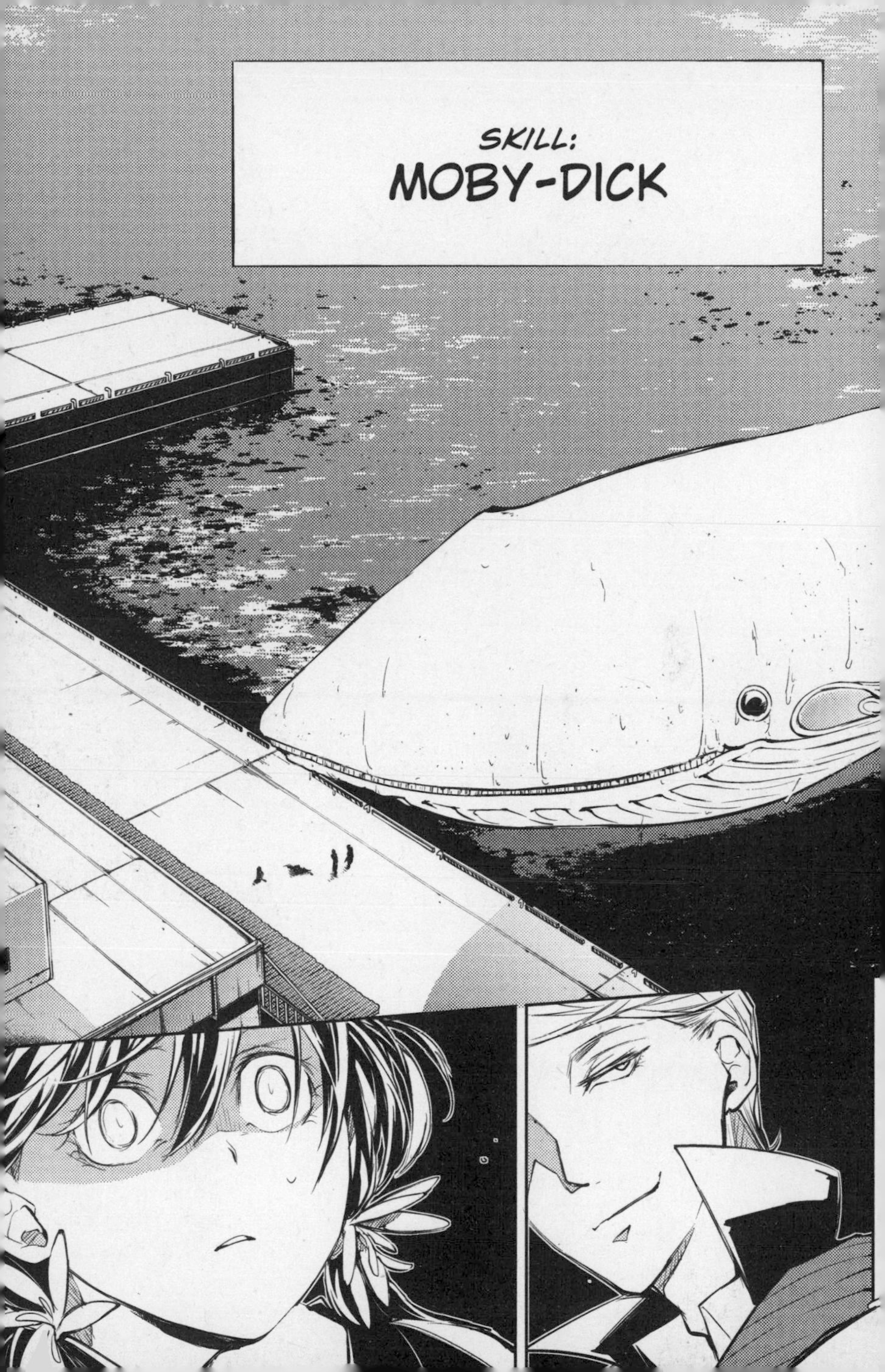
SKILL:
MOBY-DICK

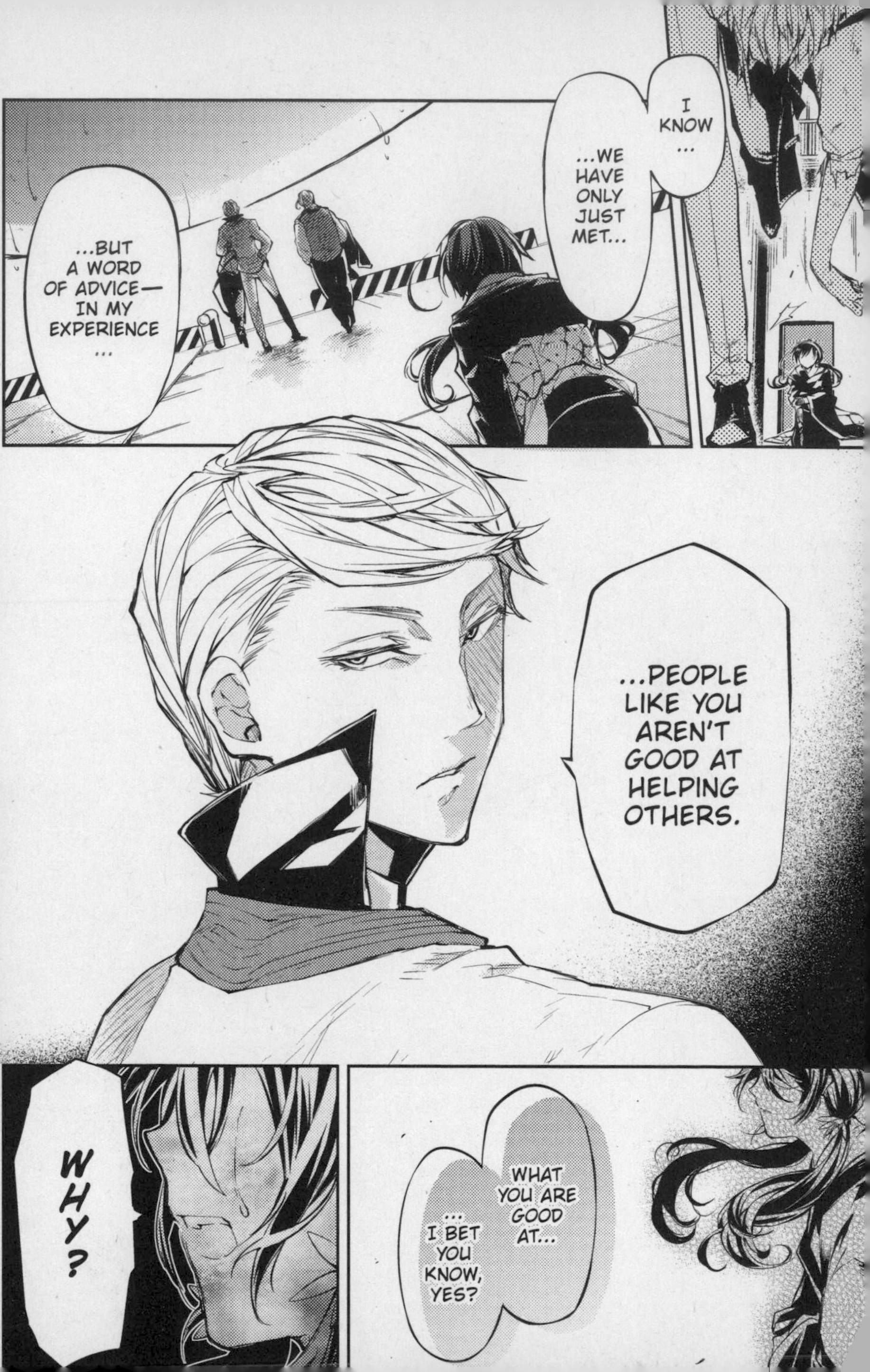
I KNOW...
...WE HAVE ONLY JUST MET...
...BUT A WORD OF ADVICE—IN MY EXPERIENCE...
...PEOPLE LIKE YOU AREN'T GOOD AT HELPING OTHERS.
WHAT YOU ARE GOOD AT...
... I BET YOU KNOW, YES?
WHY?

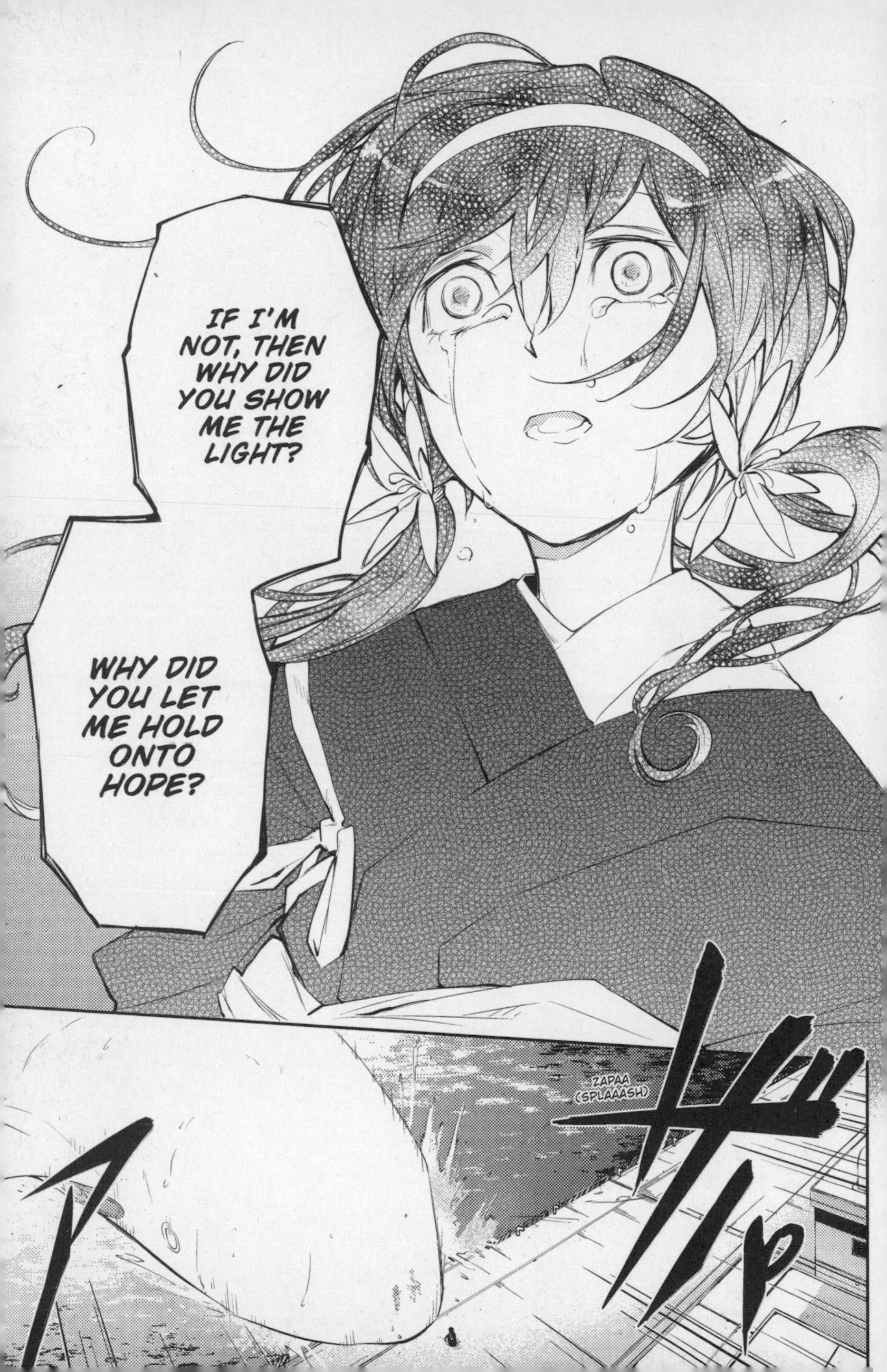
IF I'M NOT, THEN WHY DID YOU SHOW ME THE LIGHT?
WHY DID YOU LET ME HOLD ONTO HOPE?
ZAPAA (SPLAAASH)

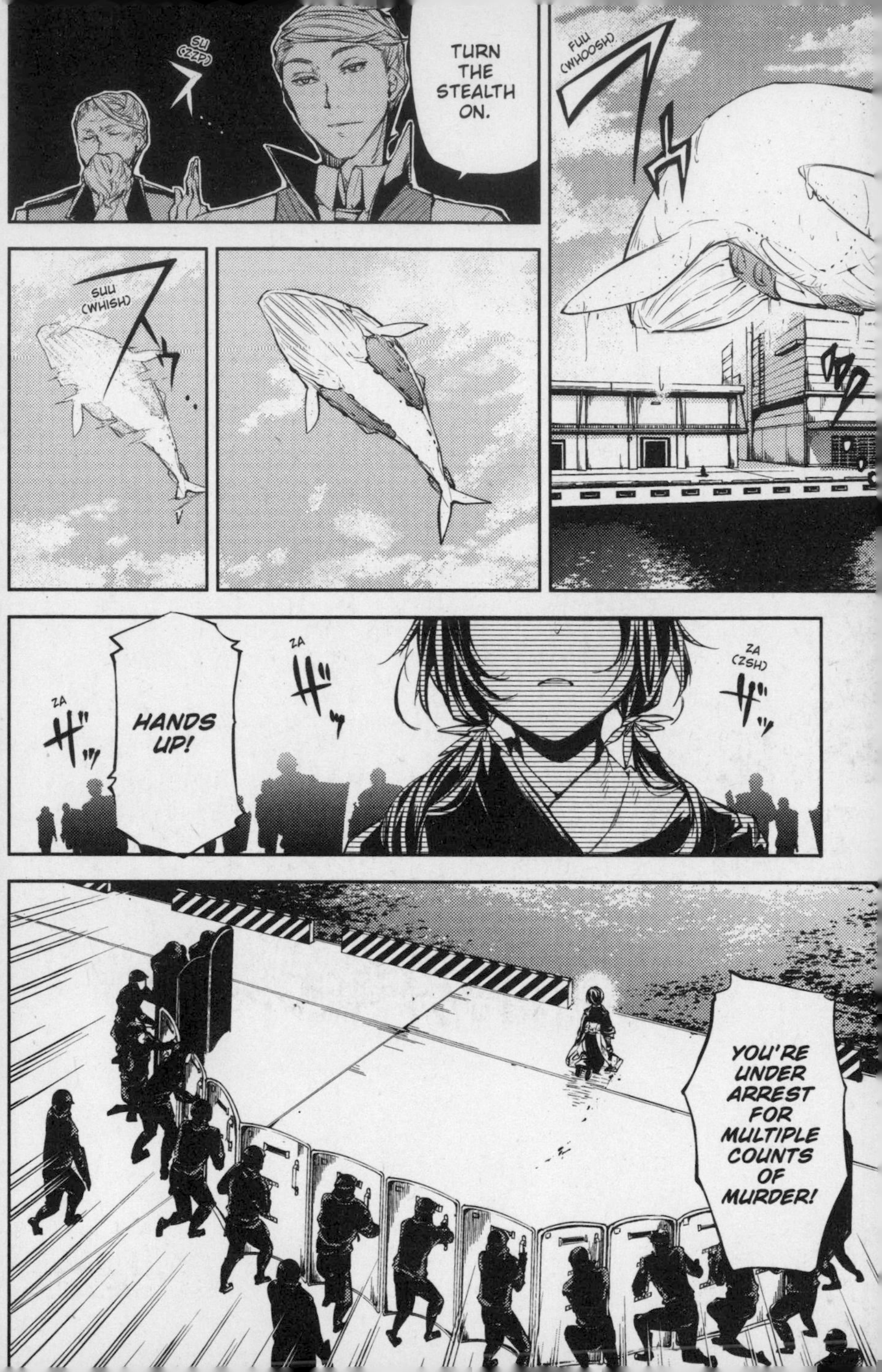
FUU (WHOOSH)
TURN THE STEALTH ON.
SU (ZZP)
SUU (WHISH)
ZA (ZSH)
ZA
HANDS UP!
ZA
YOU'RE UNDER ARREST FOR MULTIPLE COUNTS OF MURDER!

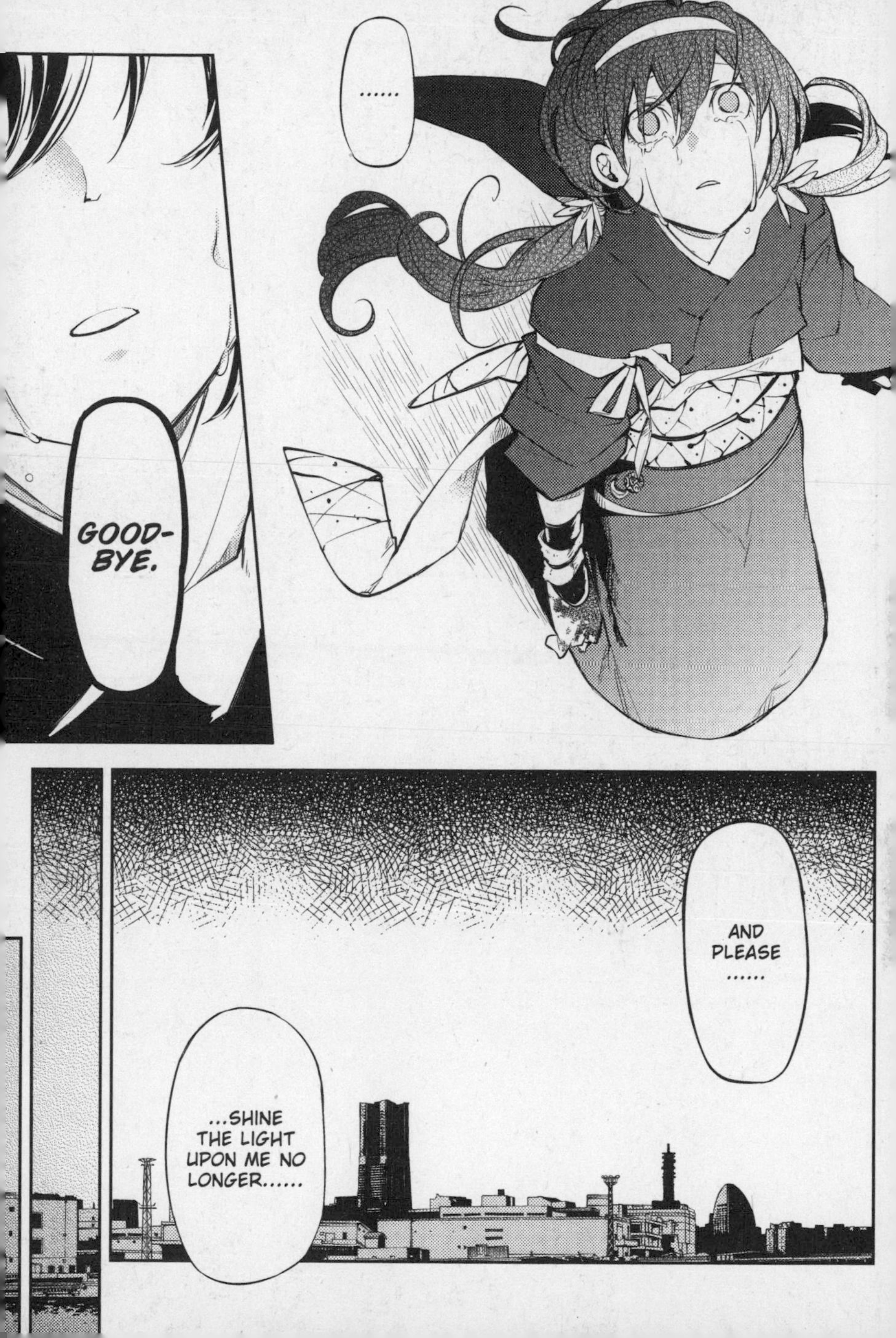
......
GOOD-BYE.
AND PLEASE ......
...SHINE THE LIGHT UPON ME NO LONGER......

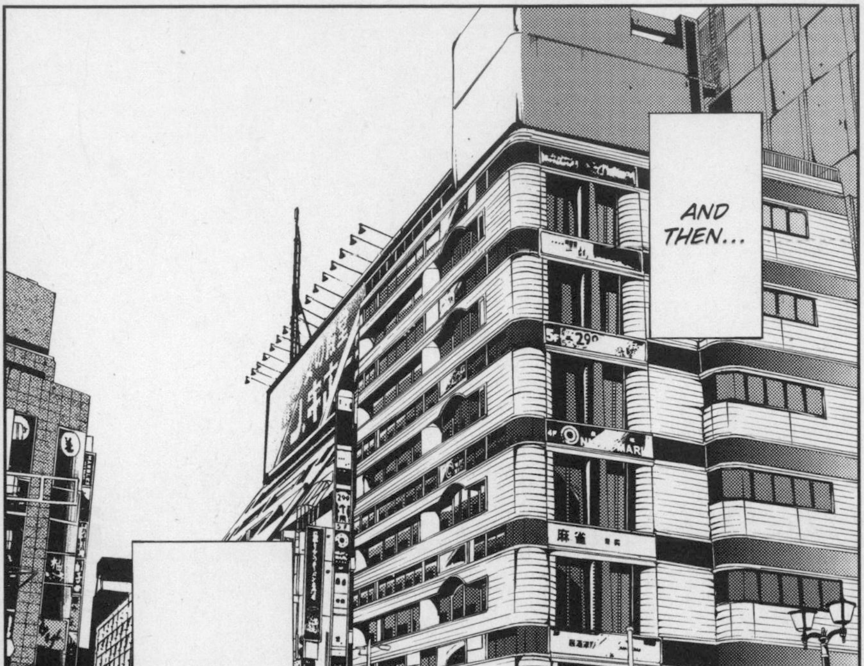
AND THEN...
...A WEEK PASSED.
麻雀

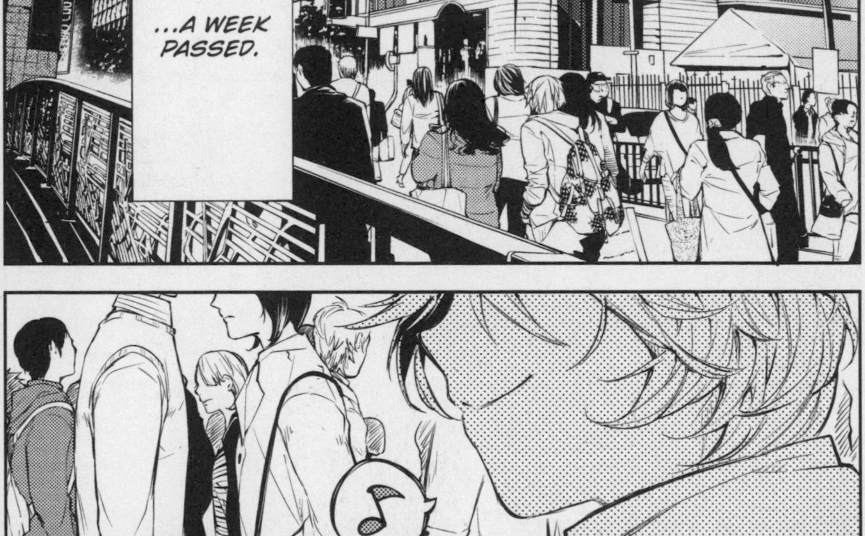

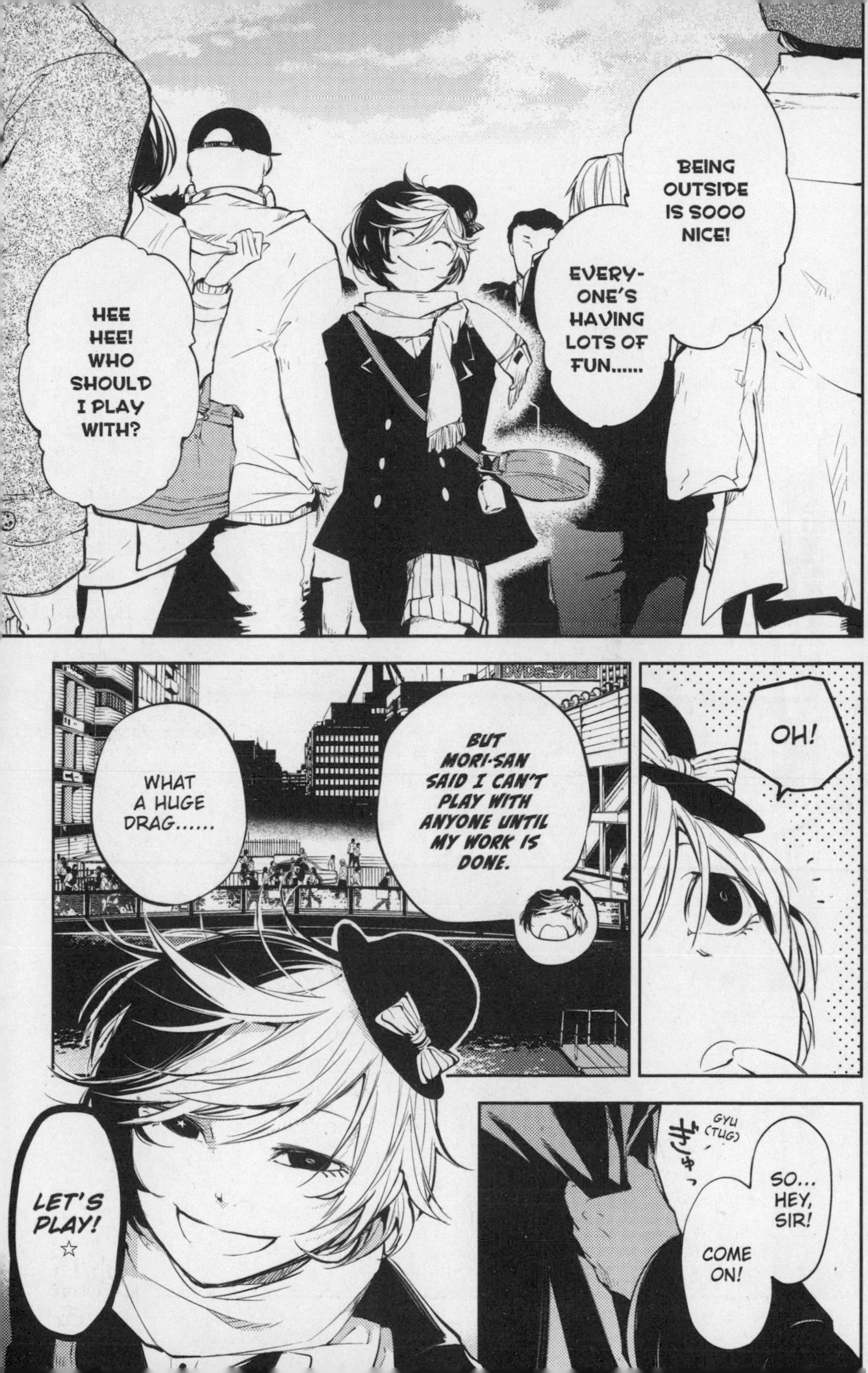
BEING OUTSIDE IS SOOO NICE!
EVERYONE'S HAVING LOTS OF FUN......
HEE HEE! WHO SHOULD I PLAY WITH?
OH!
BUT MORI-SAN SAID I CAN'T PLAY WITH ANYONE UNTIL MY WORK IS DONE.
WHAT A HUGE DRAG......
ぎゅっ
GYU (TUG)
SO... HEY, SIR!
COME ON!
LET'S PLAY! ☆

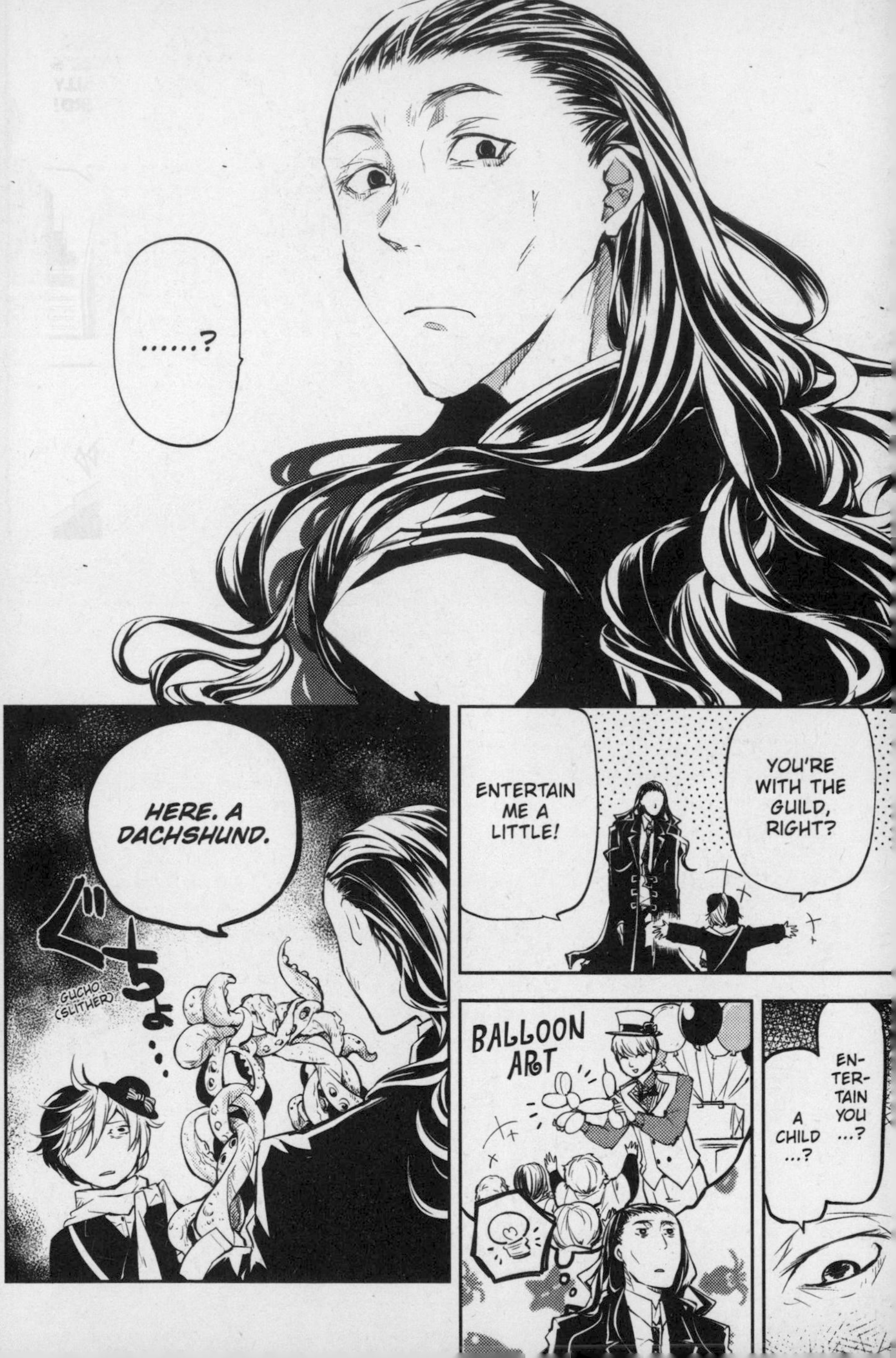
......?
YOU'RE WITH THE GUILD, RIGHT?
ENTERTAIN ME A LITTLE!
ENTERTAIN YOU ...?
A CHILD ...?
BALLOON ART
HERE. A DACHSHUND.
GUCHO (SLITHER)

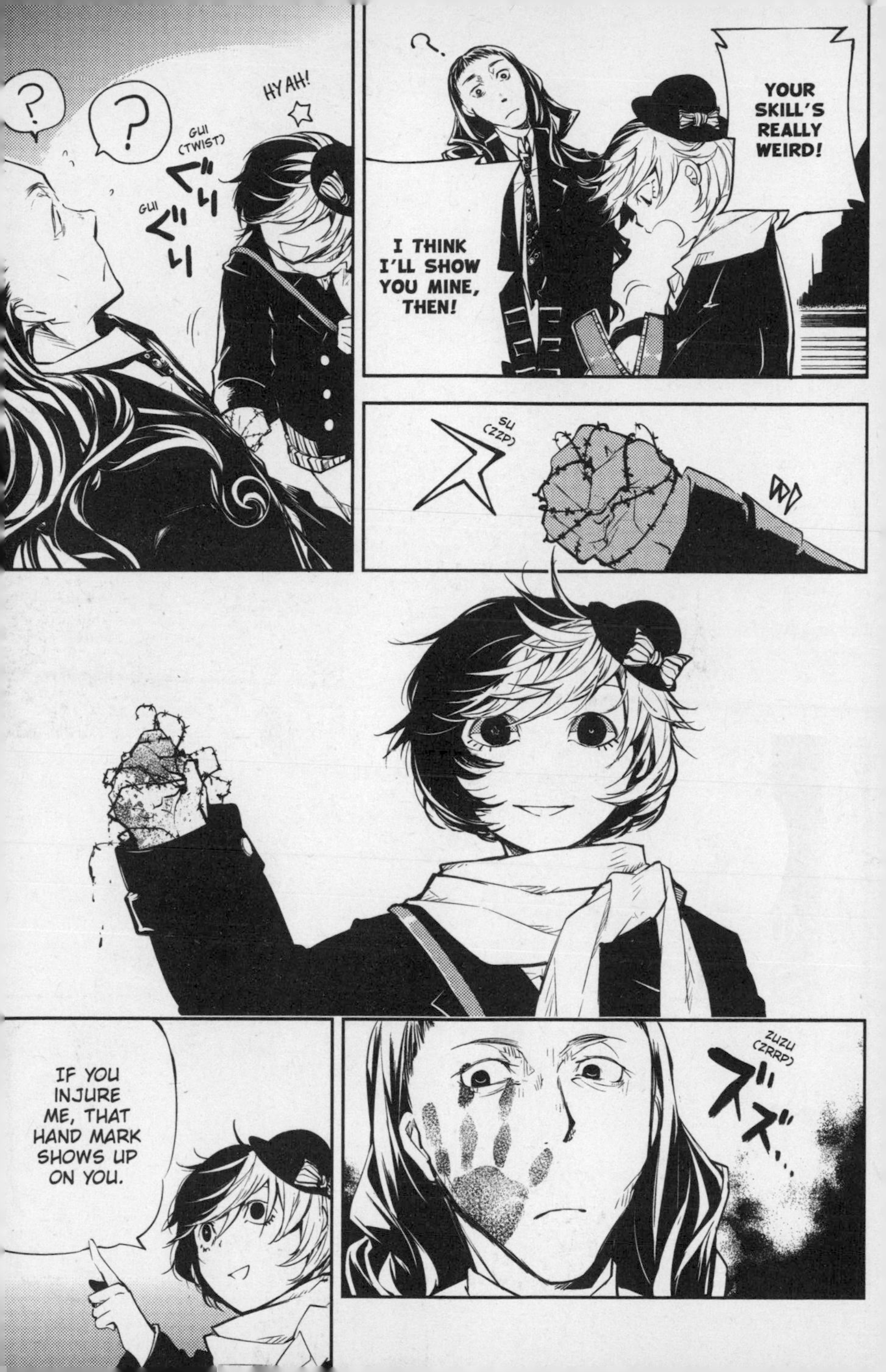
?
YOUR SKILL'S REALLY WEIRD!
I THINK I'LL SHOW YOU MINE, THEN!
SU (ZZP)
?
?
HYAH!
GUI (TWIST)
GUI
ZUZU (ZRRP)
IF YOU INJURE ME, THAT HAND MARK SHOWS UP ON YOU.

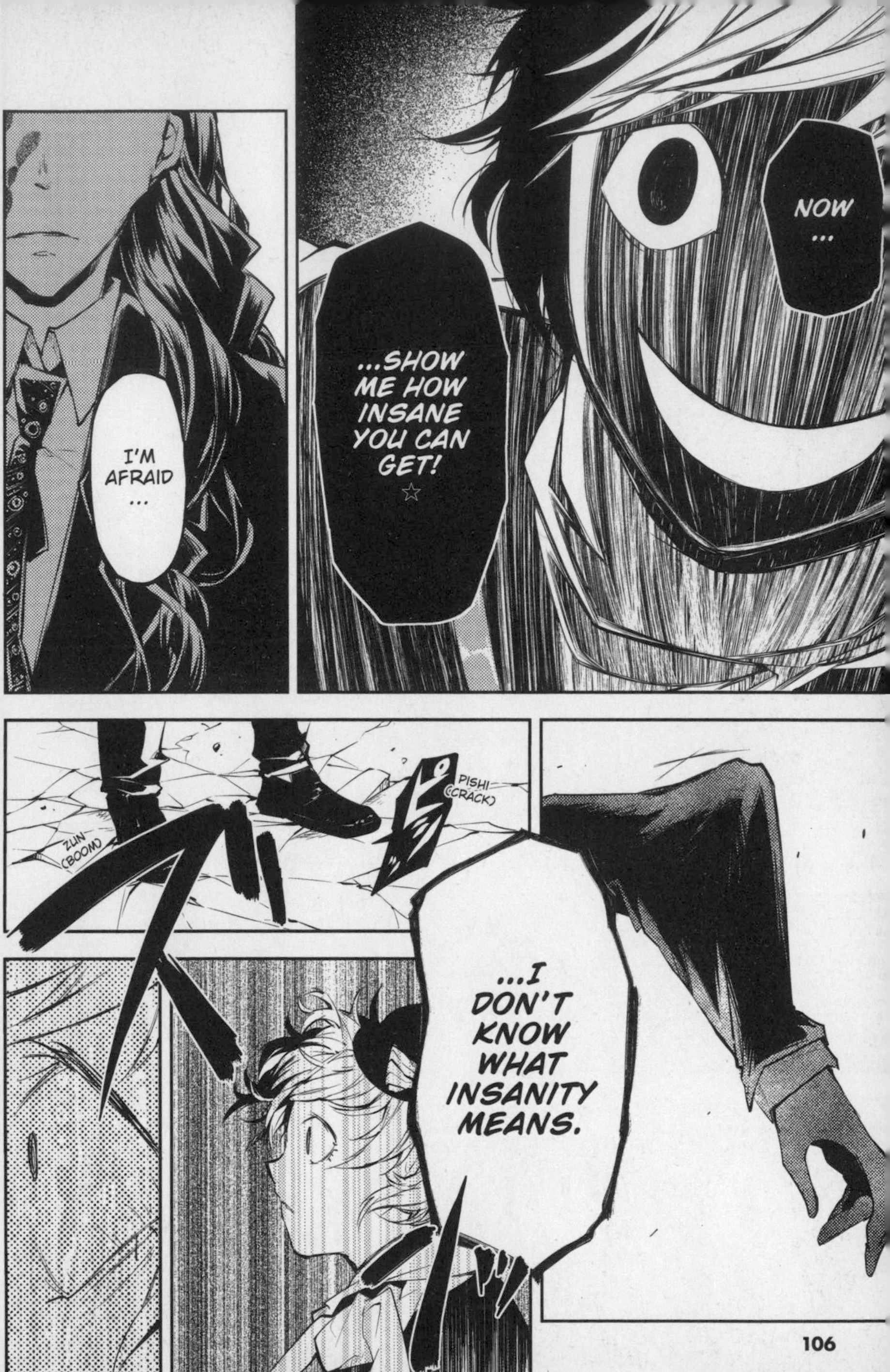
NOW ...
...SHOW ME HOW INSANE YOU CAN GET! ☆
I'M AFRAID ...
...I DON'T KNOW WHAT INSANITY MEANS.
PISHI (CRACK)
ZUN (BOOM)

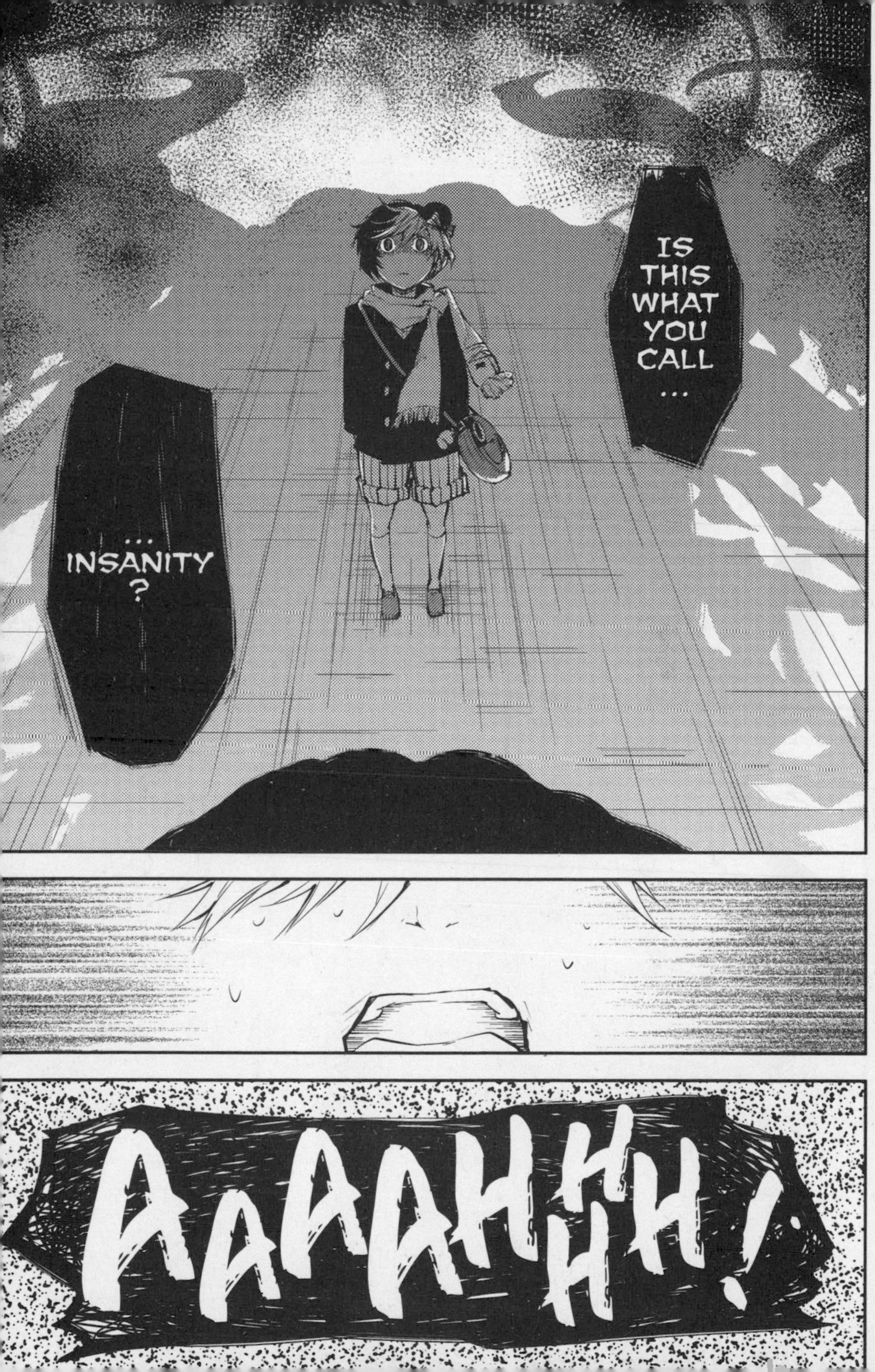
IS THIS WHAT YOU CALL ...
... INSANITY ?
AAAAHHHH!

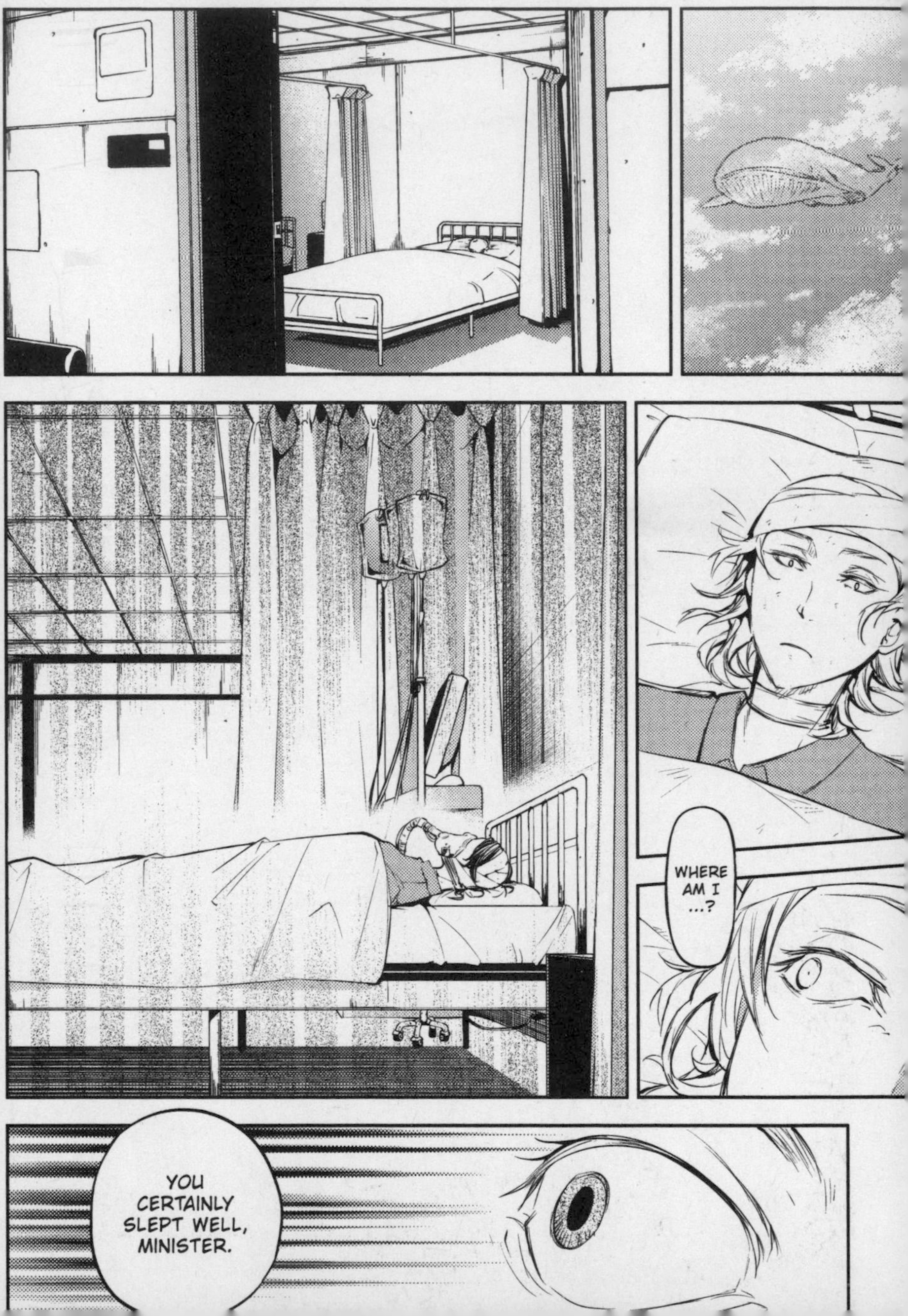
WHERE AM I ...?
YOU CERTAINLY SLEPT WELL, MINISTER.

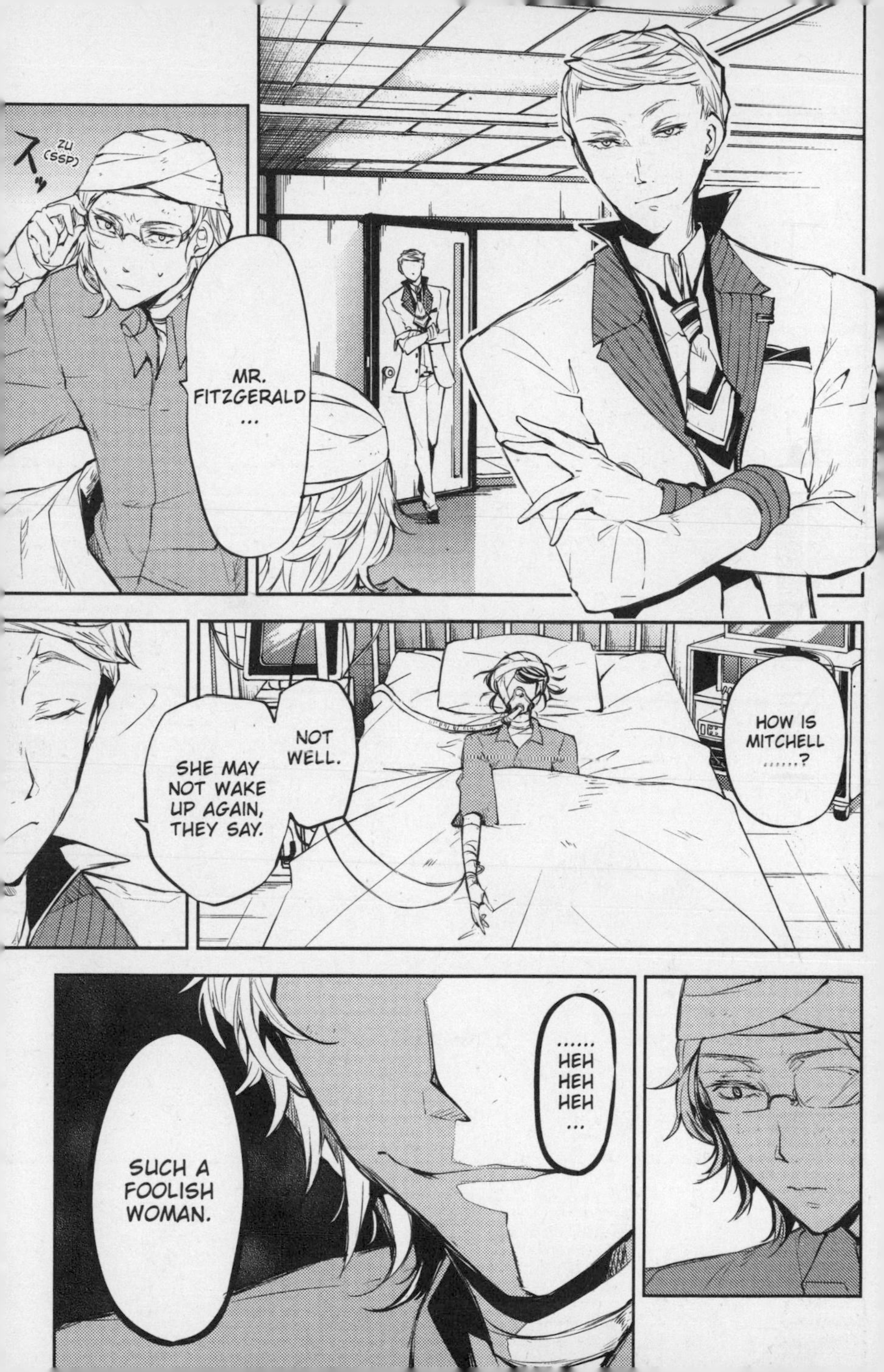
スッ
ZU (SSP)
MR. FITZGERALD ...
HOW IS MITCHELL ......?
NOT WELL.
SHE MAY NOT WAKE UP AGAIN, THEY SAY.
...... HEH HEH HEH ...
SUCH A FOOLISH WOMAN.

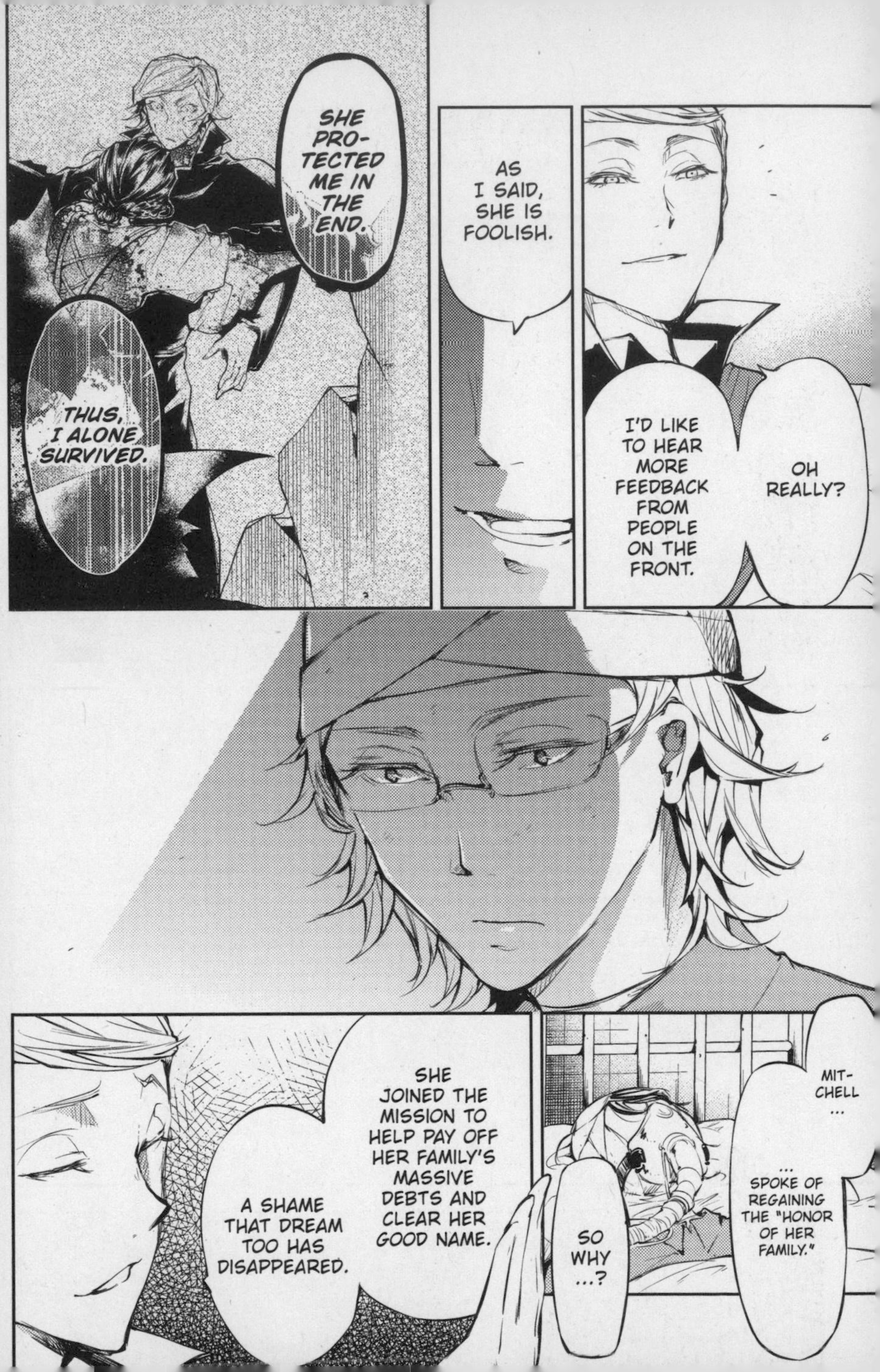
OH REALLY?
I'D LIKE TO HEAR MORE FEEDBACK FROM PEOPLE ON THE FRONT.
AS I SAID, SHE IS FOOLISH.
SHE PROTECTED ME IN THE END.
THUS, I ALONE SURVIVED.
MIT-CHELL...
...SPOKE OF REGAINING THE "HONOR OF HER FAMILY."
SO WHY...?
SHE JOINED THE MISSION TO HELP PAY OFF HER FAMILY'S MASSIVE DEBTS AND CLEAR HER GOOD NAME.
A SHAME THAT DREAM TOO HAS DISAPPEARED.

PARDON?

NOT SO.

IT DIDN'T DISAPPEAR AT ALL.

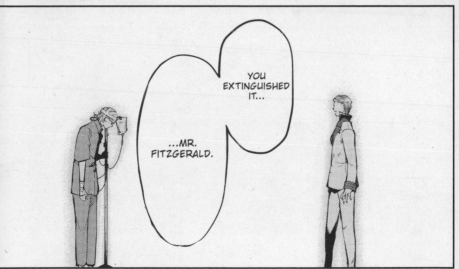

YOU EXTINGUISHED IT...

...MR. FITZGERALD.

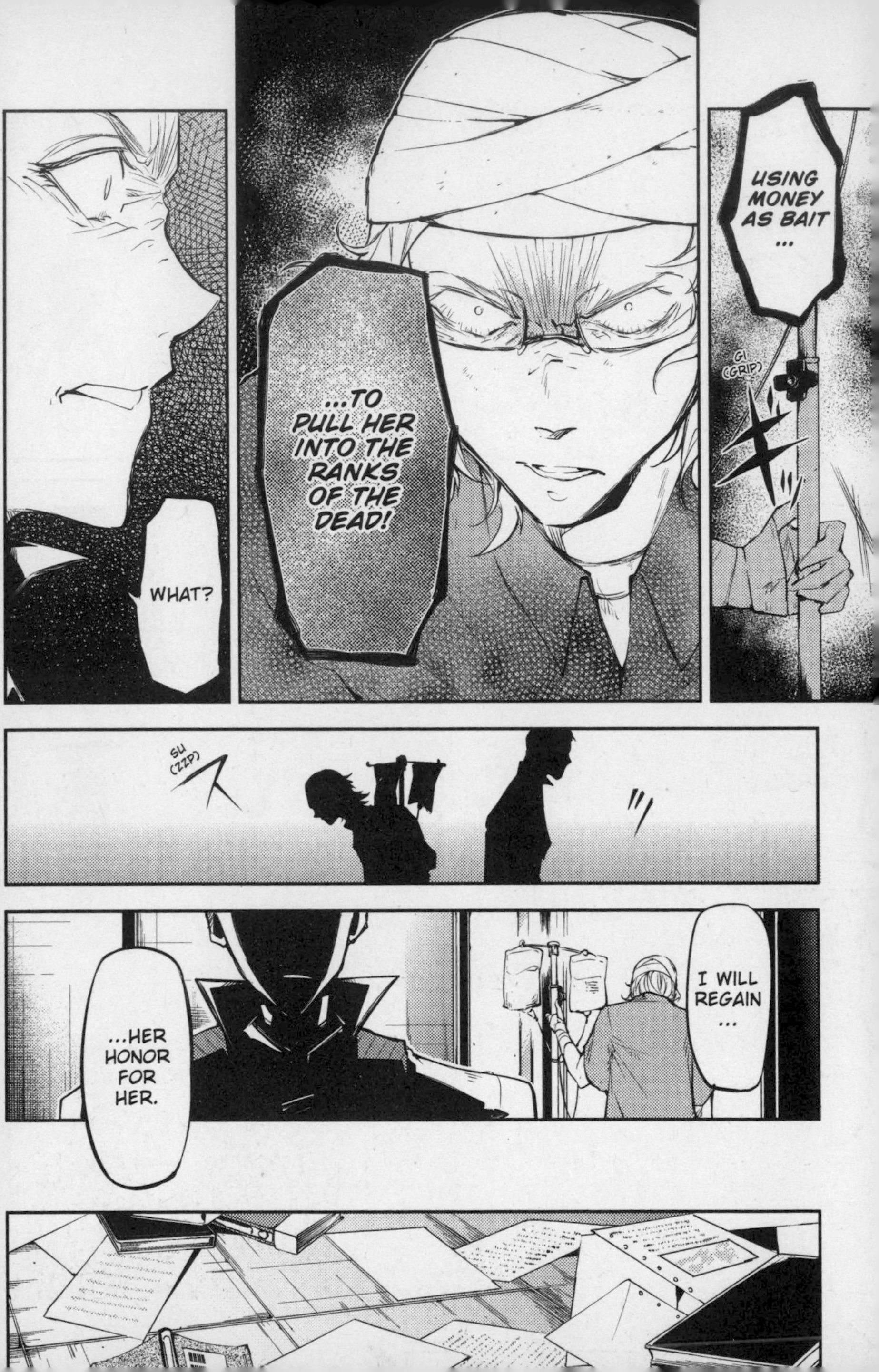
USING MONEY AS BAIT...
GI (GRIP)
...TO PULL HER INTO THE RANKS OF THE DEAD!
WHAT?
SU (ZZP)
I WILL REGAIN...
...HER HONOR FOR HER.

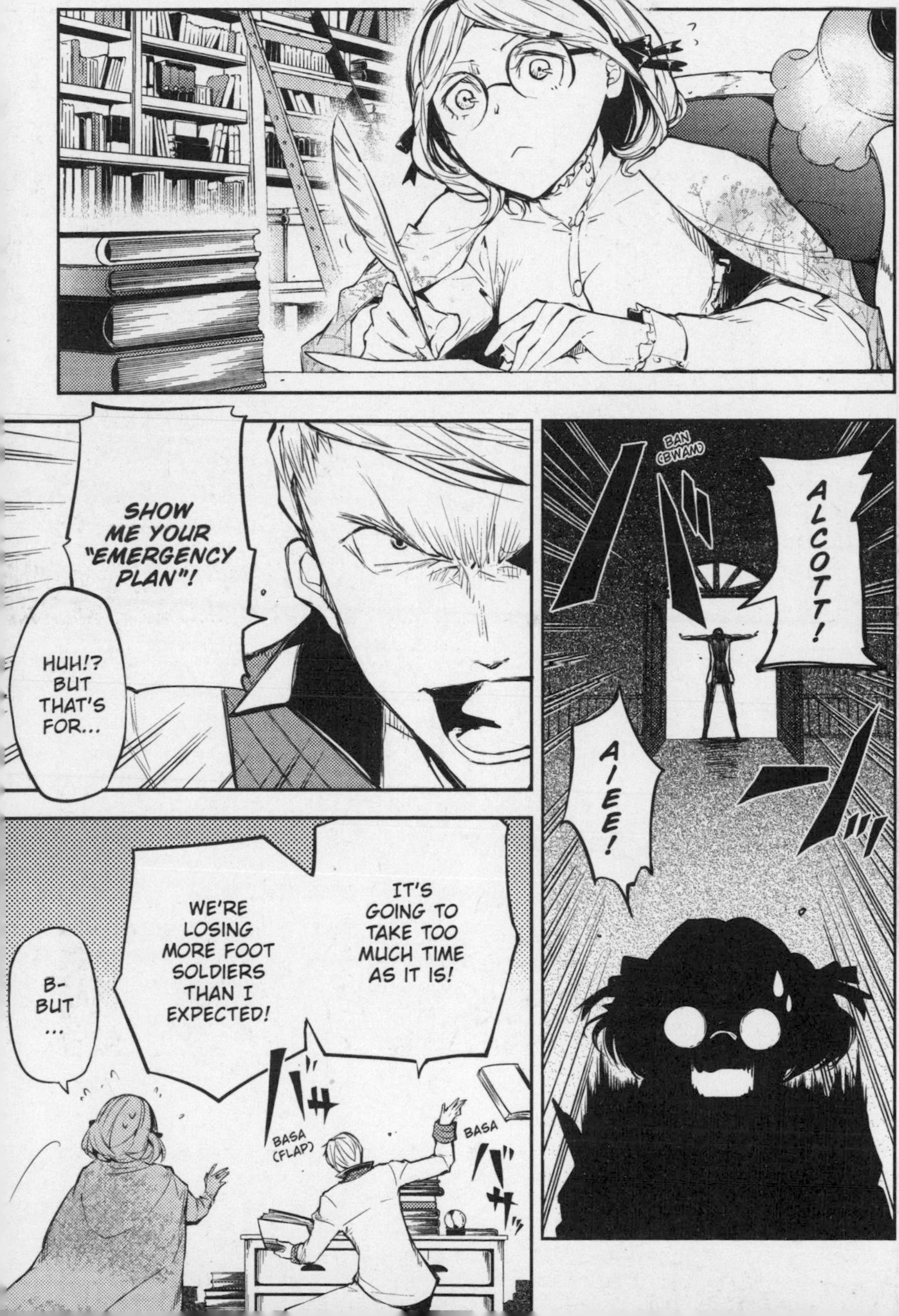
ALCOTT!
BAN (BWAM)
AIEE!
SHOW ME YOUR "EMERGENCY PLAN"!
HUH!? BUT THAT'S FOR...
IT'S GOING TO TAKE TOO MUCH TIME AS IT IS!
WE'RE LOSING MORE FOOT SOLDIERS THAN I EXPECTED!
B-BUT...
BASA
BASA (FLAP)

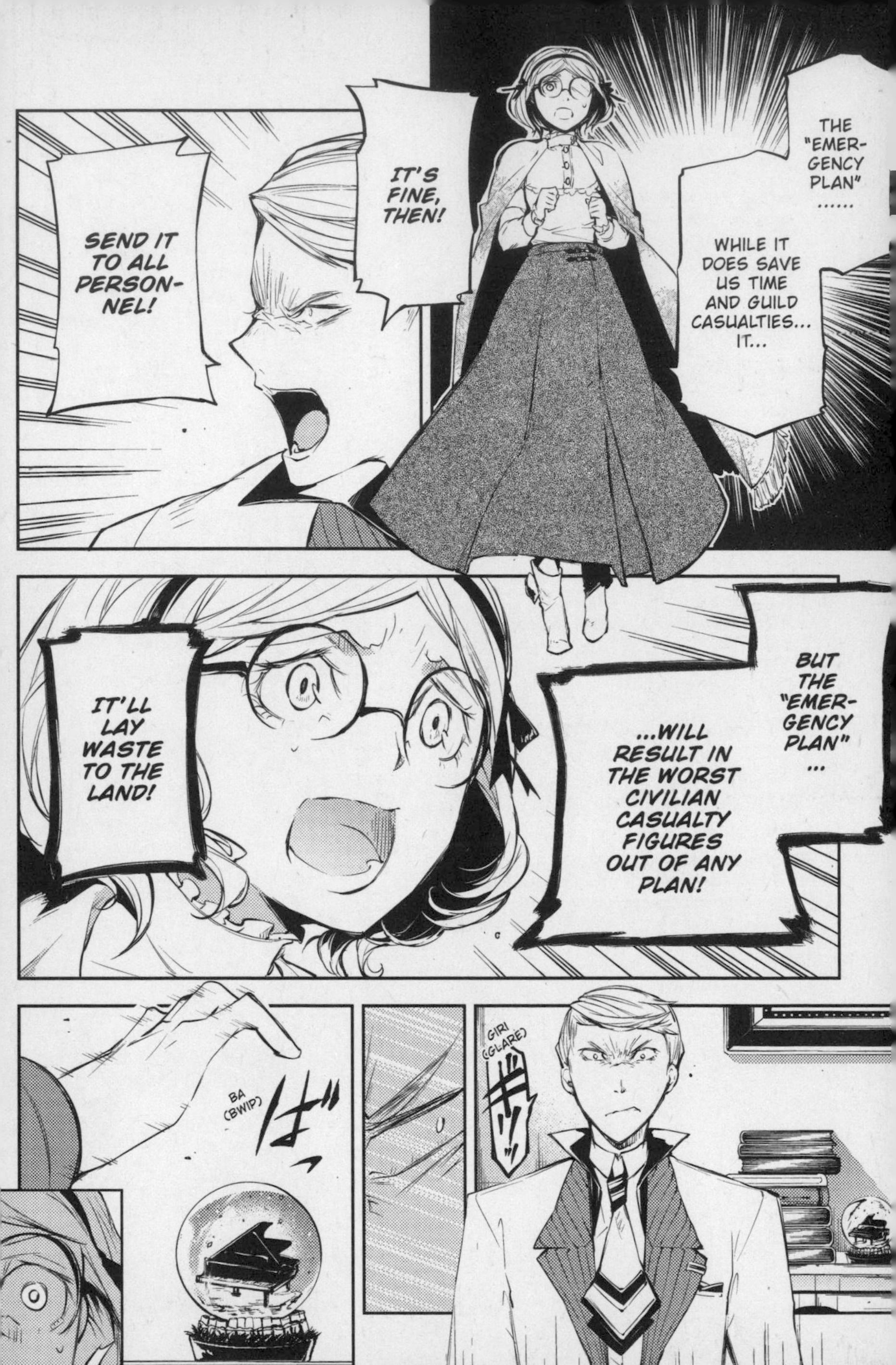
THE "EMERGENCY PLAN" ......
WHILE IT DOES SAVE US TIME AND GUILD CASUALTIES... IT...
IT'S FINE, THEN!
SEND IT TO ALL PERSONNEL!
BUT THE "EMERGENCY PLAN" ...
...WILL RESULT IN THE WORST CIVILIAN CASUALTY FIGURES OUT OF ANY PLAN!
IT'LL LAY WASTE TO THE LAND!
GIRI (GLARE)
BA (BWIP)

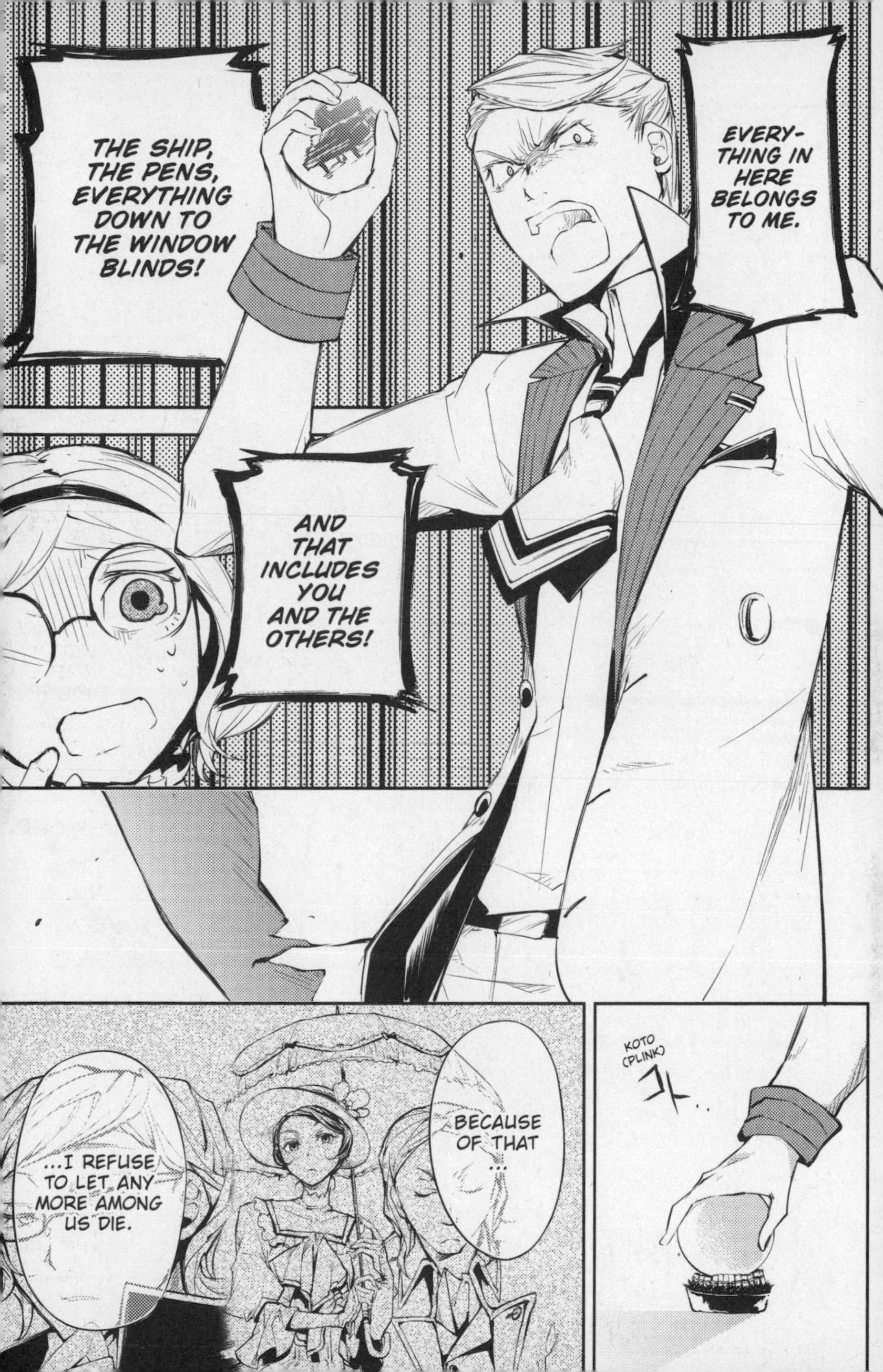
EVERY-THING IN HERE BELONGS TO ME.
THE SHIP, THE PENS, EVERYTHING DOWN TO THE WINDOW BLINDS!
AND THAT INCLUDES YOU AND THE OTHERS!
KOTO (PLINK)
BECAUSE OF THAT...
...I REFUSE TO LET ANY MORE AMONG US DIE.

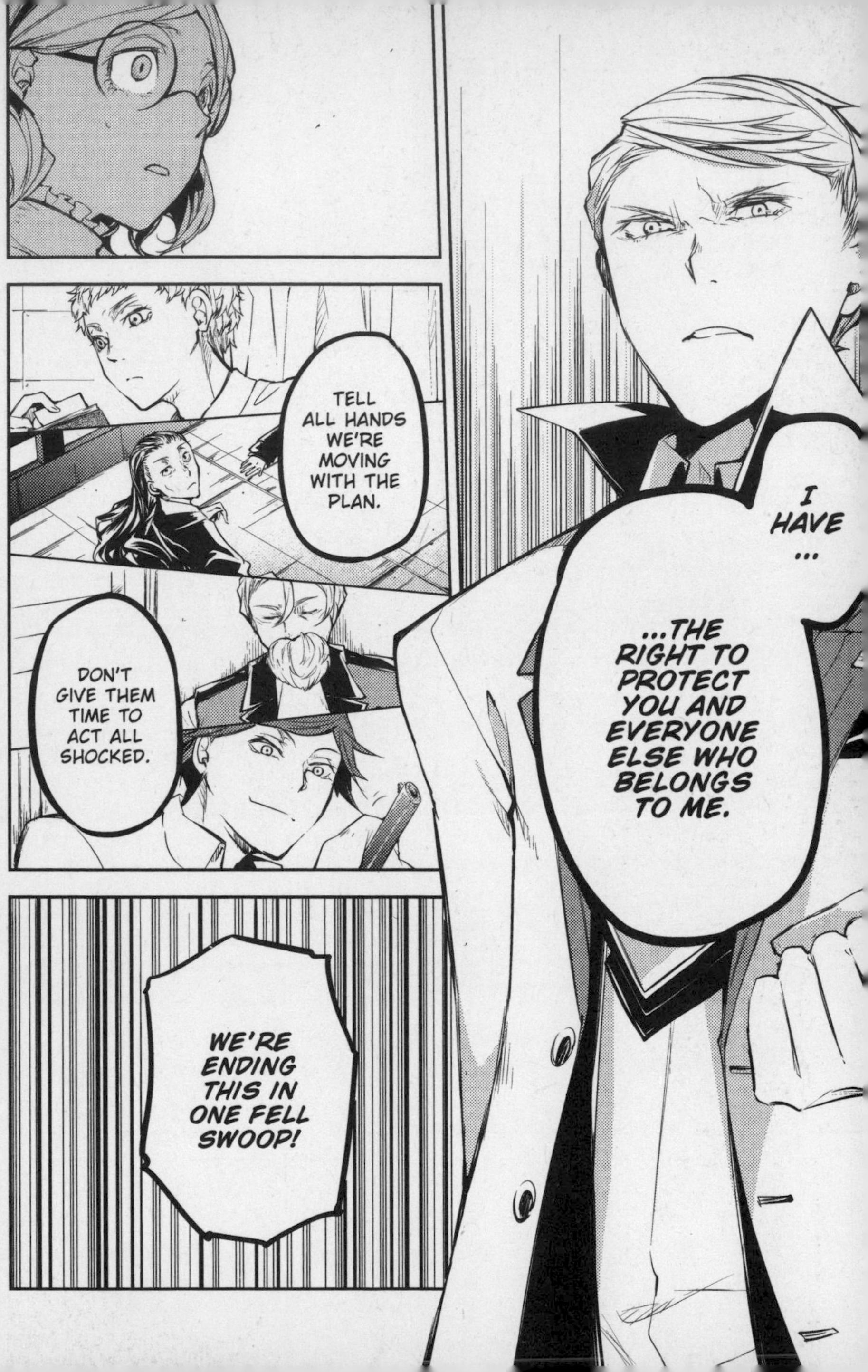
I HAVE...
...THE RIGHT TO PROTECT YOU AND EVERYONE ELSE WHO BELONGS TO ME.
TELL ALL HANDS WE'RE MOVING WITH THE PLAN.
DON'T GIVE THEM TIME TO ACT ALL SHOCKED.
WE'RE ENDING THIS IN ONE FELL SWOOP!

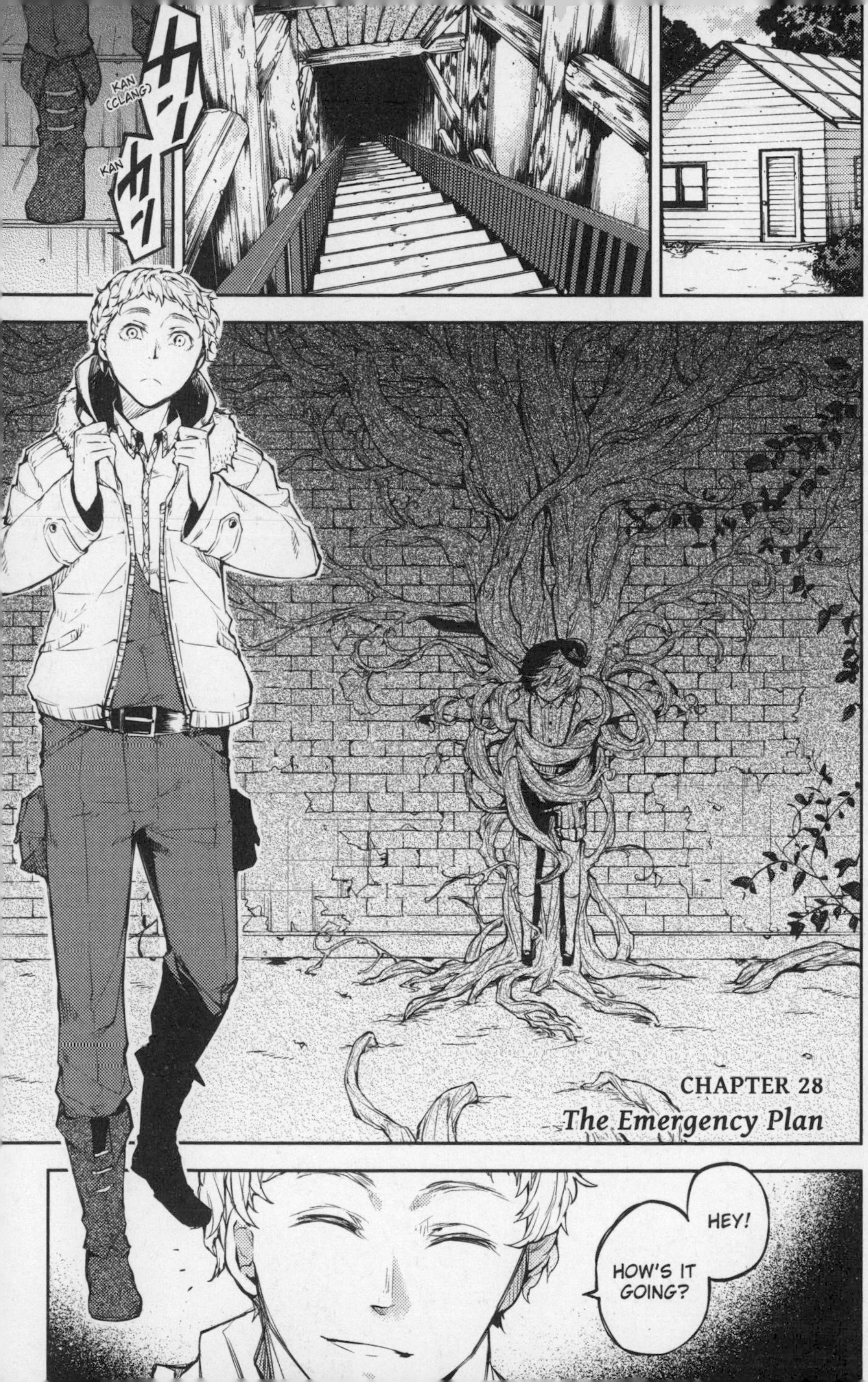
カン
KAN (CLANG)
カン
KAN
CHAPTER 28
The Emergency Plan
HEY!
HOW'S IT GOING?

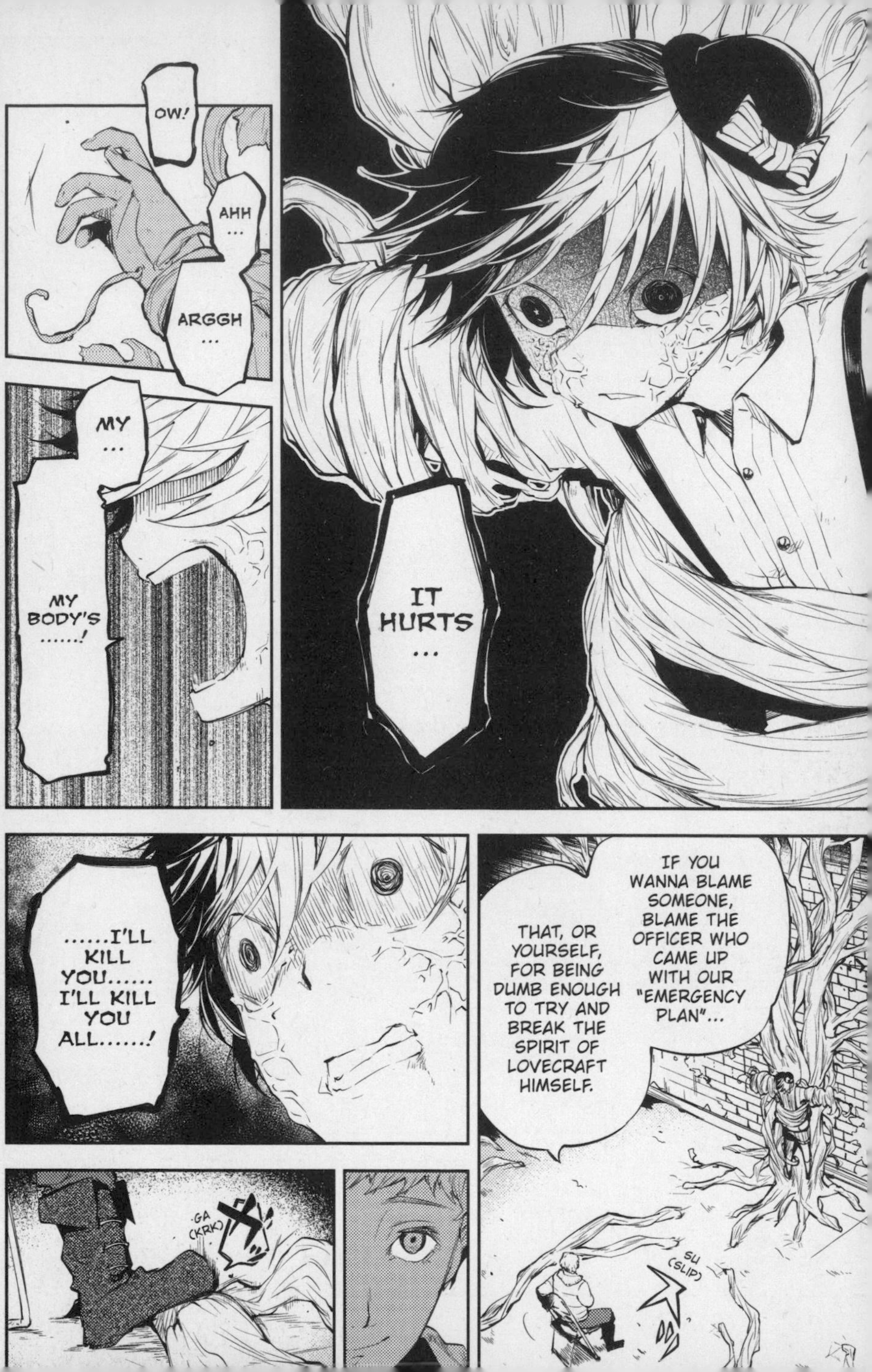
IT HURTS...
OW!
AHH...
ARGGH...
MY...
MY BODY'S......!
IF YOU WANNA BLAME SOMEONE, BLAME THE OFFICER WHO CAME UP WITH OUR "EMERGENCY PLAN"...
THAT, OR YOURSELF, FOR BEING DUMB ENOUGH TO TRY AND BREAK THE SPIRIT OF LOVECRAFT HIMSELF.
SU (SLIP)
......I'LL KILL YOU...... I'LL KILL YOU ALL......!
GA (KRK)

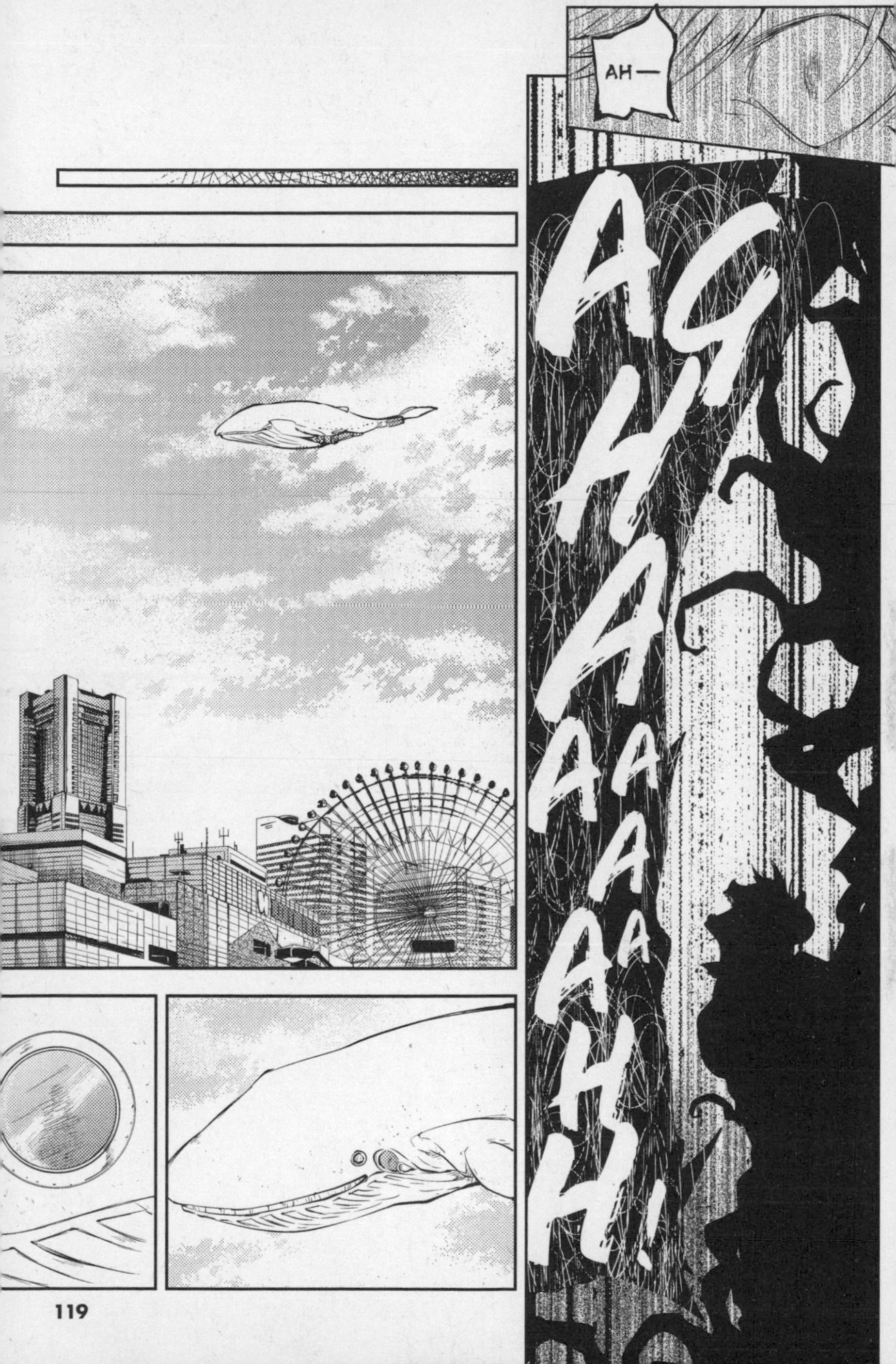
AH—
AGHAAAAAAAHH!

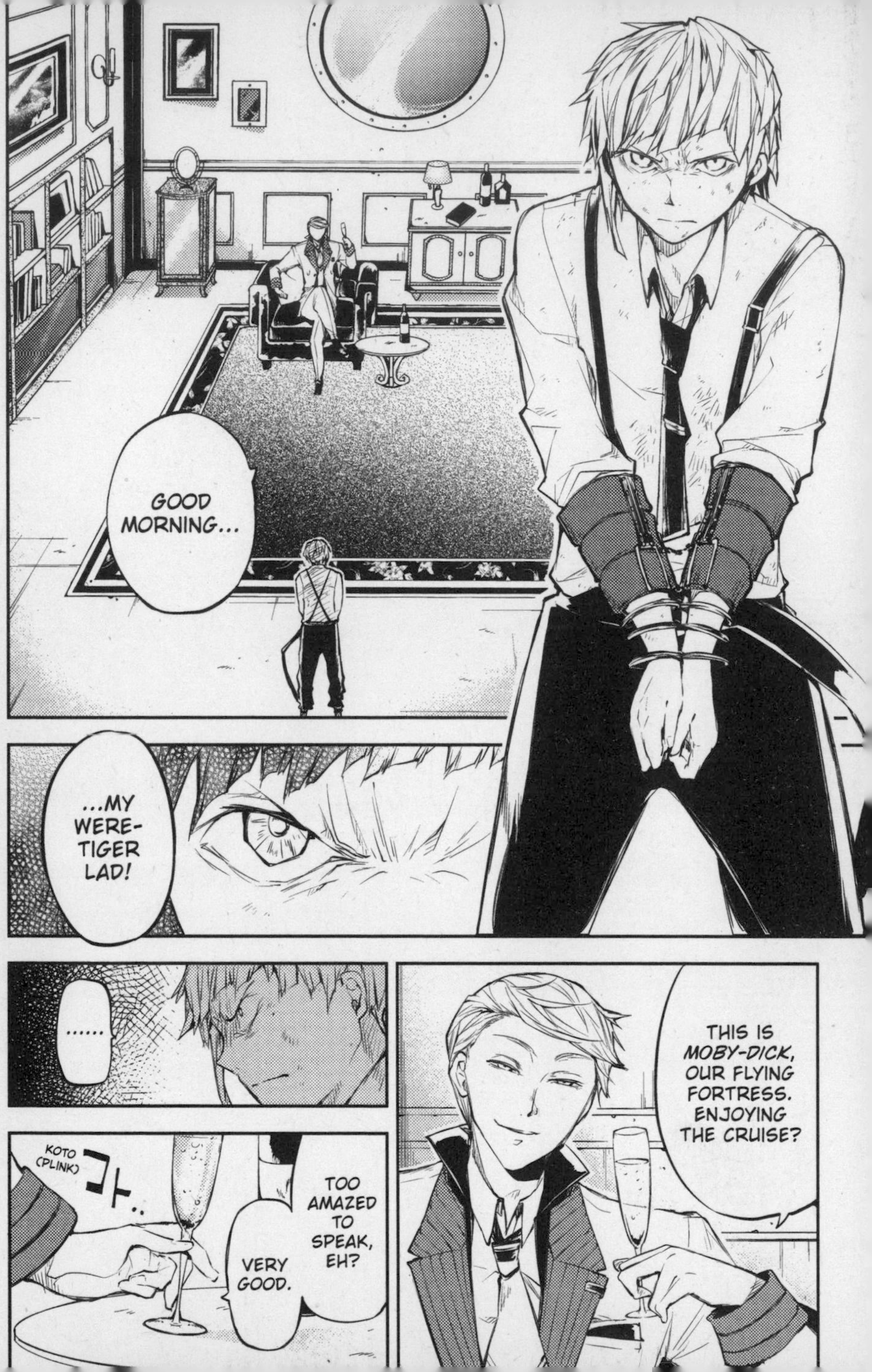
GOOD MORNING...
...MY WERE-TIGER LAD!
THIS IS MOBY-DICK, OUR FLYING FORTRESS. ENJOYING THE CRUISE?
......
TOO AMAZED TO SPEAK, EH?
VERY GOOD.
KOTO (PLINK)

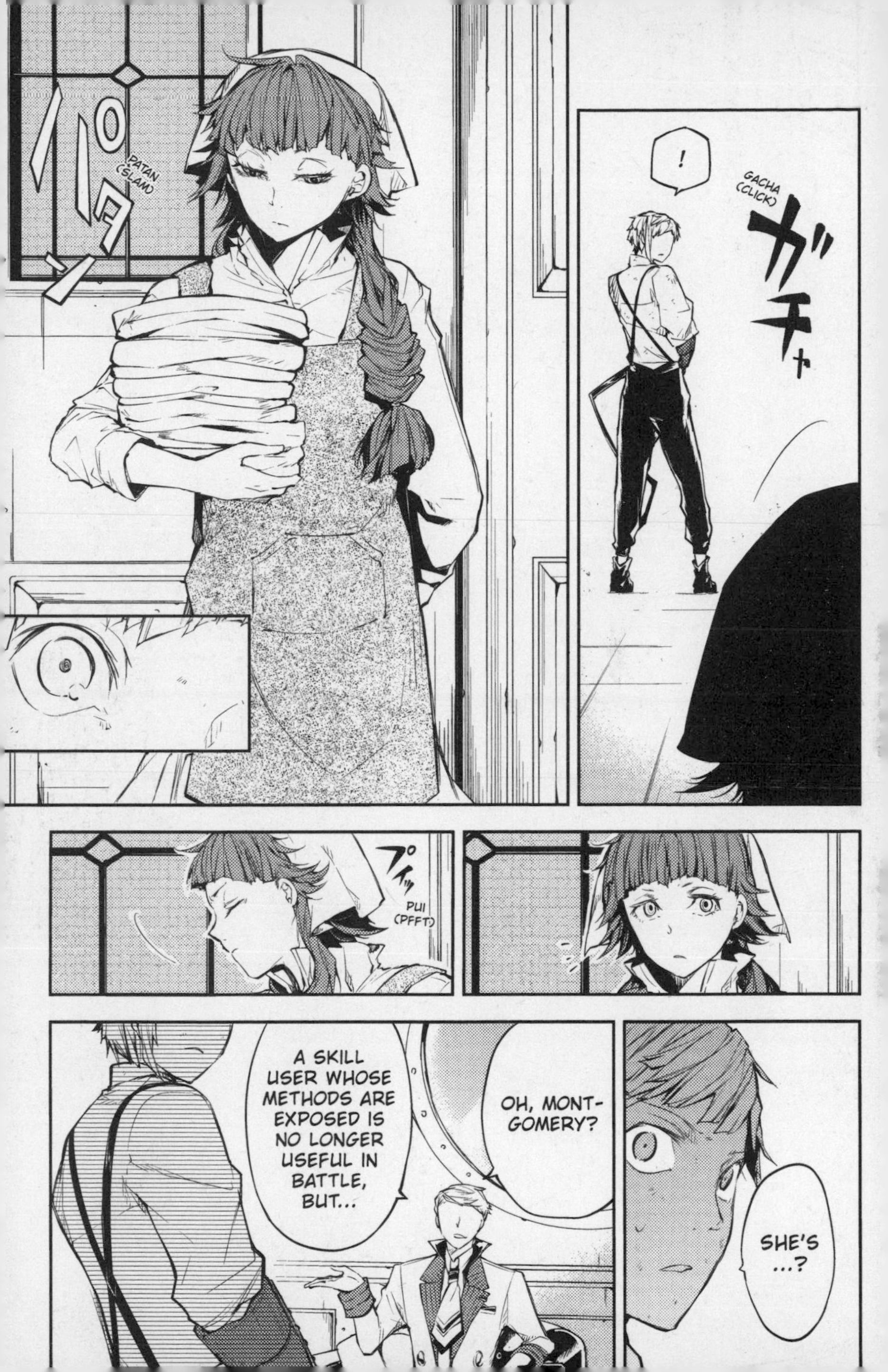
!
GACHA (CLICK)
ガチャ
PATAN (SLAM)
パタン
PUI (PFFT)
プイッ
SHE'S ...?
OH, MONT-GOMERY?
A SKILL USER WHOSE METHODS ARE EXPOSED IS NO LONGER USEFUL IN BATTLE, BUT...

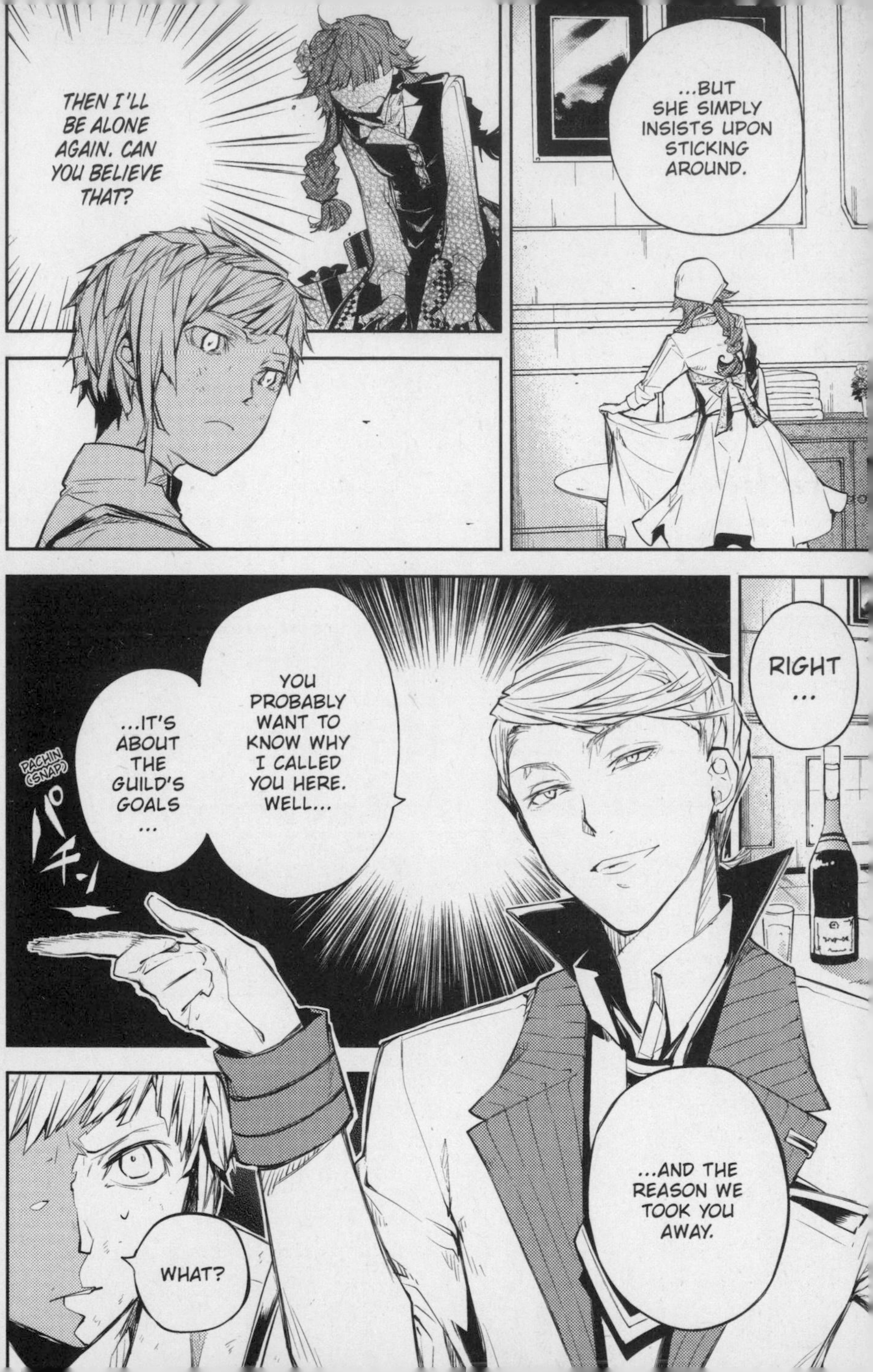
...BUT SHE SIMPLY INSISTS UPON STICKING AROUND.
THEN I'LL BE ALONE AGAIN. CAN YOU BELIEVE THAT?
RIGHT...
YOU PROBABLY WANT TO KNOW WHY I CALLED YOU HERE. WELL...
...IT'S ABOUT THE GUILD'S GOALS...
PACHIN (SNAP)
...AND THE REASON WE TOOK YOU AWAY.
WHAT?

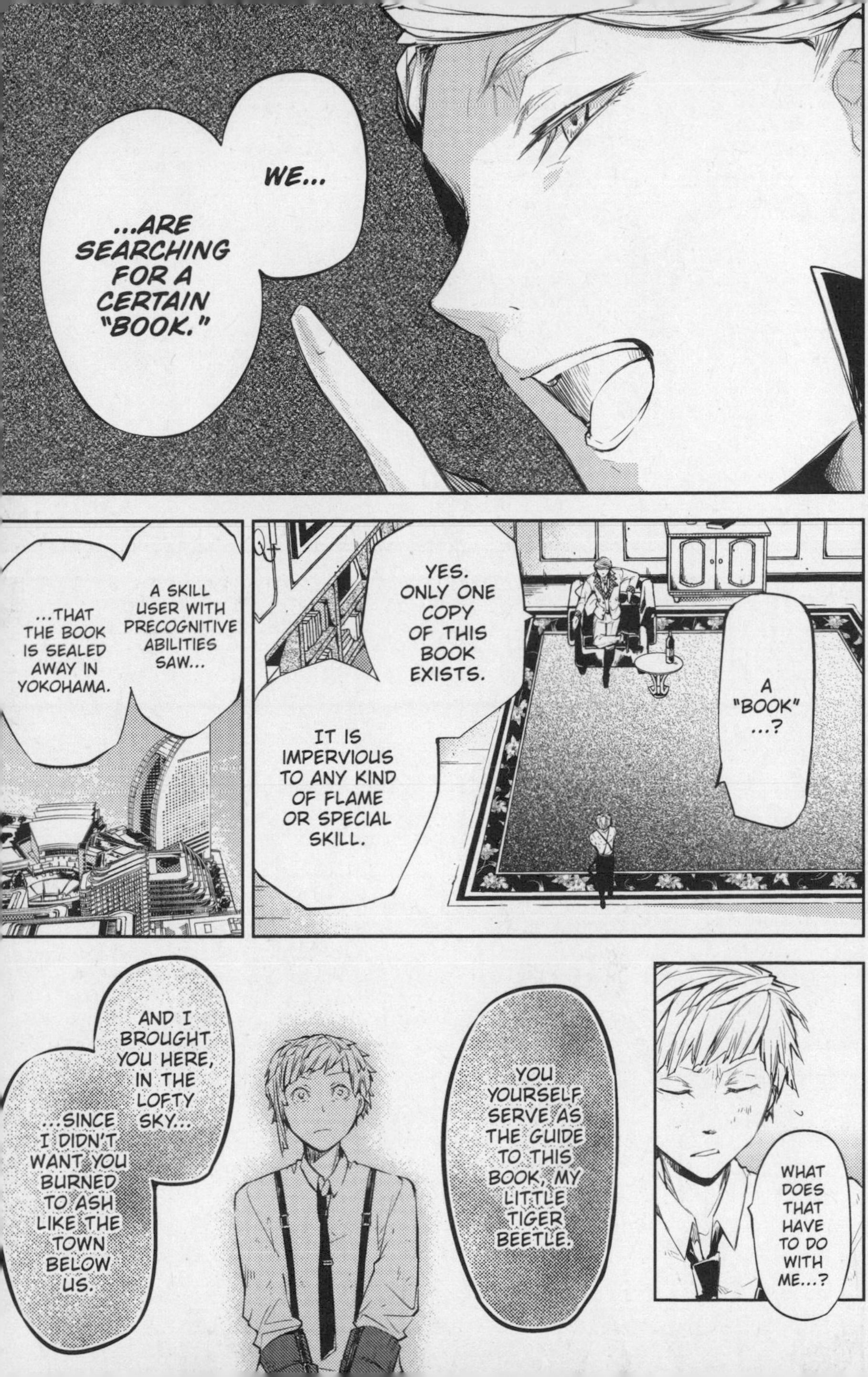
WE...
...ARE SEARCHING FOR A CERTAIN "BOOK."
A "BOOK" ...?
YES. ONLY ONE COPY OF THIS BOOK EXISTS.
IT IS IMPERVIOUS TO ANY KIND OF FLAME OR SPECIAL SKILL.
A SKILL USER WITH PRECOGNITIVE ABILITIES SAW...
...THAT THE BOOK IS SEALED AWAY IN YOKOHAMA.
WHAT DOES THAT HAVE TO DO WITH ME...?
YOU YOURSELF SERVE AS THE GUIDE TO THIS BOOK, MY LITTLE TIGER BEETLE.
AND I BROUGHT YOU HERE, IN THE LOFTY SKY...
...SINCE I DIDN'T WANT YOU BURNED TO ASH LIKE THE TOWN BELOW US.

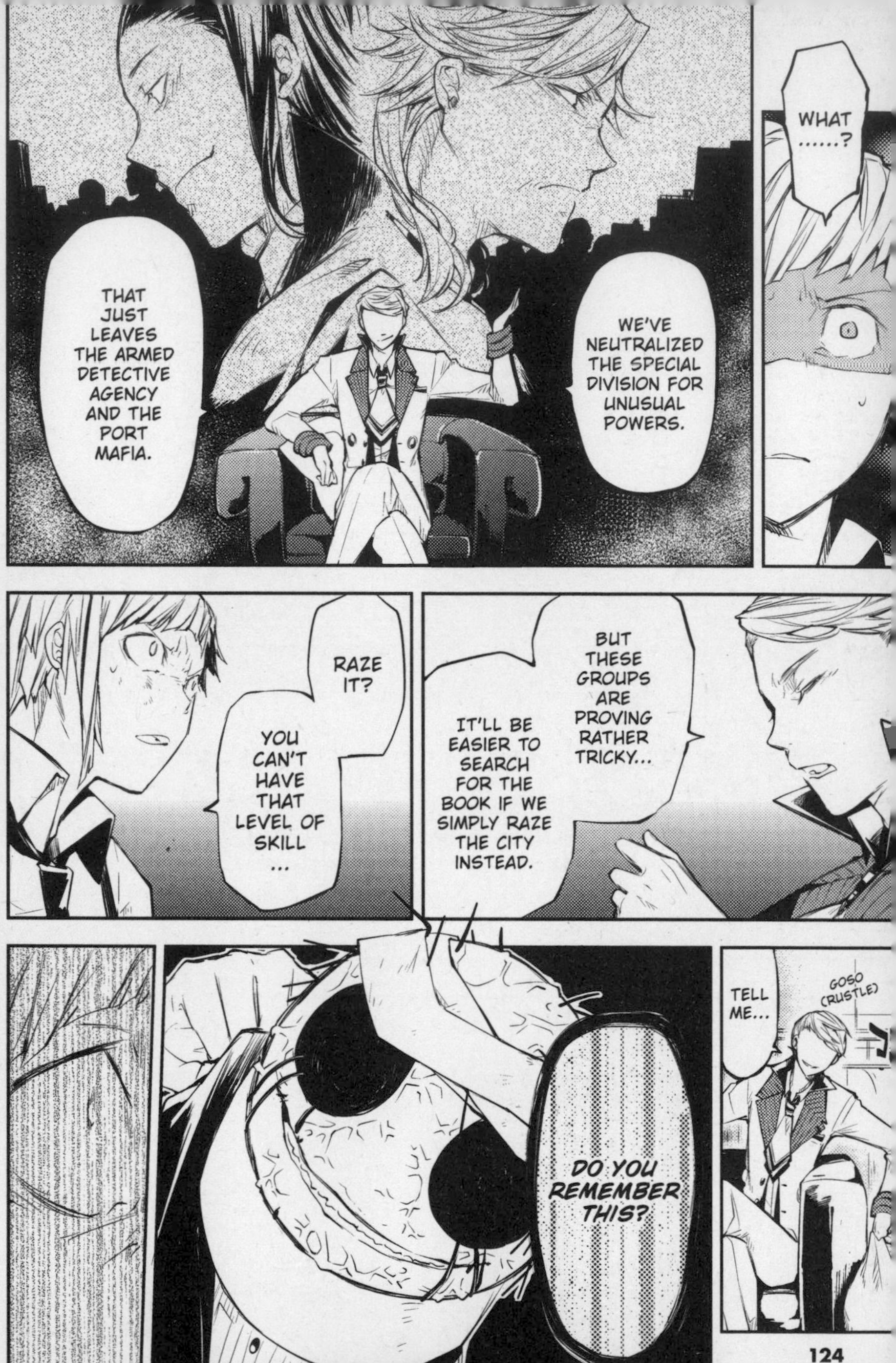
WHAT ......?
WE'VE NEUTRALIZED THE SPECIAL DIVISION FOR UNUSUAL POWERS.
THAT JUST LEAVES THE ARMED DETECTIVE AGENCY AND THE PORT MAFIA.
BUT THESE GROUPS ARE PROVING RATHER TRICKY...
IT'LL BE EASIER TO SEARCH FOR THE BOOK IF WE SIMPLY RAZE THE CITY INSTEAD.
RAZE IT?
YOU CAN'T HAVE THAT LEVEL OF SKILL ...
TELL ME...
GOSO (RUSTLE)
DO YOU REMEMBER THIS?

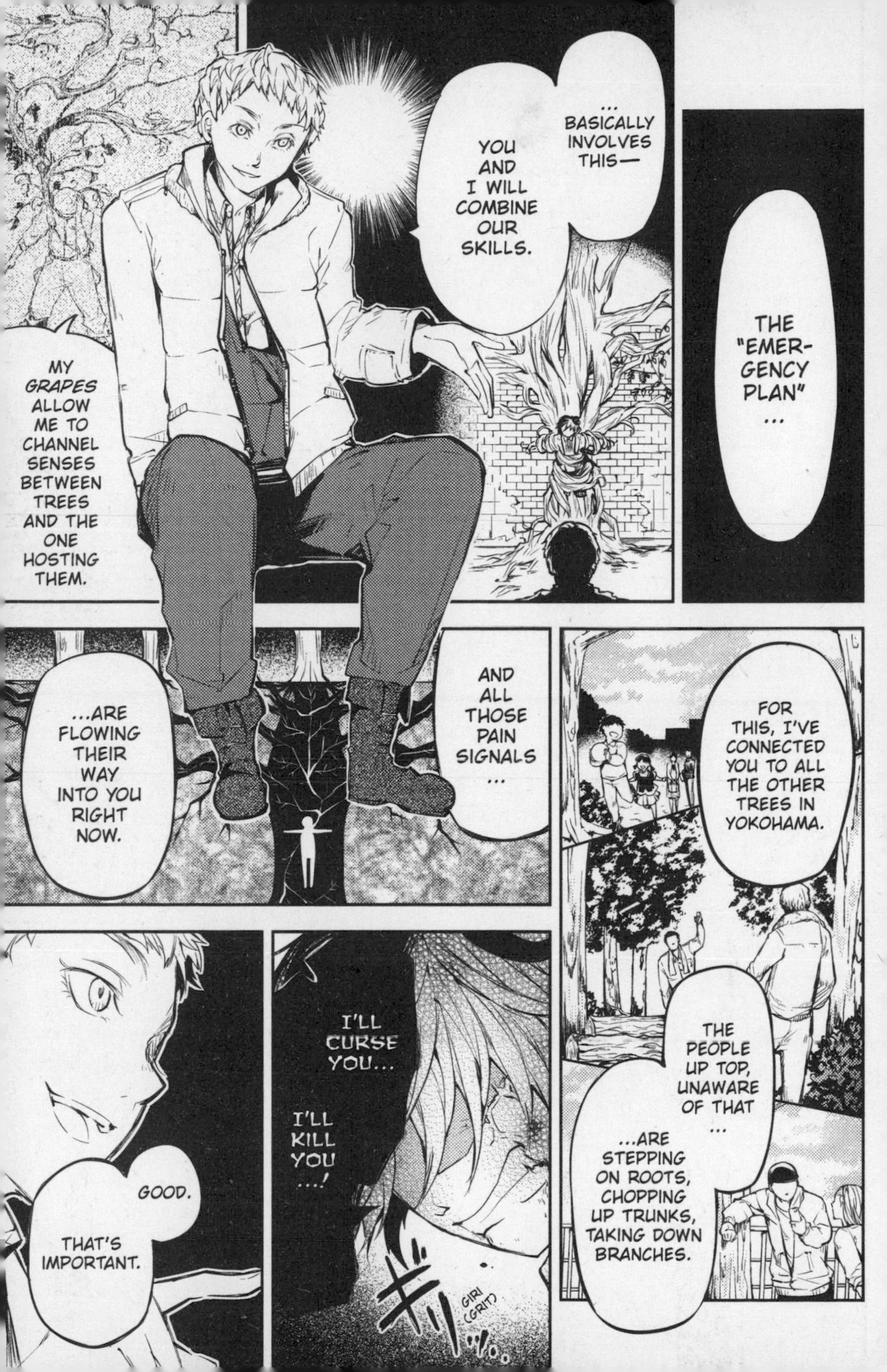
THE "EMERGENCY PLAN"...
...BASICALLY INVOLVES THIS—
YOU AND I WILL COMBINE OUR SKILLS.
MY *GRAPES* ALLOW ME TO CHANNEL SENSES BETWEEN TREES AND THE ONE HOSTING THEM.
FOR THIS, I'VE CONNECTED YOU TO ALL THE OTHER TREES IN YOKOHAMA.
THE PEOPLE UP TOP, UNAWARE OF THAT...
...ARE STEPPING ON ROOTS, CHOPPING UP TRUNKS, TAKING DOWN BRANCHES.
AND ALL THOSE PAIN SIGNALS...
...ARE FLOWING THEIR WAY INTO YOU RIGHT NOW.
I'LL CURSE YOU...
I'LL KILL YOU...!
GIRI (GRIT)
GOOD.
THAT'S IMPORTANT.

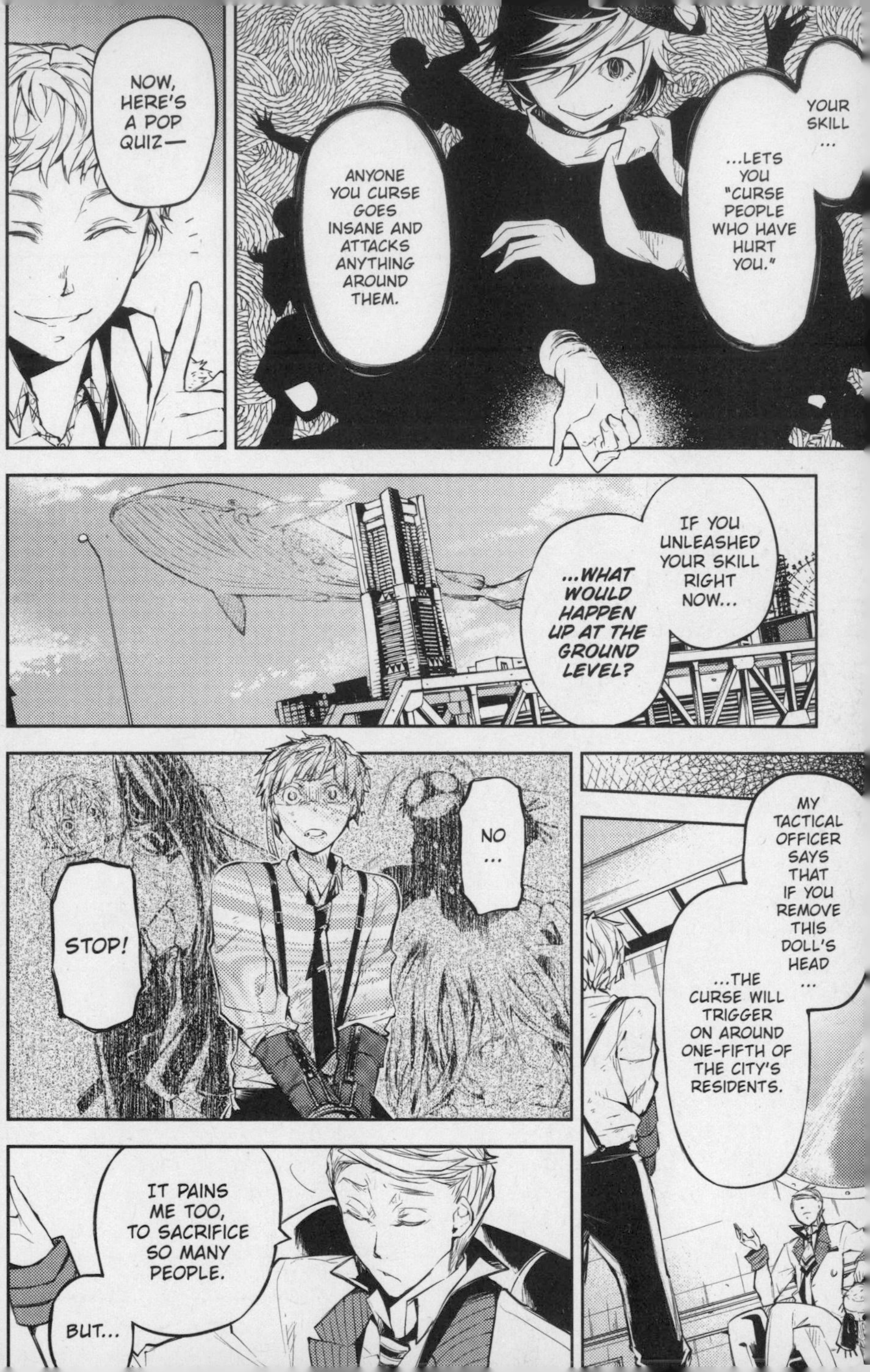
YOUR SKILL ...
...LETS YOU "CURSE PEOPLE WHO HAVE HURT YOU."
ANYONE YOU CURSE GOES INSANE AND ATTACKS ANYTHING AROUND THEM.
NOW, HERE'S A POP QUIZ—
IF YOU UNLEASHED YOUR SKILL RIGHT NOW...
...WHAT WOULD HAPPEN UP AT THE GROUND LEVEL?
MY TACTICAL OFFICER SAYS THAT IF YOU REMOVE THIS DOLL'S HEAD ...
...THE CURSE WILL TRIGGER ON AROUND ONE-FIFTH OF THE CITY'S RESIDENTS.
NO ...
STOP!
IT PAINS ME TOO, TO SACRIFICE SO MANY PEOPLE.
BUT...

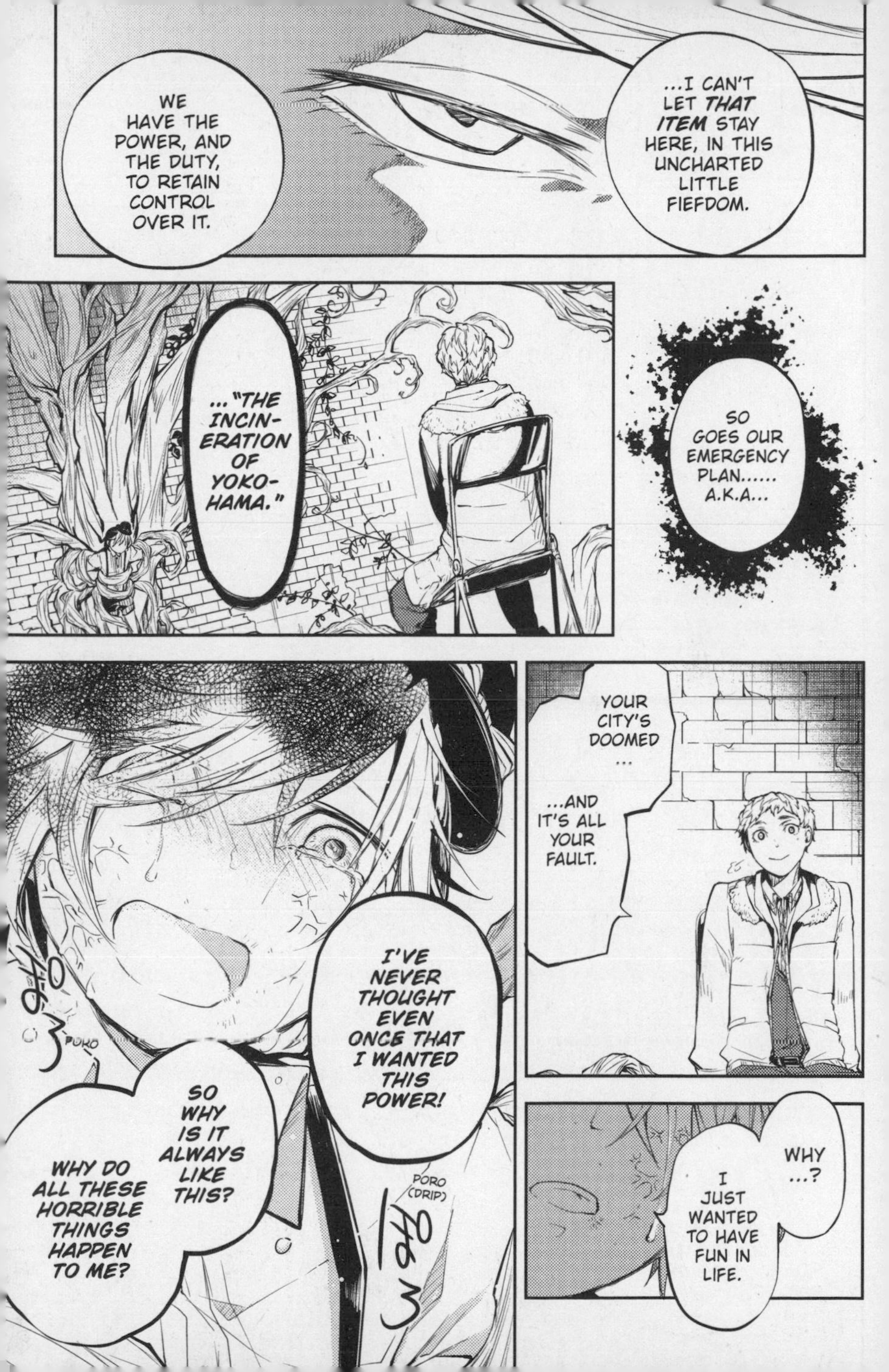
...I CAN'T LET *THAT ITEM* STAY HERE, IN THIS UNCHARTED LITTLE FIEFDOM.
WE HAVE THE POWER, AND THE DUTY, TO RETAIN CONTROL OVER IT.
SO GOES OUR EMERGENCY PLAN...... A.K.A...
..."THE INCINERATION OF YOKOHAMA."
YOUR CITY'S DOOMED ...
...AND IT'S ALL YOUR FAULT.
WHY ...?
I JUST WANTED TO HAVE FUN IN LIFE.
I'VE NEVER THOUGHT EVEN ONCE THAT I WANTED THIS POWER!
PORO (DRIP)
POKO
SO WHY IS IT ALWAYS LIKE THIS?
WHY DO ALL THESE HORRIBLE THINGS HAPPEN TO ME?

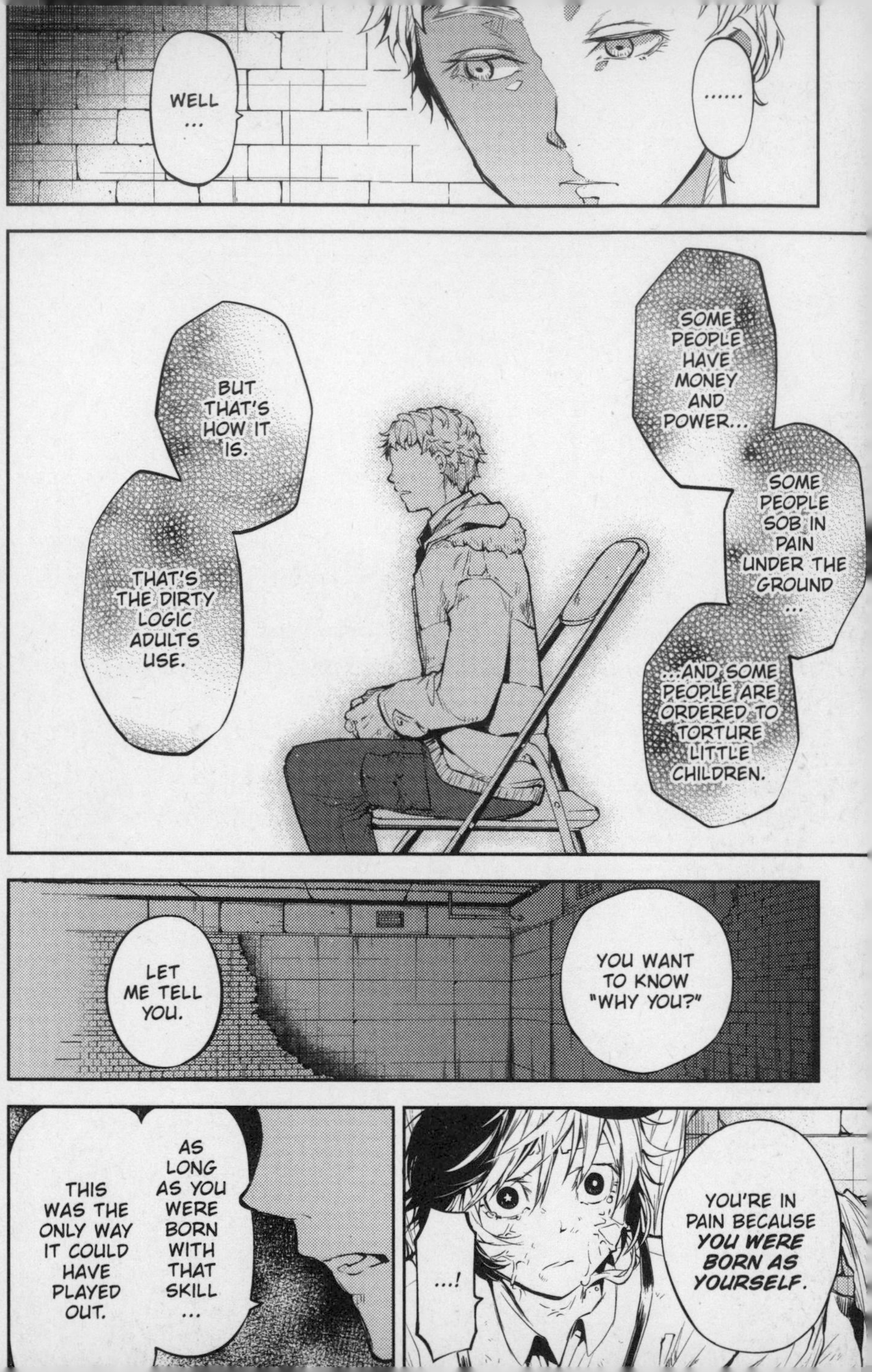
......
WELL ...
SOME PEOPLE HAVE MONEY AND POWER...
SOME PEOPLE SOB IN PAIN UNDER THE GROUND ...
...AND SOME PEOPLE ARE ORDERED TO TORTURE LITTLE CHILDREN.
BUT THAT'S HOW IT IS.
THAT'S THE DIRTY LOGIC ADULTS USE.
YOU WANT TO KNOW "WHY YOU?"
LET ME TELL YOU.
YOU'RE IN PAIN BECAUSE *YOU WERE BORN AS YOURSELF*.
...!
AS LONG AS YOU WERE BORN WITH THAT SKILL ...
THIS WAS THE ONLY WAY IT COULD HAVE PLAYED OUT.

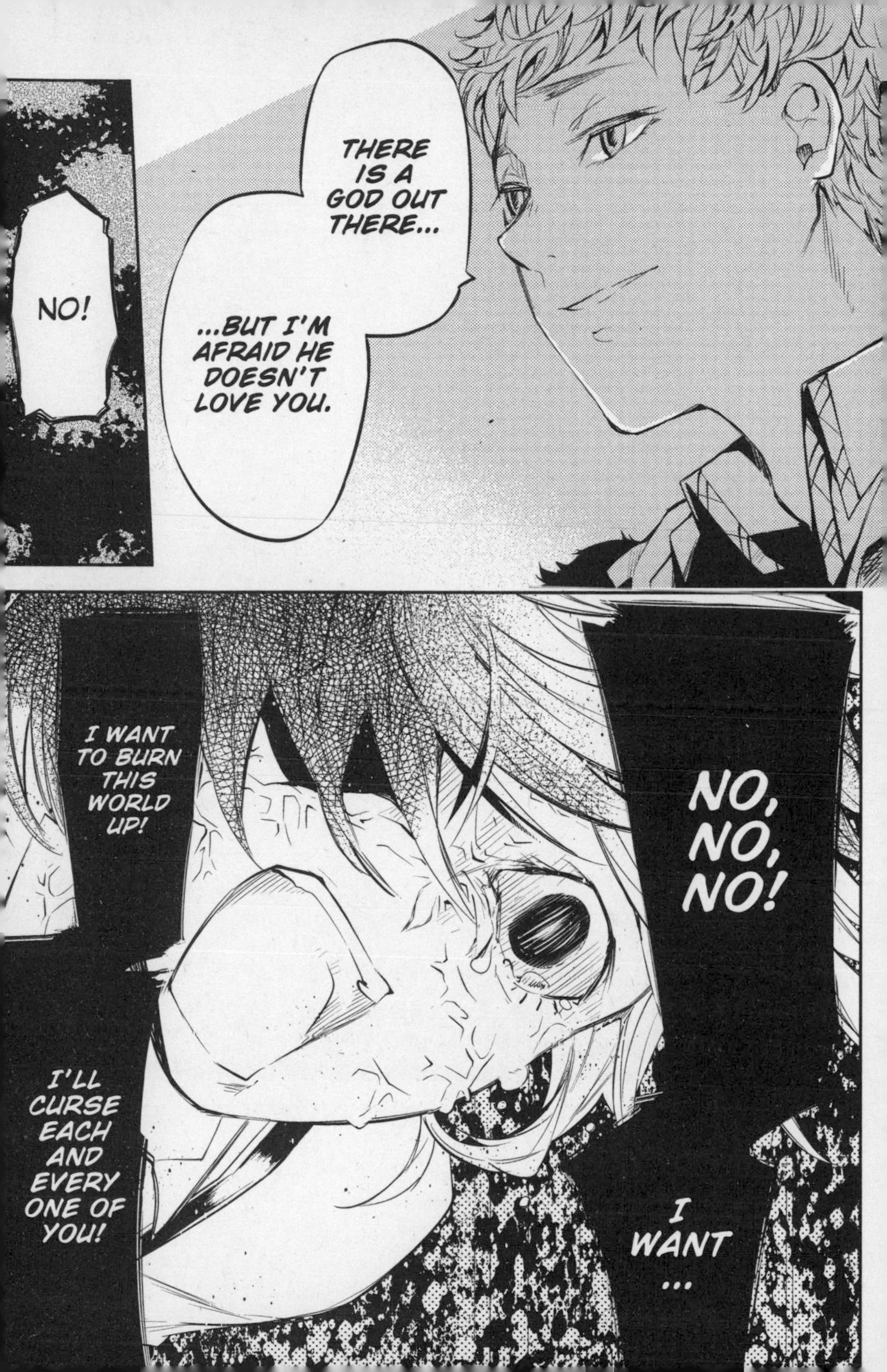
THERE IS A GOD OUT THERE...
...BUT I'M AFRAID HE DOESN'T LOVE YOU.
NO!
NO, NO, NO!
I WANT ...
I WANT TO BURN THIS WORLD UP!
I'LL CURSE EACH AND EVERY ONE OF YOU!

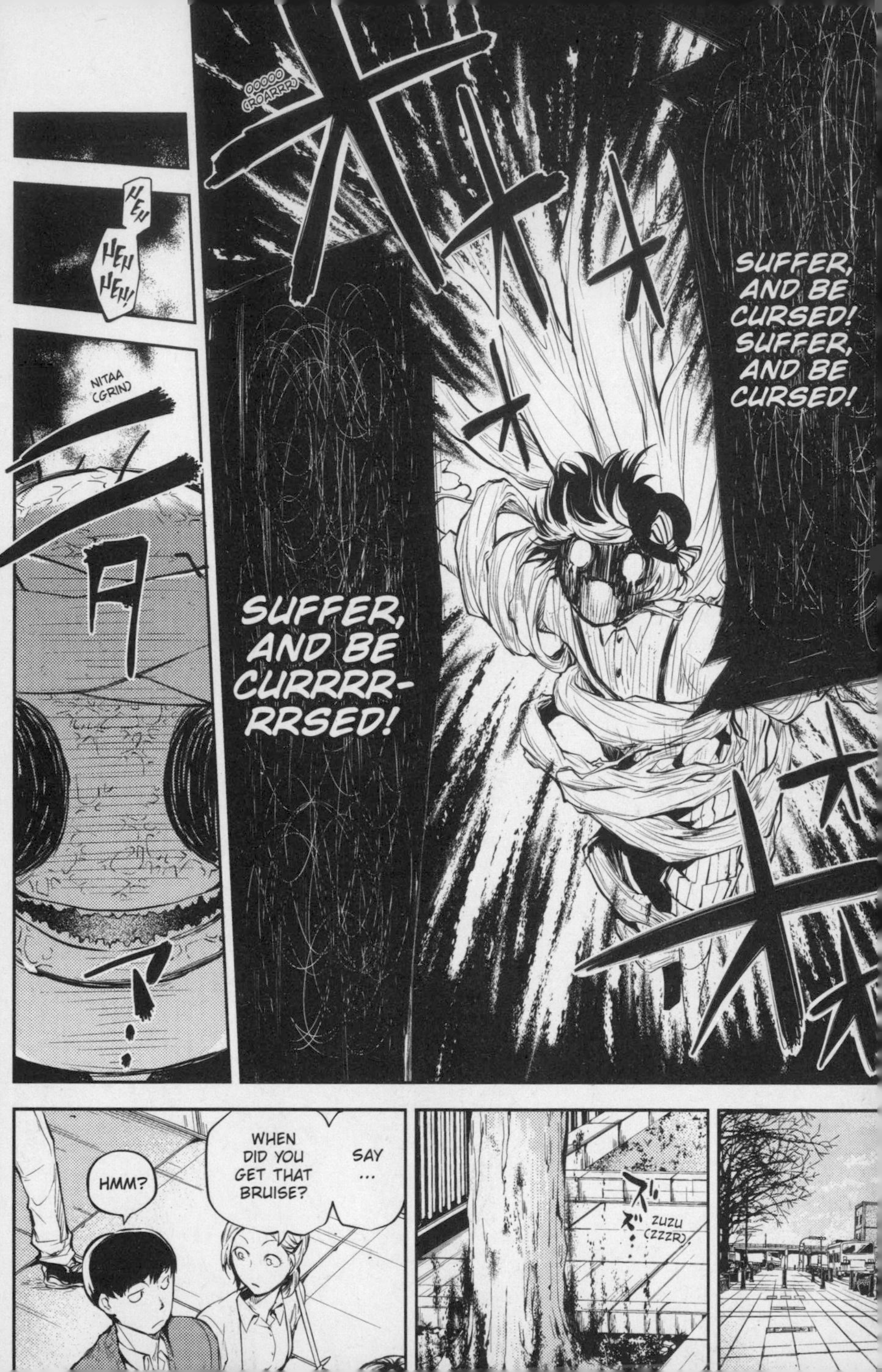
SUFFER, AND BE CURSED! SUFFER, AND BE CURSED!
OOOOO (ROARRR)
SUFFER, AND BE CURRRRR-RRSED!
HEH HEH HEH!
NITAA (GRIN)
ZUZU (ZZZR)
SAY ...
WHEN DID YOU GET THAT BRUISE?
HMM?

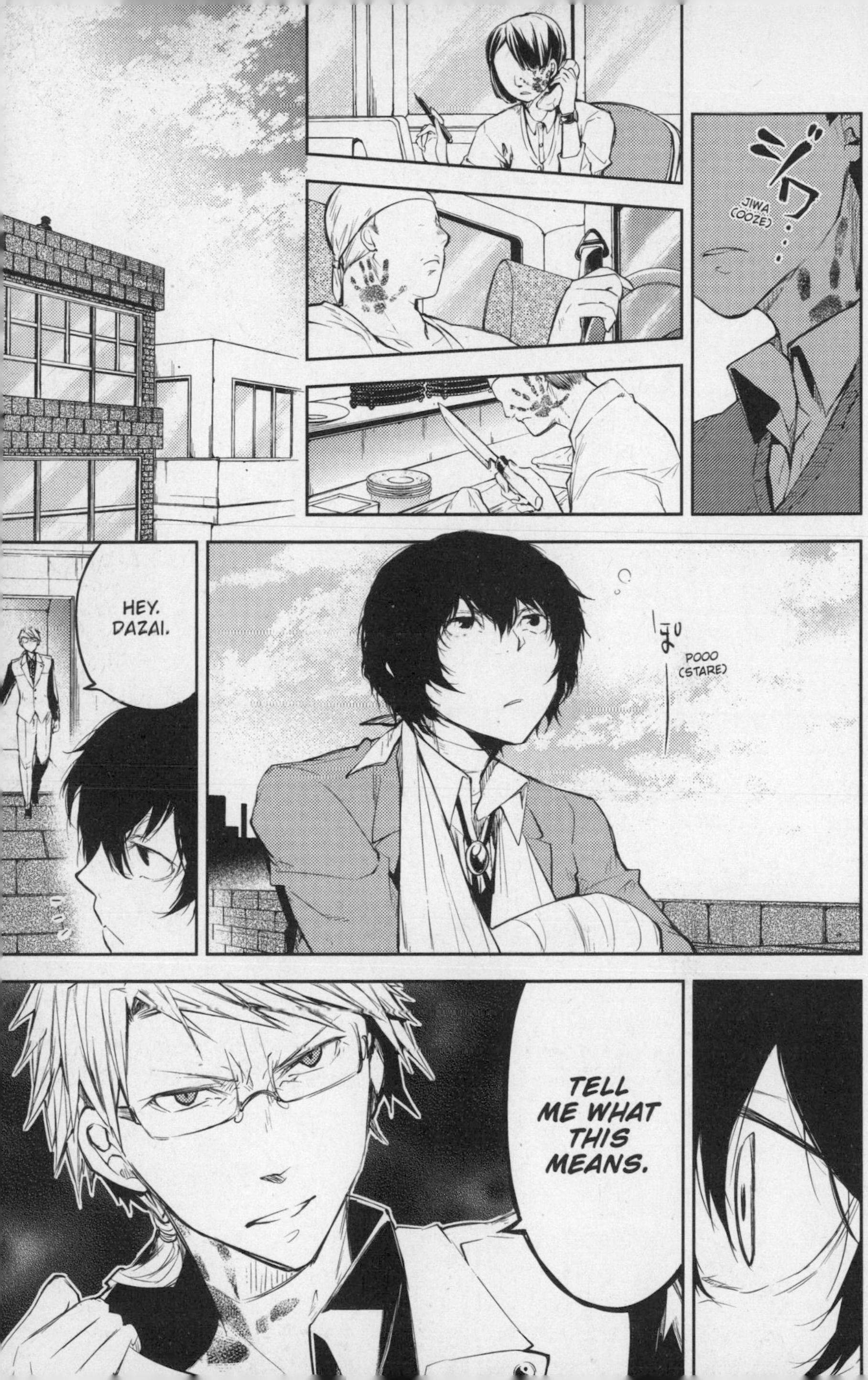
ジワ…
JIWA (OOZE)
ぽー
POOO (STARE)
HEY. DAZAI.
TELL ME WHAT THIS MEANS.

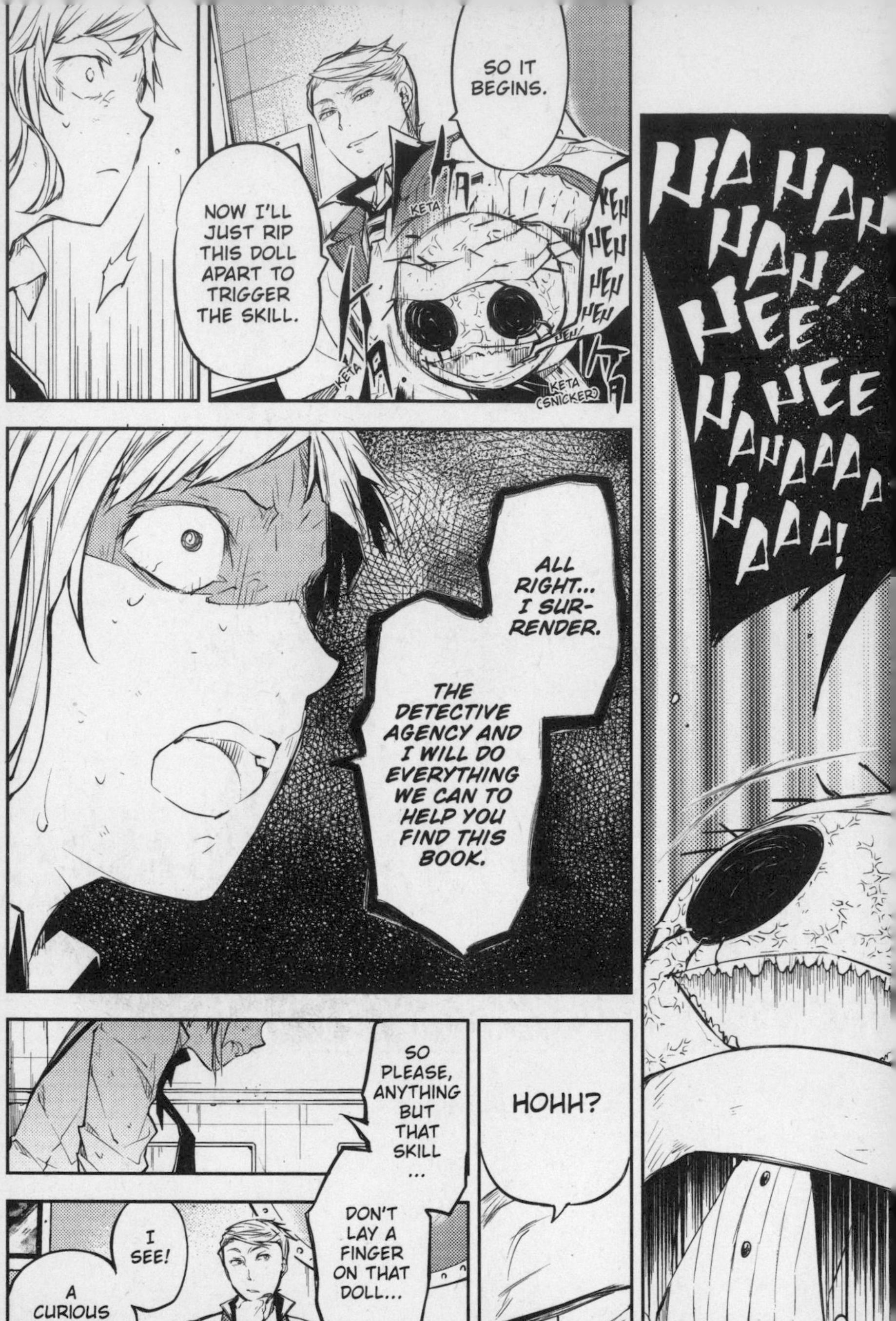
HAHAHAHAH! HEE! HAHEE HAHAAAAA HAAAA!
SO IT BEGINS.
NOW I'LL JUST RIP THIS DOLL APART TO TRIGGER THE SKILL.
KETA
HEH HEH HEH HEH
KETA
KETA (SNICKER)
ALL RIGHT... I SUR-RENDER.
THE DETECTIVE AGENCY AND I WILL DO EVERYTHING WE CAN TO HELP YOU FIND THIS BOOK.
HOHH?
SO PLEASE, ANYTHING BUT THAT SKILL ...
DON'T LAY A FINGER ON THAT DOLL...
I SEE!
A CURIOUS PROPOSI-TION.

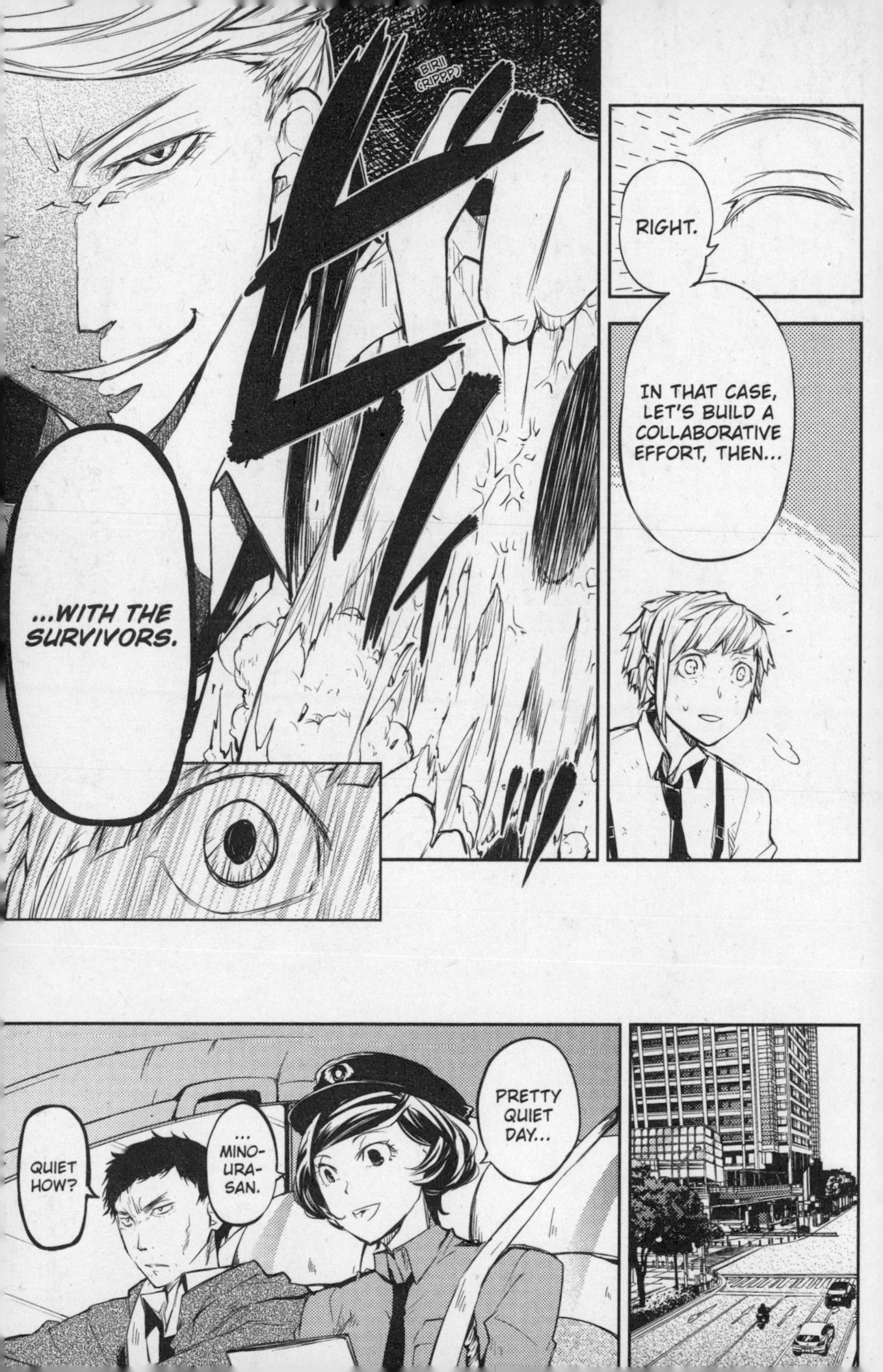
RIGHT.
IN THAT CASE, LET'S BUILD A COLLABORATIVE EFFORT, THEN...
BIRII (RIPPPP)
...WITH THE SURVIVORS.
PRETTY QUIET DAY...
...MINOURA-SAN.
QUIET HOW?

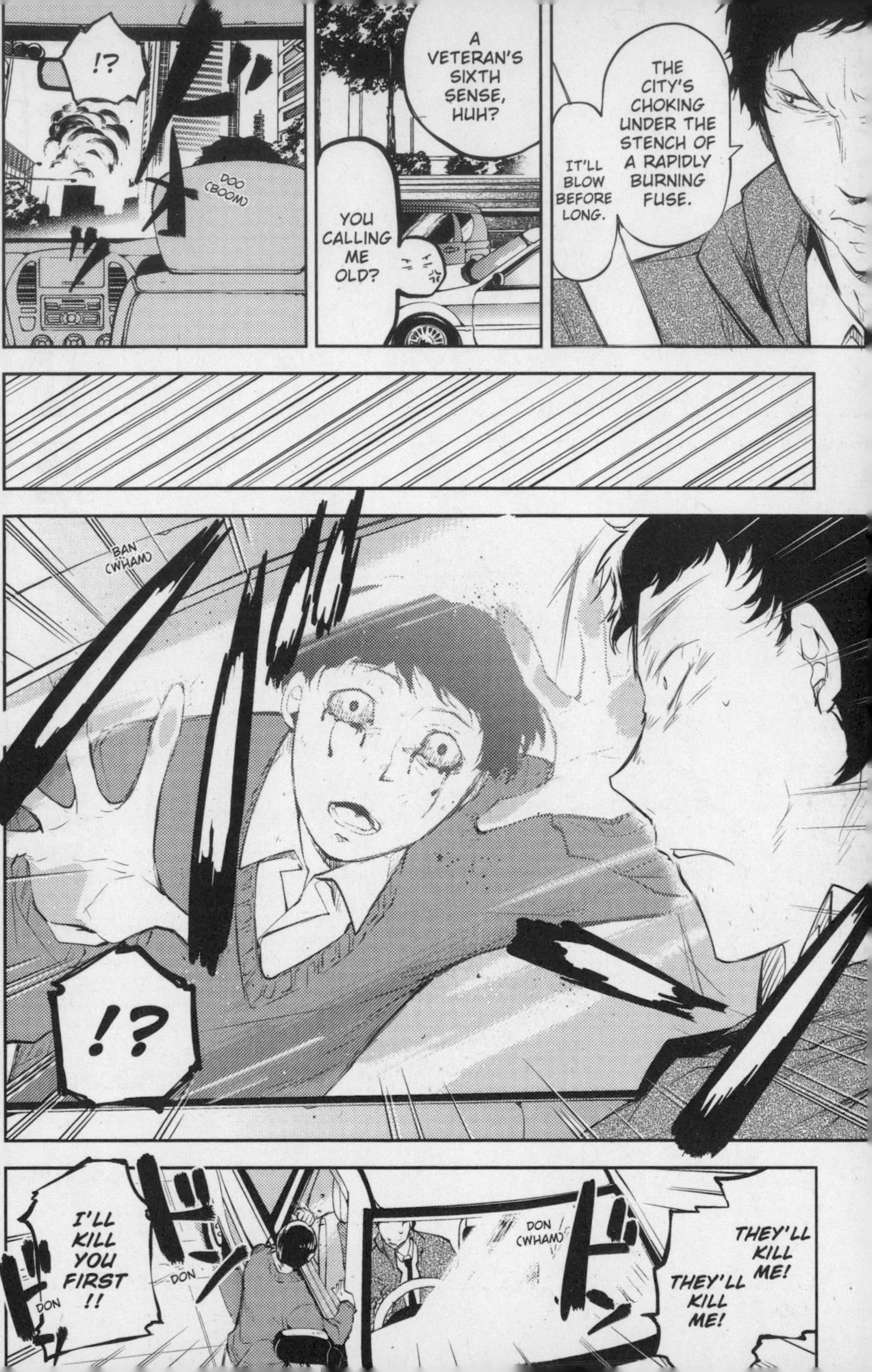
THE CITY'S CHOKING UNDER THE STENCH OF A RAPIDLY BURNING FUSE.
IT'LL BLOW BEFORE LONG.
A VETERAN'S SIXTH SENSE, HUH?
YOU CALLING ME OLD?
!?
DOO (BOOM)
BAN (WHAM)
!?
THEY'LL KILL ME!
THEY'LL KILL ME!
DON (WHAM)
DON
I'LL KILL YOU FIRST!!
DON

MINOURA-SAN!

UP FRONT!!

WHO IS THIS GUY!?

HERE WE GO!

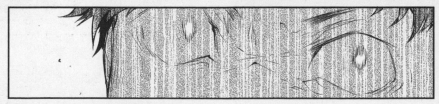

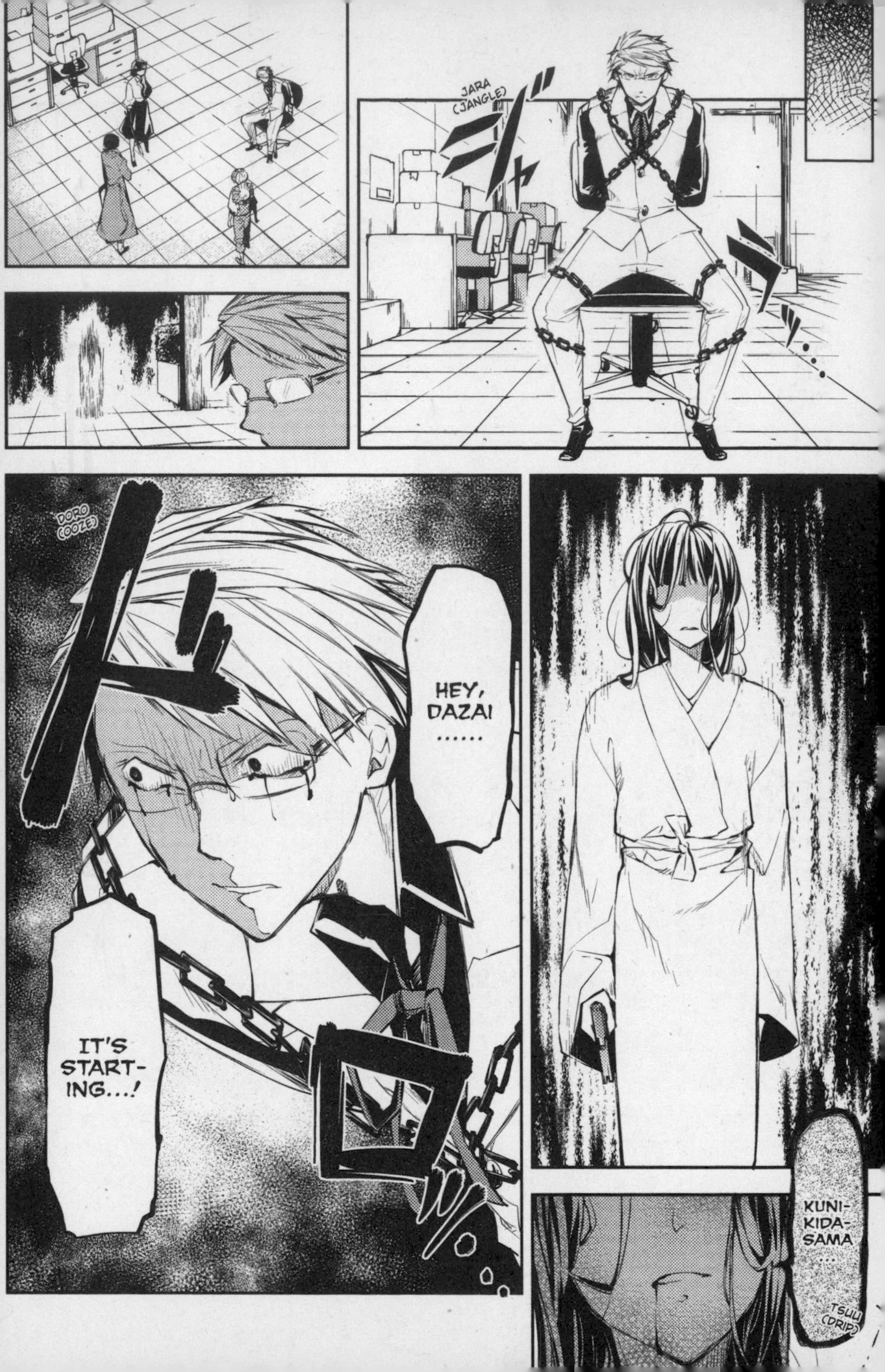
JARA (JANGLE)
KUNI-KIDA-SAMA...
TSUU (DRIP)
DORO (OOZE)
HEY, DAZAI......
IT'S START-ING...!

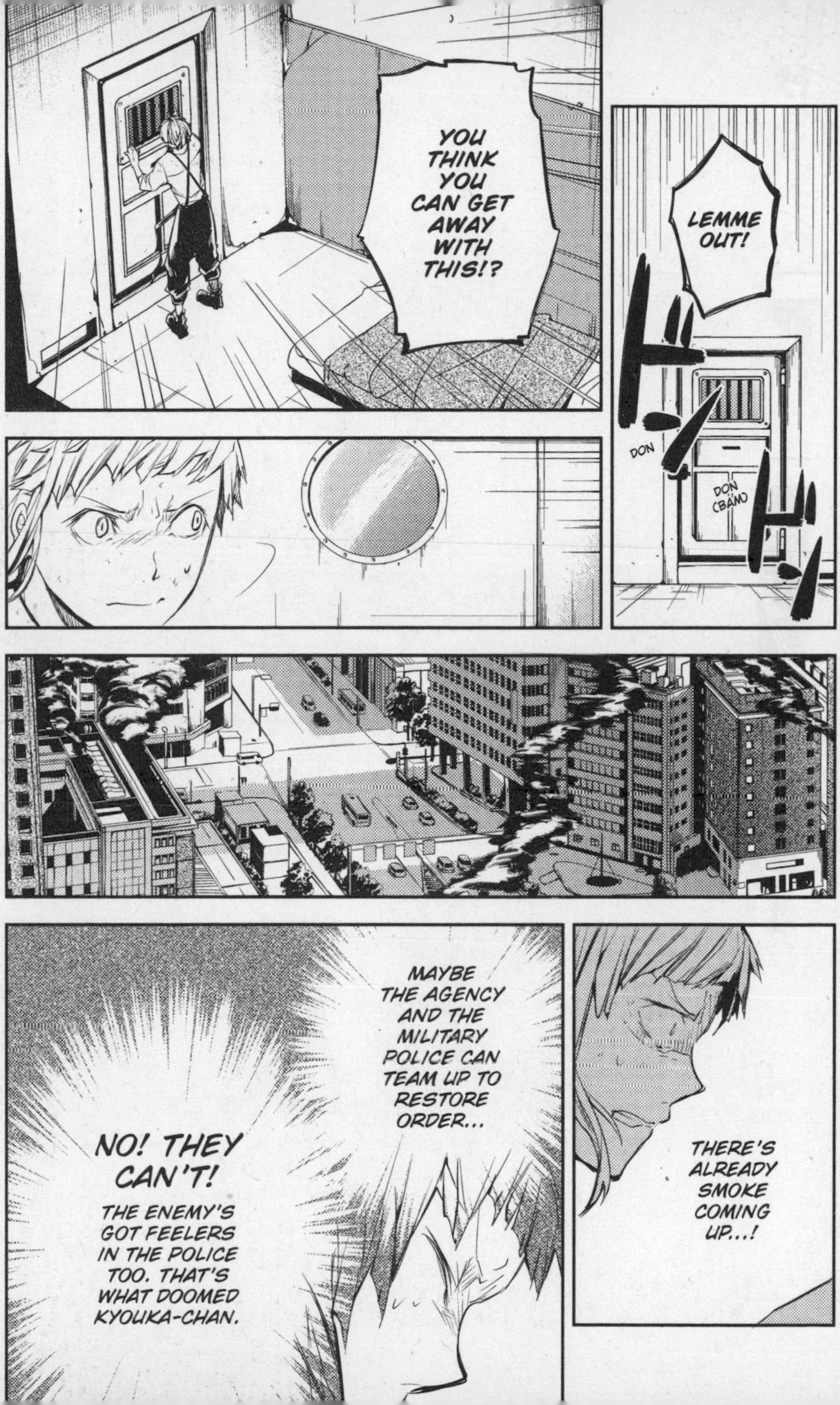
LEMME OUT!
DON
DON (BAM)
YOU THINK YOU CAN GET AWAY WITH THIS!?
THERE'S ALREADY SMOKE COMING UP...!
MAYBE THE AGENCY AND THE MILITARY POLICE CAN TEAM UP TO RESTORE ORDER...
NO! THEY CAN'T!
THE ENEMY'S GOT FEELERS IN THE POLICE TOO. THAT'S WHAT DOOMED KYOUKA-CHAN.

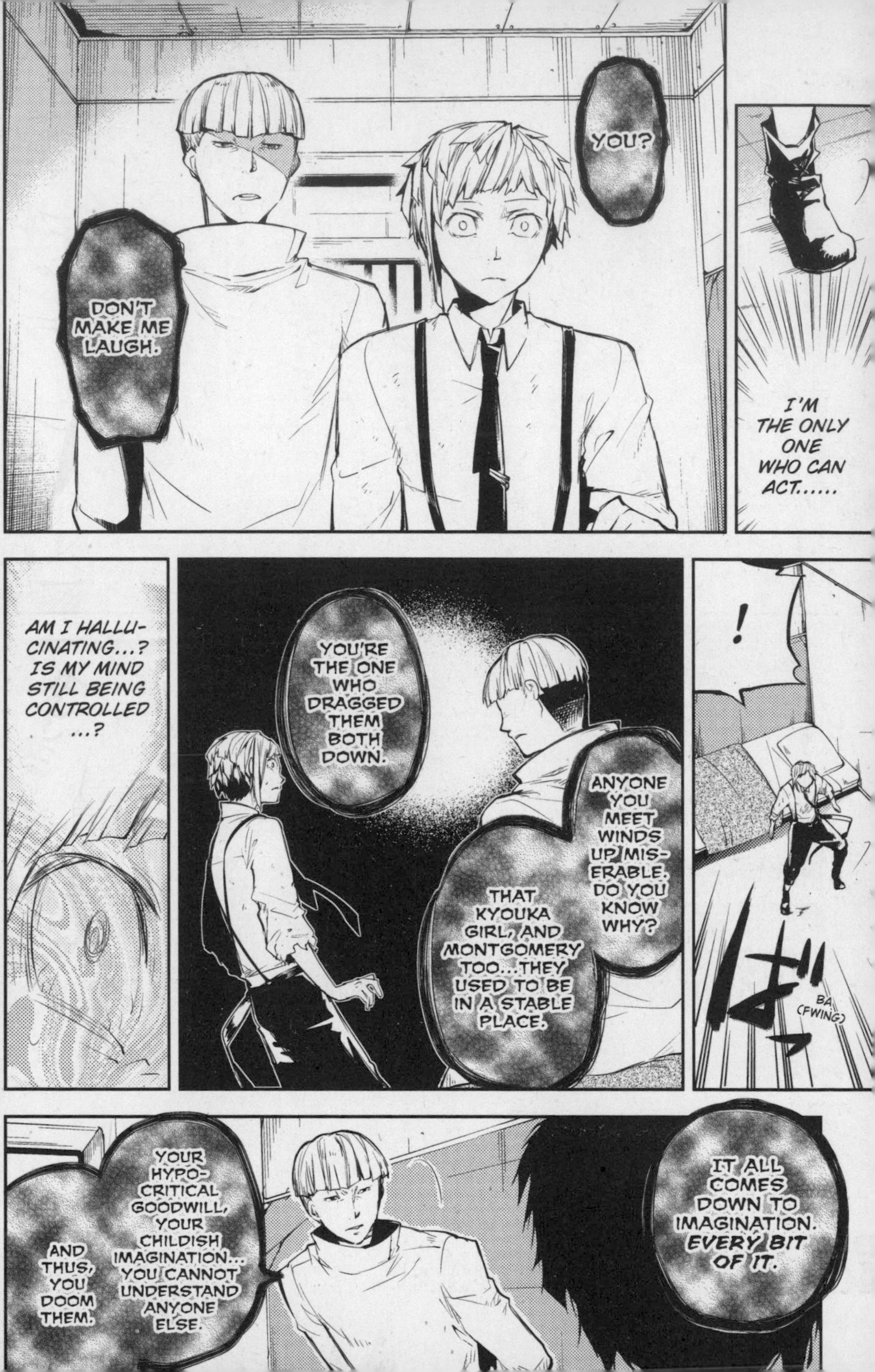
I'M THE ONLY ONE WHO CAN ACT......
YOU?
DON'T MAKE ME LAUGH.
!
BA (FWING)
ANYONE YOU MEET WINDS UP MISERABLE. DO YOU KNOW WHY?
THAT KYOUKA GIRL, AND MONTGOMERY TOO... THEY USED TO BE IN A STABLE PLACE.
YOU'RE THE ONE WHO DRAGGED THEM BOTH DOWN.
AM I HALLUCINATING...? IS MY MIND STILL BEING CONTROLLED ...?
IT ALL COMES DOWN TO IMAGINATION. EVERY BIT OF IT.
YOUR HYPOCRITICAL GOODWILL, YOUR CHILDISH IMAGINATION... YOU CANNOT UNDERSTAND ANYONE ELSE.
AND THUS, YOU DOOM THEM.

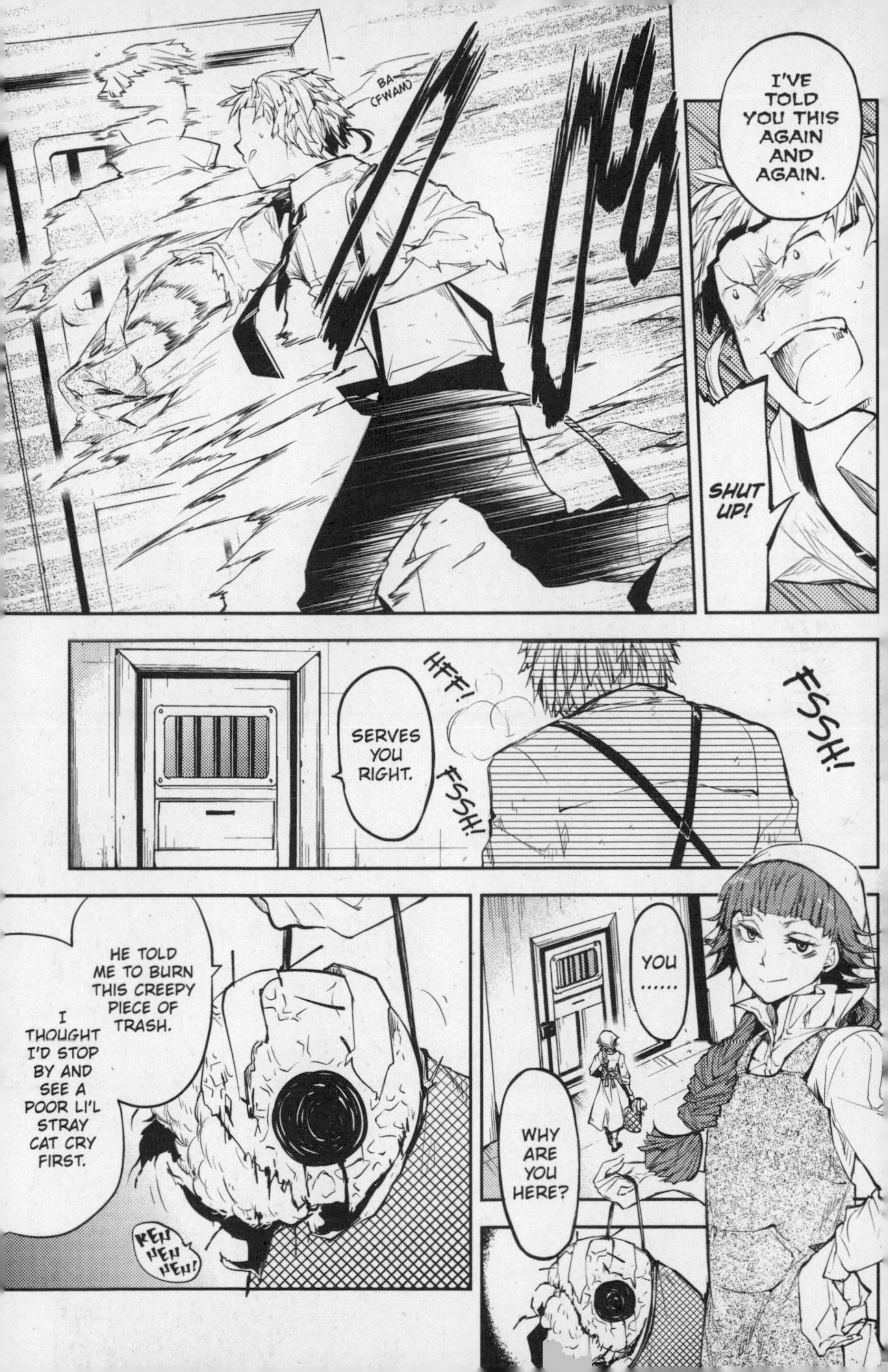
I'VE TOLD YOU THIS AGAIN AND AGAIN.
SHUT UP!
BA (FWAM)
FSSH!
HFF!
SERVES YOU RIGHT.
FSSH!
YOU……
WHY ARE YOU HERE?
HE TOLD ME TO BURN THIS CREEPY PIECE OF TRASH.
I THOUGHT I'D STOP BY AND SEE A POOR LI'L STRAY CAT CRY FIRST.
KEH HEH HEH!

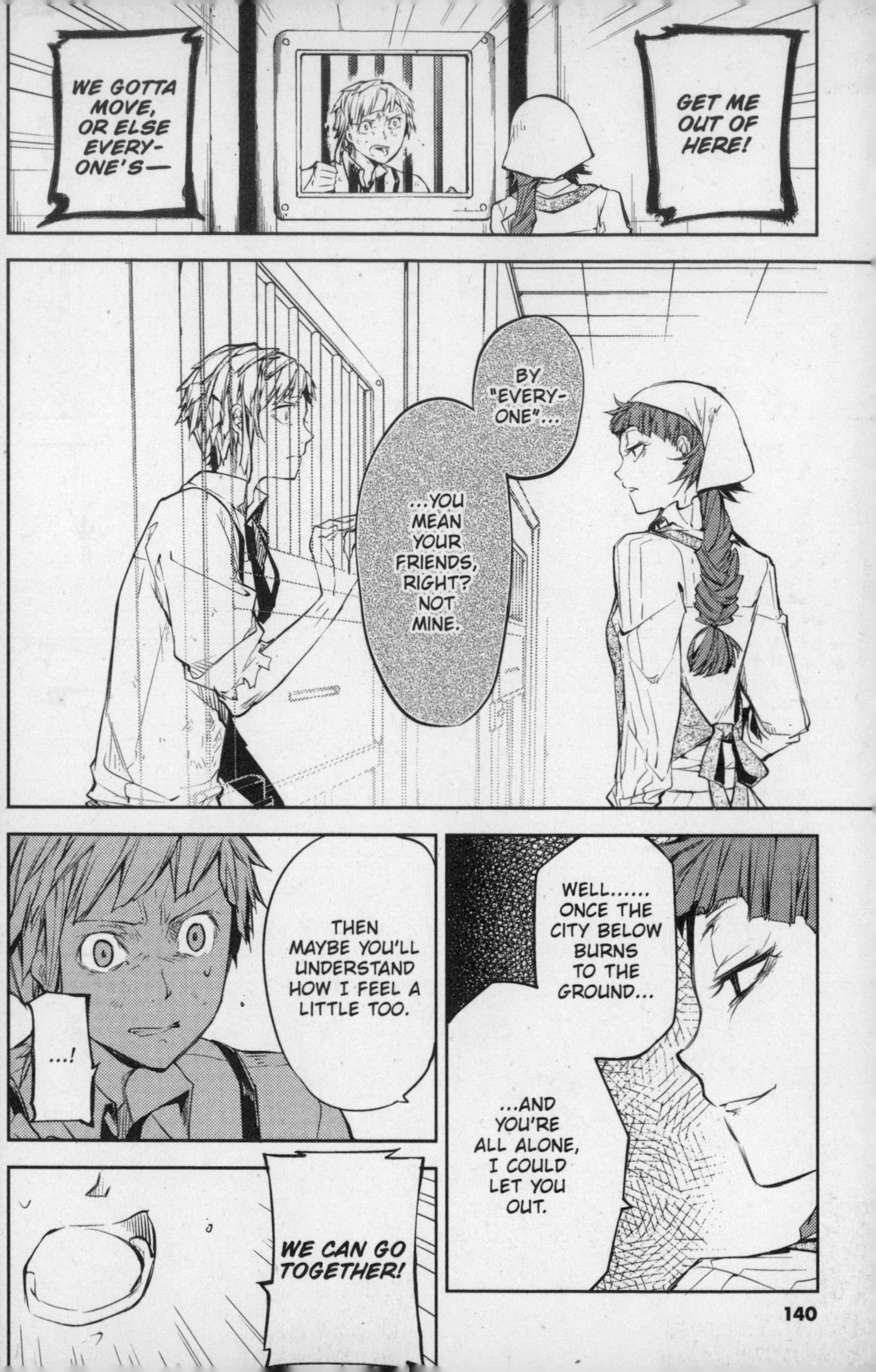
GET ME OUT OF HERE!
WE GOTTA MOVE, OR ELSE EVERY-ONE'S—
BY "EVERY-ONE"...
...YOU MEAN YOUR FRIENDS, RIGHT? NOT MINE.
WELL...... ONCE THE CITY BELOW BURNS TO THE GROUND...
...AND YOU'RE ALL ALONE, I COULD LET YOU OUT.
THEN MAYBE YOU'LL UNDERSTAND HOW I FEEL A LITTLE TOO.
...!
WE CAN GO TOGETHER!

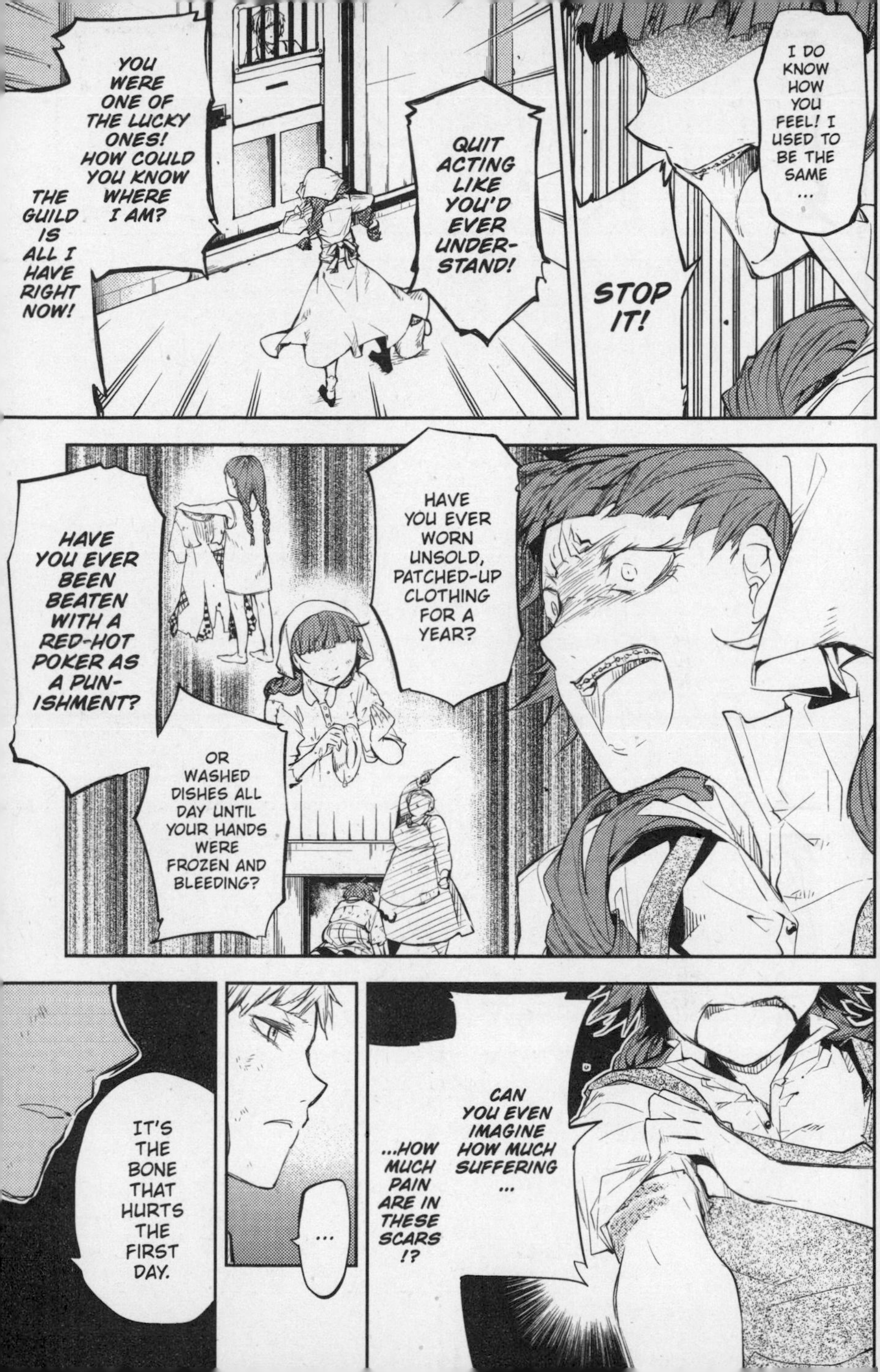
I DO KNOW HOW YOU FEEL! I USED TO BE THE SAME...
STOP IT!
QUIT ACTING LIKE YOU'D EVER UNDER-STAND!
YOU WERE ONE OF THE LUCKY ONES! HOW COULD YOU KNOW WHERE I AM?
THE GUILD IS ALL I HAVE RIGHT NOW!
HAVE YOU EVER WORN UNSOLD, PATCHED-UP CLOTHING FOR A YEAR?
HAVE YOU EVER BEEN BEATEN WITH A RED-HOT POKER AS A PUN-ISHMENT?
OR WASHED DISHES ALL DAY UNTIL YOUR HANDS WERE FROZEN AND BLEEDING?
CAN YOU EVEN IMAGINE HOW MUCH SUFFERING...
...HOW MUCH PAIN ARE IN THESE SCARS!?
...
IT'S THE BONE THAT HURTS THE FIRST DAY.

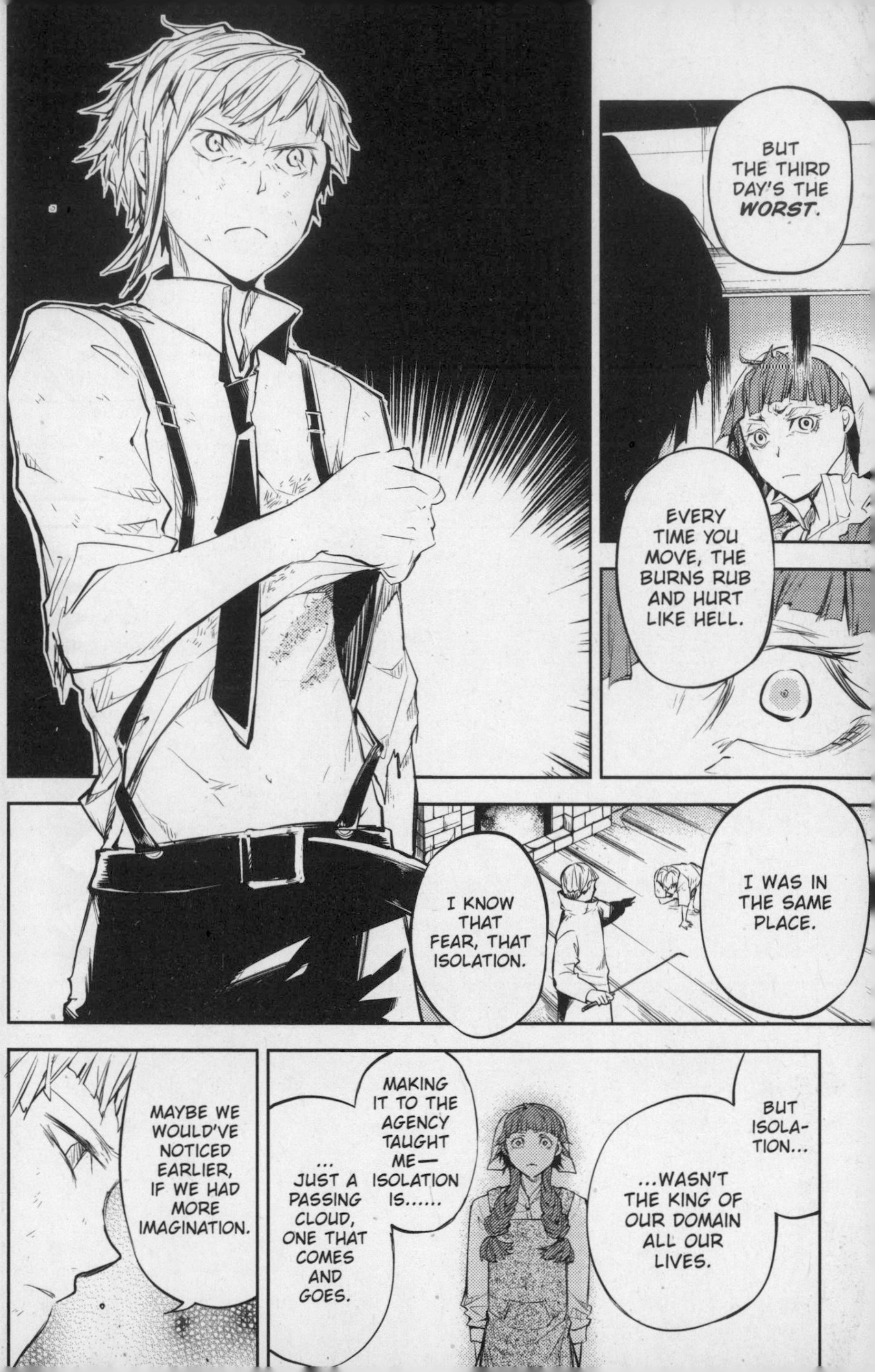
BUT THE THIRD DAY'S THE *WORST*.
EVERY TIME YOU MOVE, THE BURNS RUB AND HURT LIKE HELL.
I WAS IN THE SAME PLACE.
I KNOW THAT FEAR, THAT ISOLATION.
BUT ISOLATION...
...WASN'T THE KING OF OUR DOMAIN ALL OUR LIVES.
MAKING IT TO THE AGENCY TAUGHT ME— ISOLATION IS......
...JUST A PASSING CLOUD, ONE THAT COMES AND GOES.
MAYBE WE WOULD'VE NOTICED EARLIER, IF WE HAD MORE IMAGINATION.

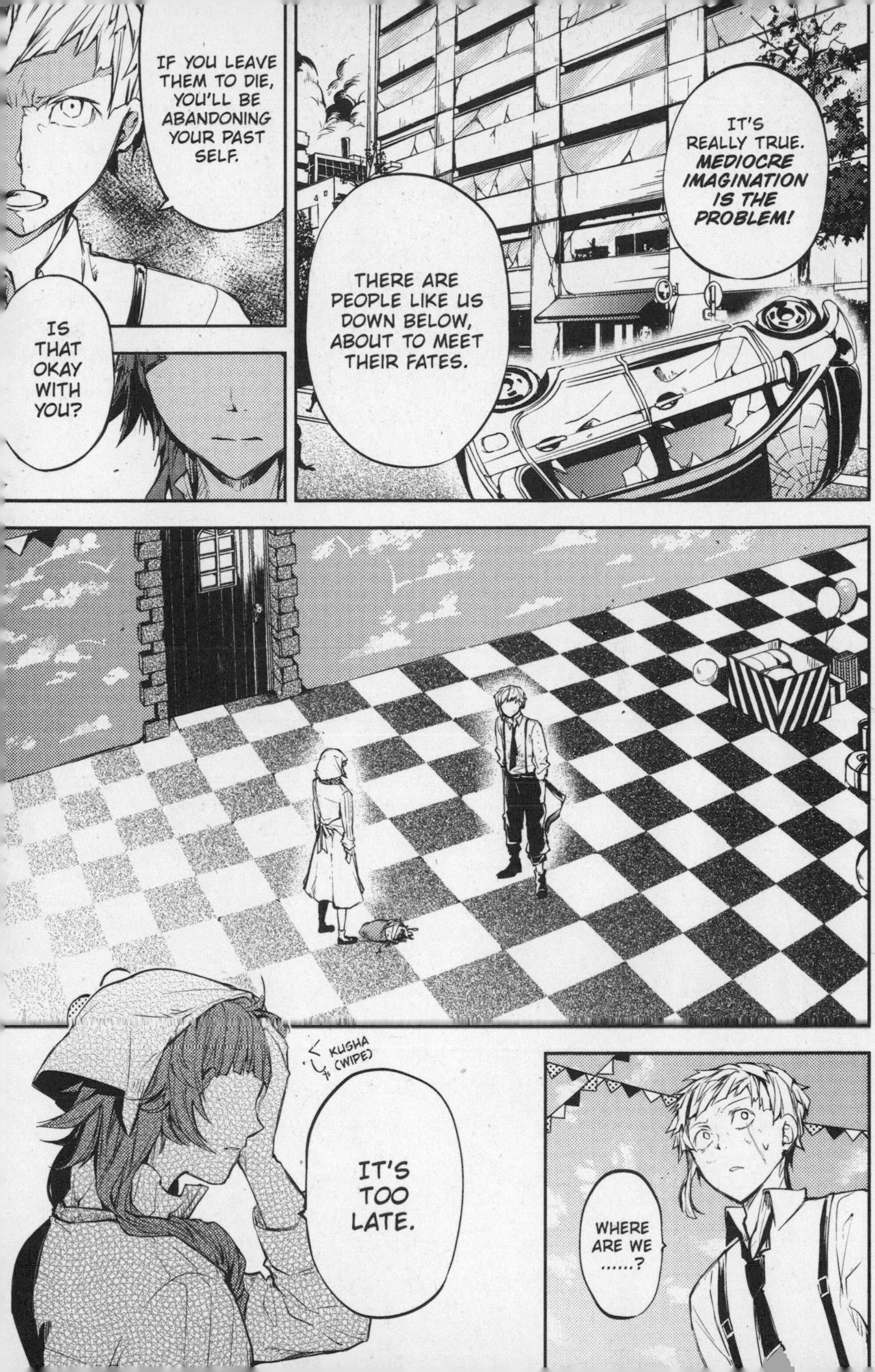
IT'S REALLY TRUE. MEDIOCRE IMAGINATION IS THE PROBLEM!
THERE ARE PEOPLE LIKE US DOWN BELOW, ABOUT TO MEET THEIR FATES.
IF YOU LEAVE THEM TO DIE, YOU'LL BE ABANDONING YOUR PAST SELF.
IS THAT OKAY WITH YOU?
WHERE ARE WE ......?
KUSHA (WIPE)
IT'S TOO LATE.

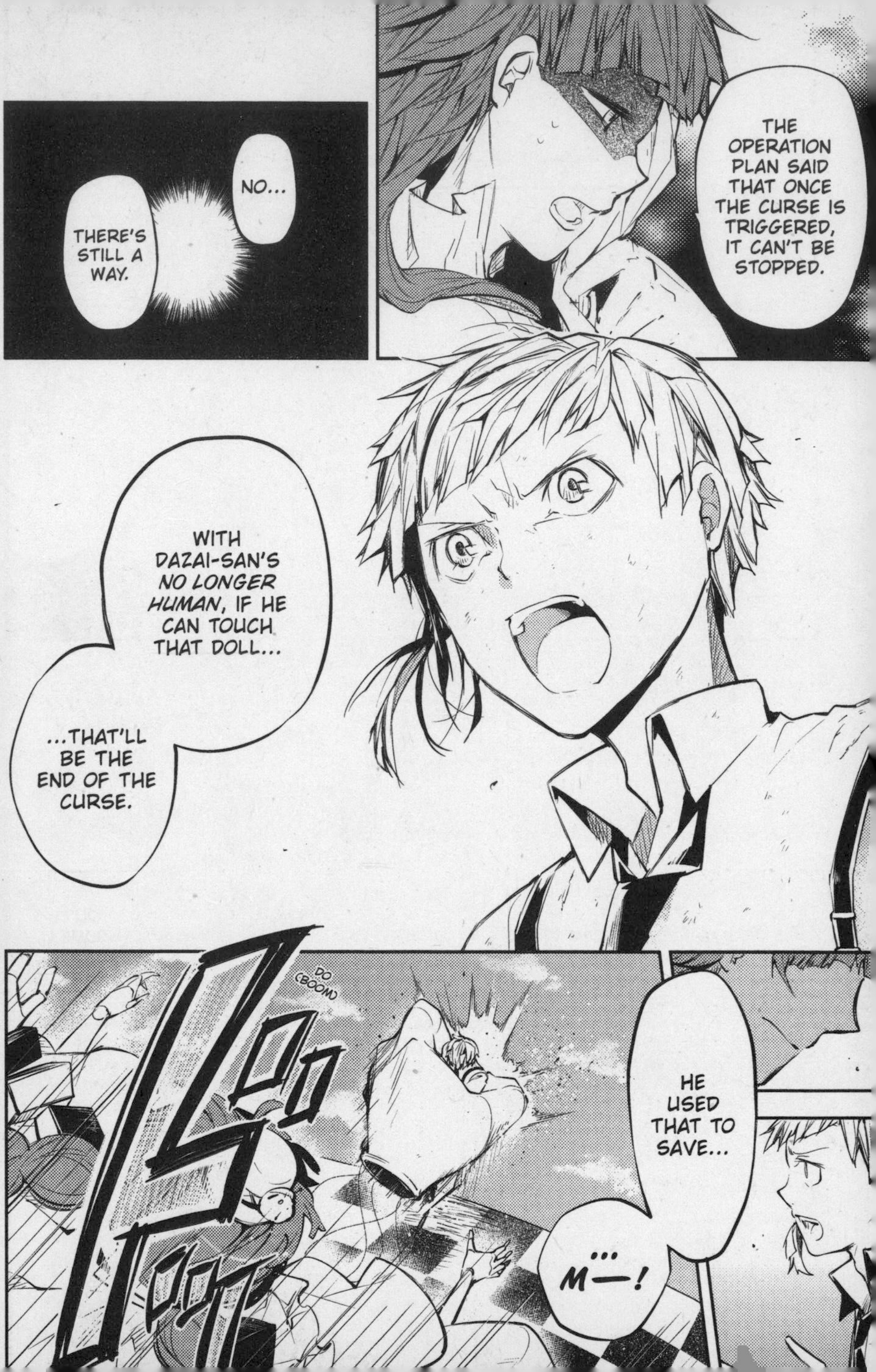
THE OPERATION PLAN SAID THAT ONCE THE CURSE IS TRIGGERED, IT CAN'T BE STOPPED.
NO...
THERE'S STILL A WAY.
WITH DAZAI-SAN'S *NO LONGER HUMAN*, IF HE CAN TOUCH THAT DOLL...
...THAT'LL BE THE END OF THE CURSE.
HE USED THAT TO SAVE...
...M—!
DO (BOOM)

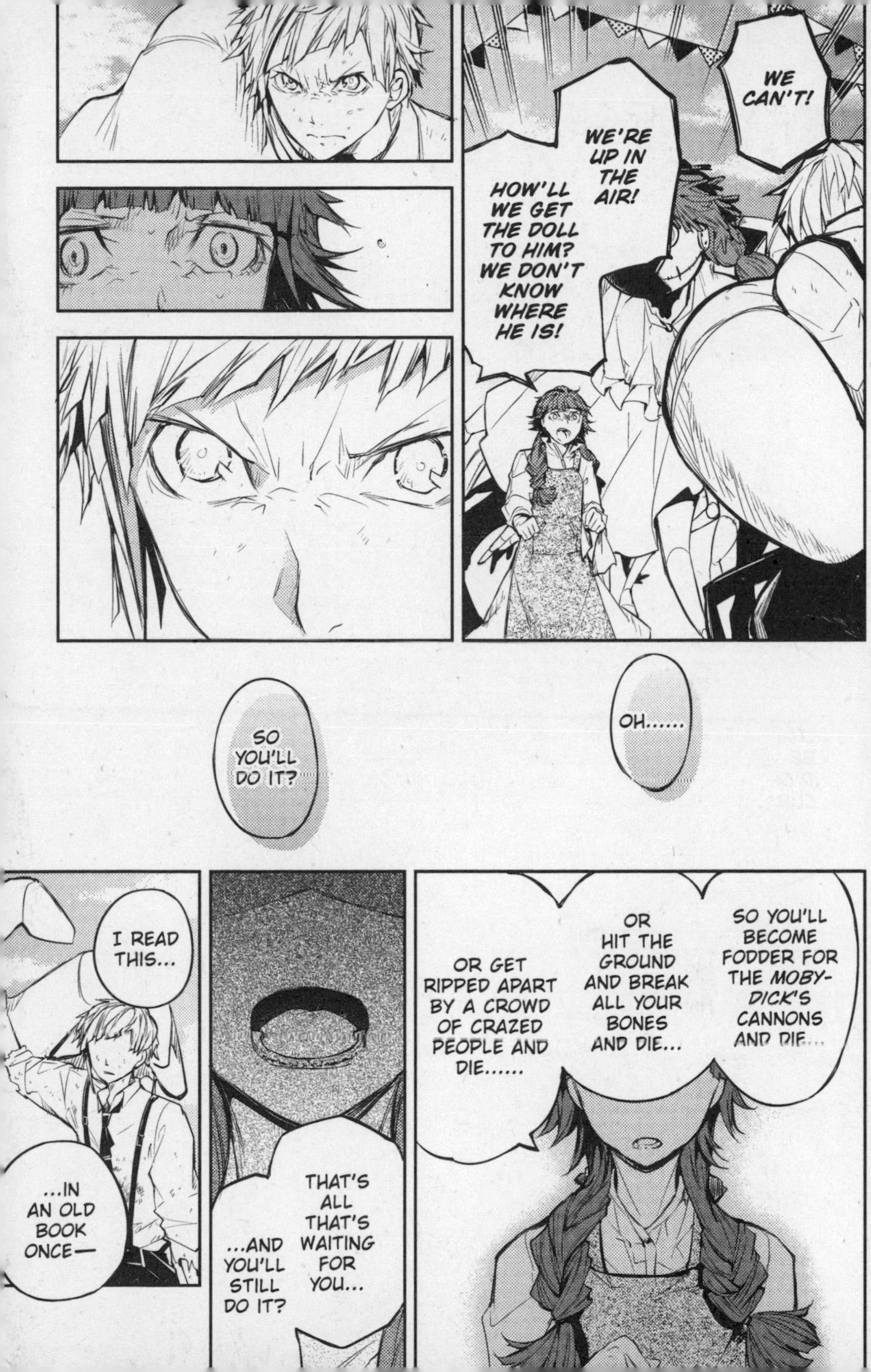
WE CAN'T!
WE'RE UP IN THE AIR!
HOW'LL WE GET THE DOLL TO HIM? WE DON'T KNOW WHERE HE IS!
OH......
SO YOU'LL DO IT?
SO YOU'LL BECOME FODDER FOR THE *MOBY-DICK*'S CANNONS AND DIE...
OR HIT THE GROUND AND BREAK ALL YOUR BONES AND DIE...
OR GET RIPPED APART BY A CROWD OF CRAZED PEOPLE AND DIE......
THAT'S ALL THAT'S WAITING FOR YOU...
...AND YOU'LL STILL DO IT?
I READ THIS...
...IN AN OLD BOOK ONCE—

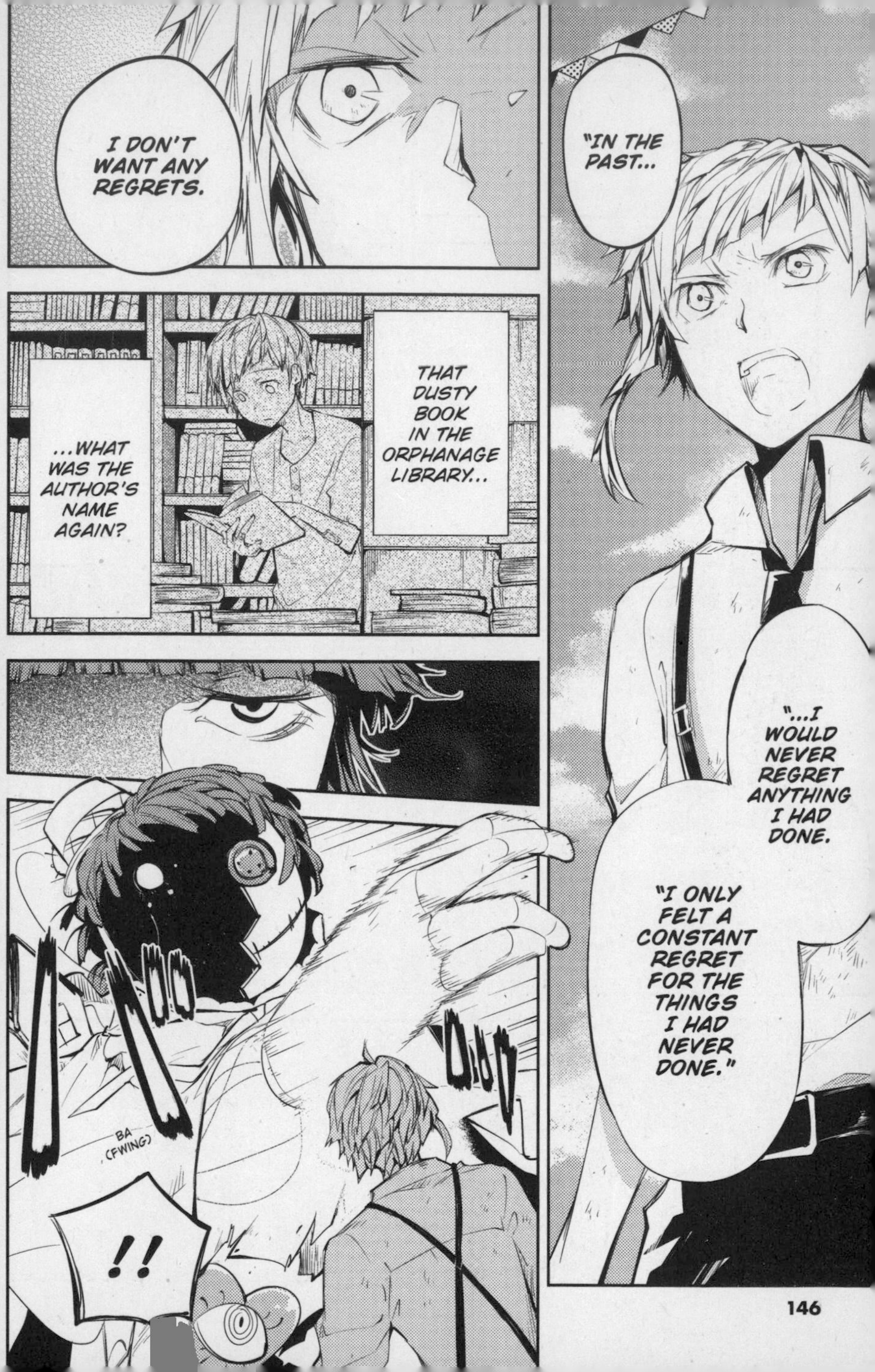
"IN THE PAST...
"...I WOULD NEVER REGRET ANYTHING I HAD DONE.
"I ONLY FELT A CONSTANT REGRET FOR THE THINGS I HAD NEVER DONE."
I DON'T WANT ANY REGRETS.
THAT DUSTY BOOK IN THE ORPHANAGE LIBRARY...
...WHAT WAS THE AUTHOR'S NAME AGAIN?
BA (FWING)
!!

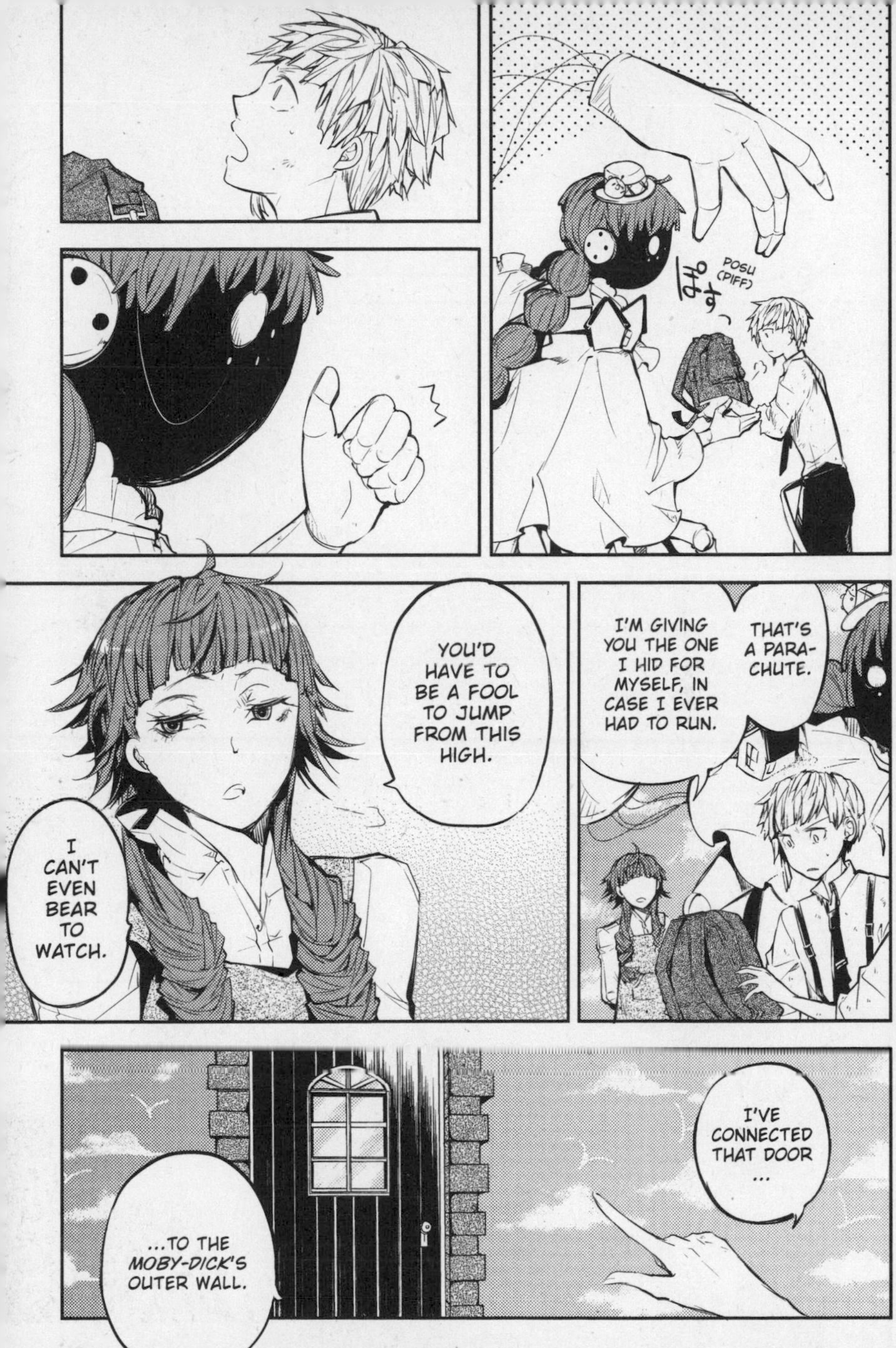
ぽす
POSU (PIFF)
THAT'S A PARA-CHUTE.
I'M GIVING YOU THE ONE I HID FOR MYSELF, IN CASE I EVER HAD TO RUN.
YOU'D HAVE TO BE A FOOL TO JUMP FROM THIS HIGH.
I CAN'T EVEN BEAR TO WATCH.
I'VE CONNECTED THAT DOOR ...
...TO THE *MOBY-DICK*'S OUTER WALL.

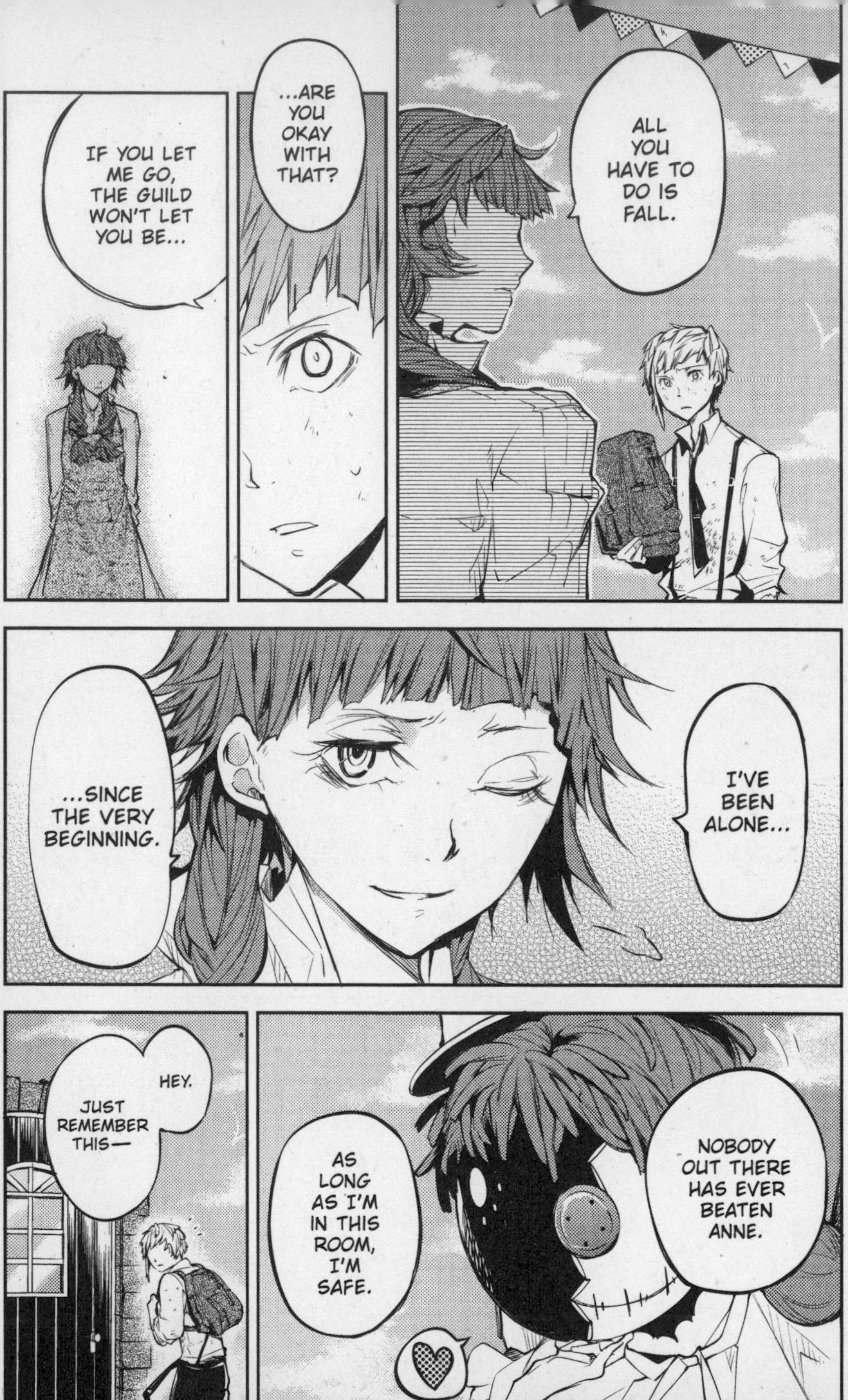
ALL YOU HAVE TO DO IS FALL.
...ARE YOU OKAY WITH THAT?
IF YOU LET ME GO, THE GUILD WON'T LET YOU BE...
I'VE BEEN ALONE...
...SINCE THE VERY BEGINNING.
NOBODY OUT THERE HAS EVER BEATEN ANNE.
AS LONG AS I'M IN THIS ROOM, I'M SAFE.
HEY.
JUST REMEMBER THIS—

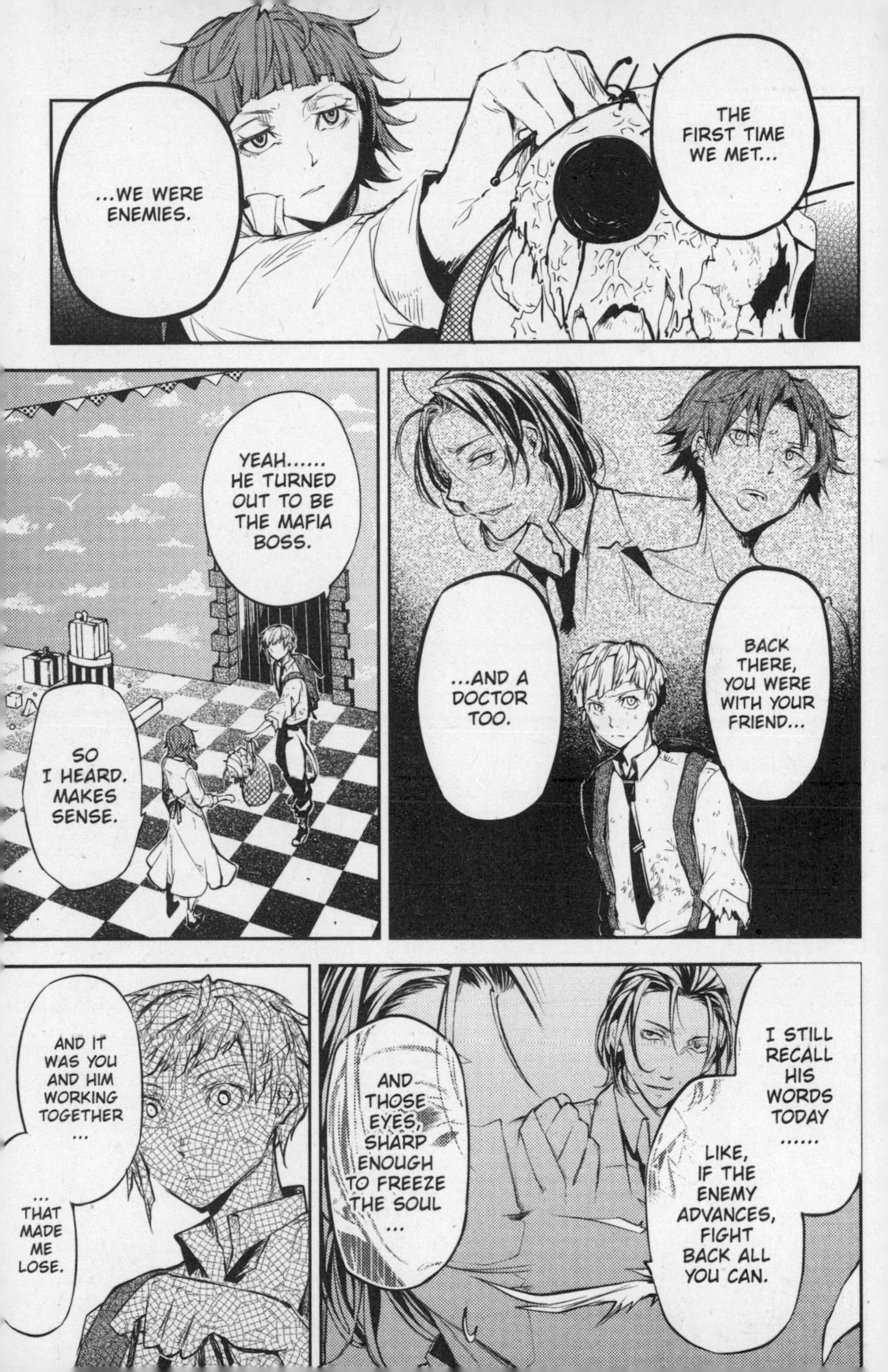
THE FIRST TIME WE MET...
...WE WERE ENEMIES.
BACK THERE, YOU WERE WITH YOUR FRIEND...
...AND A DOCTOR TOO.
YEAH...... HE TURNED OUT TO BE THE MAFIA BOSS.
SO I HEARD. MAKES SENSE.
I STILL RECALL HIS WORDS TODAY ......
LIKE, IF THE ENEMY ADVANCES, FIGHT BACK ALL YOU CAN.
AND THOSE EYES, SHARP ENOUGH TO FREEZE THE SOUL ...
AND IT WAS YOU AND HIM WORKING TOGETHER ...
... THAT MADE ME LOSE.

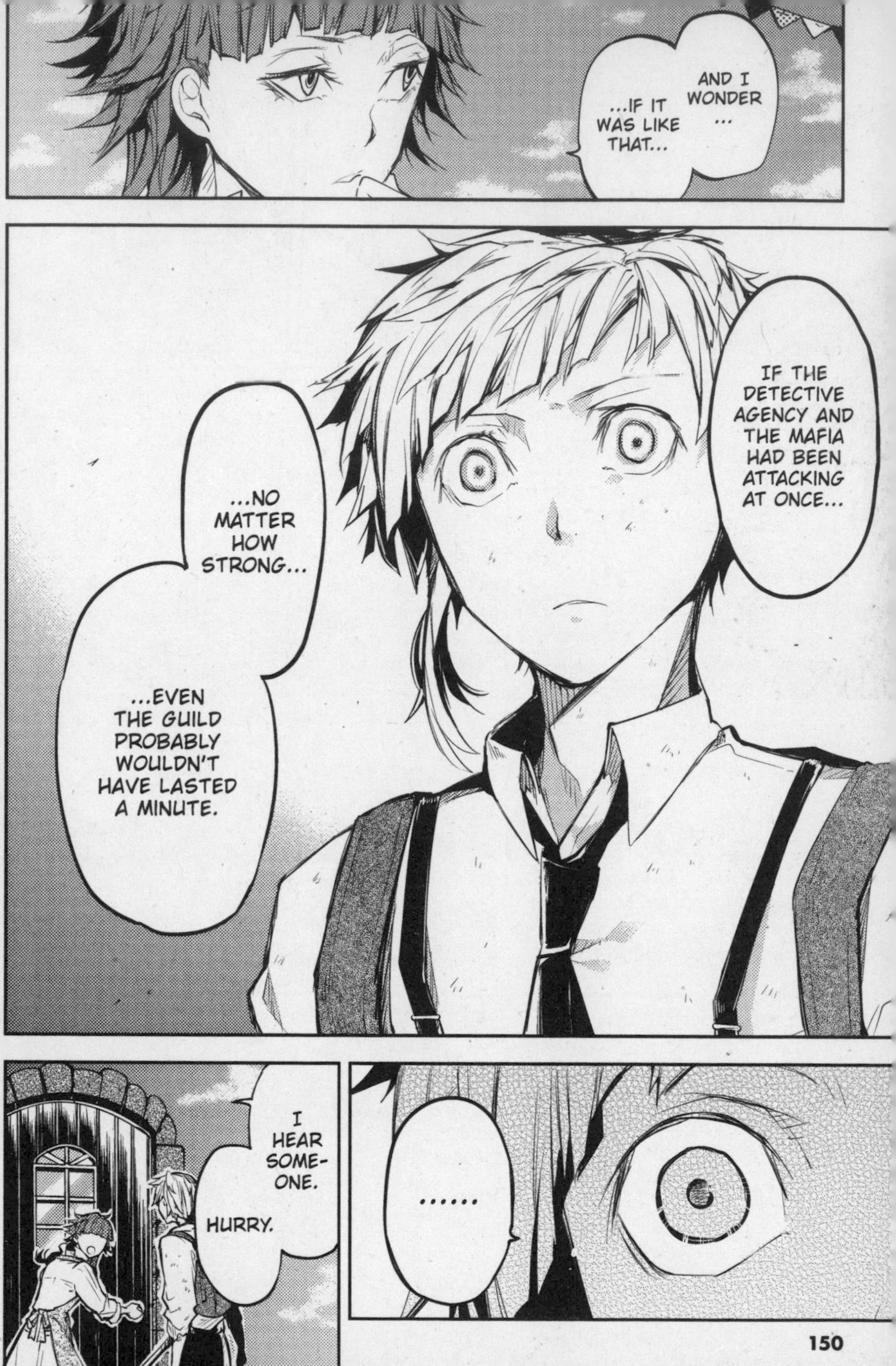

AND I WONDER...
...IF IT WAS LIKE THAT...
IF THE DETECTIVE AGENCY AND THE MAFIA HAD BEEN ATTACKING AT ONCE...
...NO MATTER HOW STRONG...
...EVEN THE GUILD PROBABLY WOULDN'T HAVE LASTED A MINUTE.
......
I HEAR SOME-ONE.
HURRY.

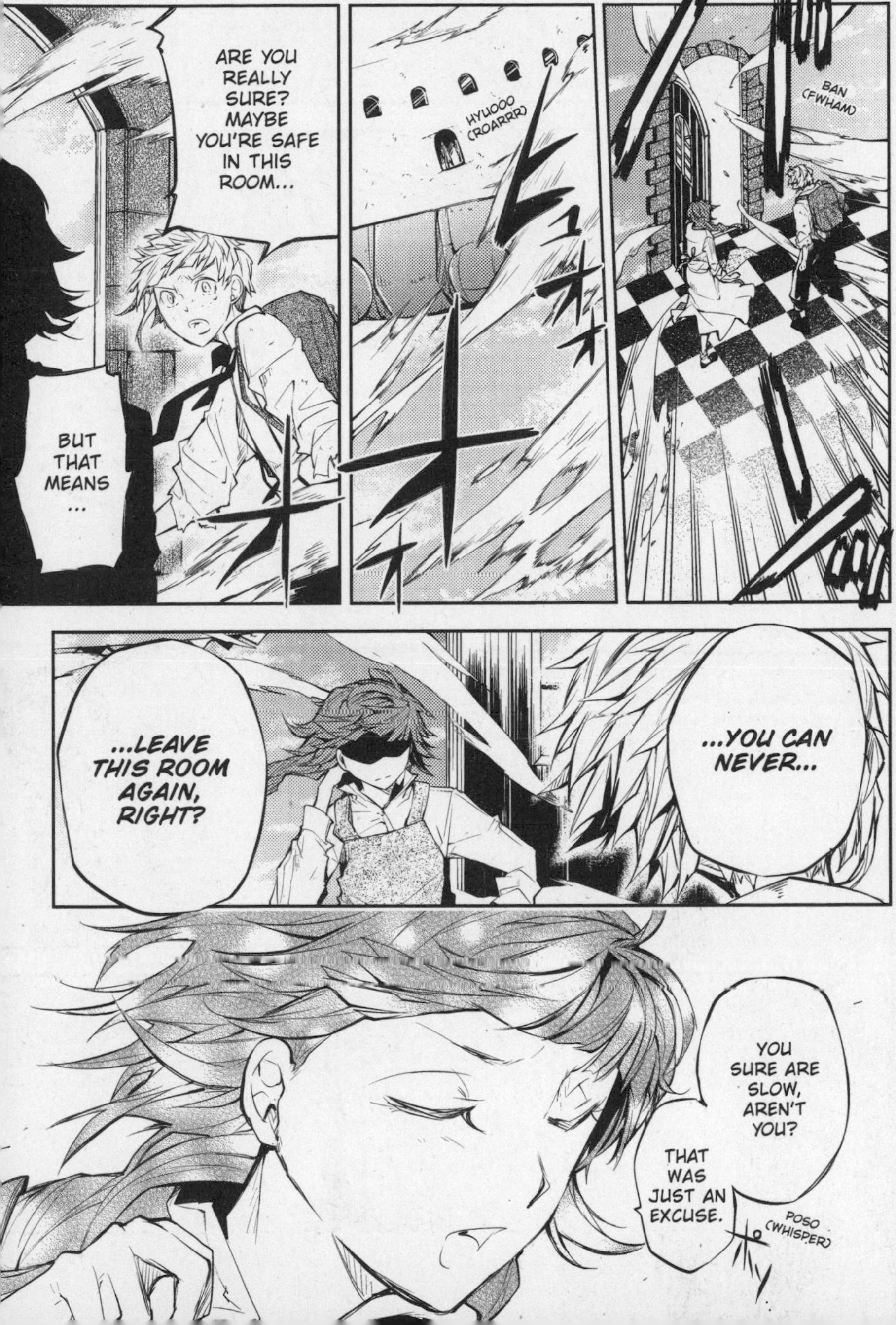
BAN
(FWHAM)
HYUOOO
(ROARRR)
ARE YOU REALLY SURE? MAYBE YOU'RE SAFE IN THIS ROOM...
BUT THAT MEANS...
...YOU CAN NEVER...
...LEAVE THIS ROOM AGAIN, RIGHT?
YOU SURE ARE SLOW, AREN'T YOU?
THAT WAS JUST AN EXCUSE.
POSO
(WHISPER)

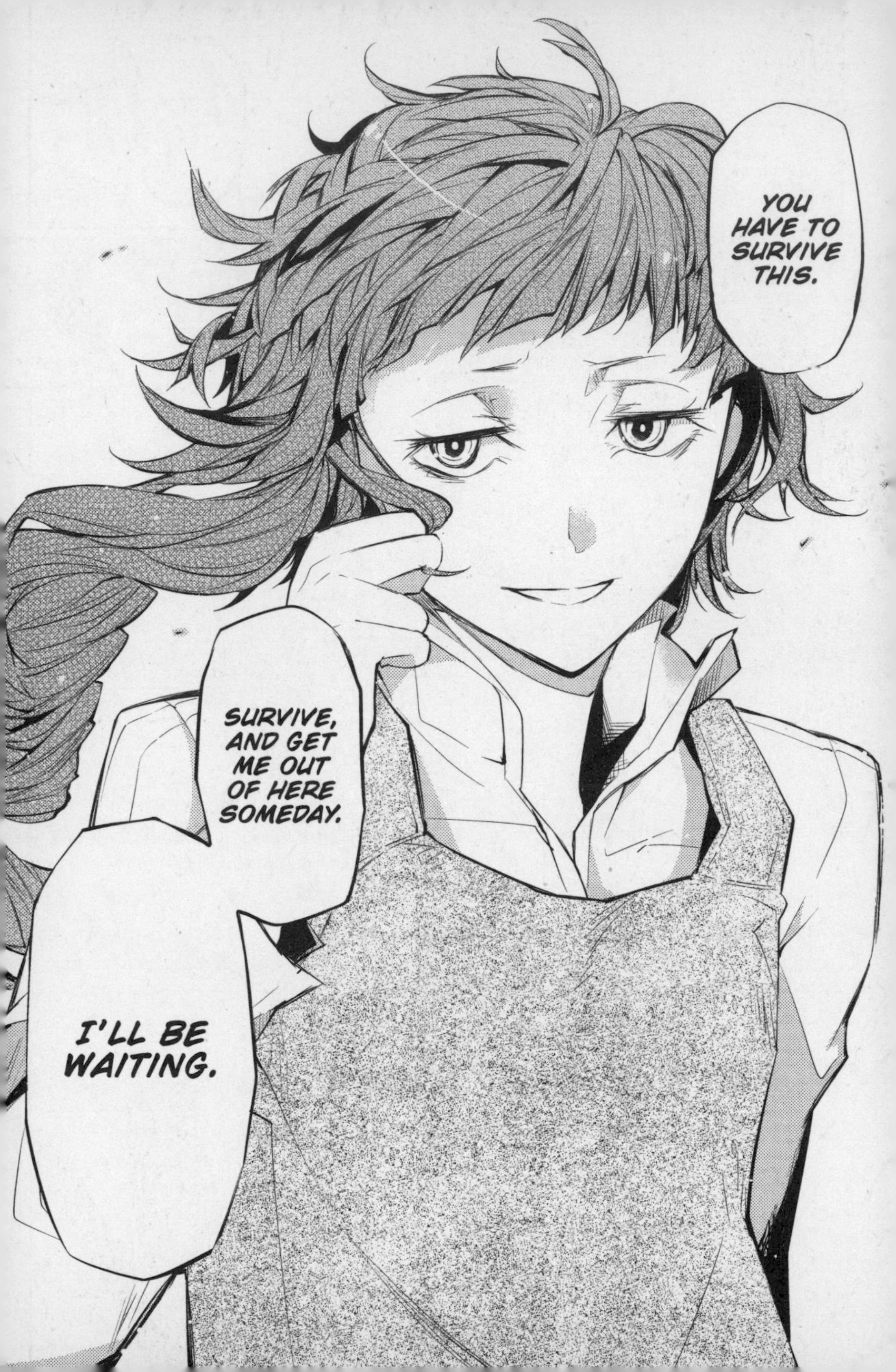
YOU HAVE TO SURVIVE THIS.
SURVIVE, AND GET ME OUT OF HERE SOMEDAY.
I'LL BE WAITING.

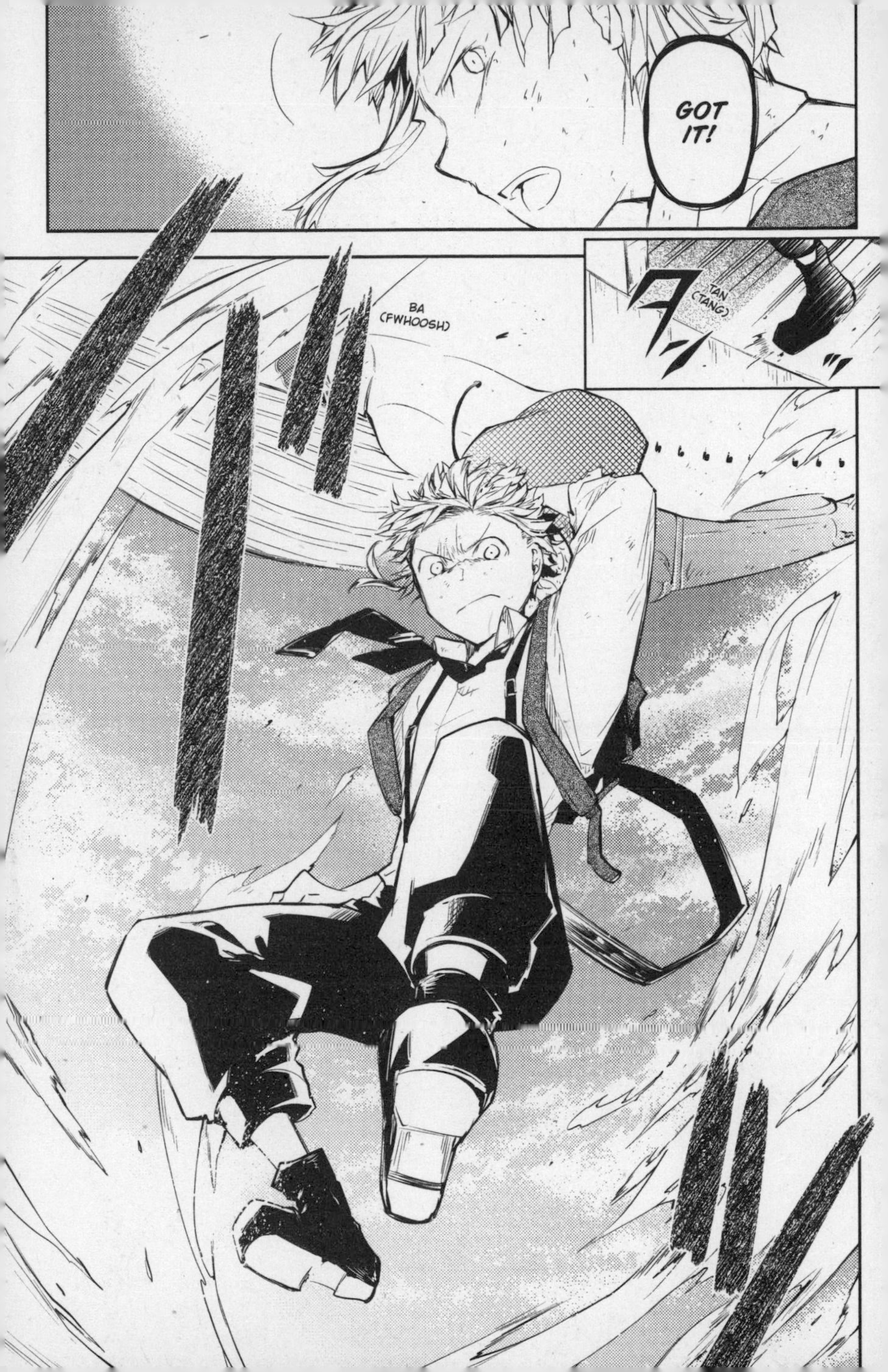
GOT IT!
TAN (TANG)
BA (FWHOOSH)

# JOHN STEINBECK

**SKILL: The Grapes of Wrath**
*Able to grow grape vines that can be grafted to other trees, sharing their senses with the host. He can also graft vines to himself to control the branches and roots of trees.*

AGE: *21*

BIRTH DATE: *February 27*

HEIGHT: *175m*

WEIGHT: *64kg*

BLOOD TYPE: *A*

LIKES: *Family, grapes, farming, the Bible*

DISLIKES: *Solitude, poverty, financiers*

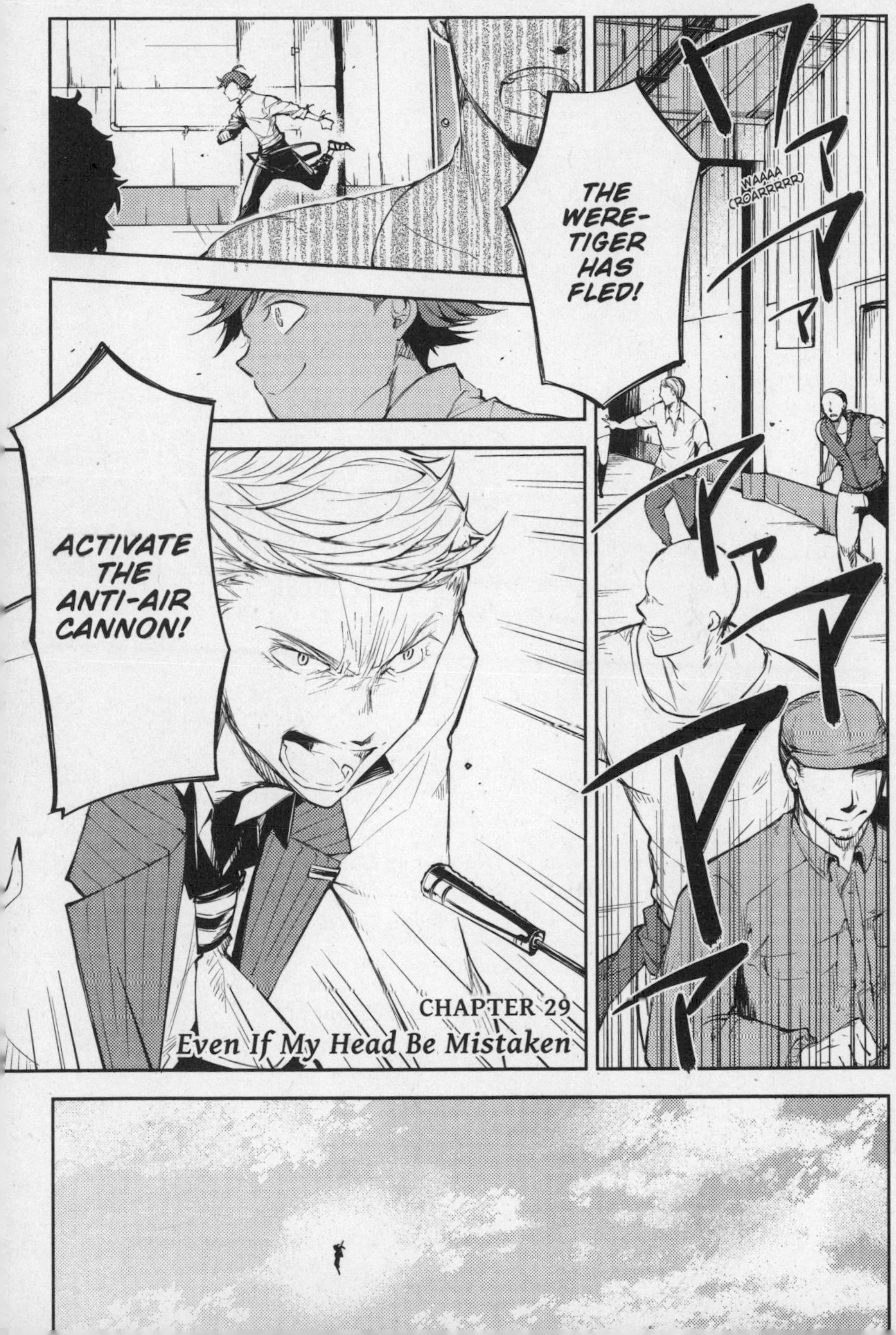
WAAAA (ROARRRRR)
THE WERE-TIGER HAS FLED!
ACTIVATE THE ANTI-AIR CANNON!
CHAPTER 29
Even If My Head Be Mistaken

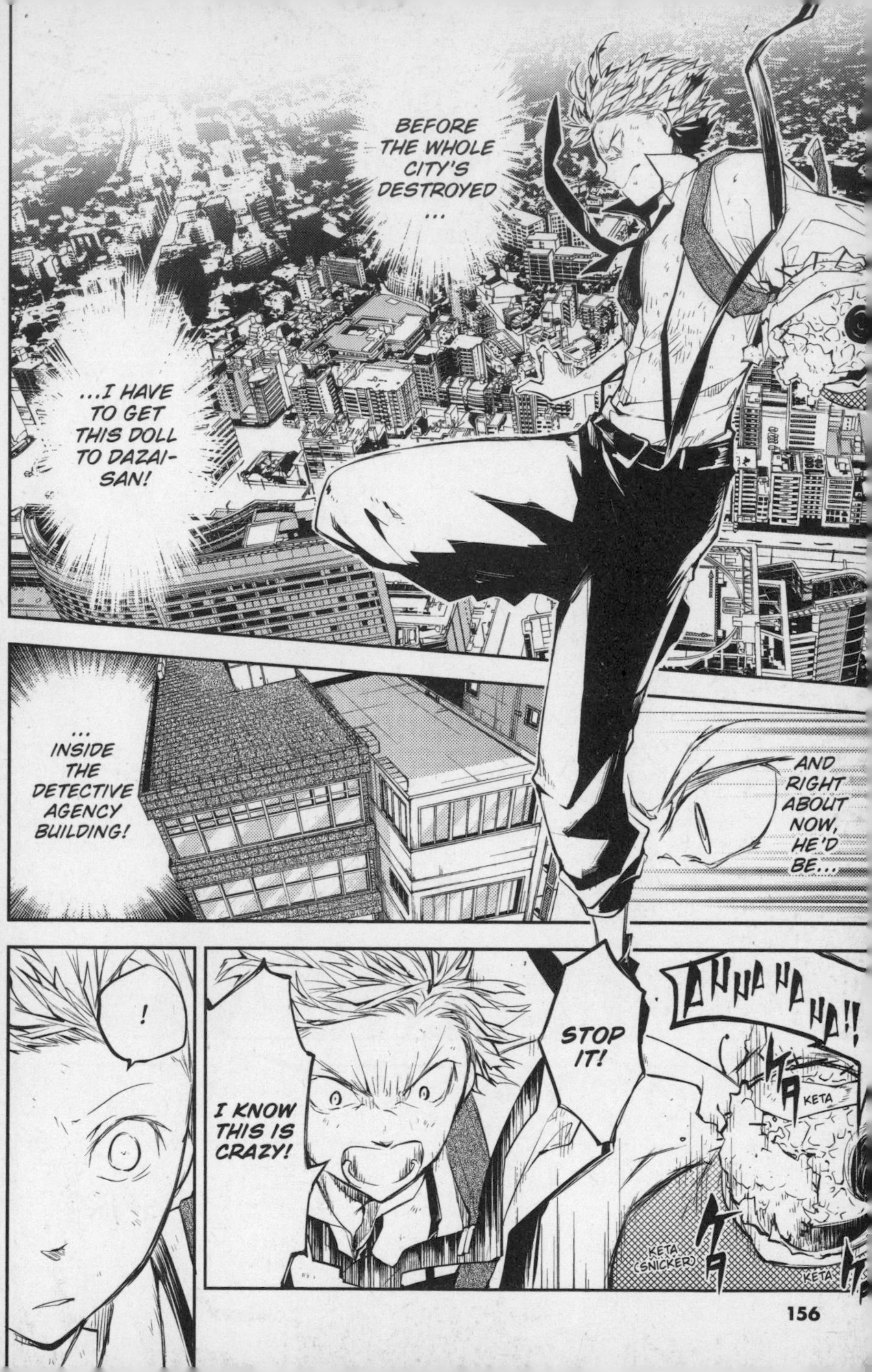
BEFORE THE WHOLE CITY'S DESTROYED...
...I HAVE TO GET THIS DOLL TO DAZAI-SAN!
AND RIGHT ABOUT NOW, HE'D BE...
...INSIDE THE DETECTIVE AGENCY BUILDING!
KETA
KETA (SNICKER)
KETA
STOP IT!
I KNOW THIS IS CRAZY!
!

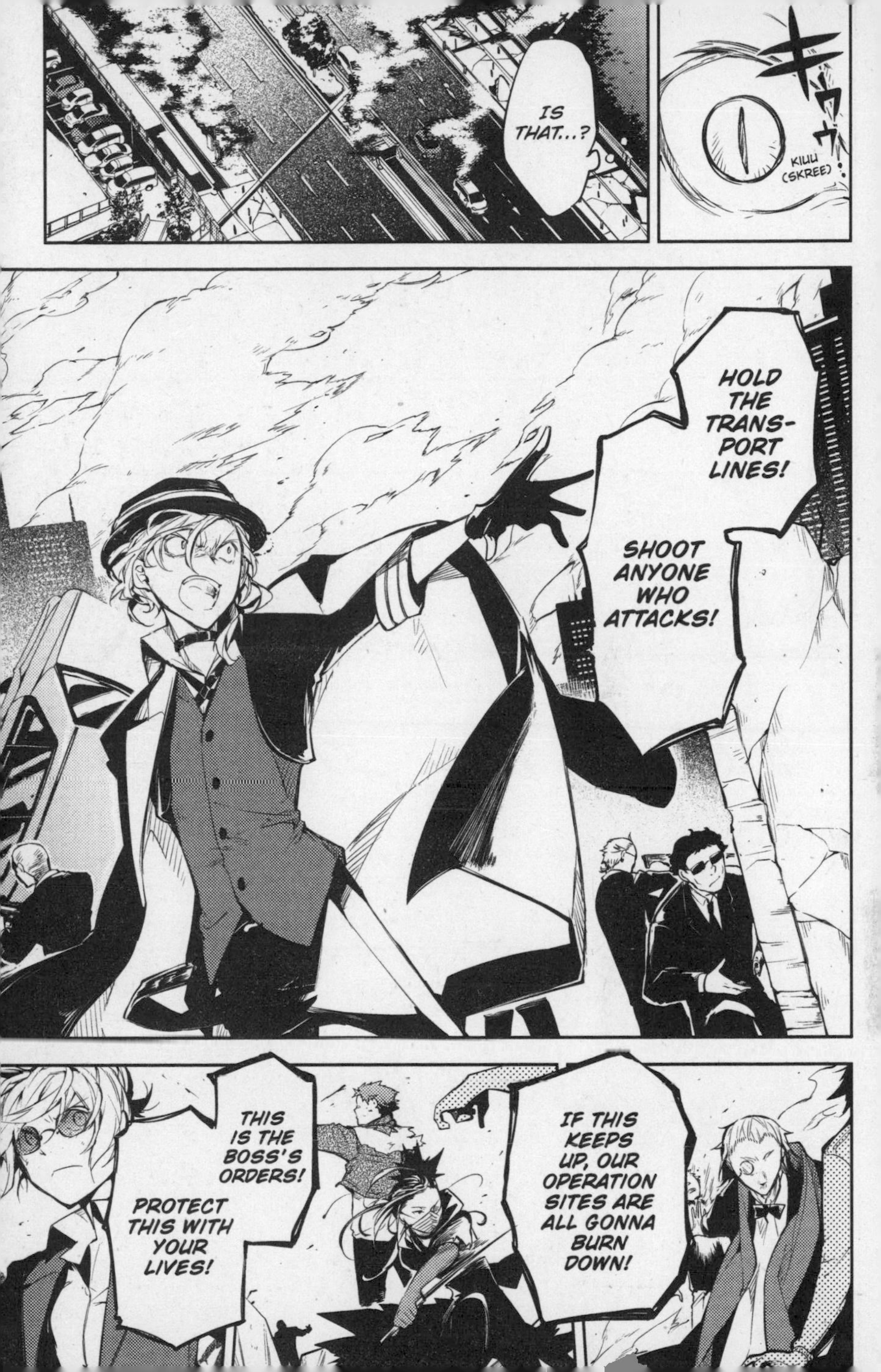
KIUU (SKREE)
IS THAT...?
HOLD THE TRANS-PORT LINES!
SHOOT ANYONE WHO ATTACKS!
IF THIS KEEPS UP, OUR OPERATION SITES ARE ALL GONNA BURN DOWN!
THIS IS THE BOSS'S ORDERS!
PROTECT THIS WITH YOUR LIVES!

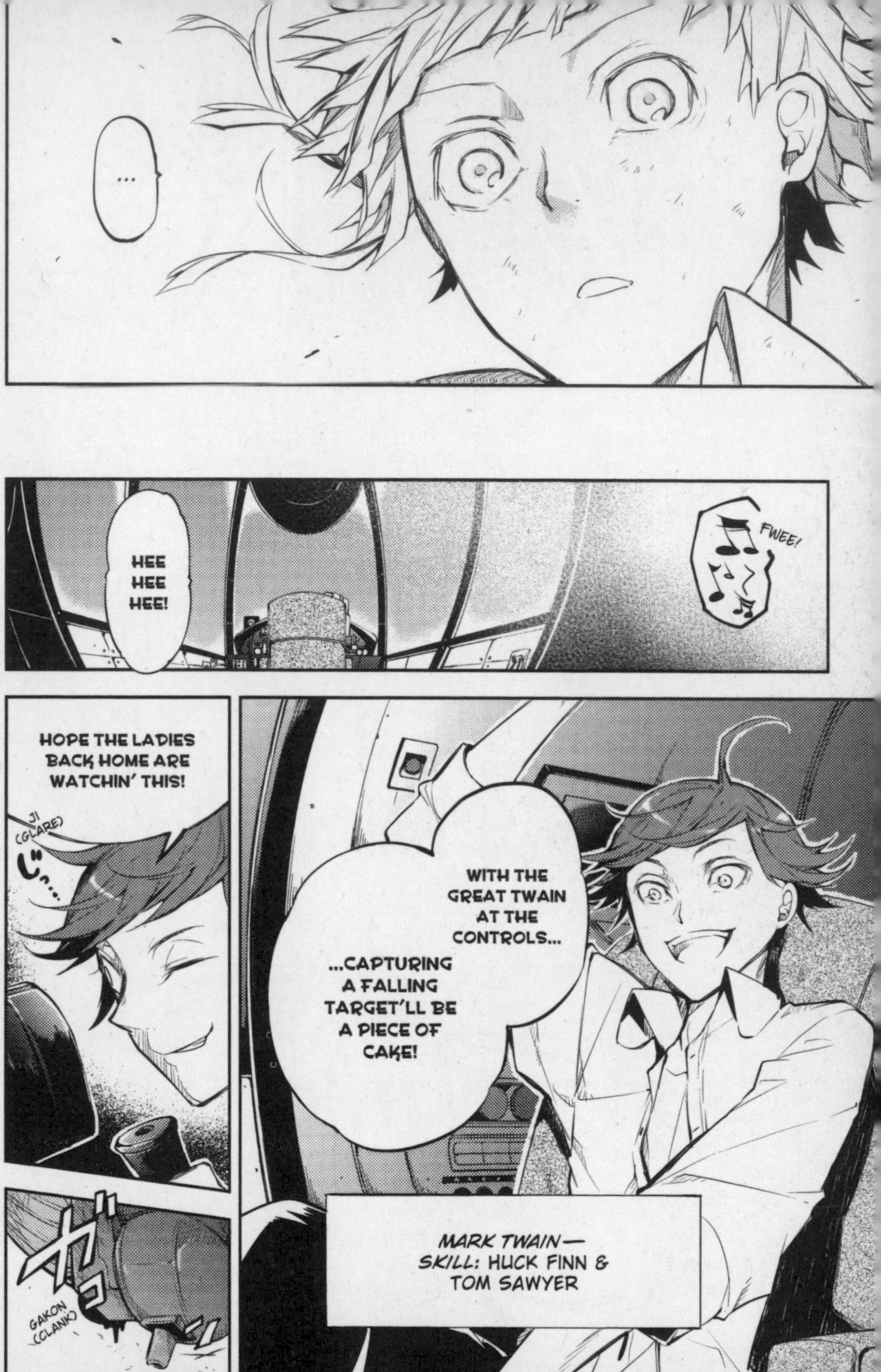
...
FWEE!
HEE HEE HEE!
WITH THE GREAT TWAIN AT THE CONTROLS...
...CAPTURING A FALLING TARGET'LL BE A PIECE OF CAKE!
*MARK TWAIN—*
*SKILL:* HUCK FINN & TOM SAWYER
HOPE THE LADIES BACK HOME ARE WATCHIN' THIS!
JI (GLARE)
GAKON (CLANK)

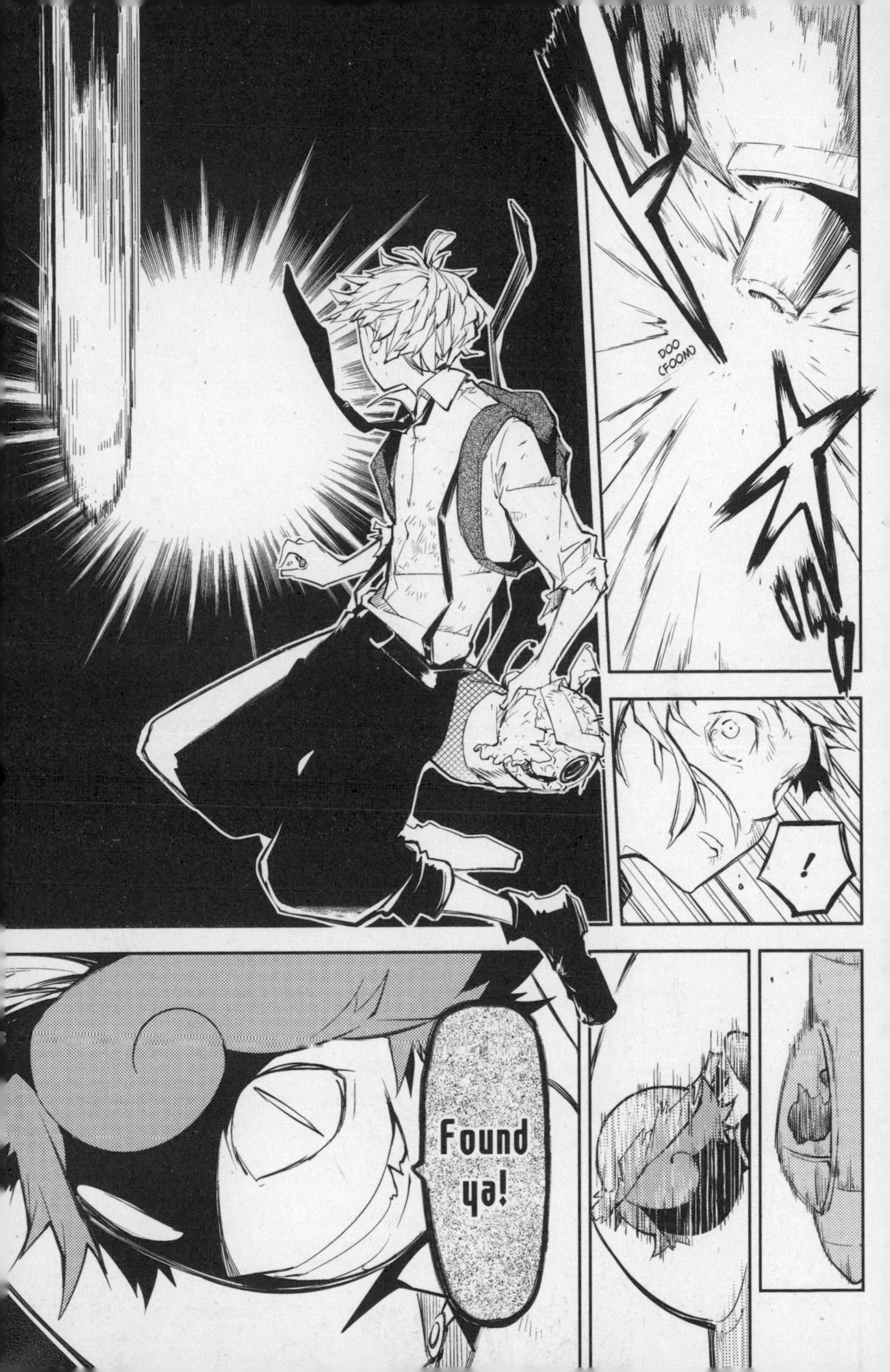
DOO
(FOOM)
!
Found ya!

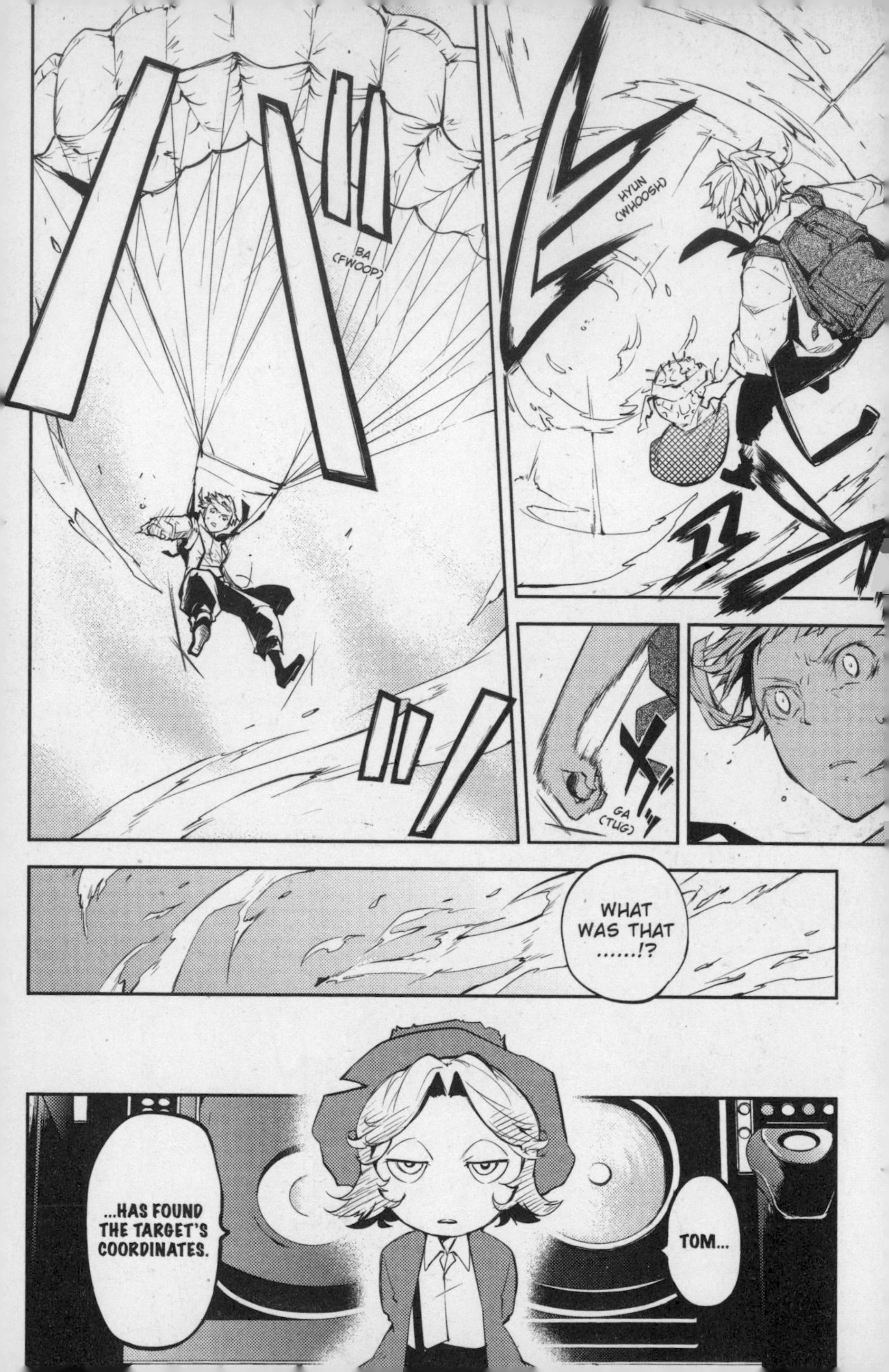
HYUN (WHOOSH)
GA (TUG)
BA (FWOOP)
WHAT WAS THAT ......!?
TOM...
...HAS FOUND THE TARGET'S COORDINATES.

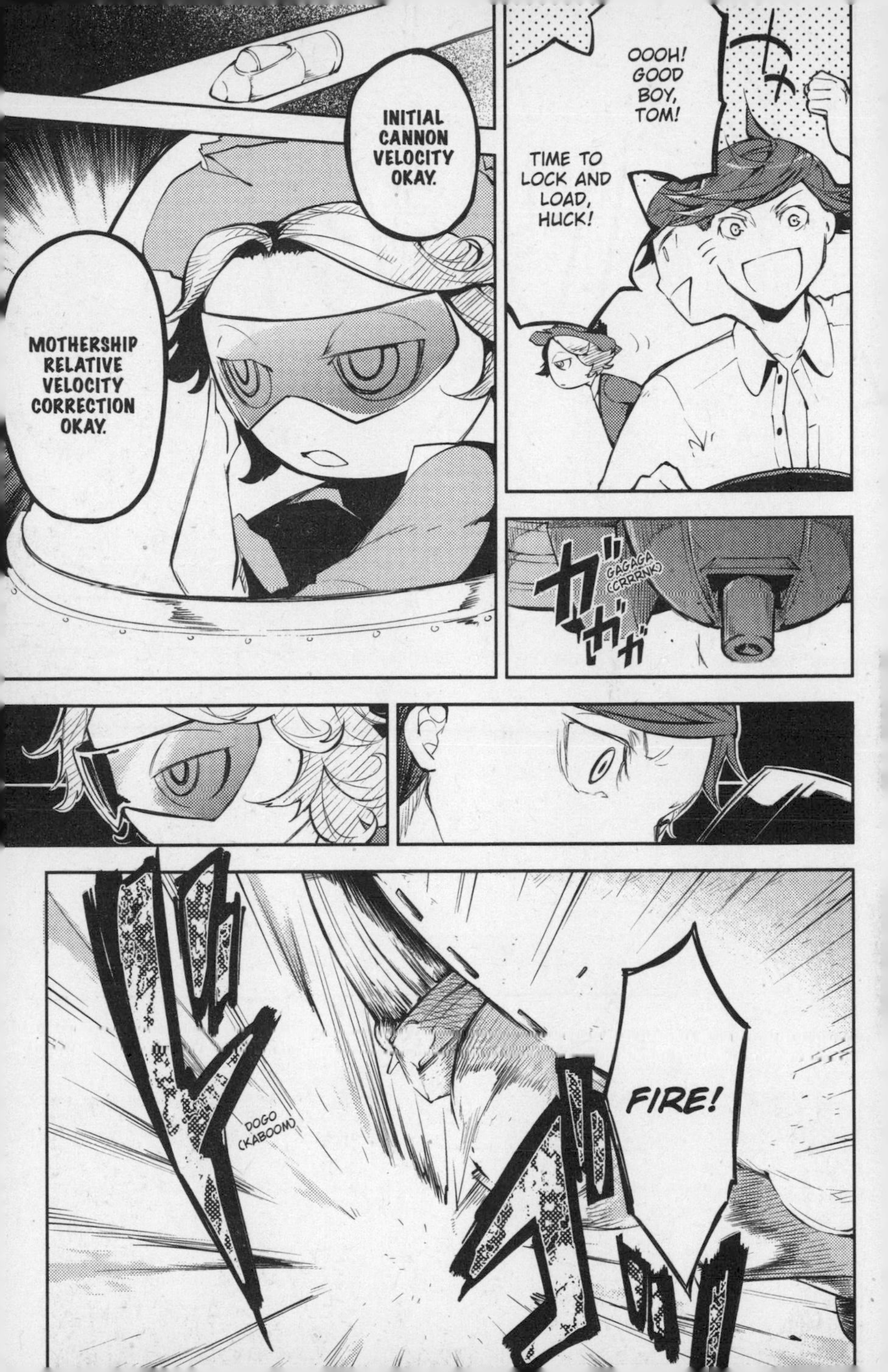
OOOH! GOOD BOY, TOM!
TIME TO LOCK AND LOAD, HUCK!
GAGAGA (CRRRNK)
INITIAL CANNON VELOCITY OKAY.
MOTHERSHIP RELATIVE VELOCITY CORRECTION OKAY.
FIRE!
DOGO (KABOOM)

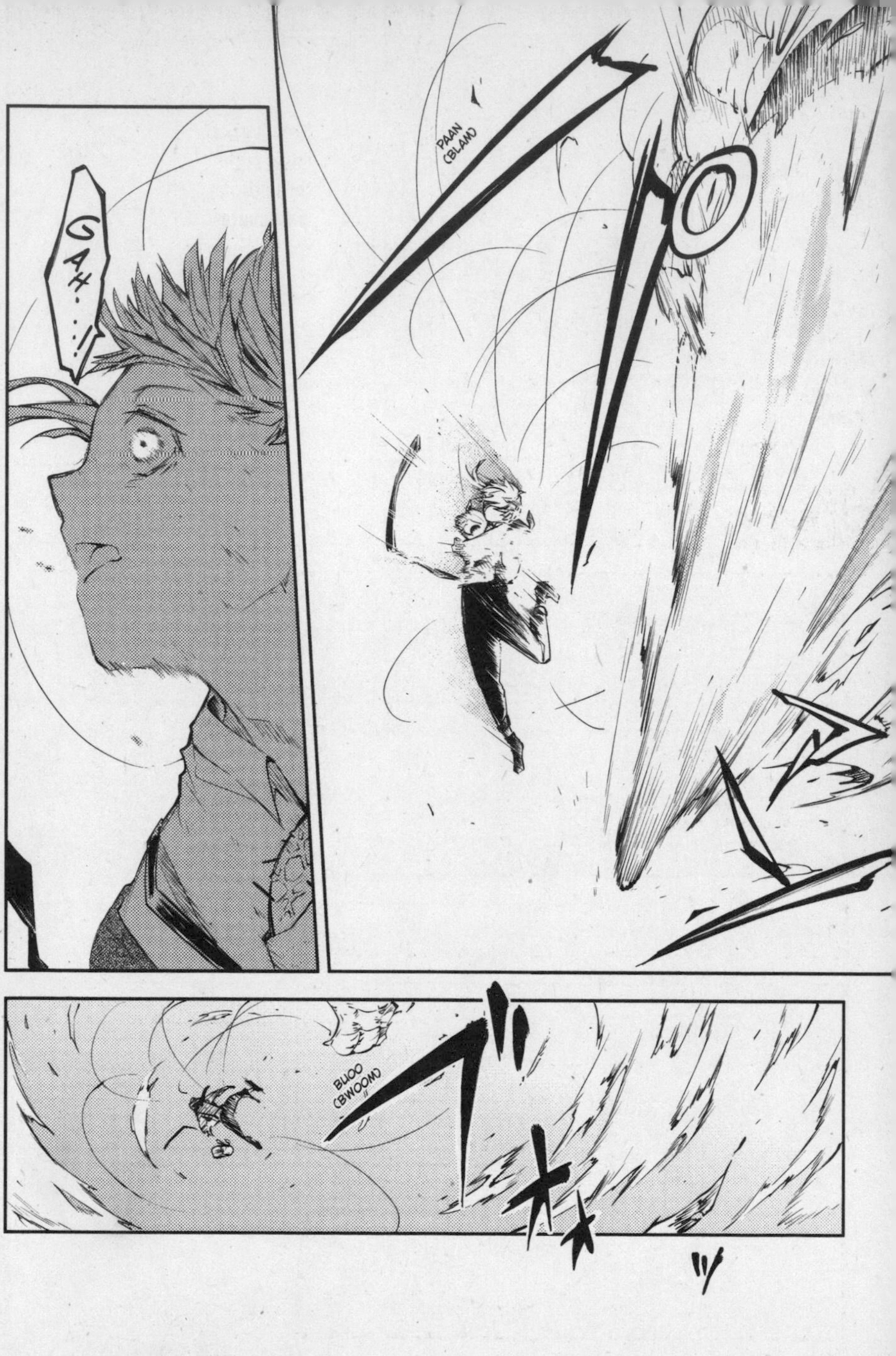
PAAN (BLAM)
GAH...!!
BUOO (BWOOM)!!

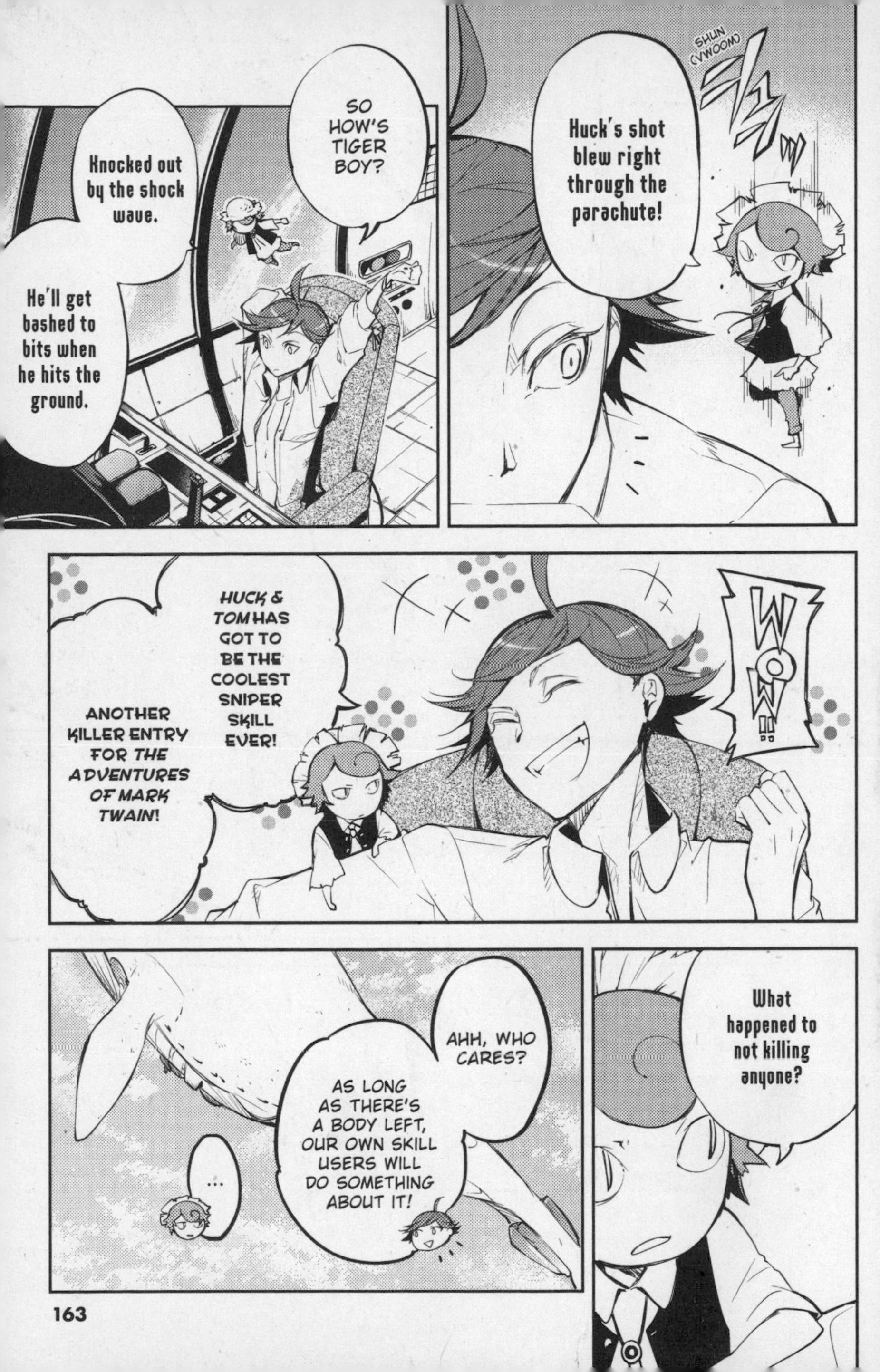
SHUN (VWOOM)
Huck's shot blew right through the parachute!
SO HOW'S TIGER BOY?
Knocked out by the shock wave.
He'll get bashed to bits when he hits the ground.
WOW!!
HUCK & TOM HAS GOT TO BE THE COOLEST SNIPER SKILL EVER!
ANOTHER KILLER ENTRY FOR THE ADVENTURES OF MARK TWAIN!
What happened to not killing anyone?
AHH, WHO CARES?
AS LONG AS THERE'S A BODY LEFT, OUR OWN SKILL USERS WILL DO SOMETHING ABOUT IT!
...

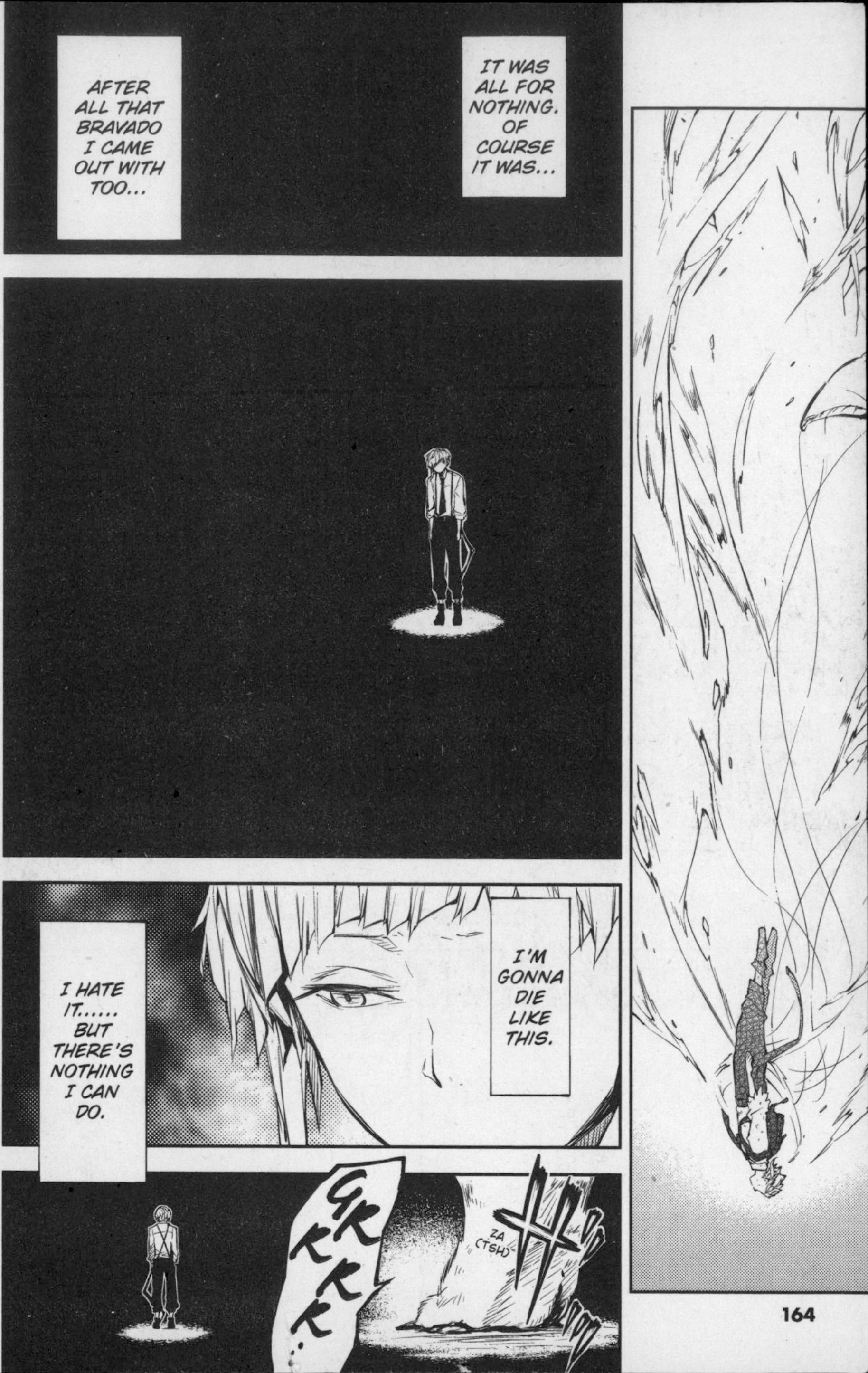
IT WAS ALL FOR NOTHING. OF COURSE IT WAS...
AFTER ALL THAT BRAVADO I CAME OUT WITH TOO...
I'M GONNA DIE LIKE THIS.
I HATE IT...... BUT THERE'S NOTHING I CAN DO.
ZA (TSH)
GRKRKK...

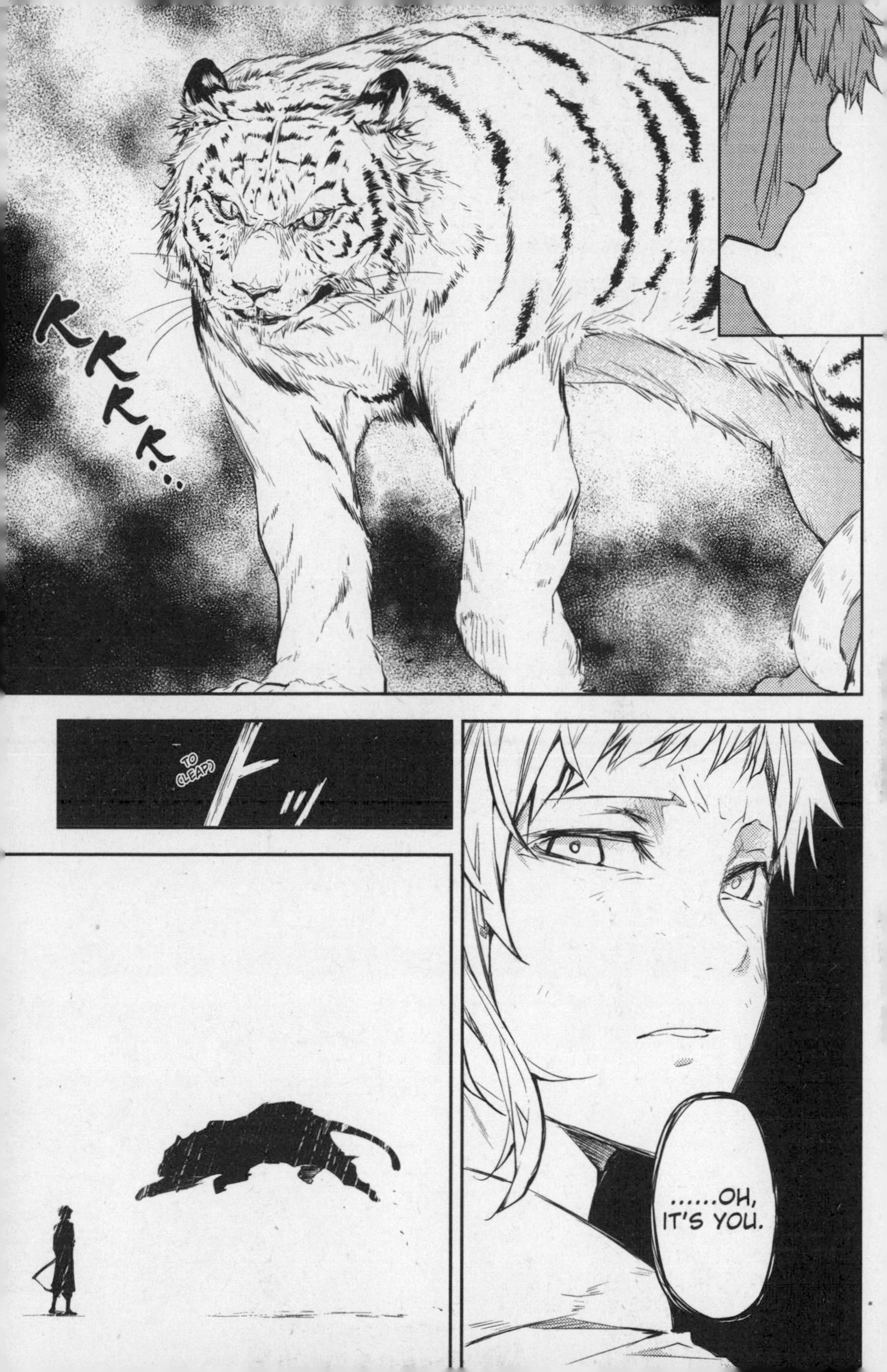
KRRRR..
TO (LEAP)
......OH, IT'S YOU.

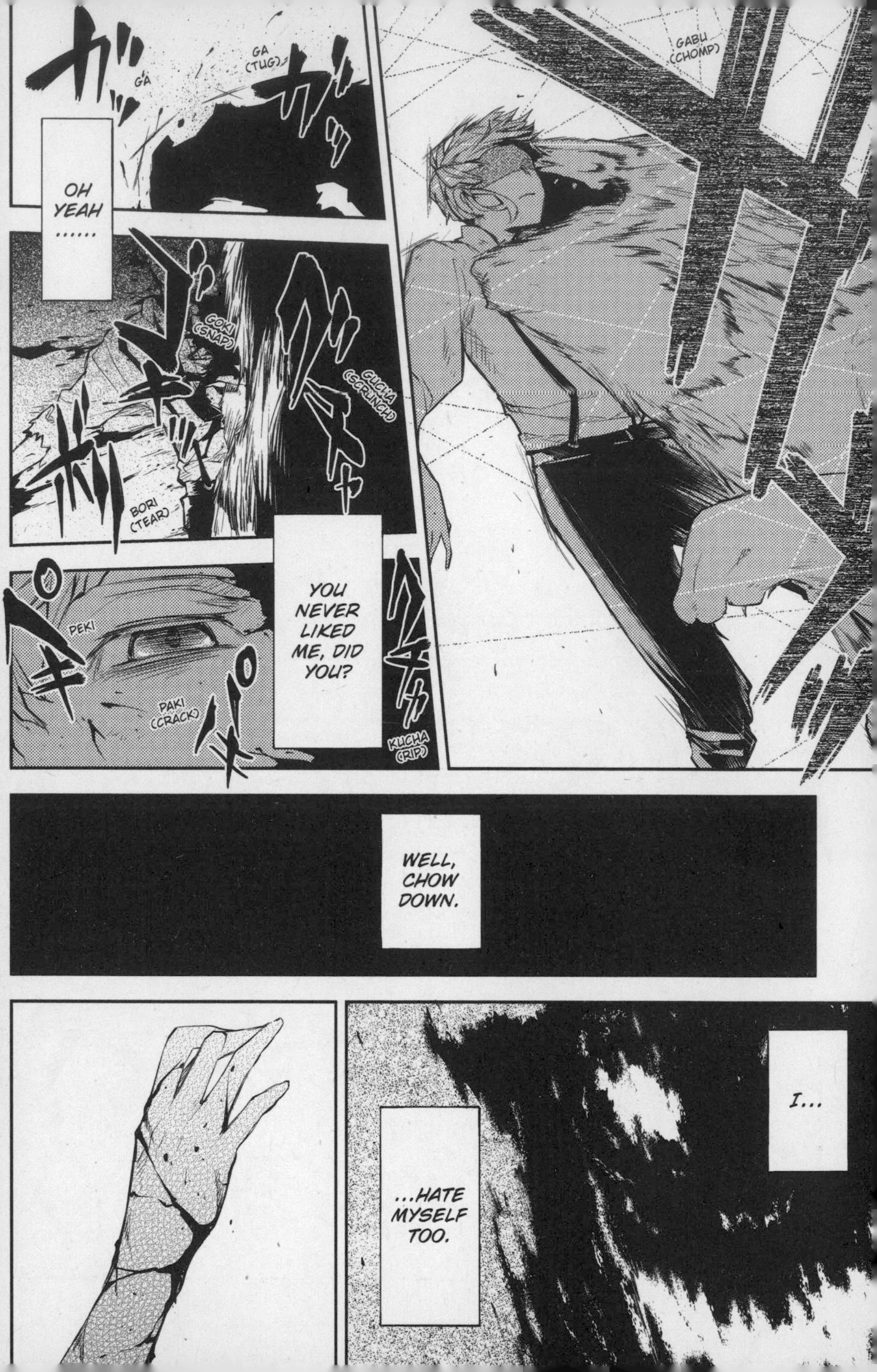
GABU (CHOMP)
GA (TUG)
GA
OH YEAH ......
GUCHA (SCRUNCH)
GOKI (SNAP)
BORI (TEAR)
KUCHA (RIP)
YOU NEVER LIKED ME, DID YOU?
PEKI
PAKI (CRACK)
WELL, CHOW DOWN.
I...
...HATE MYSELF TOO.

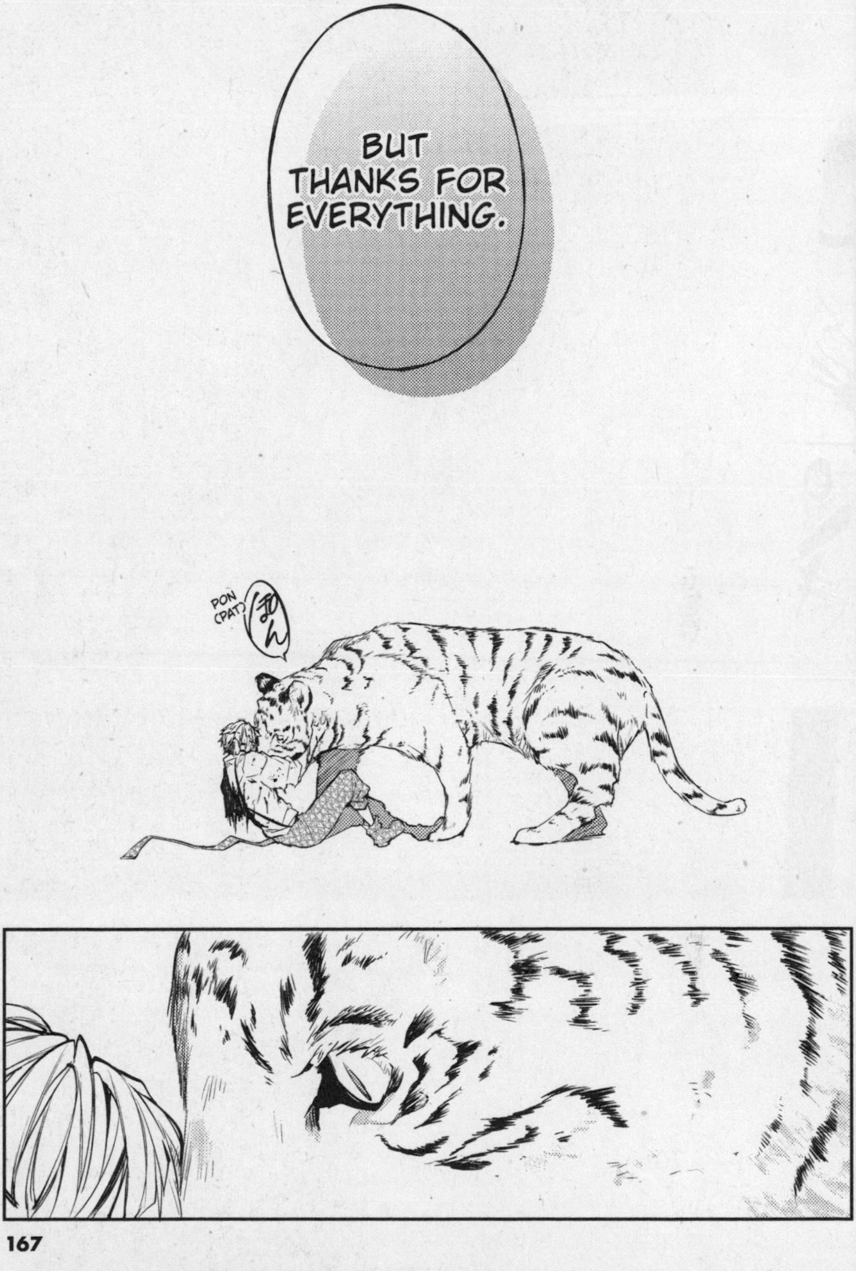
BUT THANKS FOR EVERYTHING.
ぽん
PON (PAT)

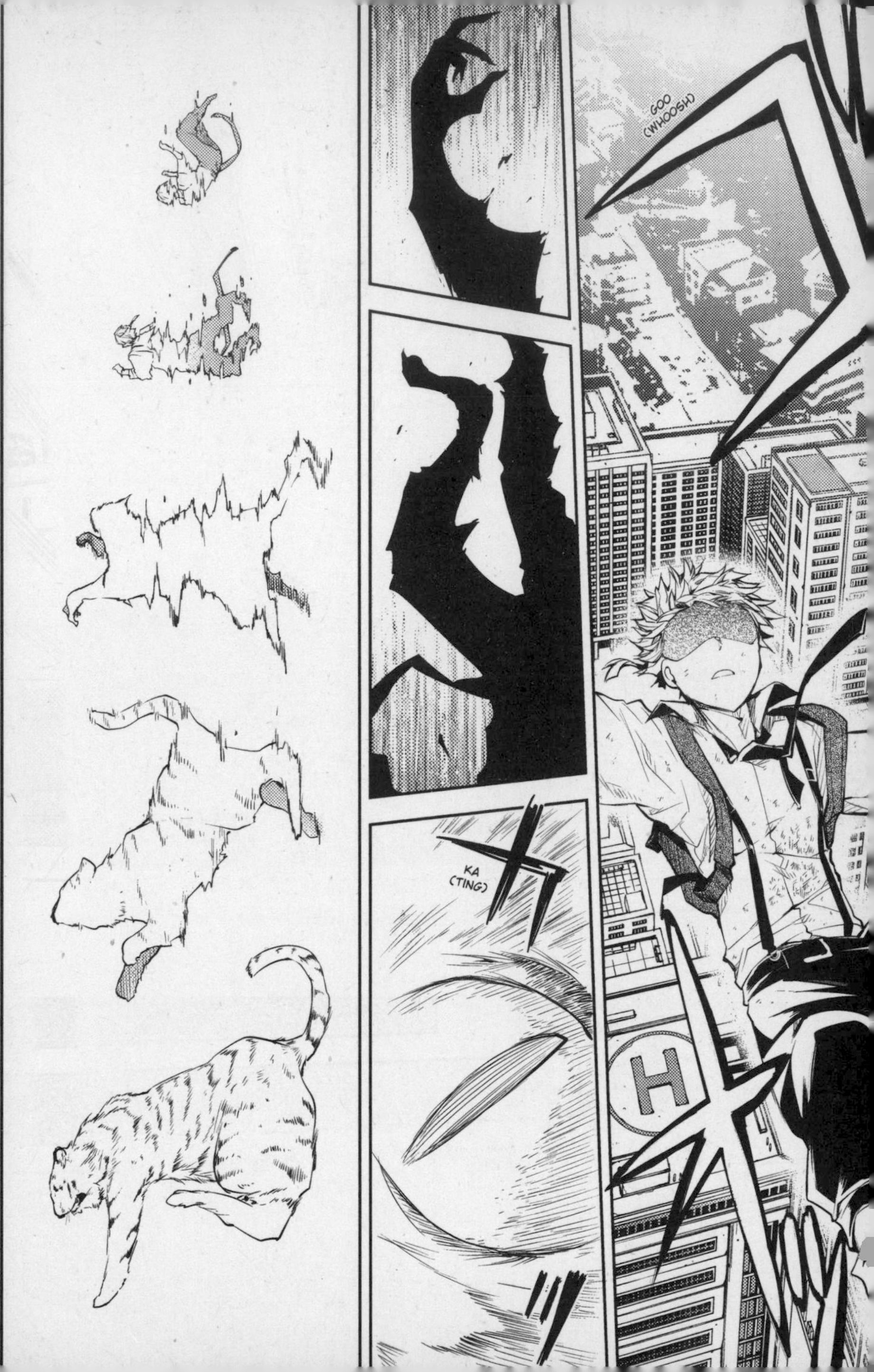
GOO (WHOOSH)
KA (TING)

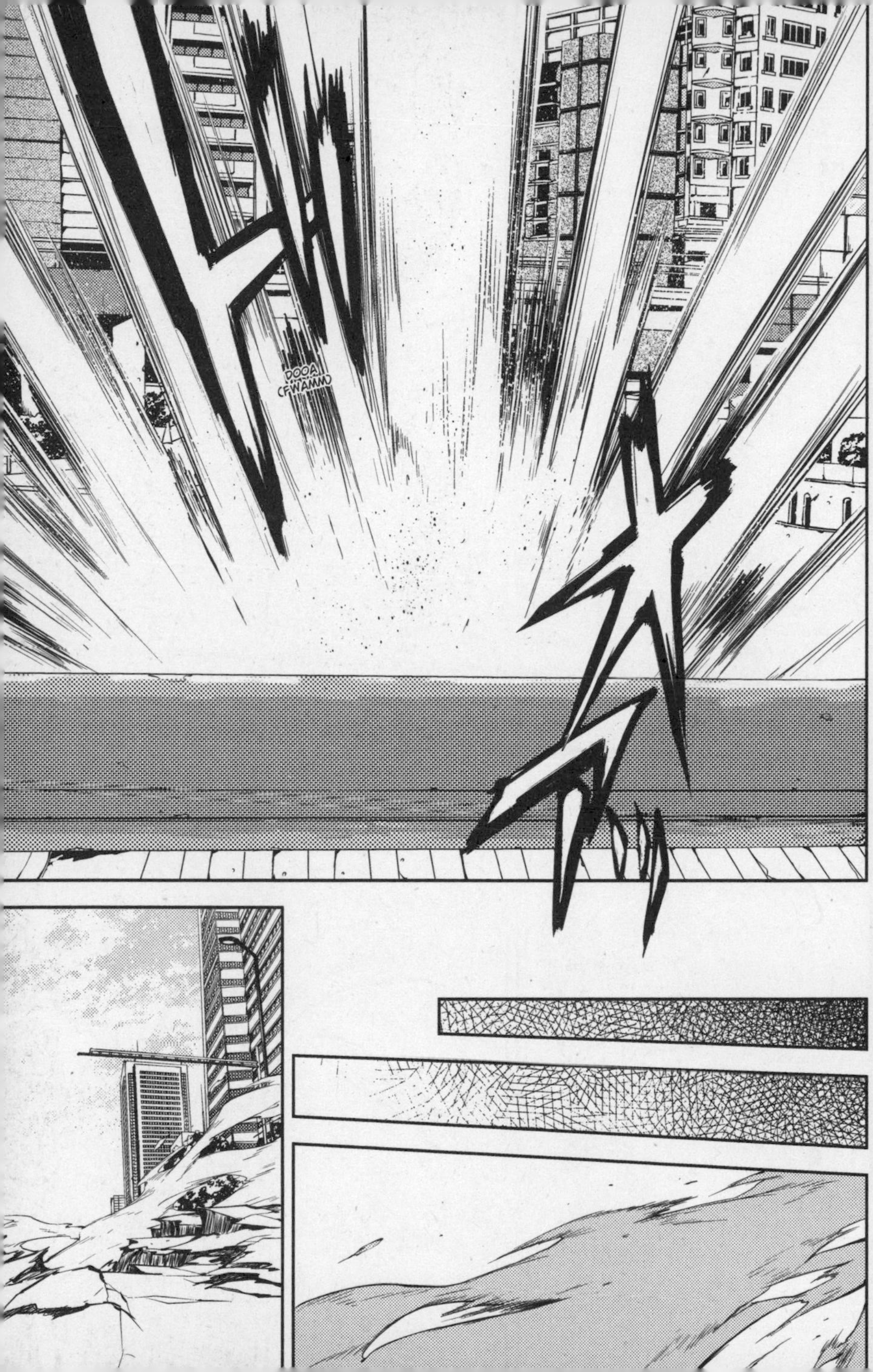
DOOA
(FWAMM)

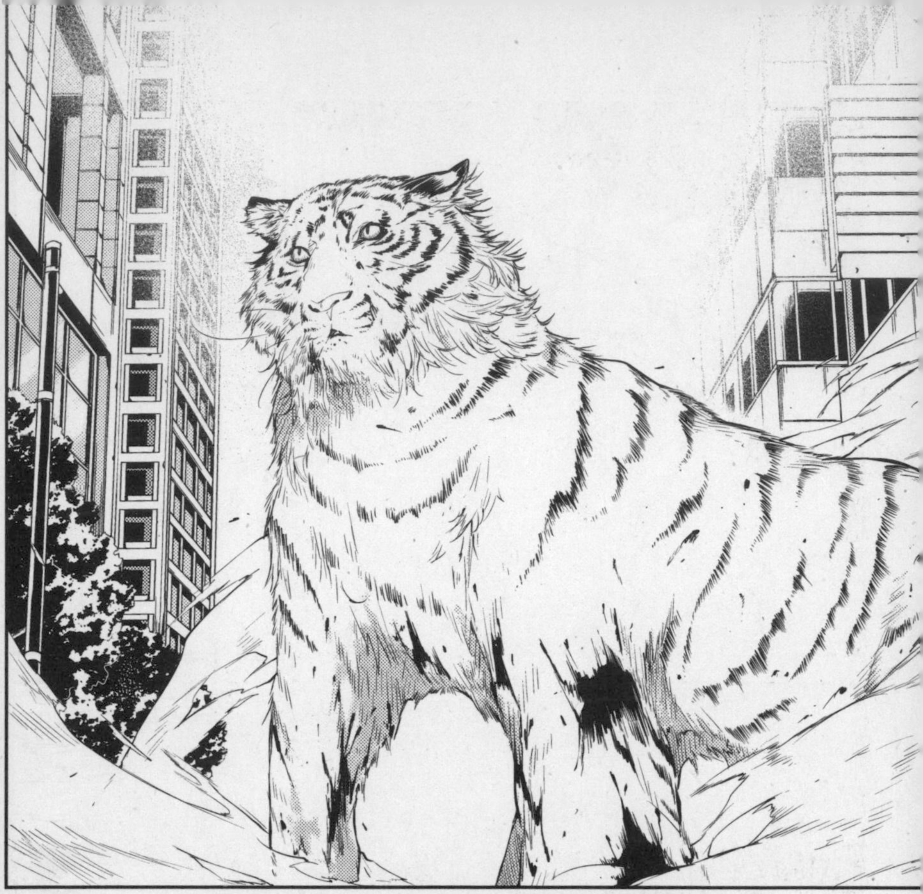

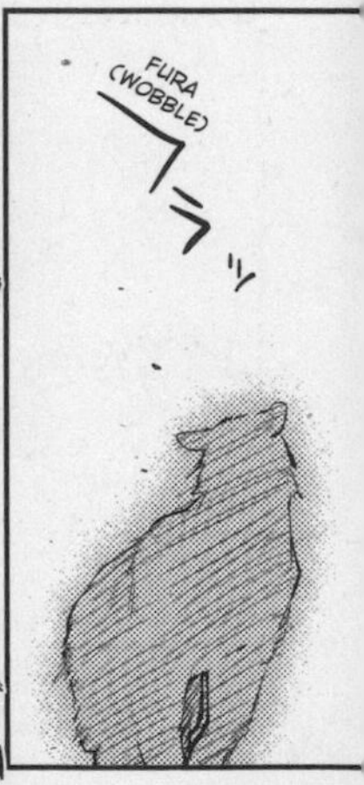
FURA
(WOBBLE)

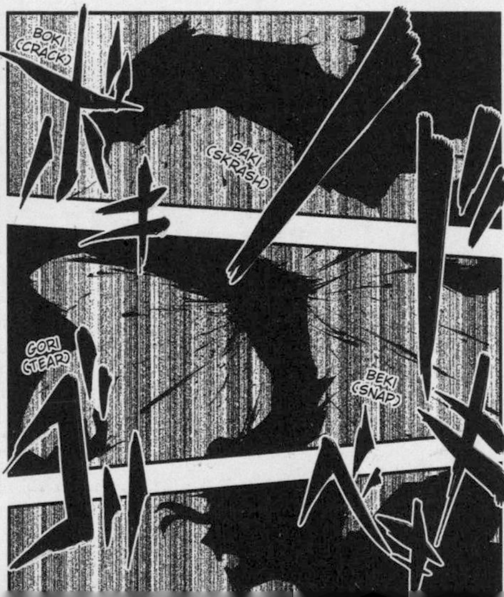
BOKI
(CRACK)
BAKI
(SKRASH)
GORI
(TEAR)
BEKI
(SNAP)

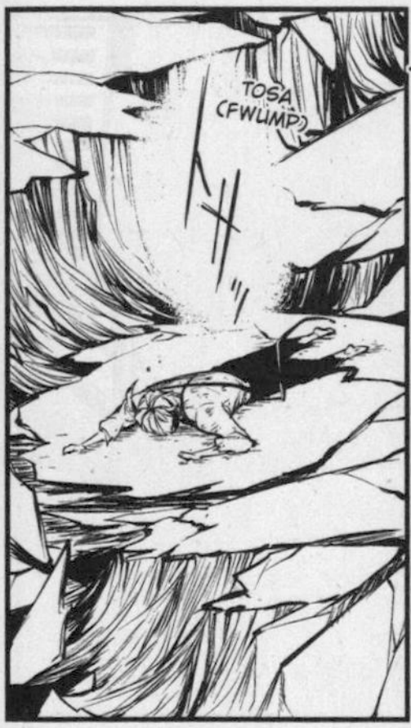
TOSA
(FWUMP)

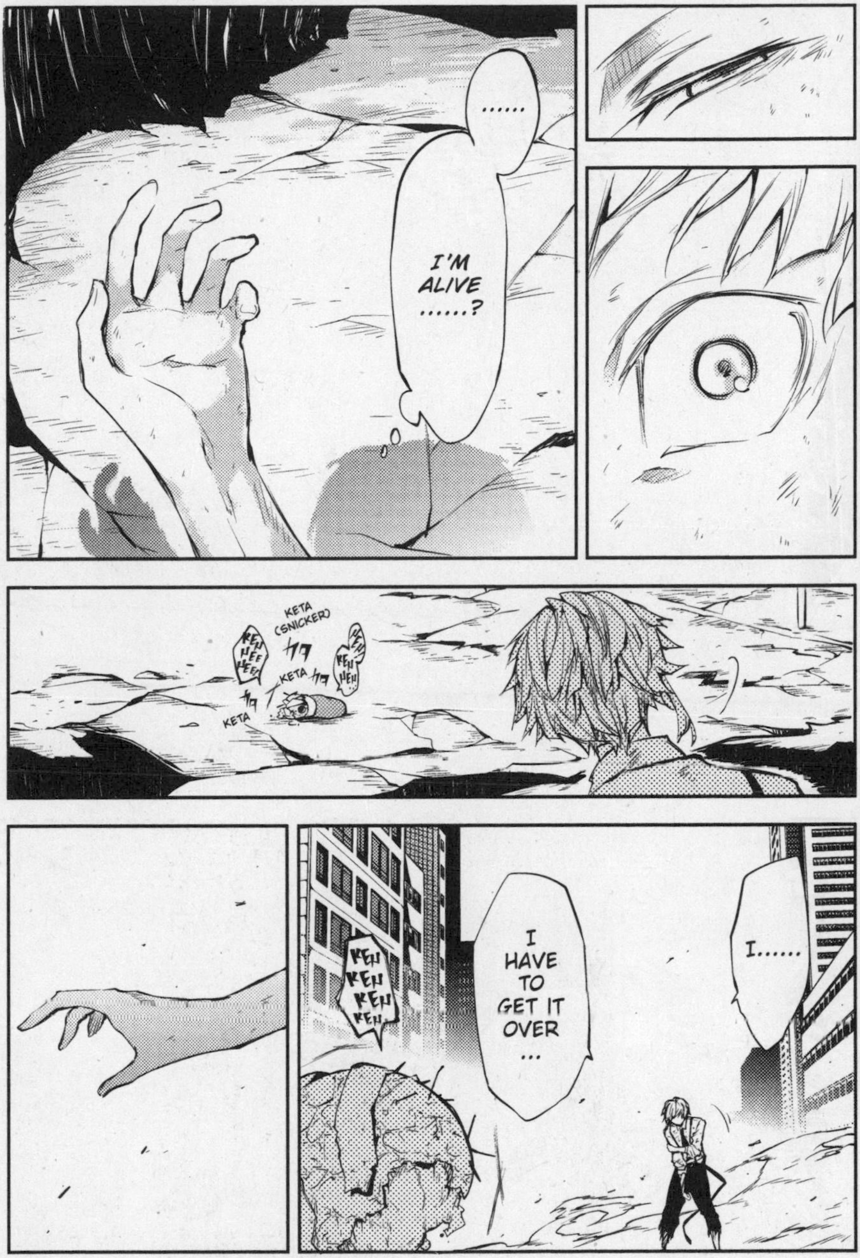
......
I'M ALIVE ......?
KETA (SNICKER)
KEN HEE HEE!
KEN HEH
KETA
KETA
I......
I HAVE TO GET IT OVER ...
KEN KEN KEN KEN

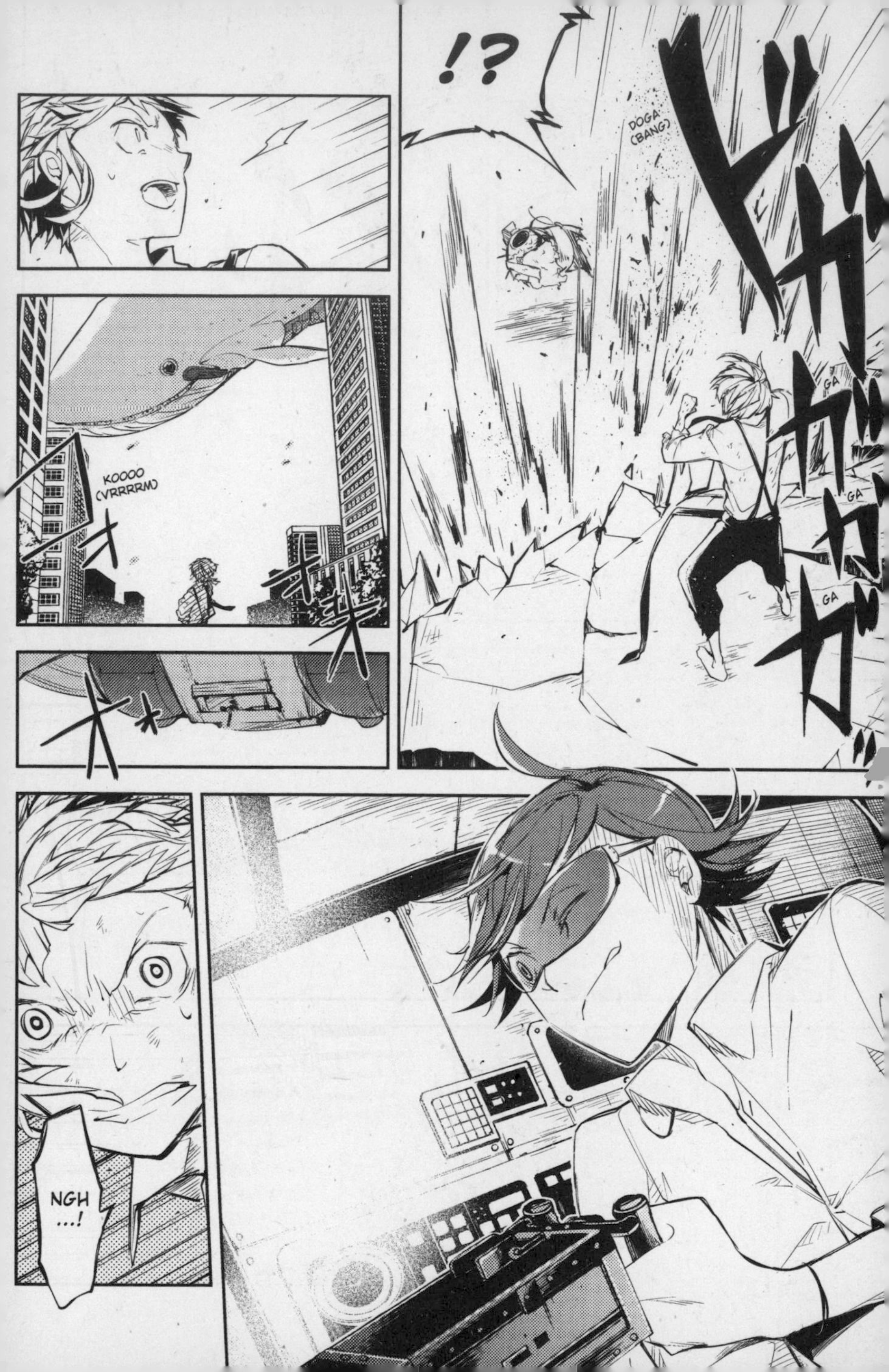
!?
DOGA (BANG)
GA
GA
GA
KOOOO (VRRRRM)
NGH ...!

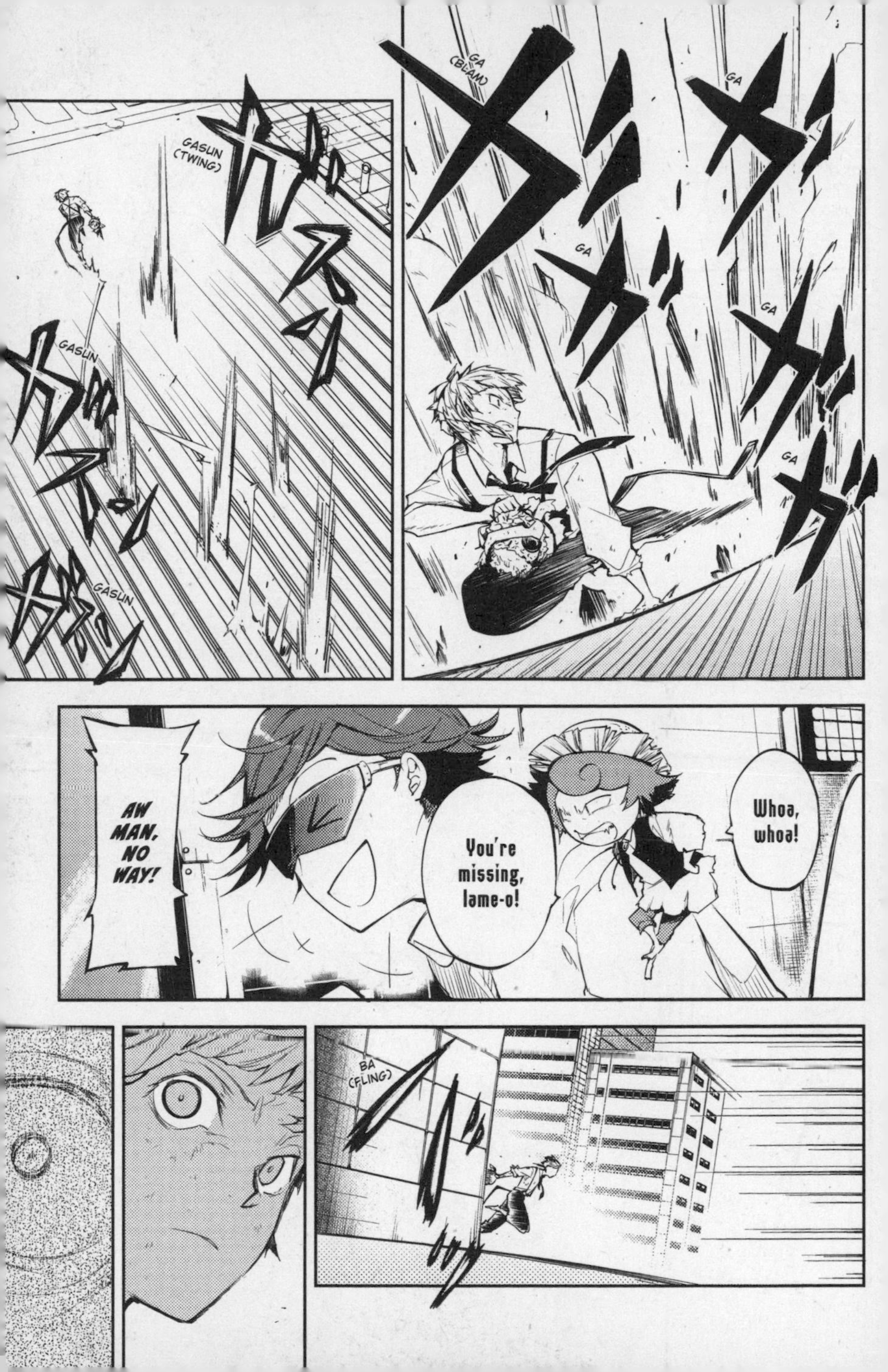

GA
GA (BLAM)
GA
GA
GA
GASUN (TWING)
GASUN
GASUN
Whoa, whoa!
You're missing, lame-o!
AW MAN, NO WAY!
BA (FLING)

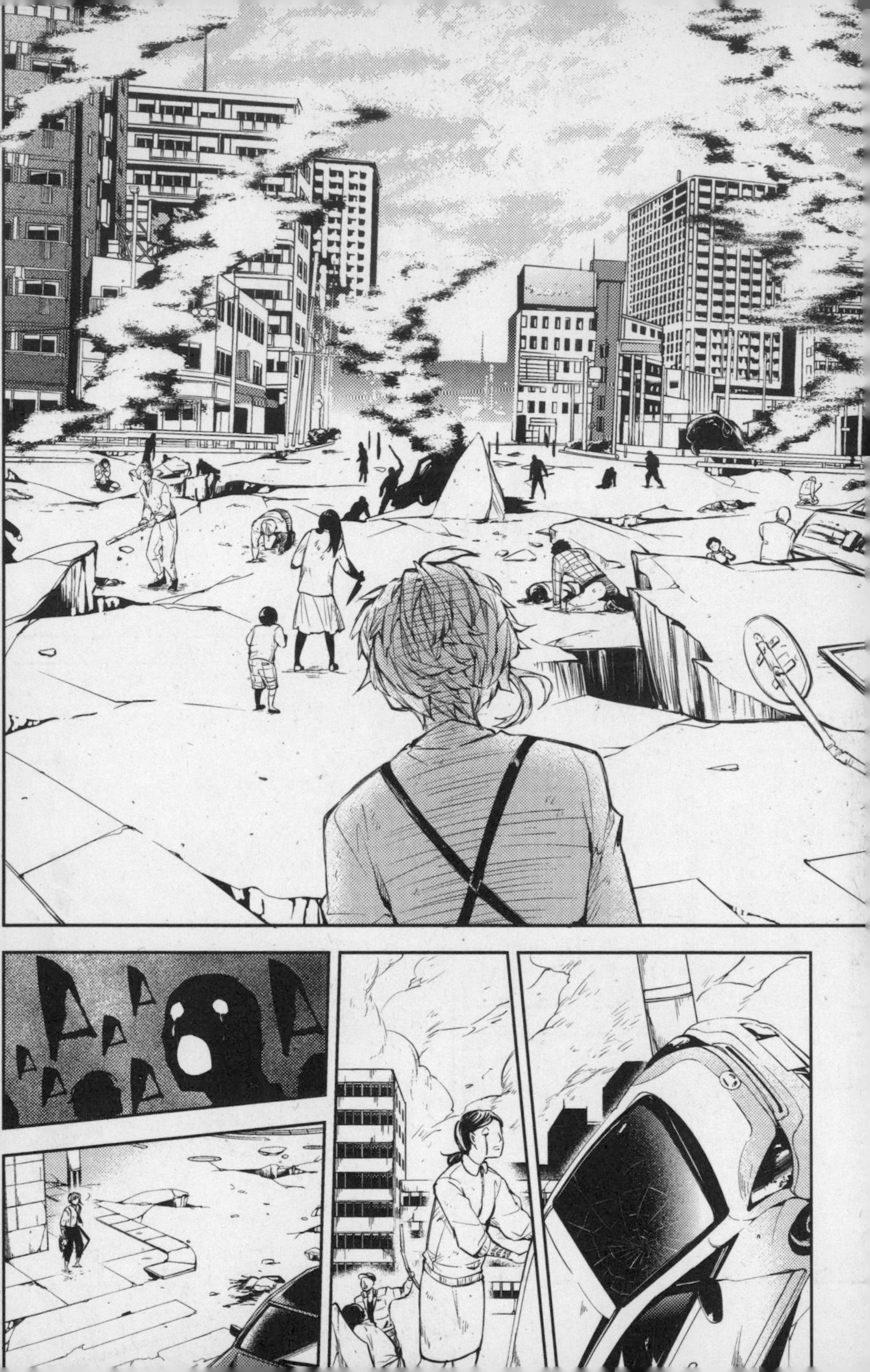

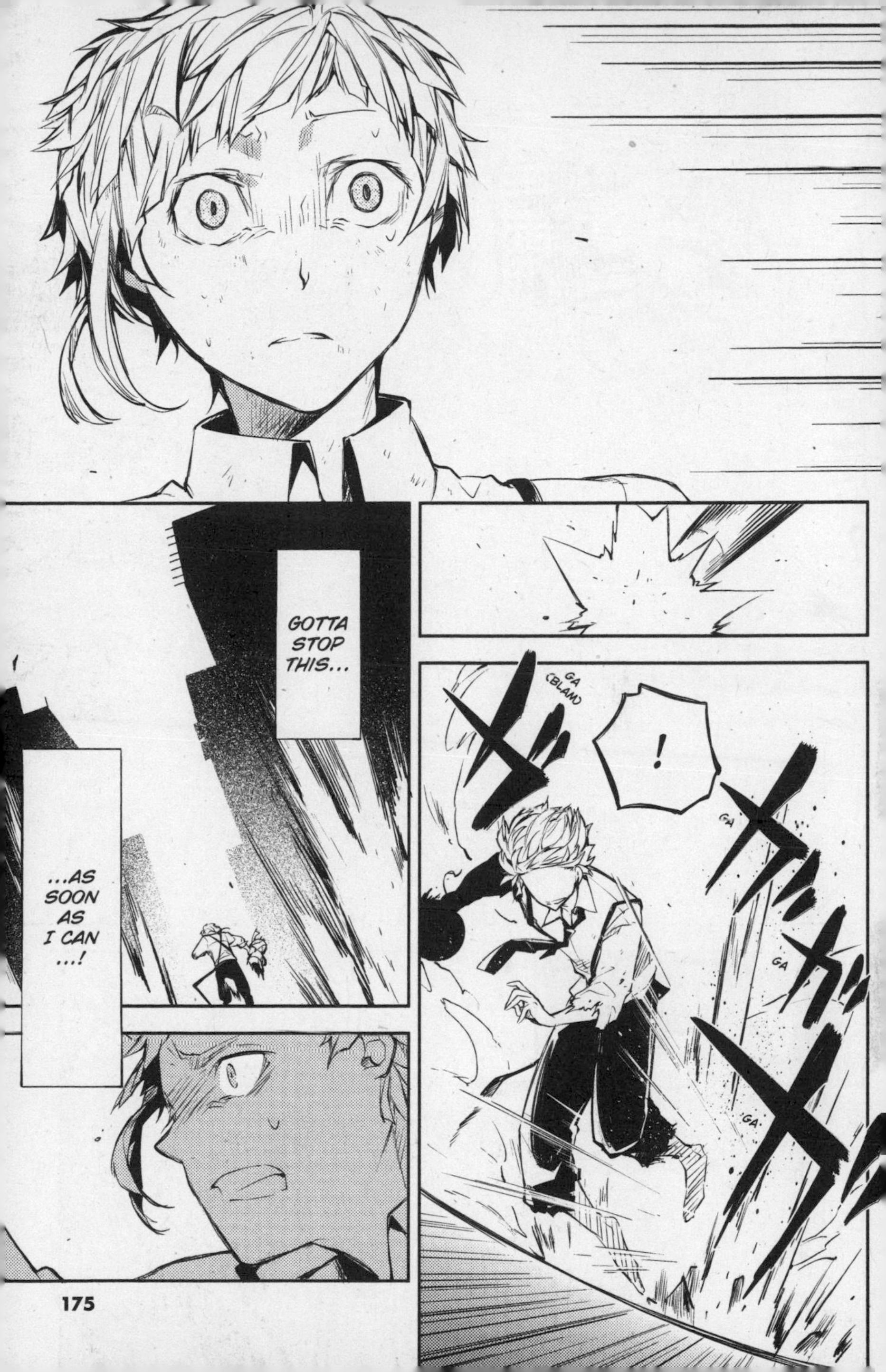
GOTTA STOP THIS...
...AS SOON AS I CAN ...!
GA (BLAM)
!
GA
GA
GA

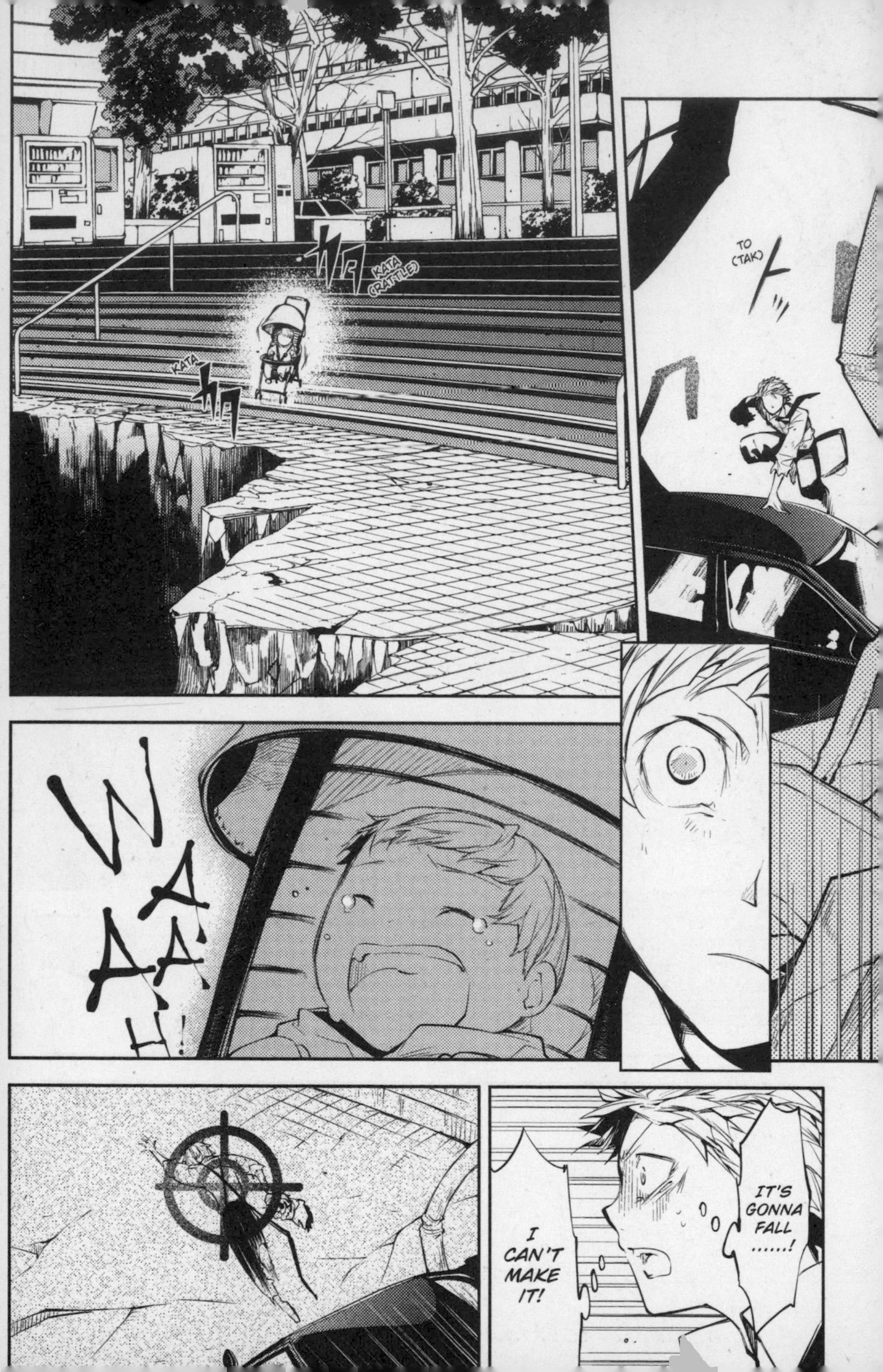
TO (TAK)
KATA (RATTLE)
KATA
WAAAH!
IT'S GONNA FALL......!
I CAN'T MAKE IT!

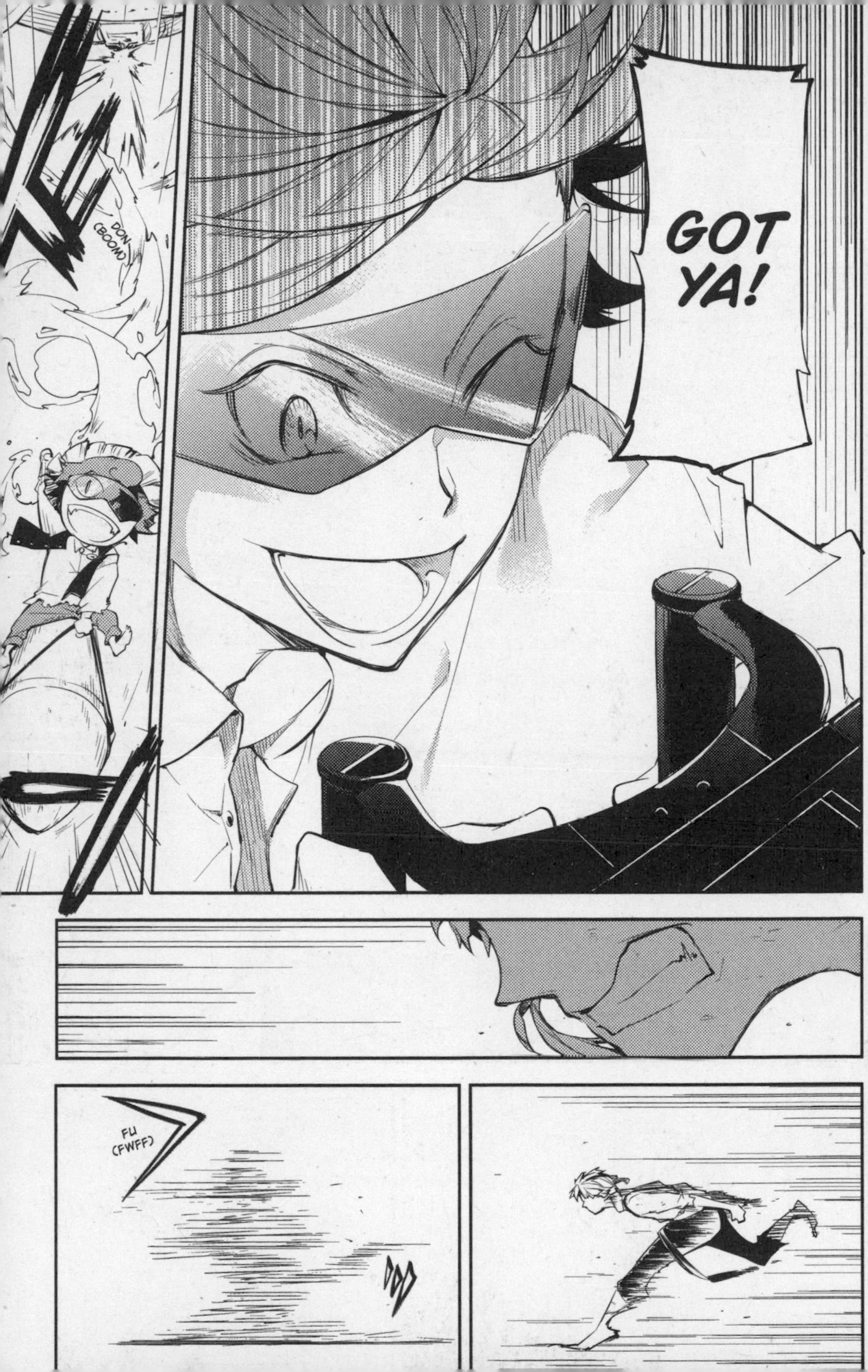
GOT YA!
DON (BOOM)
FU (FWFF)

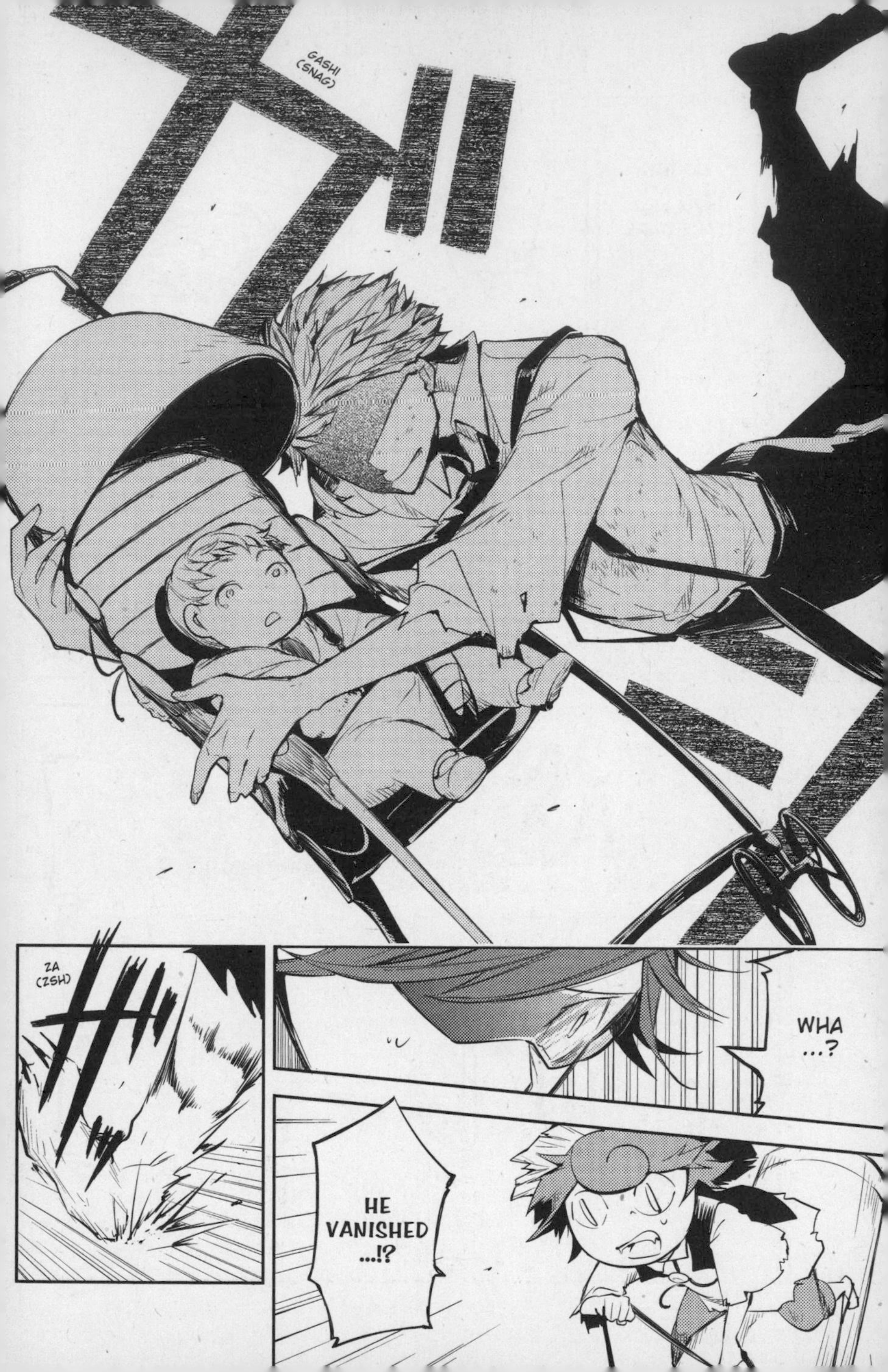
GASHI (SNAG)
WHA ...?
HE VANISHED ...!?
ZA (ZSH)

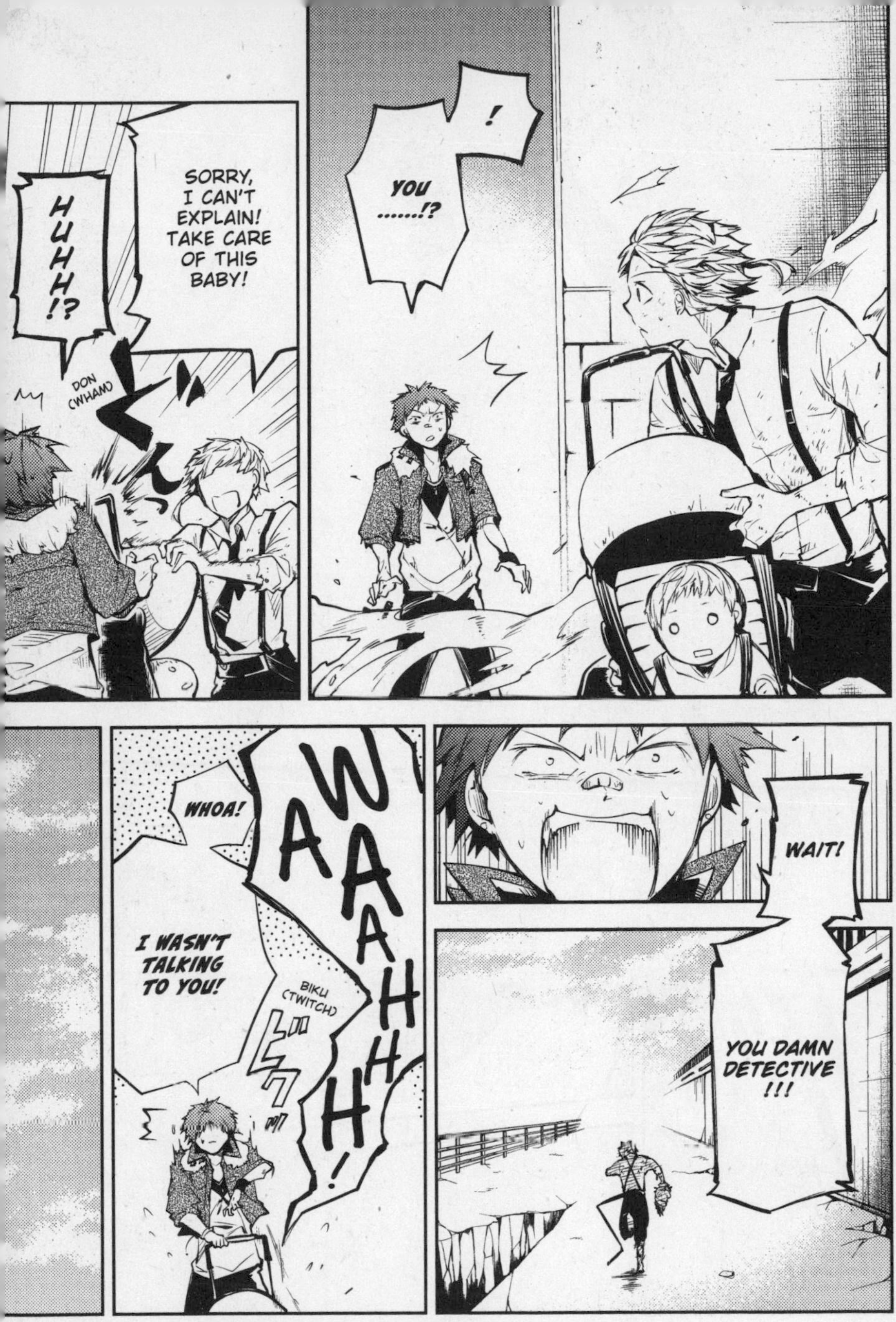
!
YOU .......!?
SORRY, I CAN'T EXPLAIN! TAKE CARE OF THIS BABY!
HUHHH!?
DON (WHAM)
WAIT!
YOU DAMN DETECTIVE !!!
WAAAAHHHH!
WHOA!
BIKU (TWITCH)
I WASN'T TALKING TO YOU!

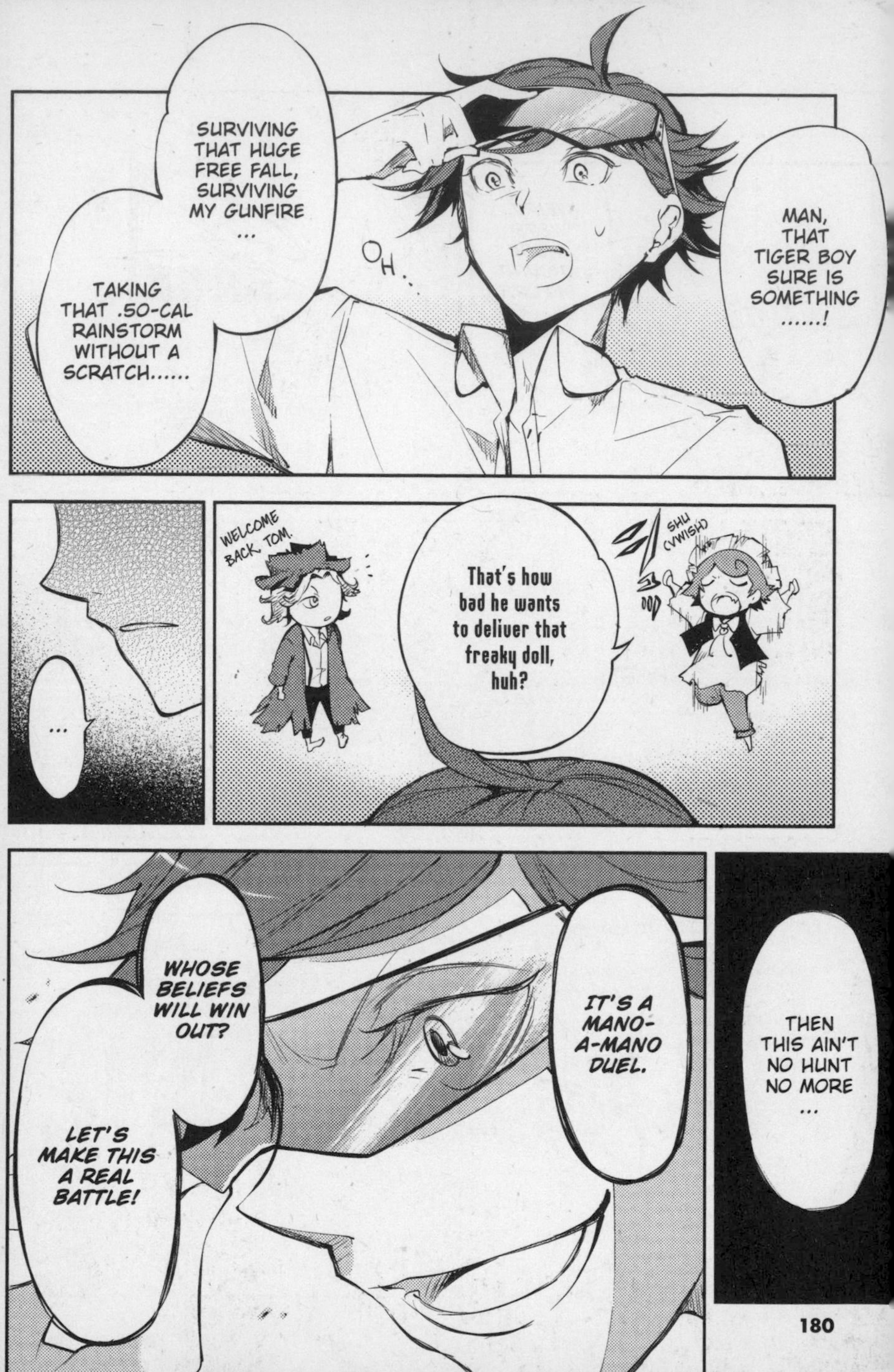
MAN, THAT TIGER BOY SURE IS SOMETHING......!
OH...
SURVIVING THAT HUGE FREE FALL, SURVIVING MY GUNFIRE ...
TAKING THAT .50-CAL RAINSTORM WITHOUT A SCRATCH......
SHU (VWISH)
That's how bad he wants to deliver that freaky doll, huh?
WELCOME BACK, TOM.
...
THEN THIS AIN'T NO HUNT NO MORE ...
IT'S A MANO-A-MANO DUEL.
WHOSE BELIEFS WILL WIN OUT?
LET'S MAKE THIS A REAL BATTLE!

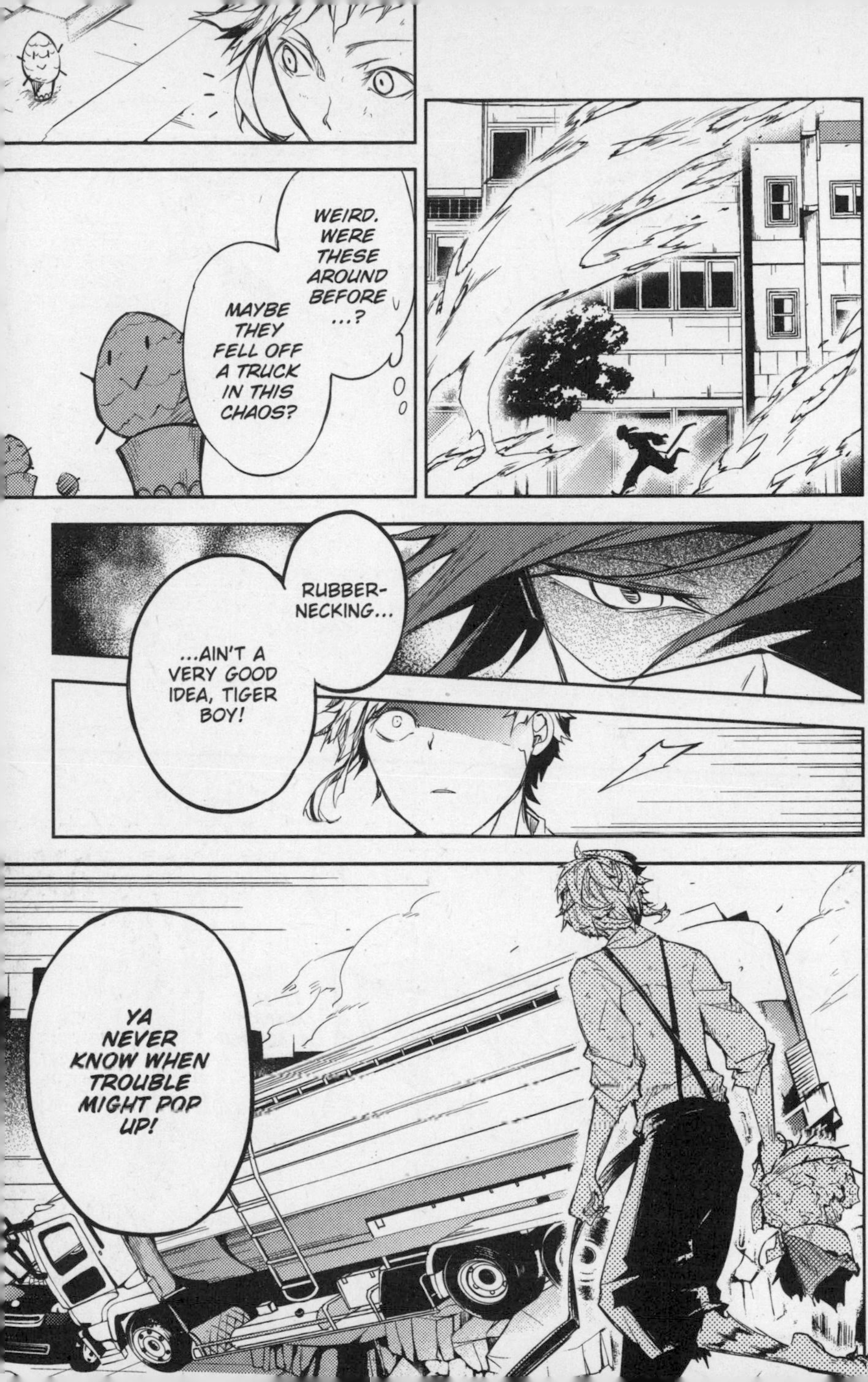
WEIRD. WERE THESE AROUND BEFORE ...?
MAYBE THEY FELL OFF A TRUCK IN THIS CHAOS?
RUBBER-NECKING...
...AIN'T A VERY GOOD IDEA, TIGER BOY!
YA NEVER KNOW WHEN TROUBLE MIGHT POP UP!

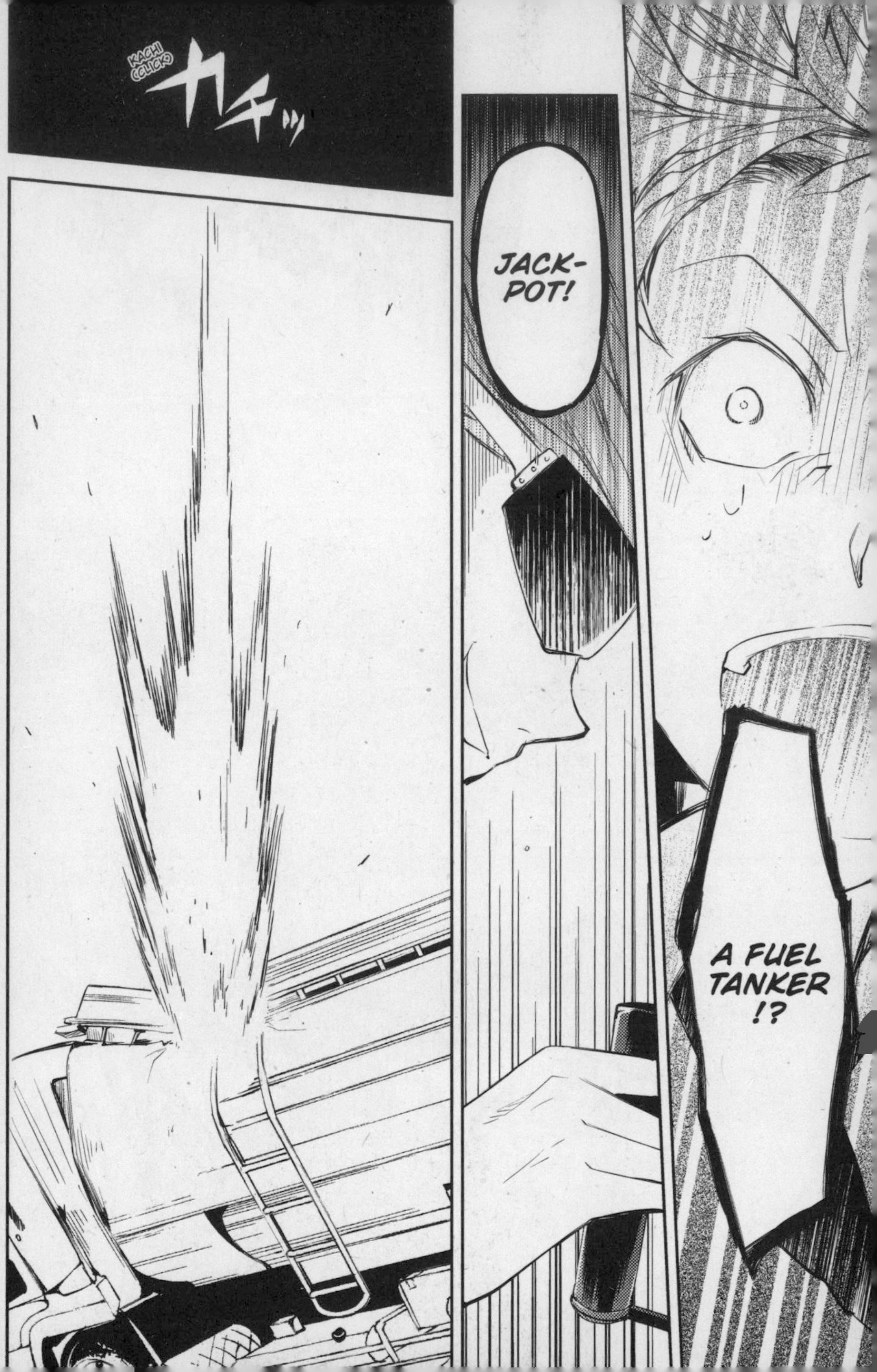
A FUEL TANKER !?
JACK-POT!
KACHI (CLICK)
カチッ

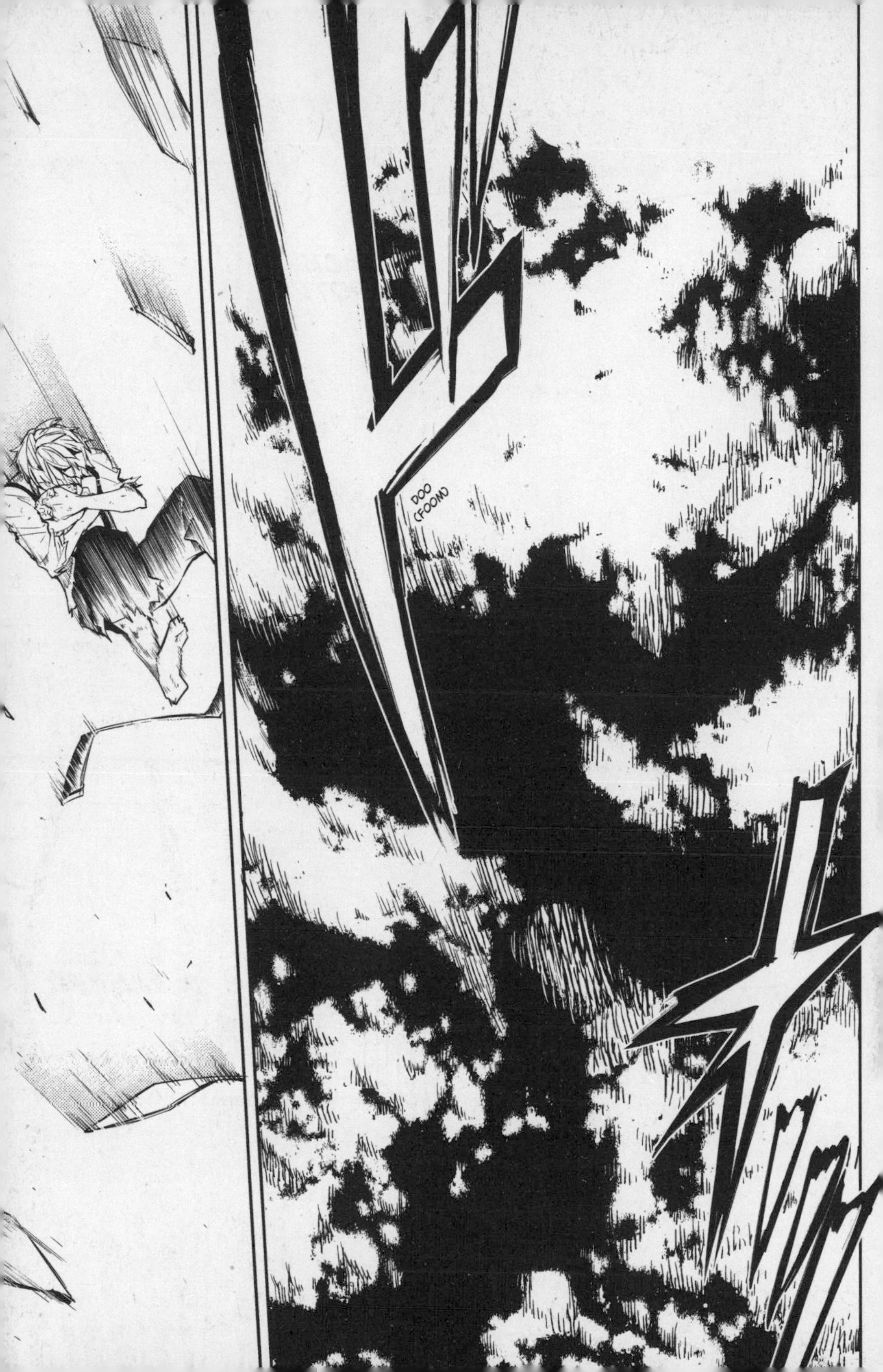
DOO
(FOOM)

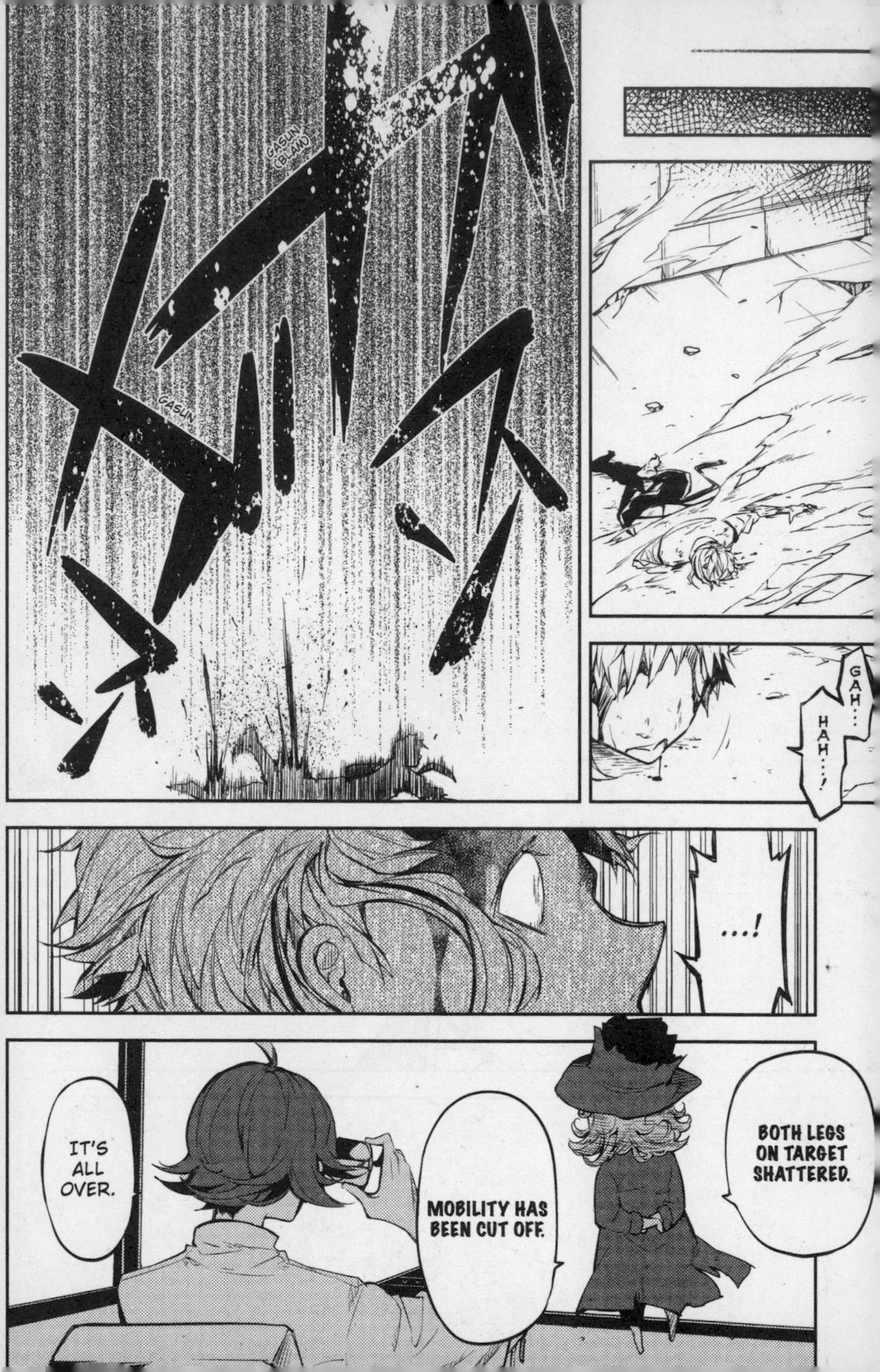
GAH... HAH...!
GASUN (BLAM)
GASUN
...!
BOTH LEGS ON TARGET SHATTERED.
MOBILITY HAS BEEN CUT OFF.
IT'S ALL OVER.

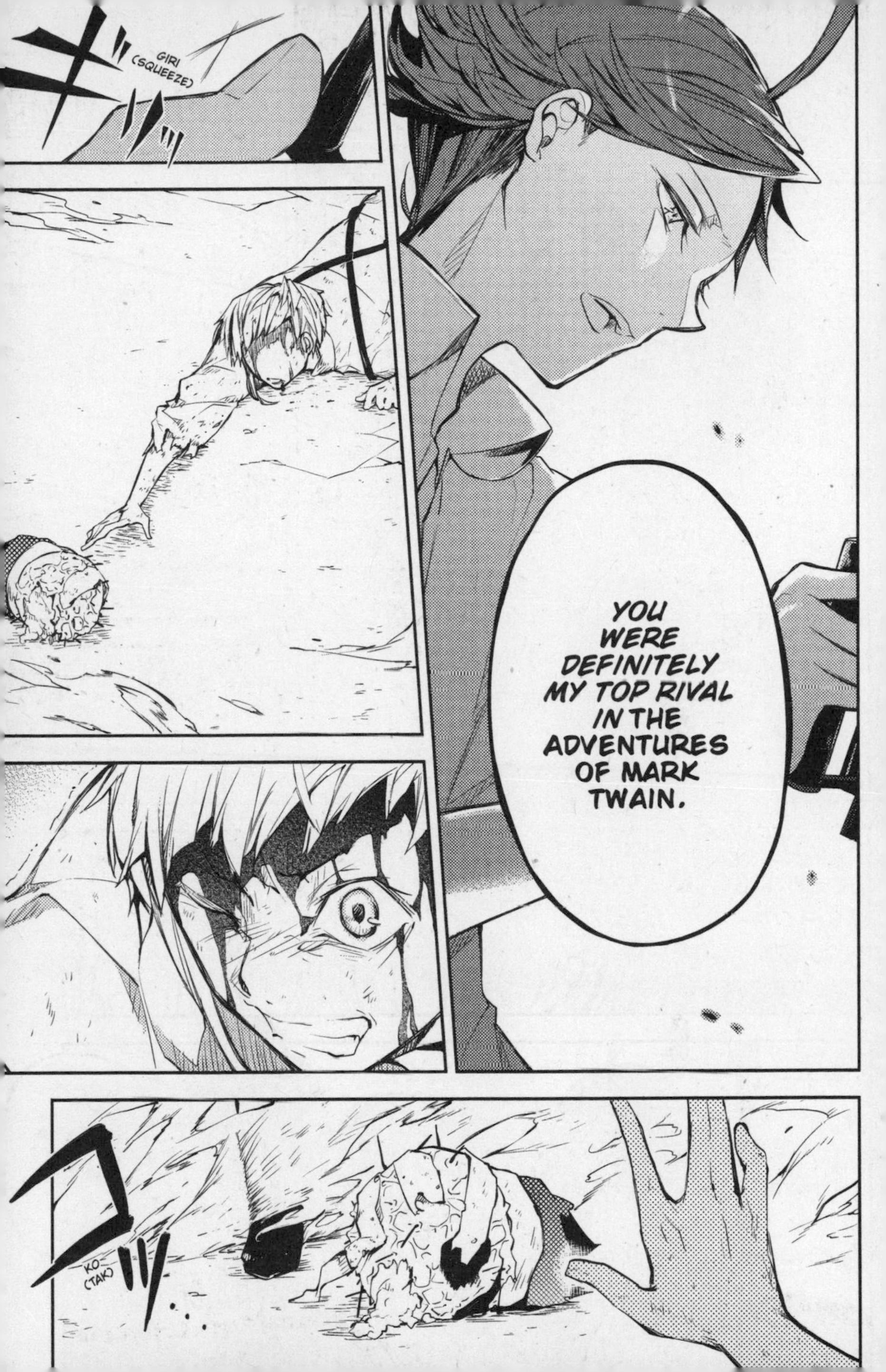
YOU WERE DEFINITELY MY TOP RIVAL IN THE ADVENTURES OF MARK TWAIN.
GIRI (SQUEEZE)
KO (TAK)

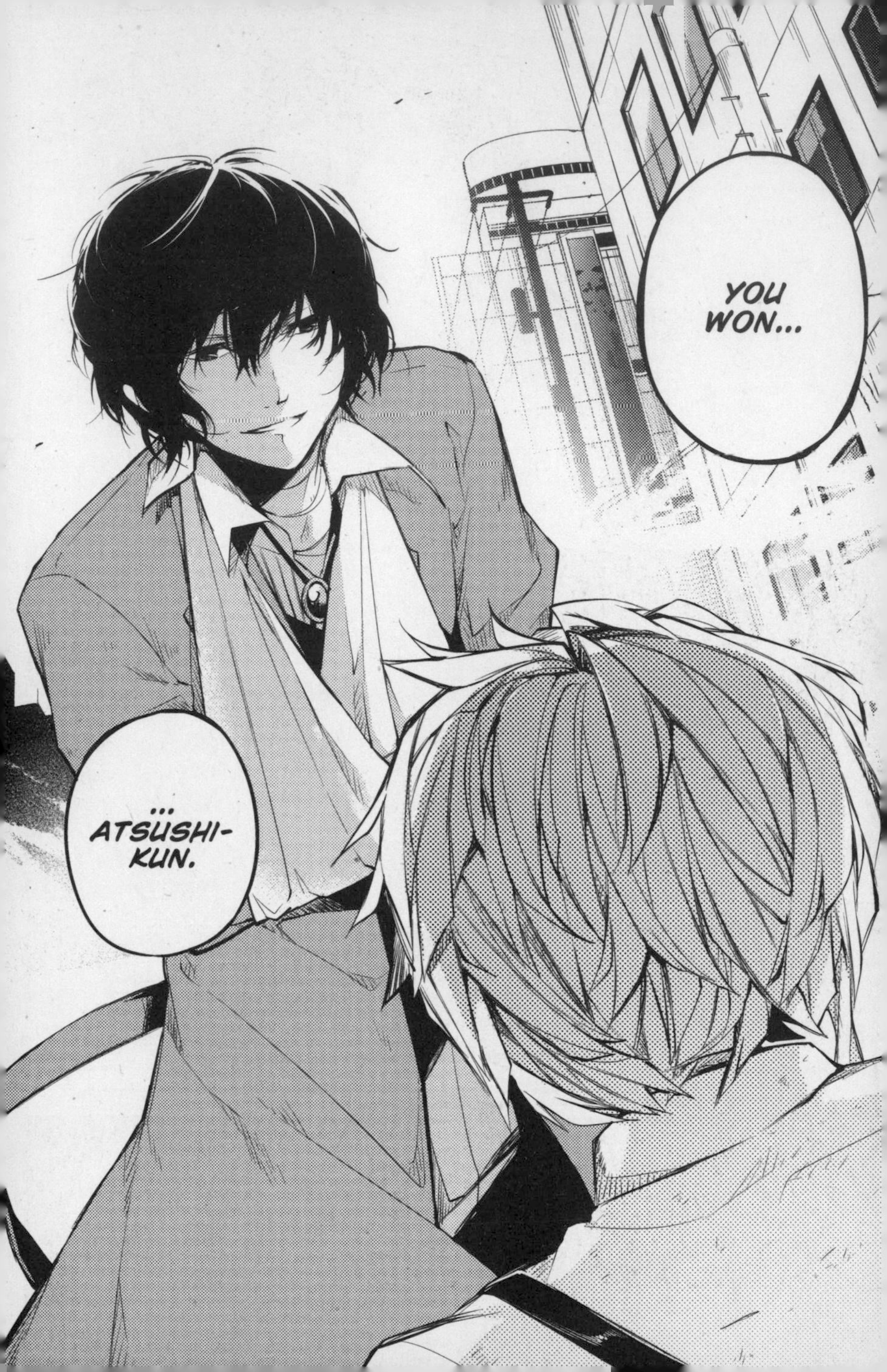
YOU WON...
... ATSUSHI-KUN.

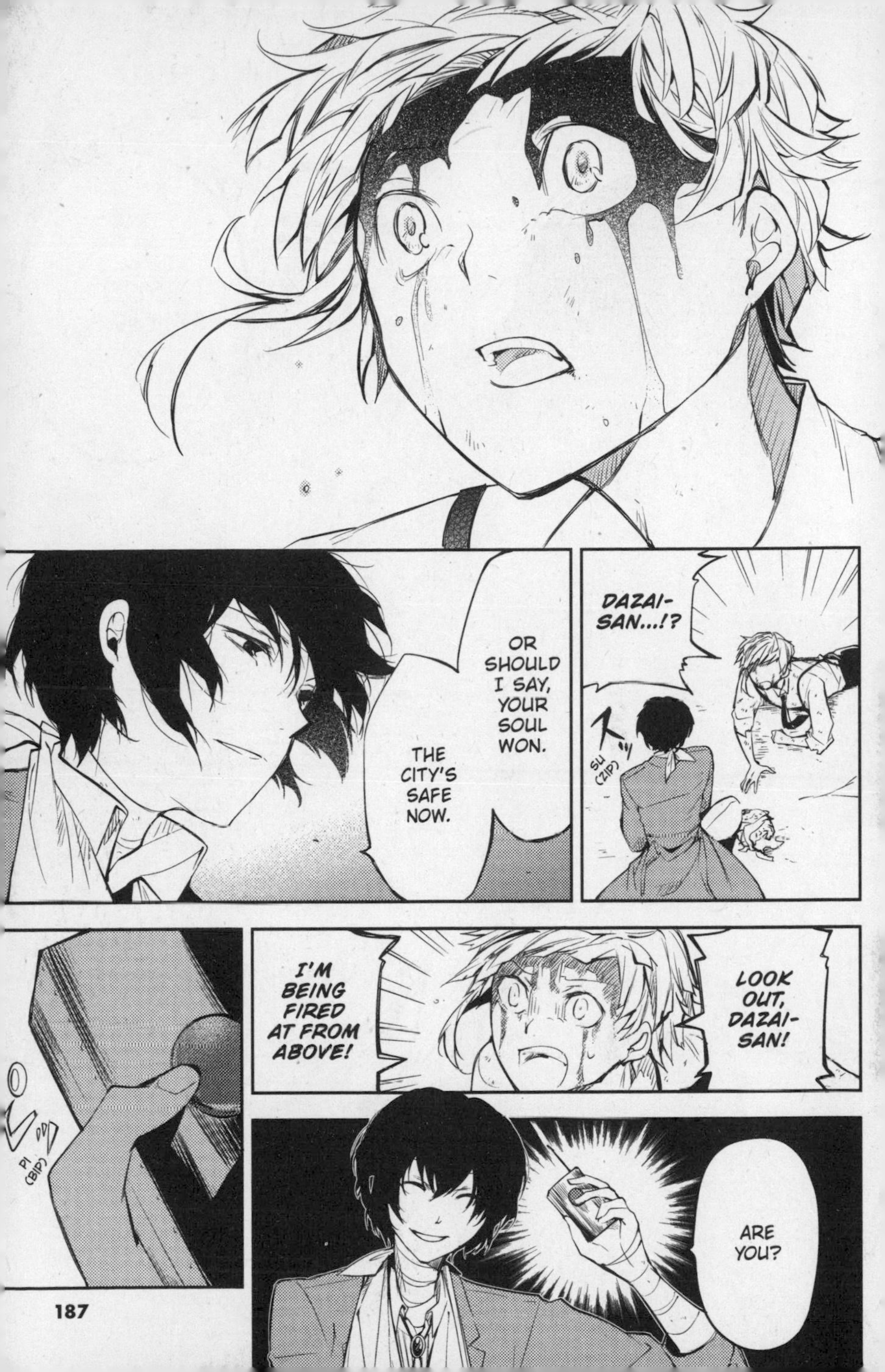
DAZAI-SAN...!?
SU (ZIP)
OR SHOULD I SAY, YOUR SOUL WON.
THE CITY'S SAFE NOW.
LOOK OUT, DAZAI-SAN!
I'M BEING FIRED AT FROM ABOVE!
ARE YOU?
PI (BIP)

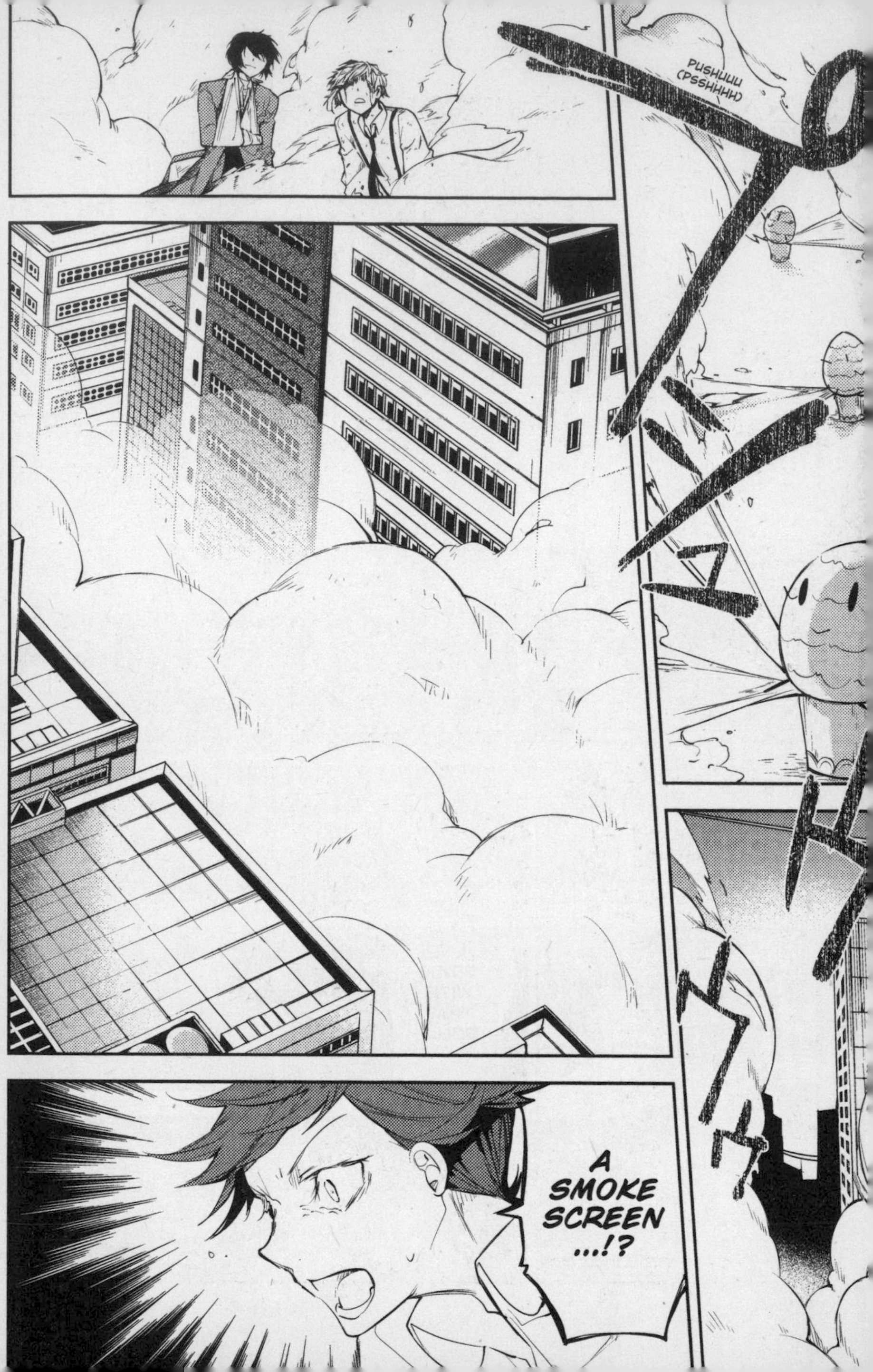
PUSHUUU
(PSSHHHH)
A SMOKE SCREEN ...!?

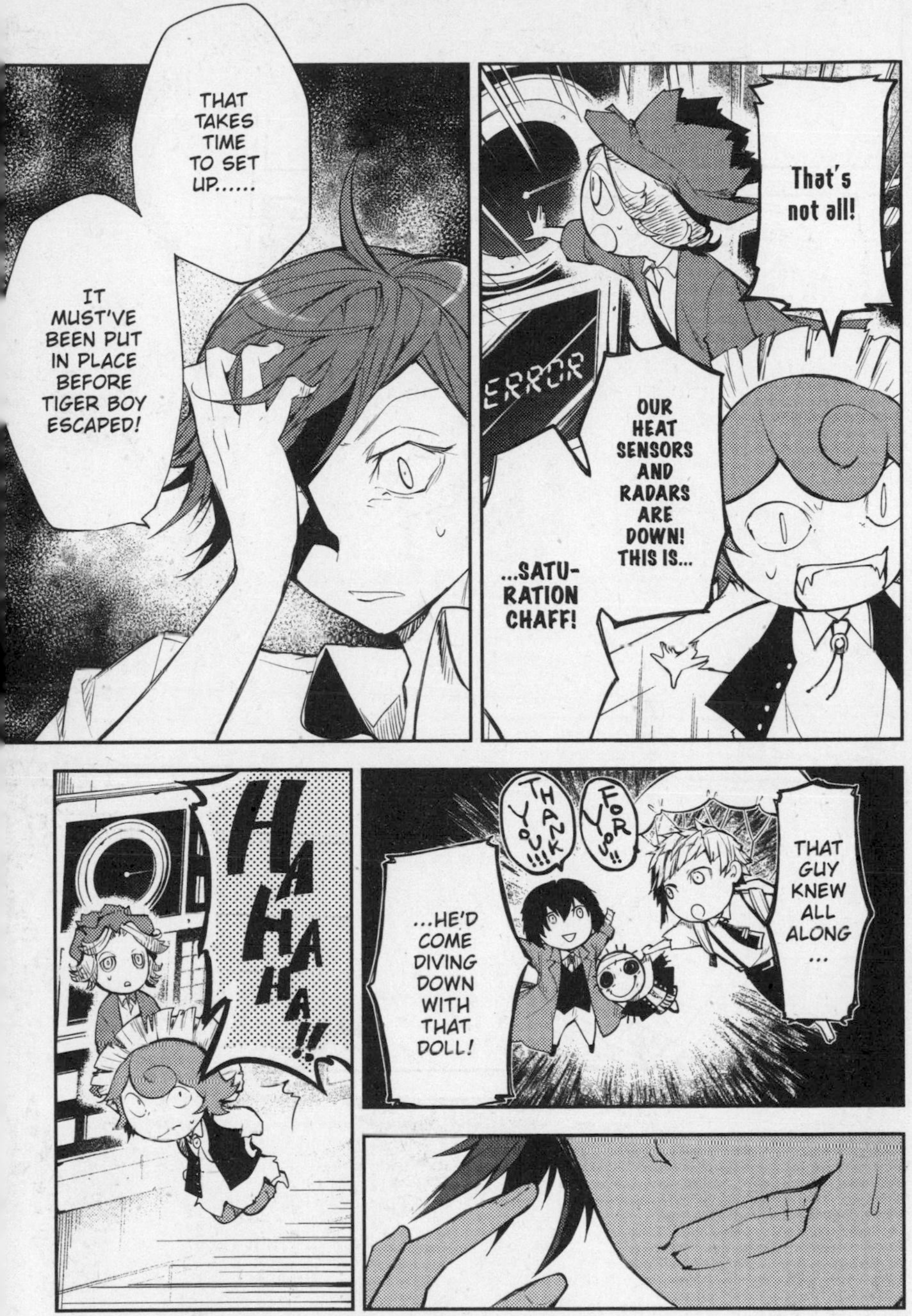
That's not all!
ERROR
OUR HEAT SENSORS AND RADARS ARE DOWN! THIS IS...
...SATURATION CHAFF!
THAT TAKES TIME TO SET UP......
IT MUST'VE BEEN PUT IN PLACE BEFORE TIGER BOY ESCAPED!
THAT GUY KNEW ALL ALONG...
FOR YOU!!
THANK YOU!!!
...HE'D COME DIVING DOWN WITH THAT DOLL!
HAHAHA!!

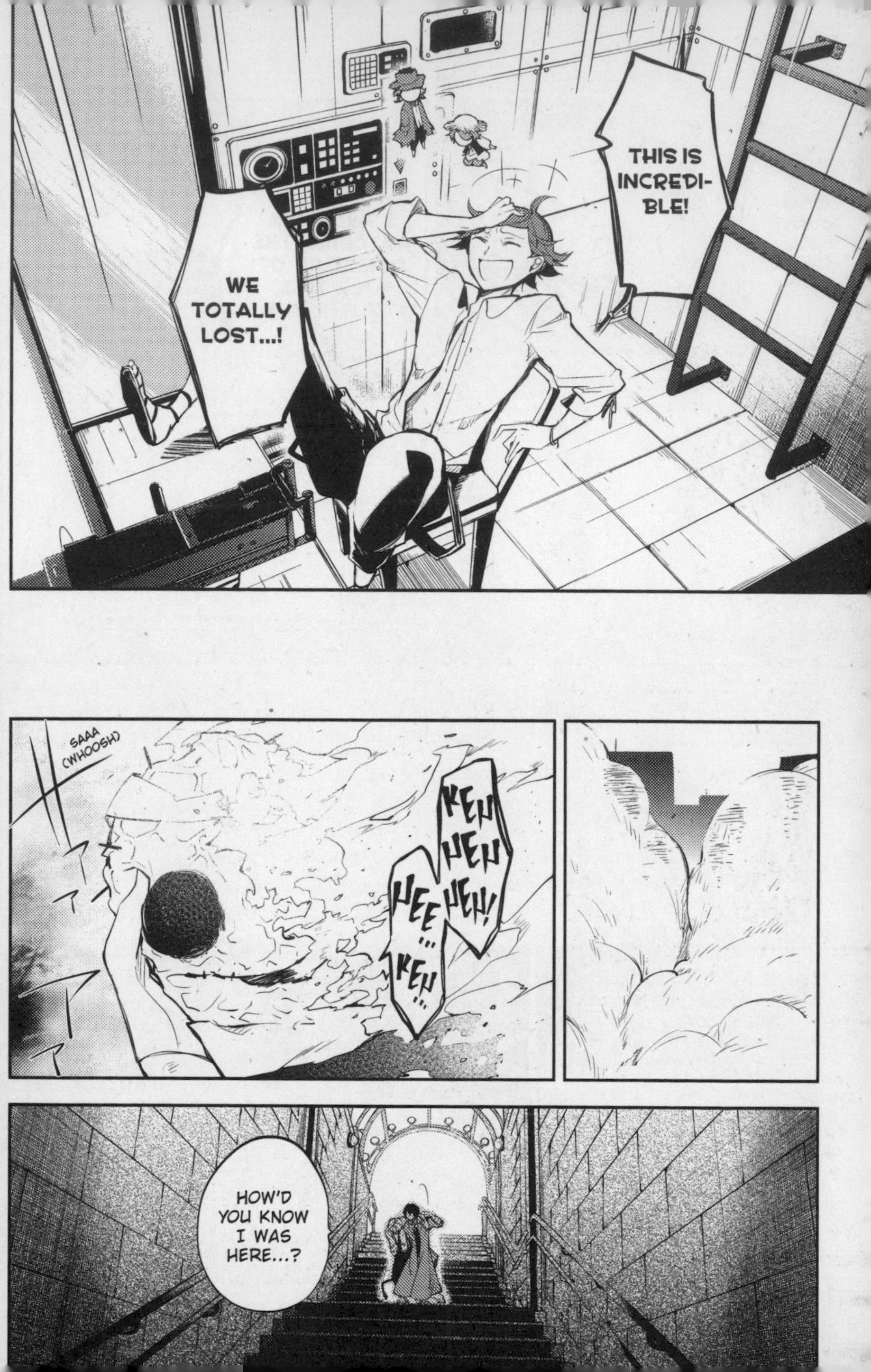
THIS IS INCREDIBLE!
WE TOTALLY LOST...!
KEN HEN HEN!
HEE... KEN...
SAAA (WHOOSH)
HOW'D YOU KNOW I WAS HERE...?

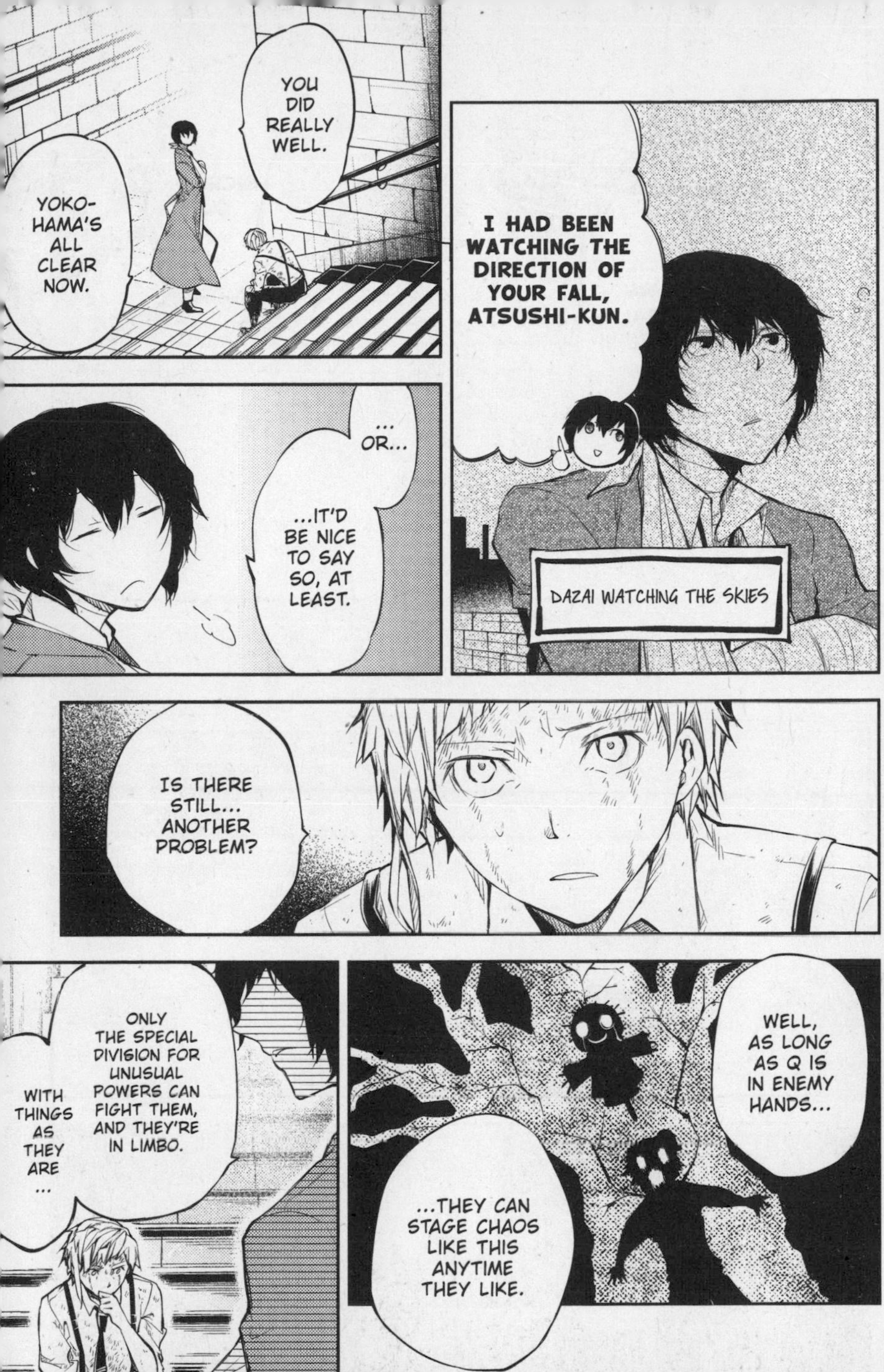
I HAD BEEN WATCHING THE DIRECTION OF YOUR FALL, ATSUSHI-KUN.
DAZAI WATCHING THE SKIES
YOU DID REALLY WELL.
YOKO-HAMA'S ALL CLEAR NOW.
... OR...
...IT'D BE NICE TO SAY SO, AT LEAST.
IS THERE STILL... ANOTHER PROBLEM?
WELL, AS LONG AS Q IS IN ENEMY HANDS...
...THEY CAN STAGE CHAOS LIKE THIS ANYTIME THEY LIKE.
ONLY THE SPECIAL DIVISION FOR UNUSUAL POWERS CAN FIGHT THEM, AND THEY'RE IN LIMBO.
WITH THINGS AS THEY ARE ...

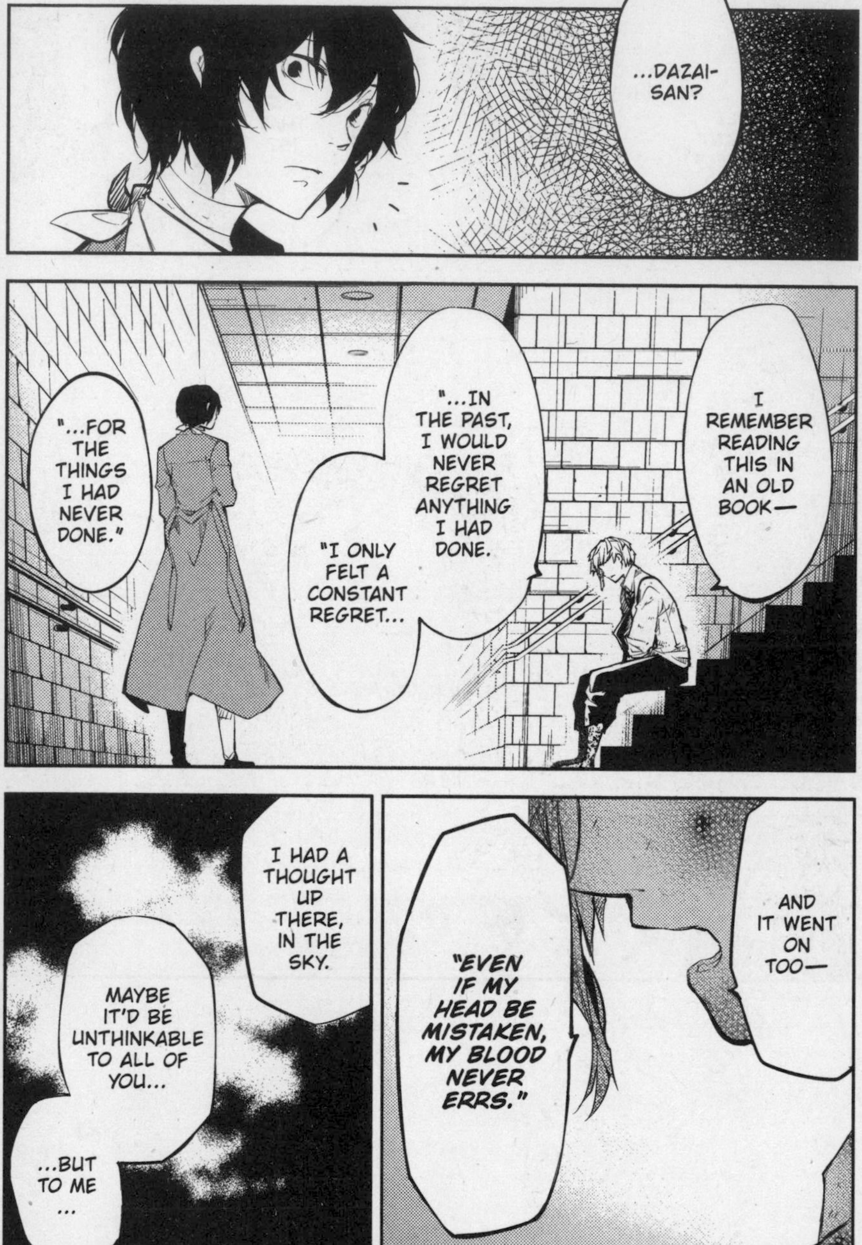
...DAZAI-SAN?
I REMEMBER READING THIS IN AN OLD BOOK—
"...IN THE PAST, I WOULD NEVER REGRET ANYTHING I HAD DONE.
"I ONLY FELT A CONSTANT REGRET...
"...FOR THE THINGS I HAD NEVER DONE."
AND IT WENT ON TOO—
"EVEN IF MY HEAD BE MISTAKEN, MY BLOOD NEVER ERRS."
I HAD A THOUGHT UP THERE, IN THE SKY.
MAYBE IT'D BE UNTHINKABLE TO ALL OF YOU...
...BUT TO ME ...

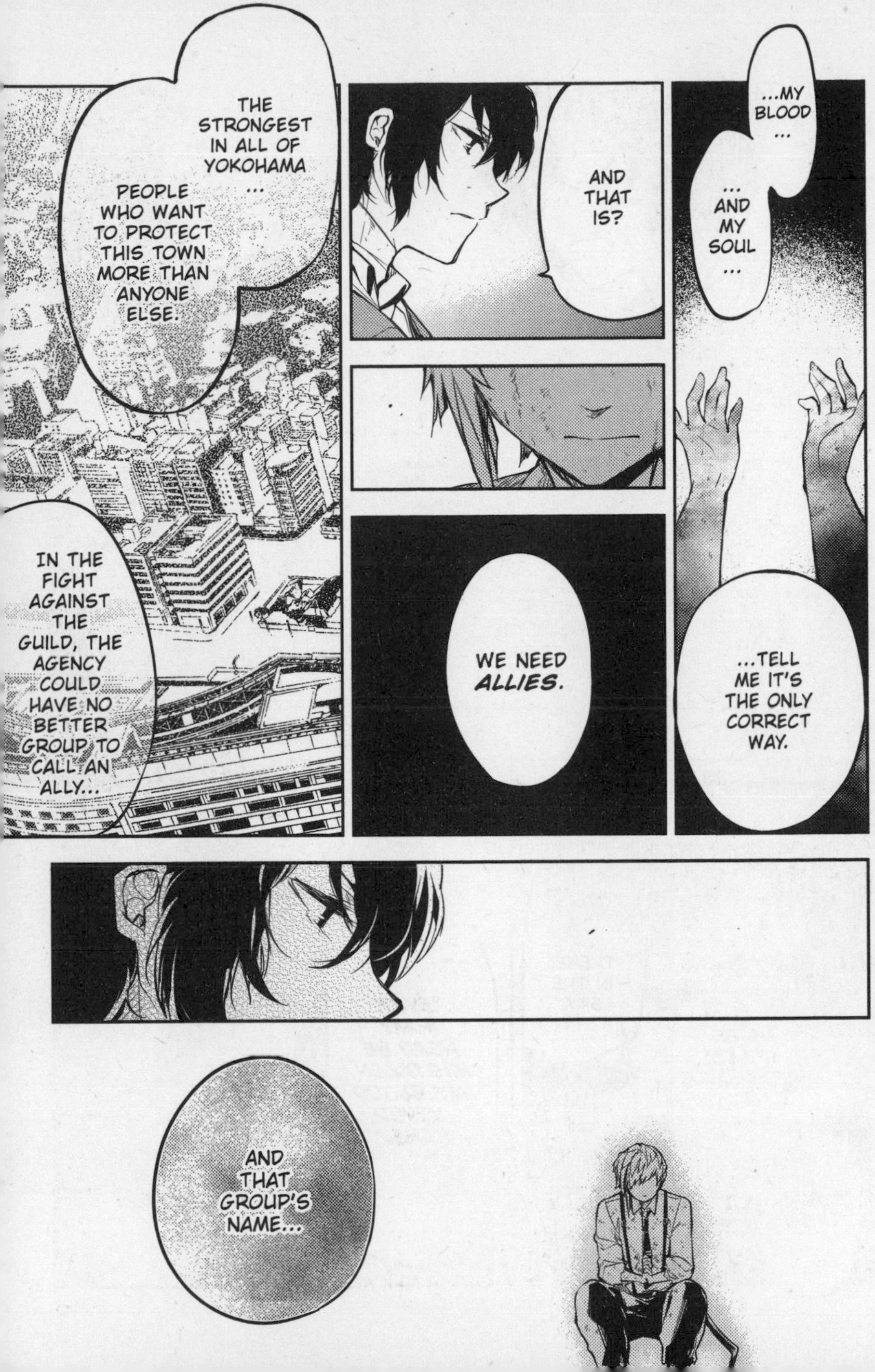
...MY BLOOD ...
... AND MY SOUL ...
...TELL ME IT'S THE ONLY CORRECT WAY.
AND THAT IS?
WE NEED *ALLIES*.
THE STRONGEST IN ALL OF YOKOHAMA ...
PEOPLE WHO WANT TO PROTECT THIS TOWN MORE THAN ANYONE ELSE.
IN THE FIGHT AGAINST THE GUILD, THE AGENCY COULD HAVE NO BETTER GROUP TO CALL AN ALLY...
AND THAT GROUP'S NAME...

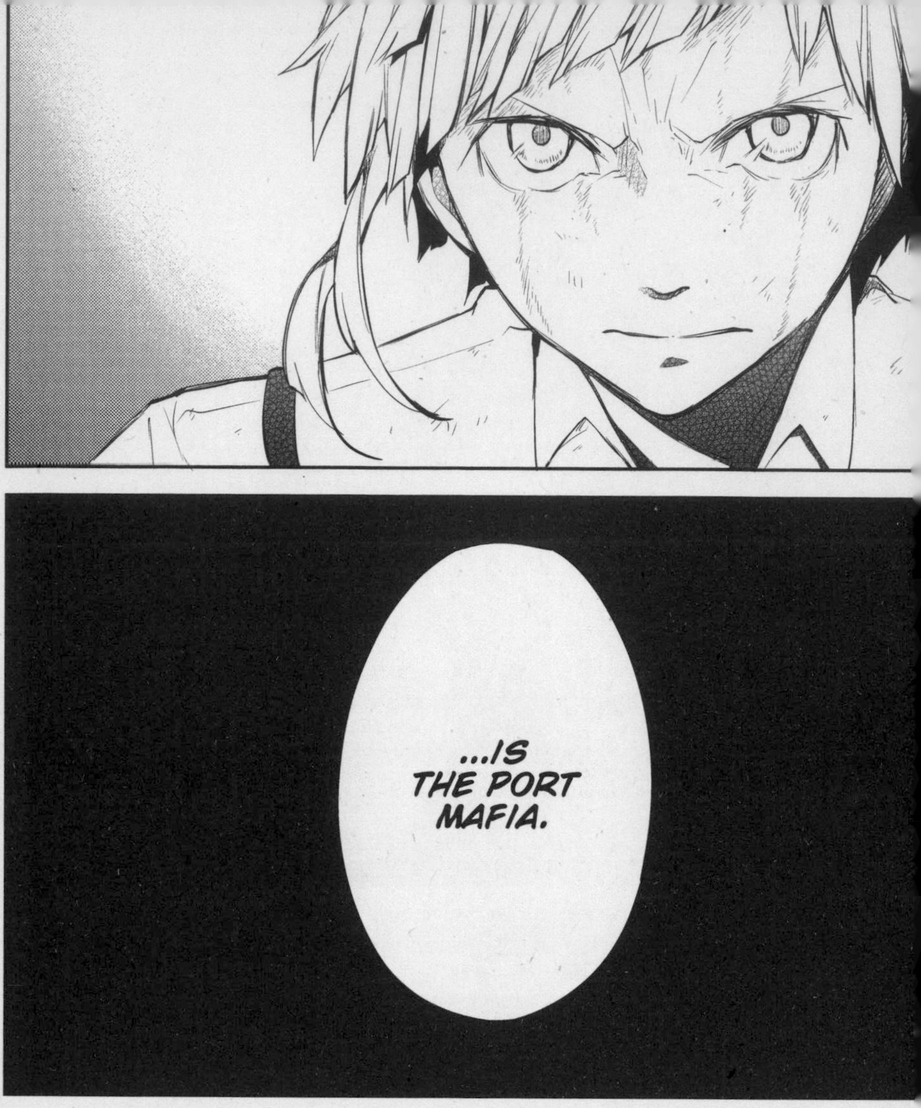
...IS THE PORT MAFIA.

"Even if my head be mistaken, my blood never errs."

—Atsushi Nakajima, *Light, Wind, and Dreams*

**To be continued**

BUNGO STRAY DOGS

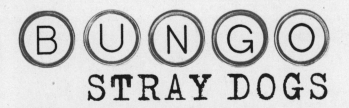

# BUNGO
## STRAY DOGS

*Story: Kafka Asagiri* † *Art: Sango Harukawa*

Translation: Kevin Gifford          †          Lettering: Bianca Pistillo

BUNGO STRAY DOGS Volume 7
©Kafka ASAGIRI 2015
©Sango HARUKAWA 2015
First published in Japan in 2015 by KADOKAWA CORPORATION, Tokyo.
English translation rights arranged with KADOKAWA CORPORATION, Tokyo through TUTTLE-MORI AGENCY, INC., Tokyo.

Yen Press
1290 Avenue of the Americas
New York, NY 10104

Visit us at yenpress.com
facebook.com/yenpress
twitter.com/yenpress
yenpress.tumblr.com
instagram.com/yenpress

First Yen Press Edition: June 2018

Yen Press is an imprint of Yen Press, LLC.
The Yen Press name and logo are trademarks of Yen Press, LLC.

Library of Congress Control Number: 2016956681

ISBNs: 978-0-316-46819-0 (paperback)
       978-0-316-46837-4 (ebook)

10 9 8 7 6 5 4 3 2 1

WOR

Printed in the United States of America